Blessings beyond the Binary

Blessings beyond the Binary

Transparent and the Queer Jewish Family

EDITED BY NORA RUBEL AND BRETT KRUTZSCH

Rutgers University Press
New Brunswick, Camden, and Newark, New Jersey
London and Oxford

Rutgers University Press is a department of Rutgers, The State University of New Jersey, one of the leading public research universities in the nation. By publishing worldwide, it furthers the University's mission of dedication to excellence in teaching, scholarship, research, and clinical care.

978-1-9788-3880-2 (cloth)
978-1-9788-3879-6 (paper)
978-1-9788-3881-9 (epub)

Cataloging-in-publication data is available from the Library of Congress.

LCCN 2023050148

A British Cataloging-in-Publication record for this book is available from the British Library.

This collection copyright © 2024 by Rutgers, The State University of New Jersey
Individual chapters copyright © 2024 in the names of their authors
All rights reserved

No part of this book may be reproduced or utilized in any form or by any means, electronic or mechanical, or by any information storage and retrieval system, without written permission from the publisher. Please contact Rutgers University Press, 106 Somerset Street, New Brunswick, NJ 08901. The only exception to this prohibition is "fair use" as defined by U.S. copyright law.

References to internet websites (URLs) were accurate at the time of writing. Neither the author nor Rutgers University Press is responsible for URLs that may have expired or changed since the manuscript was prepared.

∞ The paper used in this publication meets the requirements of the American National Standard for Information Sciences—Permanence of Paper for Printed Library Materials, ANSI Z39.48-1992.

rutgersuniversitypress.org

For Our Jewish Mothers: Cherry Cassell and Oria Rubel

Contents

Introduction   1
NORA RUBEL AND BRETT KRUTZSCH

Part I   Transforming Jews on Television

1. Rebooting Jewish Television   19
JOSH LAMBERT

2. "Happy Yom Kippur": Televising and Translating Atonement   36
NORA RUBEL

3. Melancholy and Joy: Jewish Nomadism and *Transparent*   52
RANEN OMER-SHERMAN

4. The Historiography of *Transparent*   67
MARTIN SHUSTER

Part II   Performing Judaism and Jewish Identity

5. Dancing Out the Torah: Ritual, Bodies, and Transitions in *Transparent*   83
JODI EICHLER-LEVINE

6. From *Oy* to *Hineni*: Language and Transition in *Transparent*   98
SARAH BUNIN BENOR

7. Pfefferman's Complaint: *Transparent* and the Tenacity of Jewish Familial Stereotypes   114
JARROD TANNY

8   The Gentile, the Demonic, and Collapsing Binaries
    in *Transparent*   130
    SHAUL MAGID

Part III   Transgressing and Queering Gender

9   Nostalgia, Queer Time, and the Ethnic in *Transparent*   143
    JENNIFER GLASER

10 Don't All Have Your Family: The Critique of Religion
    in *Transparent*   156
    KATHRYN LOFTON

11 From Beautiful Rabbi to Queer *Kohenet*: Gender and
    Judaism in and beyond *Transparent*   174
    SHARI RABIN

Part IV   Queering Jewish and Transgender History: Three Perspectives on *Transparent*'s Use of the Holocaust

12 Queer Temporality in Trans Times: Connection
    and Belonging in *Transparent*'s Second Season   199
    JOSHUA FALEK

13 Queering the Holocaust: Intersecting Jewish and
    Transgender Identities in *Transparent*   214
    KERSTIN STEITZ

14 Making Jewishness Transparent and *Transparent* Jew-ish   229
    MARILYN REIZBAUM

Part V   Concluding and Transitioning

15 Run from Your Parent's House: Transfeminism and
    Abraham's Blessing   247
    SLAVA GREENBERG

16 La-La-Lech-Lecha: *Transparent*'s Musical Finale   262
    WARREN HOFFMAN

    Conclusion   271
    BRETT KRUTZSCH

    Acknowledgments   275
    Selected Bibliography   277
    Notes on Contributors   279
    Index   283

Blessings beyond the Binary

Introduction

NORA RUBEL AND BRETT KRUTZSCH

In *Transparent*'s pilot episode, adult siblings Josh and Ali[1] Pfefferman are sitting together on the floor in their childhood home, listening to records. They select a Jim Croce album (1974's *Photographs and Memories*) and play "Operator." Josh, a music industry executive, holds up the record and says, "Look at that face. Look at that. They would never let me sign a guy like this right now. Look at that schnoz. You could not get that nose on TV today in a million years." Implied in this reference to Croce's face, and specifically his nose, is that Croce appears too ethnic—and possibly too "Jewish"—for TV.[2] The same could be said for *Transparent*'s Pfefferman family.

Transparent debuted in September 2014 on Amazon Prime Video. The series intimately tracks a Jewish family, the Pfeffermans, from the affluent Pacific Palisades neighborhood of Los Angeles in the aftermath of the patriarch's transition from Mort to Maura. The show emerged at a time when more transgender characters were appearing on both big and small screens. But *Transparent* was never just a transgender coming-out story. It was also a deeply Jewish one.

Although critically acclaimed, some reviewers complained that *Transparent*'s characters were "too much"—too neurotic, too pushy, too stereotypical, too narcissistic, too unlikeable, or, in Josh's unspoken words, too Jewish.[3] Others embraced the show (and the neurotic Pfeffermans) *because* of these depictions. Michael Schulman commented in *The New Yorker* that its "warped beauty was in its peculiarity, which had as much to do with Judaism as with gender. No other show I can think of has understood the exact ways that Jewish families drive one another crazy and spin trauma into shtick."[4] And creator Joey Soloway once gushed in an interview in the Jewish publication the *Forward*, "It is so Jewy. We got away with that much Jewiness? I can't believe it."[5]

In the Pfeffermans, *Transparent* presents what might very well be the most substantively and recognizably Jewish family in the history of American television. This distinction is not without competition. Jews have been on (and behind) television since the dawn of the medium. As early as 1949, *The Goldbergs* portrayed a multigenerational Jewish family as a stand-in for the American immigrant experience on the small screen. The Jewish characters in later generations of American television tended to be secular Jews with occasional religious observances (think *Bridget Loves Bernie*, *Thirtysomething*, or *Friends*) or de-Judaized ethnic stereotypes (think *Seinfeld* or the 2013 sitcom *The Goldbergs*, not related to the earlier series of the same name). As Jenny Singer, a former reporter for the *Forward* notes, "The Pfeffermans orbit between Reform and cultural Judaism, but challenge the idea that those identities are 'less' Jewish—their obsessions with memory and the past, and their supreme neediness for divine and human leadership mark them out as terminally Jewish. Their endless carping over whether a nonbinary b'nei mitzvah ceremony should be termed a 'BART Mitzvah' is a feature, not a bug."[6] The family offers an identifiably Ashkenazi presence, but—as seen by their engagement with religious practices—their contributions to Jewish American representation are not solely ethnic.

Despite the occasional side plots featuring urban-dwelling Orthodox Jews on shows like *Law & Order*, the *religious* lives of non-Orthodox American Jews have been relatively rare on television until *Transparent*. *Transparent* was the first to break free of the ethnic or religious binary. As such, the Pfeffermans were never coded so outsiders would find them recognizable as Jews (although many may do so); rather, they appear Jewish in ways that many contemporary American Jews see themselves. They are a twenty-first-century Jewish family that unabashedly identifies as Jewish, is intermarried, is affiliated with a synagogue, is annoyed by their mother, is haunted by the Holocaust, sometimes lights Shabbat candles, respects their rabbi, explores spirituality when it suits them, holds conflicting views on Israel and Palestine, and does not keep kosher (but likes a good bagel with whitefish). One Jewish journalist found this family so recognizable that he called *Transparent* "an ethnography masquerading as comedy."[7] Three years after *Transparent*'s premiere, *The Marvelous Mrs. Maisel*, another acclaimed Amazon Prime show, continued to defy this binary by also depicting the religious lives of non-Orthodox Jews—this time on the Upper West Side of mid-twentieth-century Manhattan.[8]

Although notable for its depiction of a complex twenty-first-century Jewish family, *Transparent* first received critical attention for its portrayal of a transgender woman as the show's central character. The series debuted at a moment when transgender individuals were coming out in American mass culture in significant ways. Three months prior to *Transparent*'s premiere, *Time* magazine proclaimed that the United States had reached a "transgender tipping point."[9]

With Black transgender actress Laverne Cox on the magazine's cover, *Time* declared that the country had entered a new era of media awareness about transgender people. Transgender characters, like the one Cox played on Netflix's *Orange Is the New Black*, graced Americans' television and computer screens. But the magazine also noted that although transgender people were achieving greater media attention, transgender women, especially transgender women of color, faced disproportionate rates of violence, poverty, employment discrimination, and HIV infection. Three years later, in 2017, Reina Gossett, Eric A. Stanley, and Johanna Burton published the anthology *Trap Door: Trans Cultural Production and the Politics of Visibility*, addressing this rise of violence that has accompanied the increased visibility of transgender Americans. The introduction opens with the paradox, "We are living in a time of trans visibility. Yet we are also living in a time of anti-trans visibility," and the essays included in *Trap Door* describe the legislative backlash against trans acceptance that is violently impacting the very lives that the 2014 *Time* cover sought to celebrate.[10]

Transparent premiered within the milieu of *Time*'s "tipping point" and told a story, loosely based on Joey Soloway's own family, about a transgender woman who transitioned late in life. The show would go on to mirror elements of Soloway's own transition, one that occurred contemporaneously with the series. The title itself—*Transparent*—refers to ways of seeing, but it also functions as a portmanteau centering the "parent" part as an identifier. The series is a deeply familial one and in many ways becomes more about the trajectories of the children of the trans parent as the seasons progress. Ava Laure Parsemain notes that "the main pedagogical device of *Transparent* is not its lead, but its ensemble of characters. The other queer characters (including the many transgender characters played by transgender actors) are crucial pedagogical tools that enable the series to explore a wider range of identities."[11] Through the story arcs of the Pfefferman siblings Sarah, Josh, and Ari, the show explores personal relationships to Judaism and Jewish history alongside issues of gender and sexuality.

In a 2016 interview in *New York Magazine*, philosopher and gender theorist Judith Butler discussed her enjoyment of *Transparent*, which she considered "enormously entertaining" but "much better on Jewish life than it is on trans life."[12] Other scholars and critics agreed with Butler: Hank Stuever, in a *Washington Post* review of the third season, writes, "*Transparent* is well on its way to becoming a definitive and classic work on the subject of Jewishness as 'otherness.'"[13] Josh Lambert, a contributor to this volume, wrote in *Tablet* in 2015 on the "Jewy-ness" of *Transparent*: "Transparent is not just 'Jewy,' and not just an admirable fiction about the complexity of contemporary sexuality and gender, but maybe the most important work of Jewish culture of the century so far."[14]

Building on these observations, we believe we are at a crucial moment where *Transparent*'s place as a landmark series warrants serious scholarly attention, especially by those in, or with connections to, Jewish studies. The contributors to this volume analyze, from different vantage points, *Transparent*'s portrayal of complex religious life and how it mediates or is mediated by gender beyond the binary. The chapters address the groundbreaking queerness of the show's central Jewish family (a family that includes a transgender parent and queer siblings, bisexual Sarah and nonbinary Ari). But the volume principally returns to questions of how *Transparent* depicts American Jewish identity, religious observances, and ritual—primarily, although not exclusively, through the show's portrayal of issues related to gender and sexuality. As such, *Blessings beyond the Binary: Transparent and the Queer Jewish Family* uncovers the dynamic diversity and queer creativity in contemporary American Jewish life.

Cultural Significance, Criticisms, and Controversies

Transparent garnered extensive critical praise over its four seasons and movie-length finale—amassing eight Emmy Awards (twenty-eight nominations), two Golden Globes (seven nominations)—and rave reviews from such publications as *The Atlantic* and *The New Yorker*. The series also won impressive recognition as one of the first shows to debut on Amazon's streaming service.[15]

Beyond the show's critical acclaim was real change in American Jewish communities regarding gender identity. Both the Reform and Conservative movements in Judaism issued statements (in 2015 and 2016, respectively) that affirmed varieties of gender expression and that encouraged inclusive liturgical changes for transgender Jews, among other actions. The Reform movement resolved that their "institutions [should] review their use of language in prayers, forms and policies in an effort to ensure people of all gender identities and gender expressions are welcomed, included, accepted, and respected."[16] The Rabbinical Assembly, speaking for the Conservative movement, issued a similar resolution: "The Rabbinical Assembly affirm its commitment to the full welcome, acceptance, and inclusion of people of all gender identities in Jewish life and general society; and . . . that the Rabbinical Assembly encourages all programs affiliated with the Conservative Movement . . . to work toward becoming explicitly welcoming, safe spaces for transgender and gender non-conforming people and evaluate their physical site needs, workplace needs, and language that impact gender and gender expression."[17]

Likewise, in the last decade, multiple books have been published on the Jewish trans experience, including memoirs by Abby Stein (*Becoming Eve: My Journey from Ultra-Orthodox Rabbi to Transgender Woman*) and Joy Ladin (*Through the Door of Life: A Jewish Journey Between Genders*). Jewish studies scholar Max Strassfeld published a book on the multiple gender categories in the Talmud (*Trans Talmud: Androgynes and Eunuchs in Rabbinic Literature*), and Noach Dzurma published an anthology containing both personal essays from trans Jews and scholarly articles about the Jewish trans experience by Jewish studies scholars (*Balancing on the Mechitza: Transgender in the Jewish Community*).

Although *Transparent* reflected real-life changes in American Jewish communities and garnered extensive critical praise, the show also became a source of controversy. Soloway cast Jeffrey Tambor, a cisgender Jewish man, as the show's protagonist trans woman. Although Tambor received awards for his portrayal of Maura Pfefferman, transgender viewers criticized Soloway for hiring a cisgender man to play a transgender character. In the years leading up to the show, transgender activists had been making the case that trans actors should play transgender characters, largely as a way to support trans actors and the limited roles available to them. Trans activists also opposed how cisgender actors often looked like they were in drag when they tried to depict transgender people with costumes that could be easily discarded.

Transparent emerged between two Oscar-nominated films prominently featuring trans characters, *Dallas Buyers Club* (2013) and *The Danish Girl* (2015), in which cisgender actors were cast for trans roles. Cismen Jared Leto and Eddie Redmayne were both nominated for Academy Awards for their portrayals of transwomen, with Leto winning Best Supporting Actor for *Dallas Buyers Club*. (Redmayne has since apologized for taking on that role; Leto has not.)[18] Despite the controversies that surrounded these films, Soloway reported that the criticism levied at *Transparent* caught them by surprise and that when they went to cast the role of Maura, they had their own transgender parent in mind who, they said, looked like Tambor. In Soloway's 2018 memoir *She Wants It: Desire, Power, and Toppling the Patriarchy*, they wrote, "It never even occurred to me to cast a trans woman."[19] Following backlash from the trans community, Soloway hired more transgender writers, directors, and crew to work on all aspects of the series. In subsequent years, Soloway apologized for their casting choice. Tambor's costar Alexandra Billings has noted that had the show begun in 2017, a cisman would not have been cast as the lead trans character. Describing this shift, she offers, "There have been two movies that have come out with cis people in the lead playing trans people, and they disappeared. So first of all, that speaks to our power. And second of all, that speaks to the fact that the consciousness in America is changing."[20] Real change has occurred elsewhere: transgender actors Hunter Schafer and Hari Nef (a *Transparent* alum) were cast in the prestigious shows *Euphoria* and *Assassination Nation*, and directors have increasingly promised to hire transgender actors to portray transgender characters.

Casting Tambor as a trans woman was not the only source of concern among transgender critics. Although *Transparent* depicted the difficulties Maura experienced as a trans woman, some transgender viewers worried that the show's focus on a wealthy, white trans person would skew the public's perception of the hardships most transgender people face, especially the violence and systemic oppression that poorer trans and queer people of color experience. Black transgender activist Lourdes Ashley Hunter told *The New York Times*, "I don't want people to watch *Transparent* and think this is the lives of transgender people, because it is not."[21] For Hunter and others, *Transparent* failed to depict the difficulties most transgender people endure, especially those who, unlike Maura Pfefferman, are not rich or Jewish and are not accepted by their biological family.

In 2015, one year after *Transparent*'s premiere, much of the nation followed the real-life coming out of Caitlyn Jenner as a transwoman, a development the executive director of the National Center for Transgender Equality hailed as a "teachable moment." However, many noted that Jenner's experience was not representative because most could not afford the type of transition (both medical and social) that the wealthy, white, and internationally famous Jenner experienced.[22] Connecting Jenner to *Transparent*, in an essay unambiguously titled "Amazon's *Transparent* is Transphobic Bullshit," s.e. smith laments this predominant "narrative of middle-aged and older white trans women . . . in pop culture, and while their stories are important, it's time to branch out beyond that, to face the realities experienced by trans youth."[23] Parsemain notes that *Transparent*'s Maura, like Jenner in her 2015–2016 reality show *I am Cait*, "is often positioned in the role of learner while other characters teach her what it means to be a woman and a transwoman. . . . initially focus[ing] on external attributes of femininity (clothes, hair, makeup), she eventually learns about the physical and intimate aspects of womanhood, gender politics and issues affecting the transgender community."[24] With both Caitlin Jenner and Maura Pfefferman, a wealthy white person became the media's focus for what it looks like to go through a gender transition.

This brings us to another critique of *Transparent*—its whiteness. As Taylor Nygaard and Jorie Lagerway write in *Horrible White People: Gender, Genre, and Television's Precarious Whiteness*, the series falls into a category the authors call "horrible white people" shows. Such shows "target affluent, liberal, White audiences through prestige aesthetics and innovative progressive representations."[25] They go on to indict these series for "reflect[ing] the complicity of the White Left, obsessed with its own anxiety and suffering, in the rise of the Far Right—particularly in the mobilization, representation, and sustenance of structural White Supremacy on television."[26] The Jewishness of the Pfeffermans is part of this complicity, further noting the assimilation of Ashkenazi ethnicity into whiteness.[27] On shows like *Transparent*, Nygaard and Lagerway argue that the creators "use the characters' Jewishness and [a] tradition of subaltern comedy to set their light-skinned characters outside the structures of White supremacy or to exculpate them from complicity within those structures."[28] Although Jewishness may mitigate whiteness to an extent, it complicates the truth that many Jews today benefit from white privilege, and it obscures the reality that not all Jews are white.

Although Jews of color are beginning to be seen as a larger demographic within popular culture, cultural historian Shaina Hammerman notes that they tend not to be seen on television: "I certainly can think of Black-Jewish actors, but not characters. For now, conversations about intersectionality in pop culture contexts are mostly limited to race and gender and sexuality."[29] Black Jews such as Daveed Diggs, Drake, Tiffany Haddish, Rashida Jones, Maya Rudolph, Lisa Bonet (and ex-husband Leonard and daughter Zoe Kravitz) are acclaimed by Jewish media, it seems, for just existing. But stories from the perspective of Black Jews are few and far between (a notable exception is that of Black Cindy from Netflix's *Orange Is the New Black*). As Jesi Taylor Cruz writes in a piece on Daveed Diggs's joyful "Puppy for Hanukkah" song, "It's not a coincidence that certain narratives and types of characters dominate mass media and pop culture. It's also not a coincidence that there are so few examples of Black Jewish representation in mass media and pop culture. From discriminatory hiring practices in writers' rooms to popular misconceptions about who can be and what it means to be Jewish, there are countless factors that play into the stories that are told in the mainstream."[30] As Jews have been involved in the production of television and film since the industries' conceptions, those Jews are largely white and the stories of Jews on screen tend to reflect those of the writers and directors. Jewish institutions have made tremendous strides toward racial inclusivity in recent years, but representation still lags in popular culture. We, as editors of this volume, regret that while including the strong voices of both queer and Jewish scholars on *Transparent*, we have replicated one of the show's major faults—notably that of robust racial diversity.

Another charge levied at *Transparent* (and other shows featuring Jewish characters) is that of "Jewface," explained elsewhere by contributor Jennifer Glaser as "an exaggerated performance of Jewish identity that gains its evocative force from the deep archive of Jewish stereotypes."[31] Non-Jews playing Jews on stage and screen have a long history, hence the old adage, "Write Yiddish, cast British," but this frequently has been seen as an assimilative erasure of Jewishness in Jewish roles. In *Transparent*, Maura and Shelly's children are played by non-Jews—Abby Hoffman, Jay Duplass, and Amy Landecker—and although noted in popular media, this selection has understandably caused less controversy than that of Tambor's casting.[32] Accusations of "Jewface" have most recently and publicly been issued by comedian Sarah Silverman, citing David Baddiel's *Jews Don't Count*. Silverman argues that "when Jewish roles in films are admirable or heroic . . . they are almost always cast with non-Jewish performers."[33] Without throwing unnecessary shade at the Pfefferman siblings, few viewers, as contributors to this volume note, would likely characterize them as admirable *or* heroic.

Jeffrey Tambor proved to haunt the series in more ways than just by his casting. Following *Transparent*'s fourth season, two transgender women who worked on the show (Trace Lysette and Van Barnes) reported to the press that Tambor sexually harassed them; he continues to deny the claims.[34] Soloway fired Tambor and apologized for any role they played in creating an atmosphere where abuse could take place. With Tambor gone from the cast, the show's finale, a movie-length musical, focused on the family's reaction to Maura Pfefferman's death. Consequently, this volume addresses Tambor's work on the show in depth, but the volume does not gloss or absolve the actor's history of anger, abuse, or the accusations levied against him.

Transparent, then, became a source of massive praise and substantial criticism. The show's numerous awards, critical commendations, and controversies all contribute to its status as a landmark series, and although popular media attests to the series' significance, less material can be found in contemporary scholarship. *Transparent*'s place in American popular culture and its role in imagining new ways individuals can live as Jewish, transgender, and queer religious practitioners warrant scholarly analysis. A few scholars in various fields have published journal articles on diverse aspects of the show, but no writer has centered the show's focus on Jewish identity, despite Jewishness being integral to the series; one notable exception is Slava Greenberg's 2021 essay in the *Journal of Feminist Studies in Religion*, which is reprinted in this volume.[35] This book corrects what has been overlooked elsewhere and turns to scholars primarily, but not exclusively, in Jewish studies to examine this groundbreaking Jewish series. Taken together, the essays that follow in *Blessings Beyond the Binary* interrogate what it means to be Jewish, transgender, and queer in the twenty-first century.

Transparent, Scholars, and This Volume

In December 2016, the University of Rochester hosted a symposium about *Transparent* that brought together scholars, transgender and queer activists, and show producers to consider the series' impact on American Jewish communities. The symposium (organized by coeditor Nora Rubel) was cosponsored by the University of Rochester's Department of Religion, the Center for Jewish Studies, and the Susan B. Anthony Institute for Gender, Sexuality, and Women's Studies. In 2017, the Association for Jewish Studies, the professional organization for Jewish studies scholars, featured individual papers, a roundtable panel, and a plenary session about *Transparent*. That gathering and the University of Rochester's symposium, as well as broader scholarly interest in all things *Transparent*, were the genesis of this volume.

A book about *Transparent* could cover any number of topics, from the contours of middle-age transitioning to the whitewashing of queer representations in the media; however, its designation as one of the most avowedly Jewish shows in television history prompted in this volume a focus on the show's depiction of Jewish identities, Jewish history, and the queering of Jewish gender and sexual norms. The Pfeffermans push boundaries, remix rituals successfully, transgress them unforgivably, return to Judaism, and leave again. These fluid religious practices are rarely given voice in a popular culture in which binary narratives are favored, such as those found in ABC's *The Goldbergs*, where Judaism and heterosexuality are benignly linked, or Netflix's *Unorthodox*, where observant Judaism is monolithic and immutable. Popular media simultaneously reflects contemporary culture and influences it. The depiction of LGBTQ+ people in this fictional community in Los Angeles provides both a challenge and a vocabulary for the viewer, allowing for the transformation of societal norms.

Like the series itself, this volume is divided into five sections. It opens with four essays that consider how *Transparent* revolutionized the depiction of Jews on television. The first section, Transforming Jews on TV, begins with Josh Lambert's "Rebooting Jewish Television," where he examines the current wave of Jewish popular culture in light of contemporary Jewish institutionalization and the accessibility of new media content. Lambert also addresses the privilege that the American Jewish audiences and critics held over *Transparent*'s success (as opposed to queer and trans viewers who found it less thrilling). Next, in "'Happy Yom Kippur': Televising and Translating Atonement," Nora Rubel explores Jewish religious rituals, specifically Yom Kippur, against the historical backdrop of the coverage of Jewish practice in American television. Arguing that Judaism on television has traditionally served more as a plot device than as a source for religious exploration, Rubel examines how *Transparent* takes on Jewish religious meaning and ritual, offering a step beyond the symbolic ethnicity of previous representations. Then, Ranen Omer-Sherman examines the theme of wandering, both metaphorical and physical in "Melancholy and Joy: Jewish Nomadism and *Transparent*." Situating this theme within the Jewish tradition's relation to exile, Omer-Sherman relates the series' narratives of wandering identities to those found in Genesis. And, in "The Historiography of *Transparent*," Martin Shuster explores *Transparent*'s significance as a piece of new television—that is, as a particular aesthetic object—to better comprehend its standing as a specifically Jewish work of art. Shuster argues that *Transparent* locates itself as an inventive bit of Jewish memorialization, similar in function to other ways Jewish memory has been memorialized in more traditional forms (whether in literature, song, or religious prayer).

Although *Transparent* generally avoids a heavy-handed pedagogical tone, the show occasionally explains religious and cultural practices through the character of Rabbi Raquel. Critic Sara Ivry, in her review of *Transparent*'s inaugural season, revels in what she calls "the most Jewish show to come along in years," noting that the series—beyond showcasing a standing order at Canter's deli and an overbearing mother—reveals "Jewishness with its rituals, its spiritual wrestling and doubt, its biblical stories and metaphors."[36] Benjamin Cahan goes further in applauding *Transparent*'s engagement with "less familiar [Jewish] intricacies: purifying oneself in a mikvah, studying for bat mitzvah, covering the mirrors while sitting shiva, rending garments at a funeral.... It's worth noting that one also rarely sees this kind of Judaism on television."[37] Accordingly, the essays in the book's second section, Performing Judaism and Jewish Identity, examine how *Transparent*'s characters navigate their relationship with Judaism and perform their Jewish identities through the rituals they enact, the ways they use Hebrew and Yiddish, and the cultural stereotypes they fulfill. In "Dancing Out the Torah: Ritual, Bodies, and Transitions in *Transparent*,"

Jodi Eichler-Levine explores how richly embodied actions emerge and resonate with one another throughout the series, with a focus on song, dance, and prayer in several key episodes. Eichler-Levine specifically interrogates the ritual of a solitary bat mitzvah, writing that the "performance queers and revivifies the traditional practice of chanting Torah, celebrating its spirit while unbinding it from its usual anchors." She further reflects on what it might mean to use *Transparent* as a way to think more broadly about Jewish bodies, identities, and practices in twenty-first-century America. Next, in "From *Oy* to *Hineni*: Language and Transition in *Transparent*," Sarah Bunin Benor analyzes the role of language in *Transparent*'s portrayal of two different types of transition: communal and individual. The communal transition represented in the show is how American Jewishness has moved from a primarily ethnic identity to a primarily religious one. The individual transitions include shifts in gender, sexuality, and religion. Benor tracks these transitions in identity through changes in language, from Yiddish to Hebrew and from cis heteronormative language to gender-inclusive language. As she demonstrates, all the Pfeffermans are learning new words, making mistakes, and engaging in new worlds that are opening to them. Then, in "Pfefferman's Complaint: *Transparent* and the Tenacity of the Jewish Familial Stereotypes," Jarrod Tanny examines the show's use of comedic Jewish stereotypes, especially that of the overbearing mother who is obsessed with her son. Tanny contends that *Transparent*'s exploitation of well-worn stereotypes is selective and clever, ultimately playing a constructive role beyond the elicitation of laughter. And, in "The Gentile, the Demonic, and Collapsing Binaries in *Transparent*," Shaul Magid considers the show's portrayal of gentiles, arguing that *Transparent* presents the gentile as a stranger at best and demonic at worst and that this portrayal exposes a wound in American Jewish life that even assimilation cannot heal.

The third section, Transgressing and Queering Gender, explores the myriad ways characters on *Transparent*, including cisgender heterosexual ones, subvert normative gender expectations, especially in relation to their religious identities. In "Nostalgia, Queer Time, and the Ethnic in *Transparent*," Jennifer Glaser offers an examination of *Transparent*'s ongoing engagement with the past. She argues that the series' multiple narratives of loss inspire a "diasporic and queer-inflected Jewishness" that both employs nostalgia yet resists the ethnonationalism that can come from it. Then, in "Don't All Have Your Family: The Critique of Religion in *Transparent*," Kathryn Lofton considers how *Transparent* queers religious possibilities, questioning how such a queer family might offer a roadmap for reimagining possibilities for deeply patriarchal religious traditions like Judaism. In "From Beautiful Rabbi to Queer Kohenet: Gender and Judaism in and beyond *Transparent*," Shari Rabin explores the character Rabbi Raquel and contextualizes her within the history of women rabbis. Rabin argues that Rabbi Raquel comforts viewers because, as opposed to the queer characters, Rabbi Raquel fits within normative standards of femininity, morality, and religious earnestness.

The book's fourth section, Queering Jewish and Transgender History: Three Perspectives on *Transparent*'s Use of the Holocaust, offers three essays that examine, from different points of view, one landmark episode of *Transparent*: the season 2 finale "Man on the Land." The award-winning episode brings together many of the show's themes: how Jewish history shapes Jews today, how the Holocaust annihilated thriving Jewish and queer communities, and how Jewish and queer identities interact to create new gender, sexual, and religious possibilities. The section opens with Joshua Falek's "Queer Temporality in Trans Times: Connection and Belonging in *Transparent*'s Second Season" in which he proffers that *Transparent*'s central insight is that the trauma left unspoken is the trauma that hurts us most. The chapter highlights how *Transparent* engages in a pseudo-archaeology of feeling that disturbs the ghosts and anxieties of the past, with an occasional invitation inward, rather than total rejection or sublimation of past communal traumas. Next, in "Queering the Holocaust: Intersecting Jewish and Transgender Identities in *Transparent*," Kerstin Steitz explores how Jewish and transgender histories and identities intersect in the figure and work of Magnus Hirschfeld and his Institut für Sexualwissenschaft (Institute for Sexual Science), as well as the Nazi persecution of Jews and the Weimar Berlin LGBTQ community. She proposes that Soloway chose the Holocaust as an event with which everyone is familiar—especially American Jews—to highlight the intersections and differences between the experiences of Jews and trans individuals and how they are currently remembered and commemorated, thereby successfully erecting a memorial in honor of the trans community murdered by the Nazis. And, in "Making Jewishness Transparent and *Transparent* Jew-ish," Marilyn Reizbaum examines *Transparent*'s representation of the assumed historical connections among Jewish, queer, and transgender identities through the concepts of chosenness, landedness, and deliverance. She argues that *Transparent* takes on the conceptual challenge of these historical connections and both participates in and relishes the messiness of such categorization.

The final section contains two chapters that focus on *Transparent*'s series finale. In "Run from Your Parent's House: Transfeminism and Abraham's Blessing," Slava Greenberg offers a transfeminist reading of the Abraham story in Genesis 12:1 (Lech Lecha) with Ari as a contemporary stand-in for the patriarch. By focusing on Ari's narrative, Greenberg explores trans and gender-nonconforming ways of being Jewish today. Then, in "La-La-Lech-Lecha: *Transparent*'s Musical Finale," Warren Hoffman approaches the finale through its use of the musical form and the performance of chanting Torah. Also engaging with the Torah portion of Lech Lecha, Hoffman explores the freedom that comes with both "leaving your father's house" and singing one's feelings. Although the Pfeffermans have never required permission to emote openly (or navel gaze), the musical form allows for an almost ridiculous level of self-examination; despite this silliness, Hoffman notes that the musical finale culminates in the formation of a radically queer Jewish community, a new people.

Finally, in the volume's conclusion, Brett Krutzsch reflects on *Transparent*'s legacy and its transition to a theatrical production. He questions what it means that, since *Transparent*'s trailblazing premiere in 2014, the situation for trans, queer, and Jewish Americans has become more precarious. But in reflecting on the central issues this volume raises, he considers the ways *Transparent* offers a map for how to improve the world by queering it.

Does *Transparent* provoke such inspiration? The series did not invent trans identity or queer Jewish expression, but it reflected early twenty-first-century American Jewish life and offered literacy and language for the rapid changes in gender identity. In the finale of the fourth season, Ari has an awakening at the Western Wall in Jerusalem and laments the "so binary" nature of Judaism. In the series finale, Ari celebrates a spontaneous nonbinary "bart mitzvah" in the woods. Such nontraditional ritual and life-cycle events have been increasing in mainstream Jewish settings, requiring such institutions to respond with new liturgy and language.

A March 2019 piece in *The New York Times* style section entitled "Bar or Bat Mitzvah? Hey, What about a Both Mitzvah?" describes a pangender teen's "they mitzvah."[38] In HBO's 2022 *And Just Like That . . .*, the follow-up to *Sex and the City*, Charlotte's child (who has changed their name to Rock and uses they/them pronouns) prepares for a they mitzvah. Rabbi Jen, the trans rabbi the family is excited to "get," is played by none other than *Transparent*'s Hari Nef. In June 2019, Essie Shachar-Hill produced "A Guide for the Gender-Neutral B-Mitzvah"[39] for Keshet, a national organization that bills itself as "the only organization in the U.S. that works for LGBTQ equality in all facets of Jewish life—synagogues, Hebrew schools, day schools, youth groups, summer camps, social-service organizations and other communal agencies."[40] The guide asserts: "The traditional language and practices associated with a Bar or Bat Mitzvah can exclude people who are nonbinary, agender, gender fluid, gender-queer, or any gender identity that is not girl or boy." Shachar-Hill goes on to prompt "that we are part of a Jewish tradition that is continuously evolving." The publication arm of the Reform movement, CCAR Press, subsequently published *Mishkan Ga'avah: Where Pride Dwells, A Celebration of LGBTQ Jewish Life and Ritual* in 2020. The movement itself offers a toolkit for congregations needing to adapt their liturgy and ritual to celebrate the gender diversity in their communities. The essays in the present volume, particularly those in the Ritual section, speak to these evolutions and transitions in American Judaism over the past several years.

Although the series (and this volume) employs Judaism as its lingua franca, the issues raised are not exclusive to Jews. Kathryn Reklis, in *The Christian Century*, beautifully reflects on how *Transparent*'s depiction of religion goes beyond that of American Jewish particularism: "Transparency, the show suggests, is not something we can achieve on our own. To see ourselves as we really are we need an external mirror. To change who we are we need support, compassion, and guidance. Religion—in this series a moral tradition as well as a way of knowing the divine—is offered as a possible source for this self-reflection and transformation. This makes *Transparent* one of the least cynical, most convincing shows about religion that's offered on television."⁴¹

In sum, and in the sum of its parts, *Blessings Beyond the Binary: Transparent and the Queer Jewish Family* examines the multifaceted dimensions of Jewish identity in this landmark show. The volume explores *Transparent*'s representations of Judaism, Jewish identity, and the transformation of American Jewish life through the queering of gender and sexuality and the reimagination of religious practices. As *Transparent* reveals Jews who find, transgress, and remake boundaries in their own image, it charts a path for practitioners of all religions to do the same.

Notes

1. For four seasons Gaby Hoffman's character goes by the name of Ali. In the finale, they come out as nonbinary and change their name to Ari. We will be using "Ari" going forward in this introduction and in the subsequent chapters to avoid deadnaming, the practice of referring to one who has transitioned by a name they no longer choose to use.
2. Ironically, Croce is Jewish, but he converted. He is ethnically Italian.
3. Tyler Coates, "*Transparent*'s Amy Landecker Has a Theory about Why People Find Certain TV Characters 'Unlikable,'" *Esquire*, September 23, 2016, https://www.esquire.com/entertainment/tv/q-and-a/a48808/amy-landecker-interview-transparent/; Kevin O'Keefe, "The Kids of *Transparent* Are Horrible—and They're the Best Part of the Show," *Mic*, December 14, 2015, https://www.mic.com/articles/130367/the-kids-of-transparent-are-horrible-and-they-re-the-best-part-of-the-show; Lior Saltzman, "There's a Horrible Holocaust Song in the 'Transparent' Finale," Kveller, October 3, 2019, https://www.kveller.com/theres-a-horrible-holocaust-song-in-the-transparent-finale/.
4. Michael Schulman, "What Has Changed Since 'Transparent' Debuted in 2014?" *New Yorker*, September 27, 2019, https://www.newyorker.com/culture/cultural-comment/what-has-changed-since-transparent-debuted-in-2014.
5. Debra Nussbaum Cohen, "How Jill Soloway Created 'Transparent'—the Jewiest Show Ever," *Forward*, October 21, 2014, https://forward.com/culture/207407/how-jill-soloway-created-transparent-the-jewiest/.
6. Jenny Singer, "The 'Transparent' Musical Finale: Terminally Jewish and Endearingly Hard to Watch," *Forward*, October 3, 2019, https://forward.com/schmooze/432636/the-transparent-musical-finale-is-obscenely-jewish-and-endearingly-hard-to/.
7. Eric Thurm, "*Transparent* Is the Most Jewish Show on Television," October 6, 2016, https://www.esquire.com/entertainment/tv/a49295/judaism-on-transparent-jill-soloway/.
8. Netflix's 2020 psychological drama *Unorthodox* embraced the "ethnic" or "religious" binary—starkly contrasting an American Satmar Hasidic community with that of secular artists in Berlin. In this miniseries, Shira Haas's protagonist Esti breaks with her claustrophobic community, simultaneously shedding her observance with her wardrobe (and wig) that unmistakably marked her as a religious Jew.
9. Katy Steinmetz, "The Transgender Tipping Point," *Time*, May 29, 2014, https://time.com/135480/transgender-tipping-point/.

10. Eric A. Stanley, Johanna Burton, and Tourmaline Gossett, eds., *Trap Door: Trans Cultural Production and the Politics of Visibility* (Cambridge, MA: MIT Press, 2017), xv.
11. Ava Laure Parsemain, "Realistic Entertainment: The Complex Pedagogy of Transparent," in *The Pedagogy of Queer TV* (Cham: Palgrave Macmillan, 2019), 194.
12. Molly Fischer, "Think Gender Is Performance? You Have Judith Butler to Thank for That," *The Cut* in *New York Magazine,* https://www.thecut.com/2016/06/judith-butler-c-v-r.html.
13. https://www.washingtonpost.com/entertainment/tv/better-than-ever-transparent-transitions-into-a-study-of-american-jewish-ness/2016/09/22/a61cb636-8038-11e6-b002-307601806392_story.html.
14. Josh Lambert, "Pfefferman Family Matters," *Tablet,* December 10, 2015, https://www.tabletmag.com/sections/news/articles/pfefferman-family-matters.
15. See, for example, Emily Nussbaum, "The Seductive Audacity of 'Transparent,'" *New Yorker,* December 28, 2015; Spencer Kornhaber, "The Brilliant Challenge of Transparent," *Atlantic,* December 14, 2015.
16. Union for Reform Judaism, "Resolution on the Rights of Transgender and Gender Non-Conforming People," 2015, https://urj.org/what-we-believe/resolutions/resolution-rights-transgender-and-gender-non-conforming-people.
17. The Rabbinical Assembly, "Resolution Affirming the Rights of Transgender and Gender Non-Conforming People," https://www.rabbinicalassembly.org/story/resolution-affirming-rights-transgender-and-gender-non-conforming-people.
18. "I made that film with the best intentions, but I think it was a mistake," Redmayne continued, saying that he would not take such a role on now. Chris Murphey, "Eddie Redmayne Says Starring in *The Danish Girl* 'Was a Mistake,'" *Vanity Fair,* November 22, 2021, https://www.vanityfair.com/hollywood/2021/11/eddie-redmayne-says-starring-in-the-danish-girl-was-a-mistake.
19. Jill Soloway, *She Wants It: Desire, Power, and Toppling the Patriarchy* (New York: Crown Archetype, 2018), 55.
20. "Amazon Studios Officially Fires Jeffrey Tambor from *Transparent,*" *Hollywood Reporter,* May 9, 2021, https://www.hollywoodreporter.com/tv/tv-news/jeffrey-tambor-officially-fired-transparent-wake-harassment-claims-1085236/. See also: Brenda R. Weber and David Greven, *Ryan Murphy's Queer America* (Milton: Taylor & Francis, 2022), 247.
21. See Lourdes Ashley Hunter quoted in Clyde Haberman, "Beyond Caitlin Jenner Lies a Long Struggle by Transgender People," *New York Times,* July 14, 2015, https://www.nytimes.com/2015/06/15/us/beyond-caitlyn-jenner-lies-a-long-struggle-by-transgender-people.html.
22. "It's become a national teachable moment," said Mara Keisling, executive director for the Washington, D.C.-based National Center for Transgender Equality. "Somebody made us realize we weren't alone." Lorraine Ali, "'A National Teachable Moment': What Bruce Jenner's pre-Caitlyn ABC Interview Meant for the Transgender Community," *Los Angeles Times,* April 25, 2015, https://www.latimes.com/entertainment/tv/la-et-st-bruce-jenner-interview-react-20150426-story.html.
23. "Amazon's Transparent is Transphobic Bullshit," *Global* Comment, October 3, 2014, https://globalcomment.com/amazons-transparent-is-transphobic-bullshit/.
24. Parsemain, "Realistic Entertainment," 193–214.
25. Taylor Nygaard and Jorie Lagerwey, *Horrible White People: Gender, Genre, and Television's Precarious Whiteness* (New York: New York University Press, 2020), 2.
26. Nygaard and Lagerwey, *Horrible White People,* 2.

27 For further reading on Jews and whiteness, see Eric L. Goldstein, *The Price of Whiteness: Jews, Race, and American Identity* (Princeton, NJ: Princeton University Press, 2019); Jamie Moshin and Richard Benjamin Crosby, "Liminally White: Jews, Mormons, and Whiteness," *Communication, Culture & Critique* 11, no. 3 (2018): 436–454; Karen Brodkin, *How Jews Became White Folks and What That Says about Race in America* (New Brunswick, NJ: Rutgers University Press, 1998).

28 Nygaard and Lagerwey, *Horrible White People*, 97.

29 Shannon Levitt, "Pop Culture Scholar Talks about Jews of Color on TV," *Jewish News*, August 11, 2020, https://www.jewishaz.com/community/pop-culture-scholar-talks-about-jews-of-color-on-tv/article_e815381a-dbf1-11ea-b057-e35912af4b3b.html.

30 Jesi Taylor Cruz, "So This Is What Authentic Black Jewish Representation Feels Like," *Hey Alma*, December 7, 2020, https://www.heyalma.com/so-this-is-what-authentic-black-jewish-representation-feels-like/.

31 Jennifer Glaser, *Borrowed Voices: Writing and Racial Ventriloquism in the Jewish American Imagination* (New Brunswick, NJ: Rutgers University Press, 2016), 2. It should be noted that "Jewface" was historically used to note performances *by* Jews *as* Jews. See also Michael Rogin, *Blackface, White Noise: Jewish Immigrants in the Hollywood Melting Pot* (Berkeley: University of California Press, 1996); Ted Merwin, "Jew-Face: Non-Jews Playing Jews on the American Stage," *Cultural and Social History* 4, no. 2 (2007): 215–233, https://doi.org/10.2752/147800307X199056.

32 Kristin Iversen, "Gaby Hoffman and Jay Duplass Explain What It Means to Be 'Jew-Ish,'", *Nylon* September 22, 2017, https://www.nylon.com/articles/gaby-hoffmann-jay-duplass-transparent-season-four-interview; Neda Ulaby, "The Casting of Non-Jewish Actors as Jewish Characters is Causing Controversy," *National Public Radio*, November 12, 2021, https://www.weku.org/2021-11-12/the-casting-of-non-jewish-actors-as-jewish-characters-is-causing-controversy.

33 Benjamin Ivry, "Does Sarah Silverman Actually Have a Point about Jew-Face?" *Forward*, October 11, 2021, https://forward.com/culture/476527/does-sarah-silverman-actually-have-a-point-about-jewface/.

34 Seth Abramovich, "'*Transparent*' Star Alleges Jeffrey Tambor Sexually Harassed Her, 'Got Physical,'" *The Hollywood Reporter*, November 16, 2017, https://www.hollywoodreporter.com/news/general-news/transparent-star-alleges-jeffrey-tambor-sexually-harassed-her-got-physical-1059306/; Laura Bradley, "Jeffrey Tambor Opens Up about Sexual Harassment Allegations: 'Lines Got Blurred,'" *Vanity Fair*, May 7, 2018, https://www.vanityfair.com/hollywood/2018/05/jeffrey-tambor-interview-sexual-harassment-transparent-jill-soloway.

35 Anamarija Horvat, "Haunting and Queer Histories: Representing Memory in Jill Soloway's Transparent," *Feminist Media Studies* 20, no. 3 (2020): 398–413; Parsemain, "Realistic Entertainment," 193–214. Michael N. Goddard and Christopher Hogg, "Trans TV Dossier, III: Trans TV Re-Evaluated, Part 1," *Critical Studies in Television* 15, no. 2 (2020): 162–164; Natasha Seymour, "Representing Transgender Embodiment in Film and Culture: Looking beyond the Transition Narrative in Amazon's Transparent," *Somatechnics* 9, no. 1 (2019): 84–97.

36 Sarah Ivry, "Transparent Is the Most Jewish TV Show in a While—and It's Great," *Tablet*, October 1, 2014, https://www.tabletmag.com/sections/news/articles/transparent-is-the-most-jewish-tv-show-in-a-while-and-its-great.

37 Virtual Roundtable on Transparent: Benjamin Cahan, "Sparkly Star of David," *Public Books*, August 1, 2015, https://www.publicbooks.org/virtual-roundtable-on-transparent/

38 The article depicts both b'nai or b' mitzvah's as language possibilities. Alyson Krueger, "Bar or Bat Mitzvah? Hey, What about a Both Mitzvah?" *New York Times*, March 27, 2019, https://www.nytimes.com/2019/03/27/style/gender-fluid-bar-bat-mitzvah.html.
39 "Celebrating the Age of Mitzvah: A Guide for all Genders," *Keshet,* https://www.keshetonline.org/celebrating-the-age-of-mitzvah-a-guide-for-all-genders/
40 "About Us," *Keshet,* https://www.keshetonline.org/about-us/.
41 Kathryn Reklis, "Transparent Need," *The Christian Century,* April 1, 2015, https://www.christiancentury.org/article/2015-03/transparent-need.

Part 1
Transforming Jews on Television

1
Rebooting Jewish Television

JOSH LAMBERT

Despite Jews being a tiny minority of the U.S. population, representations of Jews have played pivotal roles in the emergence and development of many new media forms, including cinema, records, radio, and television.[1] More recently, *Transparent* played this role in the history of yet another new media form: streaming video. At a moment when massive international companies including Amazon and Netflix made billion-dollar gambits to develop new media platforms and reach global audiences, *Transparent* turned out to be one of the most insistently and unremittingly Jewish shows in television history. The show also proved a website could beat out cable and broadcast television networks in the most prestigious television industry award competitions, the Golden Globes and Emmys. Before the pilot had been picked up and ordered into a series, creator and showrunner Joey Soloway told an interviewer, "The old adage is 'Write Jewish, Cast British.' You're supposed to write the Jewish anxieties, but then take out any references to Tu Bishvat and make sure that the actors look WASP-y. So I think I'm gonna subvert that and write Jewish, cast Jewish, act Jewish, fall apart Jewish, make mistakes Jewish, cry Jewish."[2] Why would a company striving for a massive global audience bet on such a highly specific representation of Jews? And why would this improbable strategy work?

One way to answer those questions would be to say that *Transparent* is just really good television: sensitively written, beautifully shot, and carefully cast to feature a range of extraordinary performers. Not gainsaying that explanation, this chapter proposes two ways of contextualizing *Transparent*'s approach to representing Jews and Jewishness, which make it seem less an outlier than a remarkable and indicative case of Jewish representation in American popular culture in the twenty-first century. The first of these contexts is the affinity between streaming media technology, as a form, and demographic minorities. The second is the increasing institutionalization of Jewish culture in America since the 1990s. Together, they give a much clearer picture of why *Transparent* looks and acts the way it does.

Streaming Media, Jews, and Prestige

The transition from broadcast and cable to streaming as the means for distributing television happened quickly. The video streaming site YouTube debuted in 2005, and within a couple of years, executives at Netflix (until then a DVD-by-mail company) realized that internet distribution speeds had increased enough to make it viable to stream television and video directly over the internet. Netflix launched its streaming service in 2007 alongside some other companies aiming for the same goal. In 2010, executives at Amazon, which was then already well on its way to becoming one of the largest companies by revenue in the world, decided to launch its own platform for distributing video entertainment.

Along the way, aspects of U.S. television viewership that had been taken for granted for decades—in which most television programs were presented in thirty or sixty-minute episodes, released serially, one per week, and interspersed with advertisements—changed seemingly overnight. This shift also brought a major change in the methods for measuring audiences. In the United States, broadcast audiences were for many decades, and are still, measured by the Nielsen Company; Nielsen relied on statistical methods to extrapolate from small samples to make general statements about audience behavior—a standard of measurement that, whatever problems it might present, has been accepted by advertisers and the television industry for decades. Because they had to be shared with advertisers and potential advertisers—the size of a program's audience determining the value of advertising sold to run during that program—these numbers were more or less publicly available. Newspapers and magazines regularly announced and discussed Nielson ratings, and major financial decisions (determining which shows continued, which were canceled, and so on) relied on those numbers. A consequence of this system was that if a show was a critical success but unpopular with audiences as measured by Nielsen, there were no reliable ways to hide that the show was not reaching a large audience. And in the competition for advertising dollars among networks, critical darlings with small audiences could rarely receive continued support.[3]

Netflix and Amazon rejected this model. These companies generally refuse to share any of their audience data, and they overtly reject the idea that Nielsen can track the viewing of their programs. In October 2017, Nielsen announced it would begin measuring audiences for Netflix shows; the trade publication *Variety* quoted a Netflix spokesman who said in response, "The data that Nielsen is reporting is not accurate, not even close, and does not reflect the viewing of these shows on Netflix."[4] Although Nielsen has ever since been hard at work strengthening its abilities in this area, the insistence by Netflix in 2017 that the Nielsen numbers were meaningless reflected the degree to which Netflix, up to that point, neither wanted nor needed its audiences to be measured by a third party.[5]

In the wake of that story, many bloggers and TV industry critics explained why Netflix neither needed nor wanted Nielsen to measure the audiences of its shows. Netflix did not need ratings because they were not selling advertising or relying on advertising revenue to produce their programs. They did not want ratings because knowing, in fine detail, what their subscribers liked to watch was one of their competitive advantages in the marketplace, and they did not want to share that data with competitors.[6] Although Netflix has been the center of these discussions vis-à-vis Nielsen ratings, the perspective was equally true of Amazon and its video streaming division in the late 2010s; after all, a 2015 article in *Fortune* referred to Amazon as "a company that hoards business metrics like state secrets."[7]

These dynamics will likely turn out to have been specific to the early years of streaming video; as business models for streaming services have developed and numerous companies have entered the field, what is and is not possible on streaming platforms continues to change; however, while it lasted, the situation created an opportunity for the television industry to operate less like magazines and newspapers (which have typically relied on advertising revenue) and more like trade book publishing (which typically has not). For at least a century, the most appealing model for most major publishers has been one based on publishing a mix of prestige products, to earn respect and awards, and popular products, to reach a larger audience—"lustre and lucre," in the words of one major American publisher.[8]

By the time *Transparent* premiered in 2014, Netflix had already established itself as the dominant streaming platform. But Amazon, a massive, complex company that does many different things—not just selling physical objects and digital content, but also maintaining server farms and selling bandwidth and storage, along with other projects—had to convince people, especially professionals in the television business, that it was serious about producing television. In terms of its relationship with audience members, the task of Amazon's original video content was to nudge its customers to subscribe to Prime, a membership service that increases the likelihood of a customer ordering more physical and digital products on the site. Because of this, at that early phase of its ambitions to produce original content, Amazon needed a critical success—a show that would attract buzz and critical acclaim in the press—much more than it needed (or could possibly produce) a ratings hit. It is worth emphasizing this: because the size of Prime membership in 2014 was nowhere near as large as the potential audience of a television show, film, or YouTube video, Amazon could not have produced a ratings hit with any show whose audience was limited to members of the service.[9]

It was crucial, then, that Amazon did not have to tell anyone how many people were actually watching *Transparent*. The audience data could be hidden from critics, fans, and other viewers, which is precisely the approach taken by publishers with critically acclaimed works of literature that turn out to have sold embarrassingly few copies. In early 2018, a leak of Amazon documents allowed a Reuters reporter to plausibly estimate the viewership for a number of Amazon shows. According to that report, *Transparent*'s third season attracted only 1.3 million viewers, a relatively small number compared to major broadcast shows (which could attract more than ten million viewers).[10] But savvy observers of the television industry understood that audience size had never been important for *Transparent*. Writing in *Vox*, television critic Todd VanDerWerff explained it this way: The number of viewers could be seriously tiny—even as small as 100,000—and still break [Amazon's] record for original programming.... Even if only five people are watching *Transparent* and they're all TV critics, the show is still a 'success' for the site, because people are buzzing about it passionately, and that gets the idea of Amazon as a content provider out there in the public consciousness. That will make it easier for future shows to break out, create new subscribers, and justify the expense Amazon is pouring into original content development."[11] A tiny audience, if the right audience, was all Amazon needed and wanted when it picked up *Transparent* in 2014. One small audience to whom the show seems to have appealed enormously is that of Jewish studies academics; this anthology provides evidence of that, as do the many other academic events that have been dedicated to discussing the show, as well as a private Facebook group in which Jewish studies academics discussed and debated *Transparent*.[12] Of course, Jewish studies academics do not typically carry much weight in Hollywood, but another group of highly educated, intellectual Jews (some of whom are not so far removed from academia themselves) were prominent among the television critics that Amazon needed to reach.

Emily Nussbaum is one prominent example. She had been named the *New Yorker*'s television critic in 2011, won a National Magazine Award for her criticism in 2014, and accepted the Pulitzer Prize for criticism in 2016. With a master's degree from New York University and a background in writing for *Lingua Franca*, the late, great magazine about academia, Nussbaum was exactly the kind of Jewish journalist to whom *Transparent* might have been expected to appeal—the kind who refers to herself self-mockingly on Twitter as a "Jew with a temper" and a "snivelling [sic] Jew."[13] Nussbaum's first review of the series, which appeared before the season became available to viewers, exclaimed, "Excitingly, it's . . . the most Jewish show I've seen on TV." Her second review referred to the show as a "stealth masterpiece"—note the implication about the size of its audience—and referred, over and over again, to the show's intense Jewishness.[14]

Many other television critics who raved in major national publications about *Transparent* likewise have personal investments in Jewishness that they have discussed in print—and many of them responded to *Transparent* with extraordinary enthusiasm. Consider Margaret Lyons, who call the show's first season "damn near perfect";[15] Willa Paskin, who reviewed the first season for *Slate*;[16] and Spencer Kornhaber, who reviewed the third season for *The Atlantic*.[17] As a gambit for critical acclaim, focusing attention on what Nussbaum calls an "aggressively specific" and "Jewy" show turns out to have been a very canny thing for the company to do, because even if only those critics and a handful of Amazon Prime members watched it, the show would have served its purpose.

It is worth considering the other small audience to whom Amazon could have been addressing with *Transparent*: trans people, and queer people more generally. Soloway's 2018 memoir, *She Wants It*, suggests distressingly how little the creators of the show thought about that potential audience as they filmed the pilot. Although they had a couple of trans consultants, it was only after the pilot was filmed and edited that Soloway showed it to trans author Jennifer Finley Boylan, and then heard, somewhat to their surprise, the prediction that "you will get a fair amount of blowback for not hiring a transgender actor or actress to play the part of Maura."[18] Of course, this is what happened when the show premiered and again when Soloway's memoir was published. Responses from trans and queer people have been, in a number of cases, intensely negative; one reviewer dismissed the show as "transphobic bullshit."[19] But that small audience did not have the same kind of media traction in 2014, especially as television critics for major publications, that American Jews did.[20] And the influence of Jews as critics and throughout the television industry might help to explain why the show is, in Judith Butler's view, "much better on Jewish life than it is on trans life."[21]

The degree to which *Transparent* had, from one perspective, pandered to Jewish audiences with its Jewish references, specifically in pursuit of industry awards, was on display in a *Saturday Night Live* parody commercial that aired in the fall of 2016.[22] The spoof pokes fun at *Transparent* having won awards as a "comedy," given the show's dark tone. But the parody also emphasizes what, to at least some observers, seems like a gratuitous representation of Jewish ritual, having the cast of its *Transparent*-like show slowly recite the *motzi*, the traditional Jewish blessing over bread. Meanwhile, *SNL*'s commercial does not reference anything about the trans or queer narratives in the show, but the prayer performed is exactly the same one the Pfefferman family sings together in a season 2 episode, "The Book of Life." As such, the parody registers the connection between *Transparent*'s emphasis on Jewishness, its small audience, and its celebration by television critics and the awards they confer.

The Reboot Approach to Ritual

It is one thing to say that a streaming video show could succeed by frankly and regularly representing Jewishness. It is another thing to specify how it does so. To explain this, it helps to keep in mind a major development in Jewish culture in America in the decades leading up to *Transparent*'s premiere. The 1990 National Jewish Population Survey, funded by the Council of Jewish Federations, sent shockwaves throughout the North American Jewish community. The most widely quoted statistic pertained to the intermarriage rate of American Jews, which was pegged at 52 percent. Although demographers objected at the time (and in retrospect) to the study's methodology (and more recent critiques have pointed to the misogyny that animates such approaches), that intermarriage figure became impossible to avoid in American Jewish life.[23]

At the same time, as historian Lila Corwin-Berman and anthropologists Joshua Friedman and Moshe Korngold have recently explored, in the wake of the Tax Reform Act of 1969, and with growing wealth concentrated in family foundations, the structures of American Jewish philanthropy changed, putting more decision-making power in the hands of individual donors and the staff of family foundations.[24] Among other effects, this led to a new stream of funding for the support and perpetuation of Jewish culture, broadly defined. Large sums of money flowed from federations, foundations, and individual megadonors to university chairs in Jewish studies divisions and to massive new experiential programs in Jewish culture, most notably the March of the Living and Taglit-Birthright.[25] One substream of such funding was motivated by a belief that arts and culture might be the key to engaging young Jews in their Jewish identities; this goal was pursued mostly through grants to individual artists and to nonprofit organizations supporting arts and artists, including the Foundation for Jewish Culture (founded in 1960, but with widely expanded programming in the 1990s, then shut down in 2014), Makor (1999–2013), the Joshua Venture (1998–), the Six Points Fellowship (2006–2013), the Jewish Book Council (founded in 1925 but revitalized in 1994), and Reboot (2002–), among other initiatives.

Whether such ventures were ever successful in inculcating the Jewish values or behaviors that their creators and funders desired—the vagueness of the aims and impossibility of measuring the success of such programs has recently been emphasized by leading scholars in the field of Jewish education[26]—one undeniable result was a flood of support for Jewish arts programming and artists. More or less directly, that wave of funding and institution building helped launch the careers of a number of contemporary Jewish artists—notably, the musician Matisyahu and novelists including Nathan Englander, Dara Horn, and Jonathan Safran Foer[27]—but rarely has the line between a Jewish cultural initiative and a cultural product been as clear and dramatic as it is in the relationship between the group Reboot and *Transparent*.

Reboot is a nonprofit organization founded in 2002 with funds from, and by the employees of, a couple of wealthy, privately controlled foundations, specifically the Andrea and Charles Bronfman Foundation and the Righteous Persons Foundation (which Steven Spielberg created using the profits from *Schindler's List*). A 2012 evaluation by the Jim Joseph Foundation, which also came to fund the organization, described Reboot as a growing network of young cultural creatives and opinion leaders working to "reboot" Jewish culture, rituals, and traditions and make them vital and resonant for young adults, the Jewish community, and the larger society.[28] Reboot has pursued this mission mainly by hosting a three-day annual summit in Park City, Utah, which brings new people into the network and connects them to one another.[29] The resulting Reboot network includes hundreds of successful media professionals in a variety of fields, as well as some rabbis and scholars.[30]

What bears emphasizing here is how clear the mission of the organization is, as phrased above: "to 'reboot' Jewish culture, rituals, and traditions." Several successful Reboot-branded projects offer clear illustrations of this mission. For example, Sukkah City was an architectural competition held in 2010, in which six hundred architects submitted designs, and twelve winning designs—updated versions of the hut traditionally built by religious Jews on the holiday of Sukkot, conforming to the *halakhic* requirements but looking radically new—were constructed in Union Square Park in New York. In short: the Sukkah, rebooted. Another example and possibly the most widely recognized Reboot project is The National Day of Unplugging, a program that, in various ways, tries to convince people to turn off their phones one day a week to restore calm and balance in their lives. In short: the Sabbath, rebooted.[31] These projects take a specific ritual from Jewish religious life and radically recontextualize it—changing its name (from Sabbath to day of unplugging) or location (from backyards and synagogue parking lots to Union Square Park) and using contemporary aesthetics to revitalize it.

Reboot is not an LGBTQ+ advocacy organization (and most of its members and leaders are cisgender and heterosexual), but it is not a stretch to understand the group's mission "to 'reboot' Jewish culture, rituals, and traditions" in relation to a larger movement of Jewish feminist and LGBTQ+ ritual "reinterpretation and innovation."[32] Inspirations for Reboot's approach can also be located in the *havurah* movement and in tech industry ideas about disruption, but it is clear that one major influence was the work of Jewish LGBTQ+ leaders and artists.[33] One "founding faculty member" of Reboot who helped to set the organization's direction was Rabbi Amichai Lau Lavie, the creator of Storahtelling and an admired drag performer. Lau Lavie's innovative approach to Jewish ritual set a template for the practice of rebooting more generally.[34] The conceptual overlap between Reboot's approach to ritual and LGBTQ+ Jewish innovation helps explain why this approach to Jewish practice would appeal to Joey Soloway, who attended Reboot's Summit in 2005.

In fact, Soloway has been outspoken about Reboot's influence on their life and work. Just around the time of the first season of *Transparent*'s release, Soloway told a reporter for the *Forward* that going to Reboot "had a major impact" on their work, and that "many of the writers on 'Transparent' are people [they] met through" that group.[35] The influence of Reboot is explicit in Soloway's films and television shows, which, in the decade after they attended the Reboot Summit, repeatedly returned to the very specific practice at the core of Reboot's mission: taking Jewish rituals and radically recontextualizing them so as to "make them vital and resonant," whether for LGBTQ+ Jews or for cisgender, heterosexual ones.

In Soloway's film *Afternoon Delight* (2013), which was released directly before *Transparent*, that rebooting gesture is somewhat awkward and devoted to strengthening the normative structure of heterosexual marriage. The movie tells the story of a suburban mom who brings an erotic dancer into her house because she and her husband have stopped having sex. The film's resolution somewhat inexplicably hinges on a scene in which the alienated husband and wife realize it is Friday night and light Shabbat candles, using two mismatched candles grabbed at random (see figure 1.1) instead of traditional candlesticks: a reboot of the ritual of Sabbath eve candle lighting that the film imbues, somewhat implausibly, with the power to overcome the resentment and distance between a struggling straight married couple.[36]

Transparent, meanwhile, explicitly invoked Reboot's programs; for example, Sarah, the eldest Pfefferman child, mentions the National Day of Unplugging at the dinner table one Friday night. The show also offers up a parody of the kind of hip Jewish event put on by the Reboot-affiliated, Silver Lake–based organization that Soloway helped to found, East Side Jews: a Havdalah event called Hineni

FIGURE 1.1 Rebooting Shabbat candle-lighting in Soloway's *Afternoon Delight*. Written by Joey Soloway, directed by Joey Soloway (The Film Arcade, 2013).

(Hebrew for "here I am") or Tacos con Torah, at which guests are asked to relinquish their phones as they enter. These moments in *Transparent*, like an episode of another streaming video show *Difficult People* (2015–2017) in which an organization called Refutz encourages Jews to unplug for Sabbath, reflect contemporary television writers' awareness of Reboot's efforts to build community among successful media professionals and encourage them to practice rebooted Jewish rituals.[37]

More meaningfully, *Transparent* instantiates Reboot's mission at least as effectively as any of the organization's officially branded projects do. The show consistently isolates Jewish rituals and traditions and recontextualizes them so as to—again in the language of Reboot itself—make them vital and resonant. A clear example is one of the most moving scenes of the show's first season. It takes place in a flashback to a 1994 weekend during which the bat mitzvah of Pfefferman's youngest daughter, Ari, was scheduled to take place. The bat mitzvah had been canceled, ostensibly because Ari expressed doubts about religion but really because the person she has known as her father wanted to attend a retreat for crossdressers. The upshot, though, is that Ari is alone in the living room of the family home when a waiter from the catering service arrives, not having been informed that the party was canceled. In the scene, Ari performs three lines of what is ostensibly her Torah portion, singing the words in the traditional *trope* (tune) to a captive audience of one, the caterer; she is barefoot and dressed in cut-off jean shorts and a rumpled baseball shirt, and at first, she is lying on a sofa before she stands to leap onto a coffee table. As she moves through these positions, she waves her arms and points her legs in gestures that look by turns expressively oratorical and vaguely balletic, and then she ends with a dramatic bow.

The scene is, unmistakably, a radical recontextualization of traditional bat mitzvah ritual, a reboot.[38] It takes the Torah reading that is part of many bar and bat mitzvah traditions and strips away the context of the synagogue and the presence of family members and rabbinical authorities and the community, as well as the physical scroll. What is left is a child singing the words of the Torah—in this case, with obvious significance, Parashat Lech Lecha, Genesis 12:1–3, the passage in which God commands Abraham to embark on a journey, trusting that he will be rewarded. It is a scene that is beautiful and moving, specifically because of what it removes from the conventional representation of a bat mitzvah: the family pressure and especially the commercial and financial encumbrances—the abandoned caterer stands, to some degree, as a negative emblem of the catered party that is not happening—that have often surrounded the ritual in America since the mid-twentieth century, much to the chagrin of clergy and other observers.[39] Instead, the scene centers on a teenager's attempt to connect with an element of the ritual that has potentially the deepest Jewish significance, the text itself, and the connection is expressed through the joyful and spontaneous movement of her body. The appreciative audience for Ari's performance of this ritual, the caterer, is played by the queer Jewish artist Mel

Shimkovitz, and that character's gender-nonconforming appearance offers a reminder that the more conventional synagogue spaces in which bat mitzvahs might be expected to take place have histories of marginalizing and excluding queer Jews. And given that in later seasons Ari comes out as queer and nonbinary, this reboot can be read specifically as imagining how a Jewish coming-of-age ritual that, in S. J. Crasnow's terms, "may be deemed heterosexist or cissexist" can be transformed into one that is "unproblematic or even affirming" for LGBTQ+ Jews.[40]

It is worth emphasizing the differences between this scene and other representations of similar Jewish rituals in American popular culture of the same period. In the video for the Canadian rapper Drake's 2011 song "HYFR (Hell Ya Fucking Right)," the joke is that he and his friends party wildly at what is staged to look like a completely traditional bar mitzvah ceremony and reception. The video was filmed at Temple Israel in Miami, Drake wears a traditional suit, tie, and yarmulke, and in one shot from the video, he stands behind a bimah next to a rabbi in the postures and position of a traditional *aliyah*.[41] When Vanessa Bayer embodied the character of Jacob the bar mitzvah boy on *Saturday Night Live* (which she did in sketches from 2011–2013), she dressed, like Drake, in a traditional suit with a yarmulke and reads from a text with a pointed finger, almost as if reading from the Torah.[42] The director of Drake's video, who goes by the name Director X, told an interviewer that he had never been to a bar mitzvah before shooting the video but that "we were very clear that the re-bar mitzvah should really look like a bar mitzvah. There was a rabbi officially there to make sure everything was straight."[43] In both examples, despite their fundamental lack of reverence for tradition and overt satirical intentions, the approach was to align with audiences' ideas about what a bar mitzvah looks like. Soloway's approach does the opposite, exploding and transforming what the ritual looks like. Drake and *Saturday Night Live* wanted to use a Jewish ritual to make their audiences laugh, but Soloway wants to use laughter and surprise to make the ritual newly resonant.

Ari's rebooted bat mitzvah is a powerful example, and it is not an exception in *Transparent*, but, very obviously, the rule. Just about every single case in which a tradition or a ritual is presented in the show is recontextualized or transformed. When a *mikvah* (ritual bath) appears in season 1, rather than serving as a pool for ritual immersions and purifications, it is out-of-service and empty of water, and two characters sit in it like a booth at a restaurant to share an intimate conversation.[44] At the Tacos con Torah event mentioned above, Havdalah—the ritual to mark the end of the sabbath—is suddenly interrupted, somewhat to the rabbi's discomfort, with a mourner's *Kaddish*, a prayer for a recently deceased person not traditionally recited at Havdalah and not traditionally recited for non-Jews, which it is in this case.[45] Indeed, the show constantly represents Jewish religious rituals, as Roberta Rosenberg has pointed out, but it is crucial that in nearly every example, they are emphatically recontextualized, rebooted rituals.[46]

One can read the larger story arcs and narrative experiments of the show, even the series' premise as a whole, as working to recontextualize major touchstones of contemporary Jewish experience specifically through a lens of trans and nonbinary experiences. The show's second season can be understood as an attempt to reboot the Holocaust, so to speak, in the sense that the episodes shift the grounds of ritualized Holocaust memory from its conventional focus on the war years of 1939–1945, the concentration and death camps, and the survivors in the postwar decades to instead focus on the traumatic break in the history of trans rights activism that occurred when Magnus Hirschfeld's Institute for Sexual Science in Berlin was destroyed and its library was publicly burned by the Nazis in 1933.[47] The show's fourth season can be understood as an attempt to reboot American Jews' ritualized and institutionalized understandings of Israel and Palestine, which are recontextualized by the show again through the perspective of Ari, who sees them first and foremost as someone who has come to question the limits of binary definitions of identity and culture, especially but not only regarding gender.[48] In that sense, the show's approaches align neatly with Reboot's mission and with the LGBTQ+ ritual innovation underlying that mission.

Is This How It Should Be?

As an example of how the properties of streaming video and the influence of Jewish nonprofit organizations can shape a contemporary television show, *Transparent* is striking but by no means unique. *Orange Is the New Black* (2013–2019), another highly successful and widely discussed early streaming video show, was likewise created by a Rebooter, writer and producer Jenji Kohan. The show was an adaptation of the memoir of Piper Kerman, whose husband, editor Larry Smith, is also a Rebooter, and a character based on Smith appeared in the series. In the show's third season, which aired in 2015, the imprisoned characters become interested in Judaism because it allows them to request better food. One widely discussed storyline featured an African American inmate Cindy, who makes the case to a rabbi about the sincerity of her desire to convert to Judaism, and then, in what is for all intents and purposes a rebooted mikveh, she ritually immerses in a pond near the prison. Not coincidentally, comedian and actress Jamie Denbo, the actress who played Shelly Ginsberg, the Jewish inmate who sits beside Cindy during her conversation with the rabbi and then oversees her ritual immersion before saying "Mazel tov" to conclude the recontextualized ritual, is also a member of the Reboot network.[49] It should be no surprise that a show whose cast, crew, and inspiration draws heavily on the Reboot network would, like *Transparent*, prominently feature a rebooted Jewish ritual.

The strangeness and specialness of the market for streaming video, in its first few years as a widely consumed media platform for longform comedy and drama, made a certain kind of cultural product possible—"aggressively specific" especially about American Jews, but also about other minority groups.[50] To say this is not to minimize the talents and achievements of Soloway, of *Transparent*'s cast and crew, or of other artists working in this period but simply to insist that the stories that are possible to tell, about Jews or anything else, are profoundly shaped by the media forms and historical moments in which they are told.

As for the factors conditioning the production of Jewish culture in the new millennium, there is room for disagreement about them. Reboot's mission, in general, may not be sympathetic to all observers. What, one might ask, does the spread of such practices of recontextualization of Jewish ritual portend? Does it mean there is no vitality left in Jewish tradition, if, to make it interesting, one needs to remove it from its traditional contexts? Or does it suggest precisely how much more room there is to find new relevance in Jewish culture, even from directions that would be astonishing to the Jews who lived a generation or a century ago?[51]

It is also worth asking whether it can be considered a positive development that a genuinely compelling, possibly enduring work of American popular culture was inspired in its representation of Jewishness by the deliberate intervention of a nonprofit foundation. Is that how the creation of art is supposed to work? *Transparent* was produced at a time of astonishing philanthropy and patronage of the arts, and it is difficult to decide what kind of systems and contexts produce the best work and which tends to churn out mediocrity.[52] The way one answers those questions—about the role of nonprofit foundations in the production of culture and about Reboot's mission to recontextualize and reframe Jewish rituals—probably correlates, quite strongly, with how much one admires, or is annoyed by, Soloway's *Transparent*.

Acknowledgments

Thanks to the Alan D. Leve Center for Jewish Studies at UCLA and to Lia Brozgal and Todd Presner for inviting me to deliver the Naftulin Family Lecture on Studies in Jewish Identity. Also, thanks to the Program in American Studies at Princeton University and to Anne Cheng and Esther Schor for the invitation to deliver the Lapidus Family Fund Lecture in American Jewish Studies. This project was strengthened thanks to the engagement of colleagues and audience members at both events. Thanks also to Jon Catlin, Nora Rubel, and Brett Krutzsch.

Notes

1. A good overview of this history is available in J. Hoberman and Jeffrey Shandler, eds., *Entertaining America: Jews, Movies, and Broadcasting* (Princeton, NJ: Princeton University Press, 2003).
2. Daniel Fienberg, "Interview: 'Transparent' Creator Jill Soloway Discusses her Amazon Pilot," *Hitfix*, February 15, 2014, https://uproxx.com/hitfix/interview-transparent-creator-jill-soloway-discusses-her-amazon-pilot/.

3. For a history of ratings practices, see Karen Buzzard, *Tracking the Audience: The Ratings Industry from Analog to Digital* (New York: Routledge, 2012).
4. Brian Steinberg, "Nielsen Says It Will Measure Audiences for TV Episodes That Stream Via Netflix," *Variety*, October 18, 2017, http://variety.com/2017/tv/news/nielsen-measurement-netflix-1202592985/.
5. John Koblin, "Nielsen Now Knows When You Are Streaming," *New York Times*, June 17, 2021, https://www.nytimes.com/2021/06/17/business/media/nielsen-streaming-metrics-netflix-youtube.html. Notably, even while expressing increased support for Nielsen's efforts in 2021, the chief executive of Netflix reiterated the company's earlier attitude about Nielsen ratings, saying, "We don't sell advertising, so it's not very relevant."
6. See, for example, Willa Paskin, "Nothing's a Hit Anymore," *Slate*, November 12, 2015, https://slate.com/culture/2015/11/tv-ratings-in-the-streaming-age-why-nothing-can-be-called-a-hit-anymore.html.
7. J. P. Mangalindan, "Inside Amazon Prime," *Fortune*, February 3, 2015, https://fortune.com/2015/02/03/inside-amazon-prime/.
8. The phrase is Victor Weybright's; see Erin A. Smith, "Paperbacks and the Literary Marketplace," *American Literature in Transition, 1940–1950* (Cambridge: Cambridge University Press, 2017), 297.
9. Though Amazon was very guarded about sharing information about the number of its Prime subscribers, the best estimate of total Amazon Prime members in 2014 was about 20 million, whereas the total number of potential television audience members just in the United States at the same time was in the hundreds of millions. See Jay Yarow, "Amazon Says It Has At Least 20 Million Prime Members," *Business Insider*, January 6, 2014, https://www.businessinsider.com/amazon-prime-members-2014-1.
10. Jeffrey Dastin, "Exclusive: Amazon's Internal Numbers on Prime Video, Revealed," *Reuters*, March 15, 2018, https://www.reuters.com/article/idUSKCN1GR0F7/.
11. Emily St. James, "Amazon's *Transparent* Gets a Second Season. But How Many People Actually Watch It?" *Vox*, October 9, 2014, https://www.vox.com/2014/10/9/6951373/transparent-renewed-amazon.
12. In addition to this symposium and anthology, there was a symposium held at Tel Aviv University in June 2018, and much attention was paid to the show at the Association for Jewish Studies conference in December 2016, where it was the subject of a roundtable, several individual papers, and a plenary session.
13. See Emily Nussbaum (@emilynussbaum), "Yes and as a Jew with a temper, I find this bad for the Jews with tempers," Twitter, July 17, 2017, https://twitter.com/emilynussbaum/status/885619887024078848, and, "@RokhlK As a snivelling Jew, I tend to be okay with that schtick," Twitter, March 27, 2015, https://twitter.com/emilynussbaum/status/581545953120759808.
14. Emily Nussbaum, "Open Secret," *New Yorker*, September 29, 2014, https://www.newyorker.com/magazine/2014/09/29/open-secret, and "Inside Out," *New Yorker*, January 4, 2016, https://www.newyorker.com/magazine/2016/01/04/inside-out-on-television-emily-nussbaum. On Nussbaum's interest in representations of Jews, see also her review of another Amazon show that followed on the success of *Transparent*, *The Marvelous Mrs. Maisel*. Nussbaum says that its premise ("a Jewish girl does standup comedy") is "so far up my alley it was practically chopping onions in my kitchen." Nussbaum, "The Cloying Fantasia of 'The Marvelous Mrs. Maisel,'" *New Yorker*, December 24 and 31, 2018, https://www.newyorker.com/magazine/2018/12/24/the-cloying-fantasia-of-the-marvelous-mrs-maisel, and her Twitter thread

about the fine points of Jewish representation on that show (@emilynussbaum), "Can I ask a weirdly specific Maisel question?", Twitter, December 6, 2018, https://twitter.com/emilynussbaum/status/1070774341116268545.

15 Margaret Lyons, "Amazon's *Transparent* Is Damn Near Perfect," *Vulture*, September 26, 2014, http://www.vulture.com/2014/09/tv-review-transparent-is-damn-near-perfect.html. Lyons was a religious studies major in college and has told an interviewer, "I was always super interested in religion and religiosity. My mom is Catholic, and my dad's an agnostic Jew, and I always had lots of questions." Claire Zulkey, "TV Guide," *UChicago Magazine*, March 24, 2015, https://mag.uchicago.edu/arts-humanities/tv-guide.

16 Willa Paskin, "See Me," *Slate*, September 29, 2014, http://www.slate.com/articles/arts/television/2014/09/transparent_on_amazon_prime_reviewed_it_s_the_fall_s_best_new_show.html. Paskin had previously been a contributing editor to the Jewish magazine *Nextbook*; see Dan Klein, "Mazel Tov, Willa Paskin!," *Tablet*, March 7, 2012, http://www.tabletmag.com/scroll/93323/mazel-tov-willa-paskin.

17 Spencer Kornhaber, "*Transparent*'s Third Season Is a Powerful Plea for Compassion," *Atlantic*, September 23, 2016, https://www.theatlantic.com/entertainment/archive/2016/09/transparent-season-3-review-amazon-prime-series/501287/. Kornhaber wrote about his identity as a queer Jew in describing a trip to Israel; see "A Queer Tour of Israel," *Atlantic*, June 25, 2014, https://www.theatlantic.com/magazine/archive/2014/07/out-and-about-in-israel/372272/.

18 Joey Soloway, *She Wants It: Desire, Power, and Toppling the Patriarchy* (New York: Crown Archetype, 2018), 75.

19 s. e. smith, "*Transparent* Is Transphobic Bullshit," *Global Comment*, October 3, 2014, http://globalcomment.com/amazons-transparent-is-transphobic-bullshit/. See also Andrea Long Chu, "Nobody Wants It," *Affidavit*, November 5, 2018, https://www.affidavit.art/articles/no-one-wants-it.

20 Trans and queer people also did not have the same level of influence as producers in Hollywood, whereas at least one of the young executives who greenlit *Transparent* for Amazon, Joe Lewis, is Jewish and has posted publicly about his self-consciousness about descending from Jewish immigrants. See Lewis (@joelewis), "In 1906, my grand-grandfather Max Lewis had to flee Russia for being Jewish, immigrating to the US at 16 and later joining the Army to fight in WW1," Twitter, November 12, 2018, https://twitter.com/JoeLewis/status/1062121274464301057.

21 Molly Fischer, "Think Gender Is Performance? You Have Judith Butler to Thank for That," *New York/The Cut*, June 12, 2016, https://www.thecut.com/2016/06/judith-butler-c-v-r.html.

22 *Saturday Night Live*, Season 42, episode 4, "Funny New Comedy," October 22, 2016, https://www.youtube.com/watch?v=AMpRJwP5y9Q.

23 On the influence of the survey on professionals at Jewish nonprofit organizations, see Rabbi Hayim Herring, "How the 1990 National Jewish Population Survey Was Used by Federation Professional for Jewish Continuity Purposes," *Journal of Jewish Communal Service* 76, no. 3 (January 2000): 216–227. On the debates about the survey's methodology and accuracy, see, for example, Nacha Cattan, "New Population Survey Retracts Intermarriage Figure," *Forward*, September 12, 2003, https://forward.com/news/8112/new-population-survey-retracts-intermarriage-figur/. For a critique of the sexual politics of "Jewish continuity," see Lila Corwin Berman, Kate Rosenblatt, and Ronit Y. Stahl, "Continuity Crisis: The History and Sexual Politics of an American Jewish Communal Project," *American Jewish History* 104, nos. 2/3 (2020): 167–194.

24 Lila Corwin Berman, "How Americans Give: The Financialization of American Jewish Philanthropy," *The American Historical Review* 122, no. 5 (December 2017): 1459–1489; Joshua B. Friedman and Moshe Kornfeld, "Identity Projects: Philanthropy, Neoliberalism, and Jewish Cultural Production," *American Jewish History* 102, no. 4 (October 2018): 537–561.

25 See Jack Wertheimer, "Mapping the Scene: How Younger Jewish Adults Engage with Jewish Community," in *The New Jewish Leaders: Reshaping the American Jewish Landscape*, ed. Jack Wertheimer (Waltham, MA: Brandeis University Press, 2011), 1–44.

26 See Ari Y. Kelman et al., "Traditional Judaism: The Conceptualization of Jewishness in the Lives of American Jewish Post-Boomers," *Jewish Social Studies* 23, no. 1 (Fall 2017): 134–167.

27 On Matisyahu's relationship with JDub Records, a nonprofit organization first funded by the Joshua Venture, see "Matisyahu Parts Ways with Longtime Management," *Billboard*, March 17, 2006, https://www.billboard.com/articles/news/59054/matisyahu-parts-ways-with-longtime-management, and Daniel Arkin, "Klezmer Punks, Gangsta Rabbis: An Oral History of JDub Records," *Brooklyn Ink*, November 12, 2012, http://brooklynink.org/2012/11/12/50511-klezmer-punks-gangsta-rabbis-an-oral-history-of-jdub-records-2002-2011/. On Foer, Horn, and the institutional support of Jewish literature in this period generally, see Josh Lambert, "Since 2000," in *The Cambridge History of Jewish American Literature*, ed. Hana Wirth-Nesher (Cambridge: Cambridge University Press, 2016), 622–641.

28 Madeleine Taylor and Pete Plastrik, "Network Evaluation Summary Report 2012," Jim Joseph Foundation, 2012, https://jimjosephfoundation.org/wp-content/uploads/2012/09/Rebppt_Eval_RADFinalReport_082720121.pdf, 4.

29 See Laura M. Holson, "You're Young and Jewish: Discuss," *New York Times*, January 14, 2011, http://www.nytimes.com/2011/01/16/fashion/16REBOOT.html.

30 Full disclosure: I attended the Reboot Summit in 2011, which means I am part of the network; I also worked with Reboot executives to bring a group of members to the Yiddish Book Center in the fall of 2017. The Reboot member directory is not a public document, but it is the source for my claims in this article about who is or is not a member of the Reboot network.

31 See Austin Considine, "And on the Sabbath, the iPhones Shall Rest," *New York Times*, March 17, 2010, http://www.nytimes.com/2010/03/18/fashion/18sabbath.html, and Fred A. Bernstein, "A Harvest of Temporary Shelters," *New York Times*, September 16, 2010, http://www.nytimes.com/2010/09/17/arts/design/17sukkah.html.

32 S. J. Crasnow describes "reinterpretation and innovation" of "Jewish tradition" as two strategies through which "Trans Jews can attain affirmation." See Crasnow, "On Transition: Normative Judaism and Trans Innovation," *Journal of Contemporary Religion* 32, no. 3 (2017): 403–415; the quote is on p. 412. Gregg Drinkwater has offered an extraordinary case study showing how "gay and lesbian Jewish leaders and their synagogues have helped reshape the relationship to healing, spirituality, and personal prayer among American Jews." See Drinkwater, "Queer Healing: AIDS, Gay Synagogues, Lesbian Feminists, and the Origins of the Jewish Healing Movement," *American Jewish History* 104, no. 4 (2020): 605–629.

33 On the *havurah* movement, see Riv-Ellen Prell, *Prayer and Community: The Havurah in American Judaism* (Detroit: Wayne State University Press, 1989). In his 2003 book *Nothing Sacred: The Truth about Judaism* (New York: Crown, 2003), Douglas Rushkoff calls the "participants of the Reboot 2002 Summit . . . the test

sample in this 'open source Judaism' project" (258) and uses the language of disruption to describe the ritual innovation of the "orange on the seder plate" (223).

34 On Lau Lavie, see Caryle Murphy, "'Storahtelling' Enlivens Worship," *Washington Post*, September 26, 2003, https://www.washingtonpost.com/archive/local/2003/09/26/storahtelling-enlivens-worship/; Nathan Gutmann, "Have We Got a Girl for You," *Haaretz*, October 1, 2004, https://www.haaretz.com/2004-10-01/ty-article/have-we-got-a-girl-for-you/.

35 Debra Nussbaum Cohen, "How Jill Soloway Created 'Transparent'—the Jewiest Show Ever," *Forward*, October 21, 2014, https://forward.com/culture/207407/how-jill-soloway-created-transparent-the-jewiest/. See also Gary Rosenblatt, "L.A. as a Model for the Jewish Future," *The Jewish Week*, March 19, 2013, http://jewishweek.timesofisrael.com/l-a-as-a-model-for-the-jewish-future/. Members of the Reboot network who have written for *Transparent* include Micah Fitzerman-Blue, Ethan Kuperberg, and Jessi Klein.

36 *Afternoon Delight*, directed by Joey Soloway (The Film Arcade, 2013), 1:29:30.

37 *Difficult People*, Season 2, episode 1, "Unplugged," directed by Jeffrey Walker, July 12, 2016.

38 It is worth noting that Soloway's own child's bar mitzvah in 2010, led by Lau Lavie, was cited in the press as exemplary of Lau Lavie's "Raising the Bar" initiative to transform b'mitzvah rituals. Soloway explained, "I was at a dinner party talking to some moms in New Jersey who were complaining about their kids hating to go to Hebrew school, hating practicing for the bar mitzvah, and I said it doesn't have to be like that, you can do it yourself . . . You don't have to even chant a portion. The portion is material you're given: make a puppet show, play, slide show—just tell the story." Julie Wiener, "A New Act for the Old Bar Mitzvah," *Jewish Telegraphic Agency*, June 2, 2010, https://www.jta.org/2010/06/02/ny/a-new-act-for-the-old-bar-mitzvah.

39 On critiques of bar mitzvah rituals as comprised by opulence—including one rabbi who proclaimed, in *Time* magazine in 1959, that the bar mitzvah was an "empty ceremony" and "conspicuous waste," see Rachel Kranson, *Ambivalent Embrace: Jewish Upward Mobility in Postwar America* (Chapel Hill, NC: University of North Carolina Press, 2017), 90.

40 Crasnow, "On Transition," 405.

41 Director X, director, "Drake - HYFR (Hell Ya Fucking Right) (Explicit) ft. Lil Wayne," YouTube, April 26, 2012, https://www.youtube.com/watch?v=oKCWqnldEag.

42 See Bayer's performances on the episodes of *Saturday Night Live* that aired on January 15, 2011; December 15, 2012; April 6, 2013; May 18, 2013; and October 5, 2013.

43 Jenn Pelly, "Drake 'HYFR,'" *Pitchfork*, April 26, 2012, https://pitchfork.com/features/directors-cut/8812-drake-hyfr/.

44 *Transparent*, Season 1, episode 6, "The Wilderness," Amazon Prime Video, September 26, 2014.

45 *Transparent*, Season 3, episode 5, "Oh Holy Night," Amazon Prime Video, September 23, 2016.

46 Roberta Rosenberg, "The Importance of Jewish Ritual in the Secular, Postmodern World of *Transparent*," *Jewish Film and New Media* 5, no. 1 (Spring 2017): 75–101.

47 See Josh Lambert, "Pfefferman Family Matters," *Tablet*, December 7, 2015, http://www.tabletmag.com/scroll/195620/pfefferman-family-matters.

48 Jackie Strause, "Blowing Up the Binary: How 'Transparent' Season 4 Is Personal for Jill Soloway," *Hollywood Reporter*, September 25, 2017, https://www

.hollywoodreporter.com/live-feed/transparent-season-4-jill-soloway-gender-binary-1042629.

49 Phil Abrahams, director, *Orange Is the New Black*, Season 3, episode 13, "Trust No Bitch," Netflix, June 11, 2015.

50 See, for example, Sara Bobolt and Brennan Williams, "If You Want to See Diversity Onscreen, Watch Netflix: And Amazon. And Hulu. Celebrate Diversity and Chill," *Huffpost*, February 26, 2016, https://www.huffingtonpost.com/entry/streaming-sites-diversity_us_56c61240e4b0b40245c96783.

51 Jack Wertheimer concludes his study of contemporary Jewish religious practice by asking some similar questions; see Wertheimer, *The New American Judaism: How Jews Practice Religion Today* (Princeton, NJ: Princeton University Press, 2018), 262–263.

52 On questions of funding and how they affect the creation of culture, see the work of Paul DiMaggio, for example, "Can Culture Survive the Marketplace?", *The Journal of Arts Management and Law* 13, no. 1 (March 1983): 61–87. On contemporary philanthropy and its effects on politics and culture, see David Callahan, *The Givers: Wealth, Power, and Philanthropy in a New Gilded Age* (New York: Knopf, 2017).

2

"Happy Yom Kippur"

Televising and Translating Atonement

NORA RUBEL

> You go explain Yom Kippur to a gentile... We're happy but we're starving, it's New Year's but we're guilty.
> —*The Marvelous Mrs. Maisel*

The family members file in, admiring the apartment, the spread, and the many accomplishments of the young people hosting. Exes are polite to each other, new relationships are beginning, and it is the culmination of a long period of prayer and self-reflection. It is the end of Yom Kippur, what Sarah Pfefferman mournfully calls "the holiest day of the year." Some of the guests have been to synagogue, some have fasted, and some have apologized for transgressions. It is time for the Pfeffermans to begin a new year. This family does have much to answer for in 5775; many of their individual choices have left others in pain and the episode entitled "The Book of Life" features Sarah, Josh, Maura, and Ari attempting to make amends in different ways (and with mixed results). As critic Eric Thurm writes, "Yom Kippur is kind of like the *Transparent* of Jewish holidays: a deeply sacred day for rigorous self-examination, shaggy spiritual pleas, and a big indulgent feast at the end."[1]

This self-examination and spiritual pleading does have some requirements. Rabbi Joseph Soloveitchik distills the Jewish approach to confession into three main components: 1. acknowledgment of sin ("I have sinned, I have acted perversely, I have transgressed"); 2. remorse ("I am contrite and ashamed of my deeds"); and 3. resolution for the future ("I will never do this again"). These stages constitute "the essence of confession."[2] All of the Pfeffermans take stabs at (some of) these components, with varied levels of success and good intentions, attempting reconciliations in the face of their own narcissism. The advertising campaign for season 2 of *Transparent* featured an image of the cast with the caption: "One family. No apologies." We should have been warned.

Jews have been featured as characters on TV since the dawn of the medium, but Judaism itself has traditionally served more as a plot device than as a source for religious exploration. *Transparent*'s Yom Kippur episode is notable for its intense and religiously specific scene in the synagogue, but it does have predecessors. In 1954, Gertrude Berg's popular series *The Goldbergs* featured a six-minute somber excerpt from a Yom Kippur service.[3] But more frequently, television shows showcased cultural Jewishness rather than religious Judaism.

Hanukkah has historically been screened for laughs as a sidekick to Christmas (such as on *Friends, South Park,* and *The O.C.*), but Yom Kippur's particularistic focus is unusual both within contemporary American Jewish practice and within televisual representation. As opposed to Jewish holidays like Passover and Hanukkah, which can be celebrated for selectively universalist themes and home-based practices, Yom Kippur is a different holiday entirely—one that speaks specifically to the relationship between Jews and their God and one that takes place primarily in the synagogue. Despite its distinct nature, Yom Kippur has been the focus of "very special" holiday episodes since the mid-twentieth century, when it was annually featured on *The Goldbergs*.

Multiple television shows have addressed both the holiday's observance and its theological significance through different lenses, but Yom Kippur has been primarily showcased in three ways: 1. as a dramatic means of displaying Jewish religiosity through liturgy and costume; 2. for its general (and more universal) theme of atonement; and 3. as a site of ethnic comedy, particularly for Jewish in-joke gags relating to the nature of the holiday's observance (such as in *The Marvelous Mrs. Maisel, Curb Your Enthusiasm,* and *Entourage*). The first two approaches serve as translation "for the goyim." The third represents a trend of "increasing proliferation of in-jokes," and Nathan Abrams has suggested that the Jews behind the scenes "neither know nor care if their Gentile audiences can share the laugh with them."[4] *Transparent*'s approach to Yom Kippur, in the second season episode "The Book of Life," remarkably employs all three approaches with a specificity never before seen.

The high holiday setting allows for a certain dramatic audiovisual gravity—prayers in Hebrew and Aramaic, the white garb of the clergy, and the collective sea of congregants beating their chests in atonement. For those affiliated Jews, this is one of the most attended services of the calendar year, occasionally requiring small sanctuaries to rent larger spaces to accommodate their regularly absent congregants. According to a 2017 Pew survey, 40 percent of American Jews fast on Yom Kippur, a greater number than those who keep kosher or light Shabbat candles. The fasting by Jews affiliated with a synagogue throughout the year is far higher, approaching 62 percent.[5] So this setting is familiar to American Jews, and although it is unlike most other year-round synagogue services, for many it serves as a stand-in for institutional religion. As Thurm argues, "That's part of why the premise for 'The Book of Life' is so great—Yom Kippur is a perfect focus for an episode of TV."[6] American Jews, regardless of their level of observance—or even their attachment to Judaism—have some understanding of this holiday and its dramatic significance. And this drama is on full display in "The Book of Life."

Explaining Yom Kippur to Gentiles

Like *Transparent, The Goldbergs* was a dramedy (to use today's parlance) and ran on television from 1949 to 1956 after almost twenty years as a popular radio broadcast. The program featured Molly Goldberg, a Yiddish-dialected matriarch of a Jewish family in the Bronx (and later, in a suburb called Haverville). According to Donald Weber, Gertrude Berg and *The Goldbergs* "performed the cultural work of . . . presenting, really re-presenting Jewish life to America in ways that made the audience members feel better about their own uprooted condition, more at ease in their New World Zion."[7] Referred to by one critic as "the most Jewish episode of any series in the history of network television,"[8] *The Goldbergs'* "A Sad Day" featured shots of the rabbi, the cantor, the separate women's gallery, and the congregants, who were chanting in Hebrew. The episode's plot involved anxiety about a possible estrangement between a father (David) and son (Sallie), and in the end, this discomfort was due to a white lie told by the son to avoid causing pain for his father. Sallie's daughter was ill, and Sallie did not want his father to worry about her. The episode concluded, after the prayer-filled service, with the reveal that the child was recovering. This plot imbues the synagogue service with a deeper meaning as the audience becomes aware of the stakes for all the family members. Notably, the bond between father and son is seen as the real meaning of the holiday—there is no explanation of either the liturgy or the holiday itself.[9]

Like many holiday episodes, the sanctity of the family is what is truly important. Arguing about the true meaning of a holiday is irrelevant; this is also evident in myriad episodes about Christmas that similarly highlight fraught family dynamics and not Jesus's birth. As sociologist Amitai Etzioni expresses in *We Are What We Celebrate,* holidays "are symbolic in the sense that their essential elements (activities, foods, rules) cannot be substantively explained—the connection between these elements and the holiday they belong to is arbitrary."[10]

On television, the parts of the holiday that are highlighted, and the meaning imbued within, are similarly discretionary.

"A Sad Day" was not the first time that *The Goldbergs* featured Yom Kippur. The series regularly noted the family's observance of Yom Kippur and Passover as part of its annual offerings—first on the radio and then later on television. Jewish viewers frequently responded to such episodes with gratitude, asserting, "I admire your courage to depict our Jewish life in such a beautiful way," and "this series from your facile pen has done more to *set us Jews right* with 'the goyim' then all the sermons ever preached by the Rabbis."[11]

"A Sad Day" aired on Erev Yom Kippur, theoretically at a time when many Jews would be unable to view it, leading one critic to suggest that the purpose of the episode was "to provide the larger, gentile audience with a positive and educational image of Jewish religious practice ... a 'teachable moment.'"[12] Remember, this religious service is entirely in Hebrew. Despite the foreignness of the tongue and the exotic nature of the costumes, this episode concluded with Molly wishing the audience a meaningful holiday at the close. "Dear friends, let me just wish for all of you God's blessings on this day and greetings from our family to your family. Good night." As Thurm observes, "Holiday episodes are a long-standing tradition.... Still, pulling off effective, relatively universal holiday episodes is a lot harder when they're part of a non-secular (or mainstream Christian) calendar."[13] In this case, the task for *The Goldbergs* is not to explain the theological underpinnings of Yom Kippur but to show what being Jewish—and celebrating a High Holiday—looks like.

In the case of *The Goldbergs*, we can see what was a stand-in for a generic immigrant family; yes, they were identifiably Jewish to New Yorkers, but to middle America, perhaps not so noticeably so. Henry Bial suggests that perhaps in today's perspective, "to anyone who is Jewish or familiar with Jewish American culture, the Goldbergs are almost too Jewish."[14] Writing in 2005, Bial had not yet met the Pfeffermans. But until *Transparent*, sixty years later, no such private and particularistic Yom Kippur synagogue scene had been made public for dramatic consumption.

The Goldbergs offered Yom Kippur to the public as a visual demonstration of specific Jewish worship, but other shows sought to theologically translate Yom Kippur to gentiles. In 1994, *Northern Exposure*—in an episode amusingly titled "Shofar, So Good"—featured a thorough account of Yom Kippur through the words of Cicely, Alaska's lone carb-loading Jew, Joel Fleischman. Explaining his fast, he says, "We're commanded to afflict our souls," then continues: "We fast so we can concentrate on being better people and stuff like that.... [Yom Kippur is] when God supposedly decides what's going to happen to everyone in the coming year. What happens is you have basically ten days between Rosh Hashanah and Yom Kippur to reverse the call.... You examine your soul, you atone for your sins." The episode features Joel being visited in a dream by his childhood rabbi in a *Christmas Carol*-ghost of Yom Kippur past/future sort of way. Joel has treated his assistant, Marilyn, poorly and is made to recognize and atone for his selfish behavior by seeing both the future consequences of his actions, as well as what could happen if he changed his ways. Having almost slept through Yom Kippur, Joel rushes to atone. He not only acknowledges his lack of appreciation for Marilyn, but he apologizes and resolves to change his conduct with concrete steps. The episode expands the theme of atonement to Cicely's gentile residents. Tavern owner Holling laments his estrangement from his daughter Jackie, confessing, "I've made a big hole in the world... that I can't fix." Holling's friend Ed offers to serve as a literal scapegoat by carrying Holling's sins into the woods, adapting an ancient Jewish tradition of the High Priest putting the sins of the community on the head of a goat and sending it out into the desert.

It is the former more universal Yom Kippur direct apology to the person who has been wronged that is the more popular takeaway. Indeed, this is the tack that *The West Wing* takes in its season 3 episode "On the Day Before." In it, Martin Sheen as President Bartlet is thinking about how to call the parents of two American Jewish brothers killed in Israel by a suicide bombing. He notes to Toby and Josh (two Jewish cabinet members) that he had just learned that "On Yom Kippur, you ask forgiveness for sins against God. But on the day before, you ask forgiveness for sins against people." Toby and Josh nod, and Bartlet continues, clearly struck, "You can't ask forgiveness of God until you've asked forgiveness of people on the day before." This theme of asking for forgiveness is one that *Transparent* highlights through the Pfefferman family's variegated observance of the holy day, featuring its characters' attempts to make amends (and excuses) while taking part in selective rituals.

Sociologists frequently categorize such observances as either tension release or recommitment holidays. Yom Kippur is in many ways the latter, one that employs "narratives, drama, and ceremonies to directly enforce commitment to shared beliefs."[15] Whether that recommitment is to a community, a faith, or a loved one, the Pfeffermans appear to be dealing with the fallout of broken commitments or choosing to break new commitments (as is clear in the case of Ari). Although these characters seem to easily embrace commitment, it is their follow-through that proves difficult to sustain.

Beyond the spiritual interpersonal dimensions of Yom Kippur, many Jews still experience Yom Kippur in a synagogue. Some comedies, most notably two other L.A.-based shows *Curb Your Enthusiasm* and *Entourage*, have used the Yom Kippur synagogue setting as a plot device, often to display a comedy of manners. In the premiere episode of season 5 of *Curb Your Enthusiasm*,[16] Larry has a near-death experience and becomes suddenly religious. Having previously ignored institutional Jewish life, Larry had not realized that he needed to purchase tickets to High Holiday services. As none were available, the episode entitled "The Larry David Sandwich" features Larry attempting to scalp tickets outside of his synagogue. As one critic put it, "It's not only the use of tickets; it's the absurd idea of scalping them as if the services were a performance. Which, come to think of it, worship has become for so many Jews."[17]

In *Entourage*'s season 3 "Return of the King" episode, a casting change suddenly puts a coveted deal on the table for manager Ari Gold. As this occurs on Yom Kippur, and his wife has forbidden cell phone use until after sundown, he and producer (and fellow Jew) Nick Rubenstein attempt to broker the deal without their phones. Much of this involves sneaking out of services to communicate with the players. In both *Curb* and *Entourage*, the participation in the pageantry of the synagogue services seeks to demonstrate the hypocrisy of the worshippers.

Sites of humor involve Yom Kippur's obligation of fasting and its subsequent feasting. In *The Marvelous Mrs. Maisel*, Yom Kippur bookends the first two seasons. When Joel Maisel goes to tell his father that his in-laws have canceled the Yom Kippur Break Fast,[18] Moishe Maisel is devastated. How can the "holiest of holy" days have been canceled? (Note: just the dinner has been canceled, not the actual day.)[19] Moishe continues, expressing his real concern about the cancellation: "Your mother is very upset. Yom Kippur is a very big day for your mother. There's kugel and she sees the kids.... You think everyday there's kugel and she sees the kids?"[20] For Moish, this holiday is about family (and ethnic food).[21]

Transparent creator Joey Soloway has spoken similarly of their family's relationship to Judaism and Jewishness: "We came from Larry David Seinfeld-y 'we are Jewish when it comes to food' people.... My parents are the post-Holocaust generation.... My mom came from parents who ran from pogroms. Nobody's proud to be Jewish, nobody believes the tradition has anything to offer. It's more 'we're not going to work on Yom Kippur because we have to but don't really know why.'"[22] In season 2 of *The Marvelous Mrs. Maisel*, the family succeeds in making it to the Break Fast, and the viewers are also granted a Yom Kippur service, complete with chanting and beating of breasts. But unlike in *The Goldbergs* and—as will be discussed later—*Transparent*, the service is comedic. Everyone is talking throughout the *Ashamnu* prayer, the wife who converted from Catholicism is emotionally wailing with over-the-top repentance, the Jews from birth are talking about food and snapping at each other, and there is even a callback to *The Jazz Singer*. Moishe makes a crack about his grandson eating so much chocolate during the service that "he looks like Al Jolson."[23] As soon as the shofar is blown, everyone runs to eat. They have performed the motions of the required ritual, and the day is over. None of these characters apologize to each other or even seem to acknowledge a need for Soloveitchik's stages of confession.

The Pfeffermans: Guilty and Starving for Forgiveness

As in *The Goldbergs, Northern Exposure,* and *The Marvelous Mrs. Maisel, Transparent* engages with displays of religiosity, themes of atonement, and various approaches to fasting but also takes on religious meaning and ritual to offer a step beyond the symbolic ethnicity of these other representations. And unlike *Curb Your Enthusiasm* and *Entourage*, *Transparent* departs from mere cultural laughs at seemingly superficial observance. When there are laughs—and there are—they dig deeper, occasionally masking real pain. What this show does so well is make explicit the Judaism of non-Orthodox Jews, signifying their Jewishness—not just by the standing order of bagels and schmear at Cantor's Deli, the Yiddishisms of Shelly Pfefferman, or the family's Holocaust gallows humor—but by specific engagement in Jewish ritual: through the lighting of Shabbat candles, the actual bat mitzvah chanting of the parasha Lech Lecha, the dressing of a body before burial and the subsequent shiva, a wedding, a Havdalah service, and the not insignificant relevance of both a rabbi and synagogue affiliation. *Transparent* further seeks to show not just what this sort of Jewishness looks like but what it feels like.

In "*Transparent*: A Guide for the Perplexed," a long-form essay about the first two seasons, Jonathan Freedman discusses how the Pfeffermans tend to engage in failed rituals, such as Ari's canceled bat mitzvah. True—these (and others) do not always work out, but it is not for the Pfeffermans' lack of trying. The "Book of Life" episode opens with Sarah attempting ritual as a means to an end. She is lost and somewhat in mourning, possibly regretting the destruction of her marriage to Len and regretting (somewhat) the fallout from the destruction of her wedding to Tammy, so she visits Tammy at work to ask for forgiveness. Tammy, a non-Jew, is understandably confused about the timing of this approach, and Sarah clumsily frames her apology in a way that only highlights her own narcissism; it is not about feeling sorry about what she did to Tammy but about her own need for absolution. "I have to come today. It's kind of like trick-or-treating. You go to the people you hurt—you think about your wrongs and apologize and then ask for forgiveness. And then you get forgiveness. And then you sort of absolve yourself."

Sarah is partially right about this. The act of *teshuvah*, literally "return," is the repentance that can occur at any time of the year but is particularly emphasized at Yom Kippur. As for absolution, one does not actually absolve oneself. Sarah's sins are quite real. She committed adultery with Tammy, devastating not one—but two—marriages. After forcing Tammy to leave her wife, Barb, and uprooting children from both families, she leaves Tammy on their wedding night. Sarah's growing awareness of her own queer sexuality is exciting—it has opened her up to new possibilities and partners—but it also appears to give her a deeply problematic license to betray the people she loves.

Tammy, whose life has twice been upended by Sarah's behavior, politely refuses to let her off the hook and wishes her a cold, firm, and deeply ironic "Happy Yom Kippur." Put off by Tammy, Sarah tries a few other things such as visiting her weed dealer, who is also her occasional paramour. Attempting to reach an altered state of some kind (notably not directly by fasting), she smokes weed and has sex. Both attempts fail, as she asks, "Have you ever gotten so high that you're like totally sober?" As Roberta Rosenberg writes, "Since successful rituals presuppose a complementary relationship between private individuals and their public worlds, the Pfeffermans often fail to access spiritual narratives, because their two worlds—Jewish community and American individualistic culture—are not always in alignment."[24] Sarah also begins to describe her desire to be dominated, one that ultimately leads to her season 3 experimentation with BDSM (bondage and discipline, dominance and submission, sadism and masochism). Is this punishment she seeks? Perhaps it is her attempt at remorse—an act she has difficulty expressing in other ways. In season 4, Len and Sarah attempt a polyamorous relationship, perhaps as a form of reconciliation, perhaps as a greater embrace of the queer family structure seen elsewhere among the Pfeffermans.

A *New York Times* review of "The Book of Life" leaves a critic dubious about the Pfeffermans' penitence:

> It is the holiest day of the year, and the Pfeffermans are making amends—or at least pretending to. The thing about Yom Kippur . . . is that it is an incredibly sacred day, but one that can also be twisted (by casual believers) into a kind of convenient get-out-of-jail-free card, a free tabula rasa. The Pfeffermans are the kind of Jews that never celebrate the Sabbath but will manipulate Yom Kippur for their own selfish purposes, and that is exactly what happens. Everyone has something to atone for, but no one is doing it with grace or humility (except of course for Raquel, who physically leads an entire congregation in voicing their sins while gracefully suffering through her own heartbreak and loss).[25]

Speaking of a lack of grace and humility, Josh—not one to be alone—tackles atonement in a different way than his sister. He chooses community, attending services with his mother. He, too, wants forgiveness from Rabbi Raquel, mourning the loss of their relationship, their pregnancy, and his son Colton, mainly the ideal of love and family life he so badly wants to attain. Raquel, like Tammy with Sarah, turns him down (although he does not ask for her forgiveness or even appear to see how he failed her).

J   I had a quick question about what I'm supposed to tell my family. Because, you know, they're just like asking me a bunch of questions.
R   That's none of my business; you can tell them whatever you want, buddy.
J   No, I know. But I just didn't want to say the wrong thing, 'cause I don't know what we want to be saying.
R   We're over.
J   Okay.

There is no remorse or resolution for Josh. An earlier episode ends with Josh telling Raquel that "I fucked up, but I don't want you to sit around collecting wrongs so you can prove to yourself that this relationship is wrong or that you're not lovable." As Freedman writes, "There is in other words the acknowledgment of transgression but neither self-recognition nor atonement—just in the end pure L.A. psychobabble."

This self-serving acknowledgment can be seen again in season 3's episode where Raquel finally loses it on Sarah: "Can you clarify for me really fast what spirituality is for you, Sarah?" says Raquel. "It's not changing your mind whenever you feel like it.... It's not following your bliss. It's not finding yourself by crawling through your belly button and out your own asshole and calling it a journey." In this season, Sarah attempts to develop a spiritual practice within Jewish institutions but is uninterested in any advice that Jewish leaders have to offer. According to Thurm, "Superstition and religion only fit into the Pfeffermans' lives when it's convenient."[26] But in that way, are they really alone? This hardly makes them unusual. Selective observance is nothing new, particularly when the rituals that are retained can be imbued with contemporary meaning.[27] Such practice, according to Amitai Etzioni, "has become the norm.... These are decisions that are increasingly made on the basis of what seems meaningful to the contemporary generation rather than what is handed down from earlier ones."[28]

After his encounter with Raquel, Josh joins his mother in the sanctuary. Shelly, meanwhile is flirting with an usher, Buzz Rackless, who flirts right back. The two continue to make eyes at each other throughout the service. For Shelly, the synagogue is a locus of social life and, therefore, a potential dating pool (even on Yom Kippur). She is not without her own hopes for new beginnings.

The episode hits an emotional climax during the communal confession of the Al Chet, known as "the long confession."

As Raquel and the cantor chant, Josh becomes more and more undone (see figure 2.1):

> We have sinned against you willingly and unwillingly/ And we have sinned against you by hardening our hearts/ We have sinned against you by acting without thinking/ We have sinned against you by speaking perversely/ We have sinned against you publicly and privately/ We have sinned against you knowingly and deceitfully/ We have sinned against you by corrupt speech/ By wronging others/ By evil thoughts/ For all these sins O God of Forgiveness, forgive us, pardon us, grant us atonement/ We have sinned against you, We have sinned against you, We have sinned against you.

And it is during this intense repetition and communal beating of chests, a full two minutes of chanting, that Josh finds himself no longer able to be with this community, to face his family, or the woman he wronged (see figure 2.2).

The scene moves from Josh outside the synagogue with the Al Chet echoing in the background to a visual of Maura—alone—feeding the ducks with a bag of challah, practicing a form of *tashlich* (literally, to cast off).

FIGURE 2.1 *Transparent*. "The Book of Life," Season 2:7. Written by Joey Soloway and Ethan Kuperberg, directed by Jim Frohna, December 11, 2015.

FIGURE 2.2 *Transparent*. "The Book of Life," Season 2:7. Written by Joey Soloway and Ethan Kuperberg, directed by Jim Frohna, December 11, 2015.

Tashlich is typically performed on the afternoon of the first day of Rosh Hashanah by symbolically casting one's sins into a body of living water and offering prayers of repentance (see figure 2.3). Maura, like Sarah and Josh, is reflecting upon her actions after a thoughtless—yet well-intentioned—conversation with her housemate Davina. By attempting to intervene in Davina's relationship, she neglected to recognize the privileges she enjoys as a wealthy, white (albeit trans) woman. Maura, at the early stages of living openly as a woman, suffers the similar myopia demonstrated by her children and ex-wife—an inability to see the consequences her actions have on others. The scene is brief but significant.

FIGURE 2.3 *Transparent*. "The Book of Life," Season 2:7. Written by Joey Soloway and Ethan Kuperberg, directed by Jim Frohna, December 11, 2015.

M You can do better than that [referring to Davina's partner].
D My God, who do you think you're talking to? . . . We don't all have your family. We don't all have your money. I'm a 53-year-old, ex-prostitute, HIV-positive woman with a dick . . . You should probably sleep somewhere else.

Davina has been Maura's chosen family since coming out. Along with Shea, she has supported Maura unconditionally through her initial immersion in an L.A. trans community. Losing that connection is a devastating possibility.

Tashlich is more traditionally performed communally, but Maura's private ritual reflects her alienation in this year of transition. This modified ritual again demonstrates the individualization of practice and selective observance. Her reflection seems to work a bit, as in later episodes (and significantly in the season 3 premiere "Eliza") she is seen performing a form of teshuvah and attempting to give back to the LGBTQ center that so readily welcomed her. She works at a suicide helpline for LGBTQ youth and attempts to understand the wider needs of her new community.

Lastly, Ari, who many argue is the true protagonist of the series, and the stand-in for Joey Soloway, chooses both ritual and community, hosting a Break Fast with their longtime best friend Syd Feldman (who is also their newish girlfriend), a gathering that ultimately brings all these previously discussed people together. While Ari and Syd are preparing the feast for their guests, it comes out that all is not what it should be. Ari does not seem to think they have anything to atone for, but Syd thinks they do—as she is beginning to suspect that she might just be a stop on Ari's foray into queerdom. (Spoiler: Syd is correct.) Having spent a night at their advisor's house, Ari is making no secret of their infatuation with Leslie (a lesbian celebrity). They want to be "open and brave"—particularly if that

FIGURE 2.4 *Transparent*. "The Book of Life," Season 2:7. Written by Joey Soloway and Ethan Kuperberg, directed by Jim Frohna, December 11, 2015.

bravery allows them to seek intimacy with women other than Syd. Like Sarah, queerness seems to offer them a license to behave badly. Rather than acknowledgment or remorse, Ari seeks what they see as honesty—one that is essentially self-serving.

And so, the Pfeffermans, the Feldmans, and friends gather at the loft and face a beautiful spread (albeit without water due to the drought, so the only beverages are wine and skim milk). Ari (see figure 2.4), clad in white with a gold orientalist border is reminiscent of the cantors leading High Holiday services, specifically in this image of Al Jolson chanting Kol Nidre at the Orchard Street synagogue in *The Jazz Singer* (see figure 2.5). Like Jack, Ari is leading a community. In the absence of someone offering the kind of identity either choose to claim, both chart their own paths. In *Acting Jewish*, Henry Bial suggests that "we might see Jack (and *The Jazz Singer*) as promoting a kind of Jewish cultural continuity, even while rejecting Judaic religious observance."[29] In this performance of Ari's, which includes a personal interpretation of the holiday as well as an enacted apology, both cultural and religious observances are met.

"I've just started wondering about and investigating my Jewishness." Ari explains Yom Kippur as an "epic yellow pages that is called the Book of Life. God—He, She, great energy—to get your name in the Book of Life you make apologies, and once it is in there, you get to live another year. So I would like to say I'm sorry." To this their mother, Shelly, replies, somewhat preemptively: "All apologies accepted."[30] Syd's mother, moved to atone by Ari's words, turns to her husband and blurts out, "I'm sorry—I was so controlling about the parking

FIGURE 2.5 Alan Crosland and Louis Silvers. *The Jazz Singer*, 1927.

space!" There is a sense of the performative here for some; Shelly is oblivious to it but to others, Ari's spiel is, well, transparent.

"Take a bagel and hold it aloft!" Ari says. Those gathered at the table join in *ha motzi*, the blessing over bread (led by newcomer Buzz because none of the Pfeffermans know what to do), and they break bread/bagels together. As Rosenberg comments, "It is into this postmodern world of absent metanarratives and religious rituals that Soloway and her series writers place the struggling Pfeffermans who, in fact, seek 'sacred times' and 'sacred spaces' but often lack the practical education and the courage to access them in meaningful ways."[31] However, not all feel helped by the ritual. Sarah, who is starving (and probably still a little high) actually eats before and during the blessing. It is at this point that things begin to fall apart and the delicately held together façade breaks. Josh, feeling overwhelmed by questions about Raquel's absence, reveals that they lost the baby. He tries to put a positive spin on the situation, saying unconvincingly, "This is a new beginning for me." Shelly, previously glowing with pride in both Ari and her prospective beau, takes this as a curse she brought on herself. She sobs and wails in mourning as Josh yells at her: "Mommy. This is not yours. It's not about you." Josh cannot bring himself to eat with those assembled, and the episode closes with him, alone, in the supermarket, binging on turkey, ham, cheese, Jello, and finally white bread (none of which is paid for).[32]

Unlike the white lies told to spare feelings on *The Goldbergs*, the attempts to bridge two cultures in *The Jazz Singer*, or the active attempts at equity in

FIGURE 2.6 *Transparent*. Season 2 advertisement. *Transparent* images provided by Amazon Content Services LLC.

Northern Exposure, the Pfeffermans are all in situations caused by their own selfishness; it is this same self-centeredness that makes it so hard for them to make amends (see figure 2.6). Notably absent from their confessions following acknowledgment and remorse is the third stage: resolution for the future—the part where one asserts, I will never do this again. The audience is tempted to yell at these characters, as Josh does to Shelly, "It's not about *you*." Buzz, in fact, attempts this with Shelly: "Good stuff happens. Bad stuff happens. You're not that powerful." Nonetheless, the Pfeffermans are trying—despite their limitations—to be their best selves. Unlike Tami's icier greeting, they warmly wish each other "Happy Yom Kippur" and are quickly corrected by Buzz, "You don't say Happy Yom Kippur, you say 'Gut Yontif.'"

Notes

1 Eric Thurm, "The Pfeffermans Fail to Starve Themselves on Yom Kippur," *AV Club*, January 4, 2016, https://www.avclub.com/the-pfeffermans-fail-to-starve-themselves-on-yom-kippur-1798186340.
2 Joseph Dov Soloveitchik and Pinchas Peli, *On Repentance: In the Thought and Oral Discourses of Rabbi Joseph B. Soloveitchik* (Jerusalem: Oroth Publishing House, 1980).
3 *The Goldbergs*, Season 1, episode 30, "A Sad Day," ABC, October 5, 1954.
4 Nathan Abrams, *The New Jew in Film: Exploring Jewishness and Judaism in Contemporary Cinema* (New Brunswick, NJ: Rutgers University Press, 2012), ProQuest Ebook Central.
5 The 2012 survey showed that 53 percent of American Jews fast on Yom Kippur. See "A Portrait of Jewish Americans: Findings from a Pew Research Center Survey of

U.S. Jews," Pew Research Center, 2013. October 1, 2013, https://www.pewresearch.org/religion/2013/10/01/jewish-american-beliefs-attitudes-culture-survey/.

6 Thurm, "The Pfeffermans Fail."
7 Donald Weber, *Haunted in the New World: Jewish American Culture from Cahan to the Goldbergs* (Bloomington: Indiana University Press, 2005), 152.
8 David Zurawik, *The Jews of Prime Time* (Hanover, NH: Brandeis University Press, 2003), 45–47.
9 Although this essay primarily explores television, I would be remiss not to also mention the first full length talkie, *The Jazz Singer* (1927). This film notably precedes *The Goldbergs* in its remarkable depiction of a Kol Nidre service. Kol Nidre is chanted on the eve of Yom Kippur and, in Ashkenazi congregations, is sung to a hauntingly beautiful melody. In *The Jazz Singer*, Al Jolson portrays Jack Rabinowitz, the son of a cantor, who leaves his religious family in order to pursue his dream of being a jazz singer. He finds great success in the secular world, but that success comes with the cost of familial estrangement. The film ultimately ends with Jack returning to his childhood synagogue and chanting Kol Nidre in his dying father's place. This three-minute scene cuts back and forth between Jack chanting in the synagogue and his father rising from his deathbed. The titles read, "Mama, we have our son again," indicating a reconciliation.
10 Jared Bloom and Amitai Etzioni, *We Are What We Celebrate: Understanding Holidays and Rituals* (New York: New York University Press, 2004), 6.
11 Weber, *Haunted in the New World*, 137. Emphasis in original quote.
12 Henry Bial, *Acting Jewish: Negotiating Ethnicity on the American Stage and Screen* (Ann Arbor: University of Michigan Press, 2005), 46.
13 Thurm.
14 Bial, *Acting Jewish*, 45.
15 Bloom and Etzioni, *We Are What We Celebrate*, 11.
16 *Curb Your Enthusiasm*, Season 5, episode 1, "The Larry David Sandwich," HBO (September 25, 2005).
17 Jeffrey Salkin, "*Curb Your Enthusiasm* is pretty, pretty, pretty, Jewish," *Religion News Service*, June 22, 2016, https://religionnews.com/2016/06/22/curb-enthusiasm-larry-david-jewish/.
18 In their 1967 study on Jewish identity and practice, sociologists Marshall Sklare and Joseph Greenblum examined the reasons why some rituals were retained by American Jews and why others were abandoned. Their findings determined that rituals are most likely to be retained when the ritual is, among other things, "capable of effective redefinition in modern terms, does not demand social isolation or the adoption of a unique lifestyle, [and] accords with the religious culture of the larger community and provides a 'Jewish' alternative which is felt to be needed." Fasting on Yom Kippur—unlike adopting a strictly kosher lifestyle—is a twenty-five-hour annual experiment; once over, there is no need to look back Marshall Sklare and Joseph Greenblum, *Jewish Identity on the Suburban Frontier: Study of Group Survival in the Open Society*, Lakeville Studies, vol. 1 (New York: Basic Books, 1967), 50–55.
19 Popular attention to the Break Fast appears later in the twentieth century, reflecting its rise in popularity among Jewish Americans (not seen so much in *The Goldbergs* or *The Jazz Singer*). See Nora L. Rubel, "The Feast at the End of the Fast: The Evolution of an American Jewish Ritual," in *Religion, Food, and Eating in North America* (New York: Columbia University Press), 234–250.
20 *The Marvelous Mrs. Maisel*, Season 1, episode 2.

21 This scene has its analogue in the 1977 Woody Allen film *Annie Hall*. Mrs. Hall asks how the Jewish family will be spending "the holidays." Mrs. Singer immediately replies, "We fast." Mr. Singer chimes in, "Yeah, no food. You know, we have to atone for our sins." Mrs. Hall responds, "What sins? I don't understand." And Mr. Singer, still shoveling food in his mouth replies, "Tell you the truth, neither do we." Woody Allen, *Annie Hall* (DVD) USA: United Artists, 1977.
22 Debra Nussbaum Cohen, "How Jill Soloway Created *Transparent*: The Jewiest Show Ever," *Forward*, October 21, 2014. https://forward.com/culture/207407/how-jill-soloway-created-transparent-the-jewiest.
23 *The Marvelous Mrs. Maisel*, Season 2, episode 7, "Look, She Made a Hat," Amazon Prime Video, December 5, 2018.
24 Roberta Rosenberg, "The Importance of Jewish Ritual in the Secular, Postmodern World of Transparent," *Jewish Film and New Media: An International Journal* 5, no. 1 (2017): 81.
25 Rachel Syme, "*Transparent* Season 2 Episodes 6 and 7: Motherhood and Making Amends," *New York Times*, December 16, 2015. https://www.nytimes.com/2015/12/16/arts/television/transparent-season-2-episodes-6-7-review-yom-kippur.html.
26 Thurm.
27 Rubel, "The Feast," 236.
28 Bloom and Etzioni, *We Are What We Celebrate*, 5.
29 Bial, *Acting Jewish*, 25.
30 Rosenberg, "The Importance of Jewish Ritual," 88.
31 Rosenberg, "The Importance of Jewish Ritual," 79–80.
32 This feast may or may not foreshadow his rejection of Judaism we then see in season 3 in his half-hearted conversion at Colton's evangelical church.

3

Melancholy and Joy

Jewish Nomadism and *Transparent*

RANEN OMER-SHERMAN

Novelist Nathan Englander once described the great preoccupation of Jewish American literature as "revolving around fluidity, of borders drawn and redrawn, of changing landscapes and altered realities."[1] Such an evocative and expansive sense of Jewish literary expression might just as easily describe the sensibilities of other forms of Jewish art, and in that respect Joey Soloway's overarching vision for *Transparent* appears as both paradoxically derivative and innovative. Soloway's painful, playful, and profound portrayals of restless, often disappointingly childish individuals morphing between religions, gender and sexual identities, partners, homes and homelands (and the intersections of these realms), are brimming with vibrant riffs on the struggle to negotiate between inherited and chosen identities. That interpretive play is inherent from the first season's stark invocation of Parashat Lech Lecha, the third weekly portion in the Jewish people's annual cycle of Torah reading (Genesis 12:1–17:27), which imaginatively comes to signify the often lonely or exilic "going forth" or unraveling of each of the Pfeffermans' individual journeys in the sunny, materialistic landscape of Southern California, America's quintessential realm of emancipatory self-reinvention and, perhaps, selfishness.[2] *Transparent* is its most imaginatively resolute in effectively repudiating its characters' nostalgic desires, especially in its pointed emphasis on each of their fraught journeys into the unknown, their weakening orientation to the bondage (or consolation) of their immediate pasts. As Soloway describes it, *Transparent* absorbed the vital rules of improv: "Yes, *and*. Go with whatever is happening, allow the soul of the *us* to expand, rather than insist on some very particular path."[3]

In Jonathan Freedman's eloquent discussion of Soloway's emphasis on the Pfeffermans' propensity for transformative change, he invokes Erich Auerbach's biblical hermeneutics in *Mimesis*:

> The Bible often reduces scale to emphasize the onerous quality of choice. As in the scene where God demands that Abram sacrifices Isaac, there are only two sentient figures here, Abram and the Deity, and they confront each other on an existential plane without any of the social texture, support, or moral injunctions that might ... reduce the onerous force of the choice with which God confronts the man. The existential quality of this moment goes even deeper. Not only must Abram do something different, but also in that quest, he must *become* someone different—which indeed he does as he accepts the mantle of prophet and journeys on his way to becoming Abraham.[4]

Enlarging on Freedman's attention to this *becoming* as one of the traditionally Jewish currents guiding *Transparent*'s narrative unfolding, I would argue that in considering the myriad struggles the series grapples with (whether in confronting myths of biological determinism or political illusions about the Middle East), it is also instructive to consider the enduring cultural force of this paradigm of beginning through the thought of Jewish philosopher Emmanuel Levinas. Over the years, viewing and reviewing the often startling trajectories of the individual members of the Pfefferman clan, I was frequently put in mind of Levinas.

For Levinas, the desert nomadism of Abraham, perceived as one who goes out from his home to an alien land, is illustrative of Judaism's prophetic indifference to boundaries and borders, its ancient inclinations to openness to movement, alterity, and otherness.[5] For those whom Levinas might seem an unlikely thinker to invoke in the context of *Transparent*'s universe, it bears considering that Levinas was dedicated to envisioning the dynamics of human relationality on a radically expansive plane. Levinas is best known for considering the primal encounter with the face of another human being as a figure for pre-ontological recognition, meaning that the ethical precedes the ontological: before there is knowledge, there is compassion. In other words, the recognition of the face of another is our primal mode of ethical contact as human beings: recognizing the complete difference of another person, recognizing that person as irreducibly separate, the subject becomes aware of their responsibility toward the Other—the face is a "moral summons," an appeal that cannot be resisted.

It is often said that after reading Levinas, it is hard not to view the entire world through a Levinasian lens, and so it was the more time I spent in the world of

Transparent. But where did I see those echoes applying to the maddeningly ego-driven characters of *Transparent*? First of all, it is important to note that Levinas makes a claim for art, that it is the revelation of the human capacity for compassion because the body is created capable of redemptive beauty and consolation. Enlarging on that premise, Judith Butler declares that "to respond to the face to understand its meaning, means to be awake to what is precarious in another life, or rather, the precariousness of life itself."[6] And from season to season, it is clear that *Transparent* affirms this principle even while startling us with the way it goes about achieving that. For one thing, the neurotic, self-obsessed, often insensitive Pfeffermans appear in a different light whenever the trauma and pain of the past rupture into their lives. This is especially evident in the second season's parallel story concerning Grandmother Rose, Maura's mother, thriving in the explosively effervescent culture that enabled the startlingly open transgender community of interwar Weimar Berlin until the Nazis annihilated all that "decadence." The fact that Rose's transgender sister Gittel (born Gershon) remained behind, trapped in Germany, intensifies that darkness and the palpable sense of intergenerational pain, the transmission of unspecified trauma. Above all, *Transparent*'s insistence on that wounding history places in the viewer's mind the impermanence of home, certainly that of any cosmopolitan utopia.[7]

Historical contingency (suppressed or otherwise) has clearly become demonstrably intrinsic to the myriad, sometimes frustrating ways *Transparent*'s characters grapple with their anxieties, especially whenever their sense of at-homeness unravels. Yet perhaps even deeper currents have shaped the underlying ethos of the series. One of Levinas's most provocative critiques is western philosophy's horror of the Other—"an insurmountable allergy" manifested in Greek culture's Ulysses. Contrasting Greek and Hebraic modes of wandering, he says that whereas Ulysses returns home to himself, a one-way movement embodying the West's perpetual self-sufficiency and self-satisfaction, Abraham leaves his homeland forever for the unknown, thus embodying a movement without return, a deferral of messianic arrival. Ironically apropos of this, in *Transparent* even the bat mitzvah in which the Torah portion would be read, is itself deferred, an absence-presence that seems to disruptively permeate everything that ensues. Expanding that premise in the second season's competing temporalities, Soloway opens a space for reimagining identity, sexual and otherwise, continually transforming, brimming with transgressive potentiality (implicitly overturning "safe" notions of what constitutes inherited Jewish tradition). In this regard, too, it is probably worth bearing in mind that Levinas's archetype of responsiveness derives from the apparent etymological relation of the word "responsibility," in Hebrew *achraiyut*, to the root *acher*, "other"—someone who is not me. Hence, there is a gravity in our relation to the alterity of the stranger, and it is this enormity that Levinas calls responsibility or obligation, a reality in which we are

FIGURE 3.1 *Transparent*. "Eliza," Season 3:1. Written by Joey Soloway, Ethan Kuperberg, and Ali Liebgott, directed by Joey Soloway, September 2016.

always already obligated to the Other, prior to any action (or failure to take action) we might perform.

It is hardly necessary to suggest that Levinas's radical thinking on alterity was in any way a direct influence on Soloway for it to enrich our appreciation of the spiritual approach Soloway takes to the Jewish story, namely as one of perpetual wandering between identities, between bodies, and between realms of belonging. Notably, in describing the show's essence (that nobody will likely surpass in its brilliant succinctness), Soloway observes, "The kids would believe they were inheriting their family home, but instead they would inherit a legacy of queerness."[8] Although *Transparent* is as arguably concerned with relationality and interdependence as untethered individualism, in the series' tense opposition between wandering and stasis, it is clear that Soloway privileges the expansive, open-ended identity of wandering over the narrowly proscribed monolithic identity that accompanies rest or arrival (perhaps the most absurd yet perhaps predictable consummation of this melancholic uprooting occurs in the third season when, at the depth of his self-hatred, Josh gets baptized).

Looking back on the narrative trajectory of the entire series, it would seem that its emphasis on loss, confusion, and unsettled indeterminacy is never expressed more exquisitely than in Rabbi Raquel's intimate musings that launch the third season, as she wrestles with finding the essence of her sermon (see figure 3.1):

Thoughts on Passover. You wake up. Two words emblazoned on your chest. It's time. You're gonna make a break for freedom. You will not be a slave anymore. You get out of bed, you grab your things, you run outside, and then[9].... there you are. Free. First light of day. Behind you is your past. Everything you came from. Everything that you thought you knew. You start running. As you run, you listen for the voice of the divine. But you hear nothing. So you stop. You listen closer. What—what is that? Is it nothing? No. It is stillness.

In this beautiful prelude exists all the vulnerability, hesitancy, and openness to revelation that the series achieved in its best moments. Notably, after a brief shot of Raquel standing alone in the cavernous space of an empty synagogue, most of this poetic utterance spills forth as the camera follows her meandering through the leafy landscape of an arboretum. Through this episode's opening burst of cinematic lyricism, we understand that we are still ostensibly in the city, yet there is also a pervasive sense that we are also nowhere at all.[10] Wandering with a sense of trepidation but not entirely letting go of a child's capacity for wonder and possibility opens up a sacred, intimate space for renewal.[11] In the rabbi's quietly intimate language, combined with the poetic visuality achieved by cinematographer Jim Frohna, this soliloquy seems one of those almost transcendent moments of emptiness, stillness, and revelation that best embody Soloway's loftiest ambitions for *Transparent*, which she once described as "this giant experiment in inclusion, art making, and love."[12]

Fittingly for a series in which every genuinely transformative moment occurs through a major character's tumultuous or abrasive encounter with another person's plight, the wrenchingly dramatic context that follows this pivotal scene focuses on Maura's inept attempt to reach out to Elizah, a trans-teen, on an LGBT hotline. After Elizah abruptly hangs up on her, Maura is left guilt-ridden and becomes increasingly agitated over her fate (which strikes me as an auditory version of Levinas's sense of the face of the Other, commanding our primal sense of unremitting obligation). In what arguably amounts to Maura's most selfless act in the entire series, she plunges into what for her (and undoubtedly the writers and producers of the series) constitutes the wilderness—the gritty, unfamiliar streets of south-central Los Angeles and the vast indoor marketplace where she finds Elizah, but where a succession of unhappy events culminate in Maura's collapse and tormented Elizah's lonely flight, no rescuer in sight, to face her destiny alone. Another Abraham. And then this elegantly bookended episode returns us to the poetry of Raquel's musings, still wandering alone herself: "You're waiting for a miracle. You're waiting for the sea to part. Well, that's an old miracle. So what about this? What if the miracle was you? What if you had to be your own Messiah? Then what?"

That powerfully disquieting nudge, an address that seems to inescapably implicate the viewer, may offer a vital clue for just why Soloway seems compelled to dissolve the marital and romantic unions of each of their characters. Indeed, to fully appreciate the urgent primacy *Transparent* places on the paradigm shifts, rupture, and the incremental expansion of human consciousness and self-understanding in the lives of its Jewish and LGBTQ characters (whether in contemporary Los Angeles or 1930s Berlin), it is essential to bear in mind the series' strikingly traditional reliance on the popular contemporary notion of Judaism's creatively productive relation to Diaspora and exilic movement. And that such a startling rebirth might even occur in the life of a retired university professor approaching seventy is all the more revealing.

One need only recall the ruptures of Genesis, the sense of felix culpa that accompanies all human exiles; from the Garden, Abraham's Lech Lecha ("Get you gone from your country and from your birthplace and from your father's house"), the expulsion of Ishmael into the desert, the narrative of Ruth the Moabite, each offering richly circuitous terrains, repetitions of wandering, wryly underscored in the uncertainties and scrambled destinies of the Pfefferman tribe. Painstakingly, each struggles to learn the discipline demanded of moving fluidly between disparate worlds. As Soloway conceived each character's unsettled and unsettling becomings, they seem to have been guided by something very much akin to the flux of what I have been describing as Levinasian nomadism. Or, perhaps Soloway's ethos can be crystallized more simply, in the way that Grace Paley so memorably expresses it: "Everyone, real or invented, deserves the open destiny of life."[13] In *Transparent*, that open destiny is rarely euphoric; it is often bittersweet, melancholic, or, especially in Josh's case, self-negating. Isaac Butler observed the paths taken by two unhappy characters in the second season:

> *Transparent*, like Josh, has few answers, because another way that the show is Jewish is that it explores its themes dialectically. The contrast between the utopian possibilities of borderlessness and the anxiety, pain, and feeling of loss that accompanies that state is in many ways *Transparent*'s true subject.... Yet the crossing of borders isn't the key to happiness on the show. Josh, for reasons best left unspoiled, realizes how badly he needs clear boundaries in his life and behavior. Sarah longs for the strict boundaries of both Jewish ritual practice and S&M, and rebels against them.[14]

Freedom is essential to any forward movement. Yet in the Pfeffermans' postmodern secularism, that aspiration never seems to culminate in the stasis of happiness. Here again, Soloway's sense of the essential nature of their characters' radically open-ended condition allies well with ancient reverberations in the Jewish tradition. As Rabbi Mark Sameth reminds us, the Hebrew Bible,

> read in its original language, offers a highly elastic view of gender. And I do mean *highly* elastic: In Genesis 3:12, Eve is referred to as "he." In Genesis 9:21, after the flood, Noah repairs to 'her' tent. Genesis 24:16 refers to Rebecca as a "young man." And Genesis 1:27 refers to Adam as "them.".... And there are even more vivid examples: In Esther 2:7, Mordecai is pictured as nursing his niece Esther. Similarly, in Isaiah 49:23, the future kings of Israel are prophesied to be "nursing kings." Why would the Bible do this? These aren't typos. In the ancient world, well-expressed gender fluidity was the mark of a civilized person.

Such a person was considered more "godlike." In Ancient Mesopotamia and Egypt, the gods were thought of as gender-fluid, and human beings reflections of the gods. The Israelite ideal of the "nursing king" may be based on a real person: a woman by the name of Hatshepsut who, after the death of her husband, Thutmose II, donned a false beard and ascended the throne to become one of Egypt's greatest pharaohs. The Israelites took the transgender trope from surrounding cultures.... Counter to everything we grew up believing, the God of Israel—the God of the three monotheistic, Abrahamic religions—was understood by its earliest worshipers to be a dual-gendered deity.[15]

As Sameth suggests here, it behooves us to remember that scientists have long intimated that gender identity, like sexual orientation, exists on a spectrum. Some of us are in greater or lesser alignment with the gender assigned to us at birth. Some are in alignment with both or with neither. For still others, that alignment is a process or journey.[16] That paradigm is certainly evident in Maura's increasingly urgent journey as she becomes more attuned and aligned with who she really is. Perhaps it is a further sign of the intrinsically Jewish nature of Maura's journey, as well as the other myriad storylines and subplots, that she and we get more questions than answers, apropos of which, as Freedman astutely observes, no character quite eludes implication in the series' loving but critical gaze, not even Rabbi Raquel, a figure many viewers find deeply sympathetic. With considerable justification, Freedman considers Raquel "the sole voice of normality and common sense in the mixed-up Pfefferman clan . . . is she right to so insistently reject Colton, the gentile son of her lover Josh? Who is right in the dialogue between the founders of the Idyllwild Wimmin's Music Festival and Maura: should there be a safe space for womyn-born-of-womyn only, or should that space be open to trans- and other-gendered folk? . . . long discussions that never end but succeed only in raising yet more questions in their wake."[17]

One of the most provocative aspects of Soloway's artistry is the degree to which, throughout the frenzied chaos of the Pfeffermans' disparate scattered orbits and sometimes fickle passions, *Transparent* slows things down, often by aligning their crises in unexpected ways to Jewish rituals and traditions precisely where we do not anticipate them. Sometimes these even drive important storylines. Arguably no ritual proves so pervasive or symbolically fraught as the prominent presence of mikveh scattered throughout the series. In recent years, artists and scholars have begun to address the liberating implications of the mikveh as a nongendered site of open expression. In one especially pertinent example of this important trend, trans scholar S. J. Crasnow suggests that "queer and trans mikveh rituals for gender transition are powerful in their centering of the queer/trans body as a holy site for transformation, and in the ways they reconfigure 'purity.' In these rituals, purification is not directed at the person immersing but at cleansing the negative effects, the filth, of engaging in the normative, queer- and transphobic secular and Jewish worlds."[18]

It seems equally pertinent to note that for every Jewish ritual or life-cycle event portrayed in the show, there is no sustained sense of celebration, arrival, or the security of stasis of any kind. Quite the opposite! Consider the first episode of season 2 where the joyous breaking of the glass at Sarah Pfefferman's and Tammy's wedding is followed moments later by the breaking of the relationship itself. Disastrous unravelings and unsettlings are pivotal, as if to suggest that complete liberation paralyzes, rather than frees, Jewish energy.[19]

Here it seems worth noting that the Pfeffermans' often dramatic spiritual and sexual transformations were undoubtedly influenced by the new paradigms of subjectivity and families presented to Soloway by queer friends, relatives, and lovers in the dizzying time that the series began to take shape.[20] Soloway's own unrest, both in defining their identity and coming to terms with their own privilege (whether whiteness or past heteronormativity), seems to have found creative expression in the open destinies of *Transparent*'s characters. Perhaps the profoundly exploratory nature of the series throughout its run also owes something to the singularly open-ended nature of the creative process Soloway always insisted on. As they declared to the cast at their first table read just before filming of the pilot began: "On most shows, they act like they're running out of money, they're running out of time, they're running out of light. On this show, let's try saying we have plenty of money, we have plenty of time, and we are the light."[21] Those who worked closely with Soloway often hail their creative process as "evolved," "organic," "utopian," or otherwise profoundly collaborative in spirit. A typical day on the *Transparent* set would begin with everyone involved with production (actors, cinematographers, and technicians) standing together in a circle to reinforce a sense of shared purpose, mission, and creative spirit. Another creative catalyst crucial to that shared purpose is what Soloway calls the "doing box" in which everyone on set gathered at the beginning of the day, and a select member of the production literally stood on a crate to share whatever was happening in their personal lives—revelations that influenced characterizations, dialogue, and story arcs.[22] The only certainty we obtain throughout the series is that wandering, whether actual or metaphorical, is ubiquitous and that all identities are in flux. Everyone is *becoming*. Yet those movements are not only forward but anchored in the past, a dynamic brilliantly evident in the episode of Ali's bat mitzvah, which is conveyed in flashback.

In perhaps the most incisive exploration of the relationship between trans and gender-nonconforming identities in contemporary Judaism and the divine imperative Abraham receives, Slava Greenberg suggests that the series' challenge of the gender divide is heavily dependent on "continual citing, referencing, and reimagining the mythological call to the biblical figure of Abraham."[23] Arguing that the secular writers' bold "interpretation of the biblical verse and the phrases of 'Go forth' and 'from your father's house' adds further questions about the meanings entailed in leaving a home, through a trans perspective of displacement, migration, and homelessness," Greenberg offers cogent evidence that a "contemporary Abraham must leave their parent's house to find a way to give back to their community by eliminating the divide." Note how much the ethos of Lech Lecha informs the destinies of each character: Maura (a flashback in which she is still trapped in the identity of Mort) runs off to a cross-dressing camp; Shelly takes shelter with a friend; Josh drives off with former babysitter Rita; Sarah is on a bus heading for a demonstration and en route, she changes her seat next to a sleeping boy to join a gay woman.[24] Above all, as Jeffrey Shoulson observes, so much of this "grapples with what it means to become a woman under the sign of specific communal strictures and outside of them, how it is possible to shatter the ritual, transgress the fiction of performance, and move outward, go forth, toward a path of self-fashioning."[25]

In ways not dissimilar to Michael Chabon in *The Adventures of Kavalier and Clay* or Tony Kushner in *Angels in America*, Soloway aligns Jews and Jewishness with other outsider identities, specifically the condition of sexual Otherness, a bridge brilliantly evident in the second season's provocative flashbacks to Weimar Germany, where the gay Jewish sexologist Magnus Hirschfeld, after a longtime engagement with homosexual rights, argued for the existence of a distinct category, that of transvestism (as it was initially labeled).[26] For actress Judith Light, the ethos of this season could be summed up with her most cherished Kierkegaard quote: "Life can only be understood backward, but it must be lived forward."[27] And it is here that I would argue that the series also reveals its fealty to George Steiner's insight that "Jews know how to say, 'We are going to suffer terribly, we are going to be pilgrims, vagabonds on Earth, but in the end we won't perish.'"[28] This is one of the salient instances where the politics and poetry of *Transparent* brilliantly converge to startle and inspire. Such artful juxtapositions of competing temporalities also remind that Diaspora is not always the blasé complacent sense of belonging that the Pfeffermans enjoy—that it is as contingent and precarious as our identities, both inner and outer realities always in more flux than most of us would like to admit. And that past trauma might anticipate future tragedy. Yet as Greenberg suggests, it might also inspire the kind of epiphany that culminates in *Transparent*'s resounding ethos, arguably its "transfeminist theology": "While some halakhic responsa (body of written decisions and rulings) base their devaluation of women, trans, and gender-nonconforming people on interpreting Abraham's covenant with God—and particularly the ritual of circumcision—as linked to the assigned-male-at-birth body, *Transparent* uses the divine call as a springboard to address trans and gender-nonconforming journeys from healing oneself to healing the world."[29]

It seems especially revealing that at the end of that pivotal third season, Maura's hopes for a completely transformed self remain unfulfilled, her strong will thwarted by the body's vulnerability. She does not "arrive." And like the rest of the Pfefferman clan, theirs remains a work in process. In one of the thoughtful Jewish bookends that often give shape and texture to each season, the family comes together for an improvised seder, which in turn evokes the season's opening with Raquel laboring over her Passover sermon. This scene transports us further back to a line from the series pilot when Maura struggled to explain to Sarah that Mort Pfefferman was the disguise, telling her, "This is me." In that moment, she was excited about coming out, letting the world see who she truly was and what she was capable of becoming. In the later episode's sadly diminished echo of that earlier triumphal declaration, she also tells Ali, "This is me" but ruefully follows that with thudding disappointment: "This is it." As far as Maura is concerned, this is not the liberating destination she intended to reach. Yet the viewer might reasonably intuit that, in one way or another, she remains in flux.

In a captivating study, *Travels in Translation: Sea Tales at the Source of Jewish Fiction*, Ken Frieden explores the ancient historical and literary tradition of Jews reporting their individual transformations after long sea journeys, beginning after the destruction of the Second Temple, in 70 C.E., and the ensuing exile, when wandering and trade involving long distances became the norm. By way of contrast, it is a little discomfiting that the Pfeffermans' sea voyage pointedly returns to its point of embarkation. Even the heartwarming premise of their improvised Passover Seder onboard ultimately unravels into the family's default mode of chaos and hyperindividualism. In at least one important context, Maura's unwelcome news that her body will be unable to withstand the medical treatments that would enable her to fully transition evokes the exilic sense of the Idyllwild festival in the second season.

Shoulson offers an observation about that abrupt, almost violent, sense of alienation: "The inclusiveness and absence of judgment, the freedom from upon which Idyllwild is ostensibly premised has its limits. One of the recurring themes of the series has been the lack of a space for trans-people, dramatically represented in Maura's wandering existence throughout the series. She is quite literally never at home, moving from one bed, one bedroom, one apartment or condo to another, excluded or walled off from a world she never feels fully a part of."[30] It bears reiterating that it is not only Maura whose growth seems stymied; other major characters get stuck in a holding pattern. Exiled from the music industry and shocked by Rita's suicide, Josh's second attempt to be a real father to Colton ends in another failure. And after flirting with Judaism only to be accused by the genuinely religious Raquel of conflating religion with self-help, Sarah reopens the possibility that her ex-husband, Len, really was her "person" after all. By the end of that season, every Pfefferman is single except for Ari, whose relationship seems on the verge of collapse when the family reunites for the cruise. Though long neglected (and perhaps underdeveloped as a character), Shelly does appear to break out triumphantly in the boldly revelatory ending of the third season. At last marching to her own drummer in ways that effectively set up the premise of the show's musical finale, Soloway's perpetually exasperating, transfixing characters are otherwise left hanging in the maritime wind at the conclusion of that season and well beyond, most notably the Pfeffermans' politically edgy season 4 journey to Israel, which only intensifies their individual self-division and rancor as a family.[31] Still maddeningly self-interested, still dissatisfied, still searching desperately for kinship, still drifting.[32] And by that point, many of us would probably not wish it otherwise.[33]

Notes

1. "On Being Jewish, American and a Writer," *New York Times*, October 2, 2017, https://www.nytimes.com/2017/10/02/t-magazine/jewish-american-novelists.html.
2. As Ariel Levy wryly puts it, this is "a family drama about California Jews who have a standing order at Canter's Deli and who bicker about which of the siblings should inherit the house where they grew up." See Ariel Levy, "Dolls and Feelings," *New Yorker*, December 14, 2015, https://www.newyorker.com/magazine/2015/12/14/dolls-and-feelings. For an earlier treatment of these issues, please see Ranen Omer-Sherman, "Nomadism and Stasis in Transparent." *Studies in American Jewish Literature (SAJL)* 41.2: 223–230: https://muse.jhu.edu/article/868212/pdf.
3. Joey Soloway, *She Wants It: Desire, Power, and Toppling the Patriarchy* (New York: Random House, 2019), 65.
4. Jonathan Freedman, "'Transparent': A Guide for the Perplexed," *Los Angeles Review of Books*, April 10, 2016, https://lareviewofbooks.org/article/transparent-a-guide-for-the-perplexed/#!. Emphasis in the original.
5. In a traditional sense, there is a monumental counterforce to this radical mobility, in the strict legal, dietary, and other weighty ordinances of 613 mitzvot that were codified beginning in the third century C.E., nearly none of which, however, remotely impact the lives of the Pfeffermans to any meaningful or sustaining degree. Naturally, some perceive the essence of the show's Jewishness in even broader terms than I am arguing. I am particularly fond of Isaac Butler's observations in *Slate*: "*Transparent* . . . isn't just Jewish because of its subject matter, or its characters, or its setting. It's Jewish in its sensibility and concerns, even as both can prove hard to define. One defining characteristic, clearly present in *Transparent*, is a sense of too-muchness. . . . It's this bubbling-forth that's most immediately visible in Jewish work. You can see it in the antic rhythms of *Annie Hall*, or the writing of Michael Chabon and Jami Attenberg. It's how we know that a character named George Costanza is actually Jewish." Isaac Butler, "Transparent Is the Most Profoundly Jewish Show in TV History," *Slate*, September 27, 2017, http://www.slate.com/blogs/browbeat/2017/09/27/transparent_is_a_profoundly_jewish_tv_show.html.
6. Judith Butler, "Precarious Life," in *Radicalizing Levinas*, eds. Peter Atterton and Matthew Calarco (New York: SUNY Press, 2010), 3–20; quotation appears on p. 7.
7. The Hirschfeld Institut für Sexualwissenschaft (Institute for Sexual Science) headed by Magnus Hirschfeld was an early sexology research institute in Germany, and Hirschfeld was a pioneer in fostering understanding and tolerance for gay and transgender (he adapted the term "transsexualism") individuals. Hirschfeld unwaveringly insisted on understanding sexual orientation as innate and not a deliberate choice. The institute thrived from 1919 until 1933 when it was destroyed by Nazi youth brigades, its library of books burned. Lisa Liebman notes that although in the season's conclusion in episode 9, *Transparent* portrays its founder as being present at the time of its destruction, the historical Hirschfeld had actually read the writing on the wall and already fled Nazi Germany on a world tour in 1930:

"Having been called out by Hitler in the '20s, he knew a gay, Jewish, trans-rights sexologist was no longer *willkommen* in Berlin. He saw the Institute's destruction in a newsreel in a Paris cinema." Lisa Liebman, "*Transparent*'s 1930s Berlin Flashbacks, Explained," *Vulture*, December 16, 2015, http://www.vulture.com/2015/12/transparent-berlin-flashbacks-explained.html.

8 Soloway, *She Wants It*, 67. Undoubtedly, it was the intermingling of art and life that helped shape this ethos, for even as Soloway was editing the pilot, they were struck by their parent's "boundarylessness" (by then Harry Soloway went by Carrie) which was "more intense now that Carrie was constantly transforming. Every time we saw her in those first few years there would be a new look, a new voice, a new Carrie." See Soloway, *She Wants It*, 68.

9 It is precisely here, at Raquel's long pause and momentary faltering, her acknowledgment that this rupture is no easy thing, that the viewer understands that the next step is filled with uncertainty; there is no reliable compass for the way forward.

10 As Esther Breger astutely observes of this episode, "*Transparent* can be bold and brazen and transgressive; it's when Soloway turns her gaze towards stillness, though, that she finds transcendence." Esther Breger, "On *Transparent*, A Family Unhappy In Its Own Way," *New Republic*, September 23, 2016, https://newrepublic.com/article/137110/transparent-family-unhappy-way. Arguably, it is due to Soloway's forsaking the latter that the series' final episode would lose its way.

11 Ariel Levy describes the "guileless delight" Soloway seeks to convey at such critical junctures in her characters' lives: "*Transparent* has a child's sense of amazement about the world—especially secret places where different rules apply. Maura seems free for the first time at a sylvan cross-dressing camp, where she bikes along the dirt road wearing a purple dress. The Michigan Womyn's Music Festival—which ended this summer, after forty years, largely because of conflicts over whether trans women ought to be included—is re-created in the second season as a muddy, magical oasis where women receive visions by staring into bonfires." Ariel Levy, "Dolls and Feelings," *New Yorker*, December 14, 2015, https://www.newyorker.com/magazine/2015/12/14/dolls-and-feelings.

12 Soloway seems to have envisioned Raquel's emerging Passover sermon as a meta-commentary on each of the characters' spiritual quests, their "questions about duality and wholeness, about knowing yourself and loneliness" and of course Maura's plight in particular: "Maura starts out the season ticking off the list of everything she's 'gotten.' She's out of the closet, has a great house, has love, but she doesn't feel better." See Soloway, *She Wants It*, 175.

13 Grace Paley, "A Conversation with My Father," *Enormous Changes At the Last Minute* (New York: Noonday Press, 1995), 162.

14 Isaac Butler, "*Transparent* Is the Most Profoundly Jewish Show in TV History," *Slate*, Sept 27, 2017, http://www.slate.com/blogs/browbeat/2017/09/27/transparent_is_a_profoundly_jewish_tv_show.html.

15 Most educated people know that science no longer views gender as a simple binary construct. But Sameth reminds us that "thousands of years ago ... ancient literature makes clear that truth was known." Mark Sameth, "Is God Transgender?" *New York Times*, August 12, 2016, https://www.nytimes.com/2016/08/13/opinion/is-god-transgender.html. Emphasis in original.

16 For some still struggling with communities hostile to their struggles, science has become an important ally. Beth Orens, an Israeli Orthodox Jew who transitioned from male to female two decades ago and runs an organization serving transgender Orthodox Jews, describes "a growing body of research that indicates that the brains

of [transgender individuals] are closer in structure to the sex they *perceive* themselves to be than they are to the sex their external organs proclaim them to be." See "I Am a Transsexual Orthodox Jew. And I Won't Apologize for It," *Haaretz*, September 8, 2016. http://www.haaretz.com/opinion/.premium-1.740993.

17 Jonathan Freedman, "'Transparent': A Guide for the Perplexed."

18 Nicki Green and S. J. Crasnow, "'Artifacts from the Future': The Queer Power of Trans Ritual Objects," *TSQ: Transgender Studies Quarterly* 6, no. 3 (2019): 403–408.

19 That the series defers its characters' family "reunification" and sojourn until the fourth season is telling, and even then, characters drift through their uneasy encounters with Israeli and Palestinian realities and the season's final scenes suggest that their identities are as ambivalently, guiltily or otherwise unhappily unresolved as ever.

20 It was not until the *Transparent* years that Soloway began to identify as nonbinary and adapt the third-person pronoun (they/them/their). In *Transparent*'s early seasons, Soloway still identified as a heterosexual woman, married to musician Bruce Gilbert and mother of two sons. But working on the show proved a catalyst for their own transformation alongside those of its fictional family members: "At first it was like, I just want to tell a small story to create a little imaginary world where I can feel safe to explore these feelings and also to make the world a safe place for my parent to be out. And then as I got to know so many trans people working on the show, I started to go through my own gender questioning and wondering." Maudlyne Ihejirika, "Exploring with Jill Soloway, 50 Years Later, Shared Childhood in Urban Renewal South Commons," *Chicago Sun Times*, September 1, 2019, https://chicago.suntimes.com/news/2019/9/1/20841369/urban-renewal-experiment-housing.

21 Soloway, *She Wants It*, 63–64.

22 Actor Jay Duplass (Josh) has described the process as a deeply cathartic experience for all involved: "People get up on the box and they talk about their problems, they talk about their breakthroughs, and you cry and you release. You might get up and say some shit but then you realize that you are infinitely a more pure vessel for what's about to happen. You go on set and you are no longer in charge and your ideas don't matter as much anymore—just your heart matters. That's the genius of the show. Genuinely, I'm not exaggerating or being saccharine about it. It's just a fact." Chris Gardner, "*I Love Dick* Cast Inherits *Transparent*'s Emotional Exercise," *Hollywood Reporter*, May 4, 2017, https://www.hollywoodreporter.com/rambling-reporter/i-love-dick-cast-inherits-transparents-emotional-exercise-997344.

23 Slava Greenberg, "Run from Your Parent's House": Transfeminism and Abraham's Blessing," *Journal of Feminist Studies in Religion* 37, no. 2 (Fall 2021): 25–41.

24 When Mort renames themselves as Maura, they are also reflecting a central tradition in Judaism. In her call for developing transgender renaming rituals, Heather Paul writes, "Avram, Judaism's first leader, received the name 'Avraham' to mark a significant transformation. In Genesis, God told him to '*Lech lecha*, from your birthplace and your father's house.' *Lech lecha* is often understood as 'go forth.'" Here Paul stresses that "a more accurate translation is 'go to yourself.' God told him, 'You shall no longer be called Avram. Your name shall be Avraham, for I will make you a father of multitudes.' [. . .] Jewish rituals do not just mark change, they effect change, and a name change should do the same." Heather Paul, "In the Torah, Name Changes Signify Moments of Transformation: In the Lives of Transgender Jews, They are Just as Powerful," *Forward* April 30, 2020,

https://forward.com/scribe/445269/in-the-torah-name-changes-signify-moments-of-transformation-in-the-lives/.

25   Jeffrey Shoulson, "The Jewish Transparent: Jewishness, Community, and Self-Definition in *Transparent*" (lecture, Modern Language Association Annual Conference, Austin, TX, January 6, 2016).

26   Soloway was drawn to the fact that Hirschfeld's "queer Jewish intellectualism as deviant was one of Hitler's first propagandistic impulses." See Soloway, *She Wants It*, 127.

27   Light quoted in Soloway, *She Wants It*, 135.

28   Laure Adler, "Interview with George Steiner," *Forward*, March 26, 2017, https://forward.com/culture/366594/he-may-be-our-greatest-jewish-thinker-but-what-does-he-think-about-jewish-t/.

29   Slava Greenberg, "Run from Your Parent's House": Transfeminism and Abraham's Blessing," 41.

30   Jeffrey Shoulson, "The Jewish Transparent: Jewishness, Community, and Self-Definition in *Transparent*," (presentation at the Modern Language Association Annual Conference, Austin, TX, January 2016).

31   The premise, which takes up most of *Transparent*'s final regular season, is that Maura has been invited to present at a Tel Aviv University conference, accompanied by Aly, and the others eventually join the trip, leading to a plethora of encounters with predictably hilarious and maddening encounters with the exotica of Bedouin tents, Israeli machismo with which Josh flirts with a predictably disastrous outcome, the Occupation (including Aly's somewhat feverish sojourn with Palestinian hipsters and gay activists in Ramallah and a utopian West Bank community), Zionism's morally complex relation to the Holocaust as well as important revelations about the family's previously hidden Holocaust history. It proves an ambitious and largely successful story arc filled with arguments about roots, politics, and human rights, all of which are left ingeniously unsettled, debates that will undoubtedly continue in the minds of many viewers. As Isaac Butler observes, "Is it any wonder . . . that this most Jewish of shows, with its obsession with boundaries and borders, would do its own version of making *aliyah*? *Transparent*'s treatment of Israel is just as ambivalent, contradictory, anxious, and overflowing as its explorations of anything else"; see Butler. In Soloway's memoir, they describe their own visit to Ramallah and the West Bank prior to filming that season and the painful shock of coming to terms with their Jewish privilege. See Soloway, *She Wants It*, 196–199.

32   Candor requires that I acknowledge my profound disappointment with *Transparent*'s sole episode in season 5 (and conclusion to the series), formally titled Musicale Finale and which, though a feature-length film marked by a tonal shift from melancholy to unadulterated joy, resorted to hasty sitcom fixes to resolve the narrative complexities and heal dysfunctional relationships (perhaps most notably, the cringe-inducing resolution of Rabbi Raquel and Josh's breakup) that many critics and viewers found so reliably compelling in previous seasons. Undoubtedly, much of its long-sustained nuance and ambitious emotional and intellectual spectrum was thwarted by the stridently didactic lyrics (perhaps Sondheim might have managed better?) as well as the choice to privilege bombastic statements over the introspective intimacy that many viewers anticipated. Even the cinematography, so poetic and immersive in previous seasons, seemed curiously flat (the accomplished cinematographer Jimmy Frohna had moved on to other series by then). As Ben Travers complains, it landed like "a desperate flailing for attention that betrays

what the show did best and, worse still, such contradictory pomp comes from a series that knows it should've gone quietly into the night, rather than clawing tooth and nail for another day of sun." Ben Travers, "*Transparent* Review: Amazon's Musical Finale Strikes the Wrong Chord, Too Many Times," *IndieWire*, September 28, 2019, https://www.indiewire.com/2019/09/transparent-finale-review-musical-ending-amazon-1202177103/. Or, as Robin Bahr suggests in a similar vein, the finale felt "hastily composed, a tacked-on coda from a visionary who has already moved onto brighter horizons, such as the underrated *I Love Dick*.... The show has always been invested in dissecting performativity, but perhaps a musical is just too literal an interpretation." Robin Bahr, "*Transparent*: Musicale Finale," *Hollywood Reporter*, September 15, 2019, https://www.hollywoodreporter.com/review/transparent-musicale-finale-review-1239775.

33. Here it seems worth noting that the Exodus narrative, evident throughout the series but of course especially prominent in this third season, also has striking resonance for the lived experience in the small but increasingly vocal transgender community in Israel. As reported in *Haaretz*, Yiscah Smith, a 65-year-old woman, chooses to describe the story of her coming out as transgender as "*coming out from slavery into freedom*" (emphasis mine). Smith was born in 1951 into a New York Jewish family. Today she lives in Jerusalem, where she is a well known figure in the religious LGBT community, works as a Jewish educator, and teaches Hasidic thought. After meeting transgender people in the nonreligious world, Smith understood she was not alone, but as time passed, she returned to religion and the religious community. "I asked God to help me, because I couldn't breathe any longer. I understood that I needed to start on a journey of gender change, and God would guide me. The minute I understood that, my life changed. As if God had stretched out his hand to me and said: 'Yiscah, I am guiding you.' So there is not just gender change here, but spiritual correction. I started to live who I really am." Ariel Horowitz, "Transgender Jews Attempt to Reconcile Identity, Religion," *Haaretz*, October 4, 2016, https://www.haaretz.com/jewish/.premium.MAGAZINE-transgender-jews-attempt-to-reconcile-identity-religion-1.5444802.

4
The Historiography of *Transparent*

MARTIN SHUSTER

The philosopher and conceptual artist Adrian Piper mused that imposing constraints on her art made her work "potentially as accessible as comic books or *television*."[1] After noting how socioeconomic difference often makes impossible a connection between artist and audience, she also noted that "this is not to say that I think art could conceivably *solve* any socioeconomic problems, no matter how accessible or integrated into the culture it is. But if it were accessible to wider segments of the culture, it would be informed by the more various types of critical feedback, would effect a more various and richer quality of experience for people, *would be responsive to more of what in fact constitutes our social reality*."[2] I mention this in broad strokes because I want to flag two themes that Piper raises. The fundamental accessibility of television—and thereby its prospects for works of art—is important to how this chapter orients itself.[3] Relatedly, I am in broad agreement with Piper's suggestions about the (potential) role of works of art, especially televisual ones, in the constitution of social reality.

This chapter revolves around *Transparent*'s relationship to Jewish historiography, to the writing of history. My argument is twofold. First, *Transparent* powerfully diagnoses and responds in a politically and ethically sensitive way to the suffering that the present historical moment generates (including how the suffering of the past remains with and affects the present to create even more suffering). Second, in doing so, *Transparent* locates itself explicitly as an inventive bit of Jewish memorialization of that suffering, similar in function to other ways in which Jewish memory has been memorialized in literature, song, or religious prayer.[4] Ultimately, I suggest that this twofold procedure allows us to rethink the very possibilities of what Judaism or being Jewish might amount to in the future and especially the way *Transparent* conceives the very construction of history involved in modern memorialization as full of ruptures, in part due to the fragmentation of modernity, and, in part, to the ways in which suffering is inherited and yet forgotten and repressed.

Television, Film, and the Present Moment

Transparent's standing as a work of televisual art must be related as much to television history as to the history of film and literature. The common thread between new television and these other media is their ability to reflectively address the present and the past. *Transparent* fits into the rubric of what might be termed new television,[5] which denotes its standing as a work of art, no different in its aspirations than a serious film or novel. Unlike something created solely for the purpose of generating profit, *Transparent* appears to admit to other— perhaps even conflicting—motives or purposes (and does so without denying that profit is also a motive). *Transparent* thereby invites interpretation of and reflection on its intentions and aspirations as a work of art.[6] On one hand, it is obvious that *Transparent* responds to the present sociopolitical moment in the United States, especially to how queer culture is and is not being recognized.[7] On the other hand, there is something significant to *Transparent* being a series made for the "small screen" (a euphemism I invoke here to highlight that *Transparent* is fundamentally television and that it does not appear on a "regular" television channel; this says more about the current possibilities of the medium itself than about *Transparent*).[8] After all, because one can respond to and make similar sociopolitical points by means of a novel or a comic book or a film—is there something significant to this medium in this case?

Take the view of an artistic medium as a "mediator... a go-between... artist and perceiver."[9] In this way, we might compare a medium to a form of speech, where it provides a particular way "to get through to someone, to make sense."[10] Just as certain forms of speech are more effective in certain contexts (say, legal speech in a legal context, religious speech in a religious one, and so forth), it may be that a particular medium is more effective in one context than another. To the extent that they have their genesis in photography and to the extent that they both rely on moving images, the medium of new television shares much with the medium of film[11] and can thereby be partially situated in the context of film history. As many have noted, film is the modern art form par excellence.[12] One way to cash out this idea is through the thought that film attends to significant features of modernity. Thus, the early twentieth-century social critic Robert Warshow and contemporary philosopher Stanley Cavell respectively claim that

> [Social] criticism finds its best opportunity in the movies, which are the most highly and most engrossing of the popular arts, *and which seem to have an almost unlimited power to absorb and transform the discordant elements of our fragmented culture.*[13]

> [People see films] in their experience as memorable *public events, segments of the experiences, the memories, of a common life.* So that the difficulty of assessing them is the same as the difficulty of assessing everyday experience, the difficulty of expressing oneself satisfactorily, of making oneself find the words for what one is specifically interested to say.[14]

Warshow and Cavell both highlight the fragmented nature of experience. The reasons for such atomization are surely varied and range from the rise of capitalism[15] to the disintegration of various forms of authority[16] and the difficulty of establishing new ones;[17] to the rise of science and a concomitant disenchantment of the world;[18] to the spread of colonialism and racial thinking;[19] to the shock and spectacle of the modern world[20] and to the sort of dissonance[21] and loneliness that it produces and exacerbates.[22] I mention these not because I have the space to address them in the depth they would require but to stress the shared and common nature of films: that they are addressed to a common experience—felt at a variety of and because of different sites—but nonetheless experienced regularly and generally. Film's power—more so than, say, the novel, which also addresses itself to similar concerns[23]—is that it, through its orientation around essentially natural motion[24]—requires very little training to appreciate; this is one way in which we might say film is democratic. As Cavell puts it, "Rich and poor, those who care about no (other) art and those who live on the promise of art, those whose pride is education and those whose power is power or practicality—*all care about movies, await them, respond to them, remember them, talk about them, hate some of them, are grateful for some of them.*"[25] I think all of the same is true of new television, which has deep connections to film in this regard[26] and which has itself sometimes been understood as "cinematic."[27]

Walter Benjamin, a German-Jewish thinker at the turn of the last century, appraised modernity in similar tones but noted an even more insidious consequence of the atomization of modernity. According to Benjamin, our powers for constructing a meaningful narrative about our lives have greatly waned, exactly because the traditions that would animate such narratives have themselves been undermined, lost, or become lifeless.[28] And this problem is so serious that our very capabilities for doing history have also been undermined—again, exactly because the very traditions that modernity has undermined were in fact the traditions that gave us access to the past in various forms and ways. And here Benjamin might be said to have had in mind—but also radicalizing—an idea that animates historian Yosef Yerushalmi's suggestion that every people produces traditions (Yerushalmi playfully calls them *halacha*):[29] "Only those moments out of the past are transmitted that are felt to be formative or exemplary for the *halakhah* of a people as it is lived in the present; *the rest of 'history' falls, one might almost say literally, by the 'wayside.'*"[30] The same is true of moderns, except that our traditions have become qualitatively poor and so have our capacities for historical narration. Concomitantly, as the last century—with its legacy of genocide—made clear, the capacity for doing history has taken on an ethical import; we owe it to the dead to construct a history that does not forget or neglect them. Strikingly, Benjamin thinks that film can somehow address this state of affairs. In his journals, he writes, "[About the past:] Do not cry. The nonsense of critical prognoses. *Film instead of storytelling.*"[31] And as I have been suggesting, anything that film can do, new television can also. On one hand, by means of Warshow and Cavell, film and new television might give our present experience a certain unity. On the other hand, Benjamin also thinks that film can do something more radical than this—it can also revive our access to the past. How?

Television and the Past

One way we might think about this issue is to note that Benjamin, in responding to the crisis of modernity, thought that the way forward was essentially through modernity; that is, in this context, one must find a way to do history in such a way that both acknowledges this basic fragmentation (as opposed to avoiding or denying it) and uses that fragmentation to produce an entirely novel understanding of what history might be. Benjamin goes so far as to call it a "Copernican revolution," defining it as follows: "The Copernican revolution in historical perception is as follows. Formerly it was thought that a fixed point had been in 'what had been,' and one saw the present engaged in tentatively concentrating the forces of knowledge on this ground. Now this relation is to be overturned, and what has been is to become the dialectical reversal—the flash of awakened consciousness . . . the facts become something that *just now first happened to us, first struck us; to establish them is the affair of memory.*"[32]

One element of Benjamin's radical thesis is thereby to reverse our common sense understanding of the past: the past is not something that is given and out there waiting to be discovered. Instead, Benjamin's suggestion is that any understanding—in fact, any actuality of the past—emerges from the present. The past only becomes what it is by virtue of the intervention of human subjectivity in the present. On this point, he and Yerushalmi agree: present traditions determine the nature of the past.[33] Thus, we acknowledge the status and sway of modernity. Furthermore, as Warshow and Cavell suggest, film (and new television) might allow us to organize our present experience in a common way, with viewership requiring only the tiniest bit of training (really, all one needs to know is that one cannot enter the world of the screen and vice versa).[34]

At the heart of Benjamin's glorification of film is a challenge to think about how film can organize our experience of the past. To get some grip on this challenge, consider, for example, how the Western or the gangster film has organized the American experience of its history.[35] More recently, think of how, say, a show like *House of Cards* has organized our understanding of the historical office of the U.S. presidency (see figure 4.1).[36] To stress film and new television's power, think of the ways in which contemporary concerns might organize our very invocation and involvement with history, indeed our very understanding of what happened and how it all fits together. In this context, consider the glut of recent films and television series that stress the 1980s (*A Most Violent Year, Dallas Buyers*

FIGURE 4.1 Top: Trump meeting Putin (2017), Bottom: *House of Cards* (2015). From *The Sun*, https://www.thesun.co.uk/news/3967298/donald-trump-vladimir-putin-house-of-cards-g20/.

Club, Argo, Guardians of the Galaxy, The Americans, Halt and Catch Fire, Stranger Things, Deutschland 83, Dark, and so forth).[37] As art, and as stories—and as contributions to how we frame and tell our histories—these works are animated by the fact that the problems of the 1980s are very much with us,[38] indeed that our problems have their genesis there (in a way that might not otherwise be apparent), and, in fact, they have become more exacerbated, and we might need to deal with and acknowledge even our own yearning and nostalgia and desire for a period where history seemed to hang for us between good and evil in a way it no longer seems to do.

The Contemporaneity of *Transparent*'s Past

It is in this context that I want to turn to *Transparent*. As other chapters in this volume have discussed, the Jewishness of the Pfeffermans is essential to the success of the show, including its deepest ambitions to give voice to the trans and queer community.[39] One way to put this point is to see *Transparent* as a sort of Trojan horse: by leveraging a television trope that viewers were already familiar and enthralled with (the Jewish sitcom),[40] *Transparent* is able to get viewers to take an interest in another sort of show: a "fun-comfortable" or "funerable" show whose protagonist is Jewish *and* trans.[41] In this way, *Transparent* makes its televisual form reflect the queerness and complexity of its portrayals of gender and sexuality.[42] What is especially remarkable about *Transparent*, however, is not merely this seeming sleight-of-hand on its part, but rather how it helps us understand Benjamin's ambitions vis-à-vis history.

In fact, *Transparent* itself performs Jewish history. In the second season, the show exhibits the history of the Pfefferman family in Nazi Germany, thereby connecting the suffering of the present to the suffering of the past, creating a constellation of suffering that makes available a sequence of experiences that might otherwise remain separate, inflecting the present with the past and vice versa. Here, we might think of Talal Asad's understanding of suffering as constituted by "sufferers ... [who] are also social persons," where "their suffering is partly constituted by the way they inhabit, or are constrained to inhabit, their relationship with others."[43] The question is who one allows oneself to cohabitate with—or acknowledges oneself as perhaps already cohabitating with.[44] In this vein, *Transparent* explicitly links the struggles of present-day Maura and her transition with the struggles of her ancestor Gittel, and her living as a trans woman in 1930s Berlin, under the auspices of Magnus Hirschfeld's Institute for Sexual Science (Institut für Sexualwissenschaft).[45] When the Nazis storm the institute, burn its books, and capture its members (see figure 4.2), the show connects not only the suffering of these two trans women but also the suffering of the Jews and all other groups the Nazis targeted—indeed, marginalized people targeted anywhere, anytime (as the connection to the present makes explicit). Putting things in this way calls to mind the dedication philosopher

FIGURE 4.2 *Transparent*. "Man on the Land," Season 2:9. Written by Ali Liebegott, directed by Joey Soloway, December 11, 2015.

Emmanuel Levinas, himself a Jewish survivor of the Nazi genocide, attaches to his book *Otherwise than Being*: "To the memory of those who were closest among the six million assassinated by the National Socialists, and of the millions on millions of all confessions and all nations, victims of the same hatred of the other man, the same anti-semitism."[46]

The sequence where this happens in *Transparent* is remarkable as it is embedded in a broader arc where the Berlin timeline appears to Maura's daughter, Ari Pfefferman. The attack on Hirschfeld's institute visually parallels and is tied to Maura's lack of acceptance at the Idyllwild Wimmin's Music Festival due to Maura having so-called "male physiology." The Berlin past almost involuntarily flashes up to Ari, giving her access to some sort of seemingly archaic self and history.[47] Importantly, though, this occurs a few episodes after Ari first experiences a vision of the Berlin past, here, originally, in the context of her discovery of the transgenerational inheritance or "epigenetic" effects of trauma. Talking to her friend, Ari muses: "Oh my god. This shit is fascinating. Did you know there is such a thing as inherited trauma in your actual DNA? They did this study on bunnies where they give them electric shocks where they were smelling cherry blossoms and the bunnies's babies and their babies, the grandbabies, they were all afraid of cherry blossoms. [...] It was inherited in their DNA. It's incredible. It's called epigenetics."[48]

The introduction of the Nazi era in *Transparent* performs Benjamin's procedure by linking the past and present in exactly the way in which he suggests,[49] and the introduction of epigenetics raises questions about our very notion of history. Importantly, given the show's first season, it would never be obvious or suggested to any viewer that this is where the show would go. History did not seem to be a serious concern. And yet, it is exactly because of its ethical impulse with respect to the present moment that *Transparent* moves to the past. Even histories of the Nazi genocide often gloss over the suffering of homosexuals and others targeted for their sexuality by the Nazi regime,[50] a history that *Transparent* recuperates without in any way minimizing the suffering of Jews, instead showing—as Levinas insists—that although undeniably distinct, these are all of a *kind,* "victims of the same hatred of the other man, the same anti-semitism." It is in this sense that we ought to understand Benjamin's remark: "The only historian capable of fanning the spark of hope in the past is the one who is firmly convinced that *even the dead* will not be safe from the enemy if he is victorious."[51]

Conclusion

Such a procedure thereby forces on the viewer a very sophisticated call for reflection. *Transparent* urges the viewer to reflect on how they are situated in relation to the suffering that the show exhibits. The reference to epigenetics asks the viewer to reflect on her own relationship to what is on screen and thereby to suffering more generally: what does it mean to acknowledge suffering? Is it mere spectatorship or voyeurism? Or, as *Transparent* models the procedure, must we make sense of it by placing it into a broader context, drawing contemporary conclusions, and training our vision to take stock of the contemporary United States and its violence toward its queer minorities? An analogous thread is suggested in the second Berlin sequence (episode 9), when after a poignant and dramatic scene of violence in Berlin, the screen fades to black, lingering there for a moment before transitioning to the next scene, inviting us to reflect on how the problem is not just a problem of the world in the screen but a problem of the world of the screen. In the face of a black screen, we are forced back into our world, into ourselves, dismissed from viewing the world of *Transparent*.

In this way, *Transparent*, like all successful televisual art—indeed all art—acknowledges the extent to which art is a form of human expression. Because it is screened and comes to an end, it demonstrates the fragility of human expression; because it speaks to us, exhibits before us a world of suffering akin to our own, it reminds us of the possibility of human expression and thereby of its power. And, perhaps most importantly, because it alleges historical connections between the past and the present, even if only amidst fictional beings, it inspires us to understand how we might presently comport ourselves differently and how we might ourselves relate to our past. Or, in a modification of what philosopher Ludwig Wittgenstein once said about fiction, we might say that nothing is more important for understanding our sites of suffering—sites that we enable and allow—than the construction of fictitious ones.[52] All good fiction is always "an act of culture making."[53] *Transparent* might be said to train our vision, affecting the way we inhabit and perceive the world and the ways we might draw connections between it and the past, in turn making for us "new affective structures" and "lighting up the world in different ways."[54]

When *Transparent* memorializes the Pfeffermans as a family essentially woven by the Nazi genocide (here in more ways than one, i.e., both as Jews and as trans women),[55] it also presents a distinct understanding of the possibilities of Jewish historiography. By giving voice to those who are minimized, ignored, marginalized, or discarded by contemporary society, *Transparent* suggests—as Benjamin did—similar procedures for the past. By linking events that may not otherwise seem connected, we may begin to move away from a linear conception of history—a conception that always leaves something out. In this way, *Transparent*, Benjamin, and—once again—Yerushalmi are of one mind: "The task can no longer be limited to finding continuities in Jewish history . . . perhaps the time has come to look more closely at ruptures, breaches, breaks, to identify them more precisely, to see how Jews endured them, to understand that not everything of value that existed before a break was either salvaged or metamorphosed, but was lost, and that often some of what fell by the wayside can become, through our retrieval, meaningful to us."[56]

Notes

1. Adrian Piper, "Notes on Mythic Being, I–III," in *Out of Order, Out of Sight: Selected Writings in Meta-Art, 1968–1992* (Cambridge: MIT Press, 1999), 122. Emphasis added.
2. Piper, "Notes on Mythic Being," 122. Emphasis added.
3. I will have more to say about this shortly, but let me note that my (and Piper's) use of "accessibility" is a point about the *formal* qualities of the medium: that it is a sophisticated (and on my argument modernist) art form that requires very little training to appreciate (unlike other modernist art forms like the novel or the abstract painting or atonal music). This point is separate from (although not entirely unrelated to) a point about how socioeconomic conditions intersect with questions of accessibility. For example, in noting these formal qualities of television, I do not mean to minimize the extent to which *Transparent* has a particular economic or material threshold (i.e., Amazon requires a subscription service fee, it requires a device for viewing, and so forth—these features are exactly in tension with the aforementioned formal qualities). This is why questions of accessibility cannot be settled purely at the formal level and require discussions and commitments around, for example, preservation and—literal as opposed to formal—accessibility in the form of public archives or other sites of availability. For an excellent summary of the issues involved here, see William Boddy, "Statement by William Boddy, Baruch College and Graduate Center, City University of New York," *Historical Journal of Film, Radio and Television* 16, no. 3 (1996): 393–396. There are also, of course, important questions here around accessibility from the point of view of disability studies where notions of accessibility require even deeper and more nuanced contextualization and understanding. For more on this, see Marja Evelyn Mogk, ed., *Different Bodies: Essays on Disability in Film and Television* (Jefferson, NC: McFarland, 2013).
4. I am especially thinking of Yerushalmi and the way in which he highlights how Jewish memory often actualized itself not merely by means of the writing of history,

but also by art and religion. See Yosef Hayim Yerushalmi, *Zakhor: Jewish History and Jewish Memory* (Seattle: University of Washington Press, 1996), 45.

5. Many incredibly complex issues are glossed by my remarks here. Above all, I imagine that many scholars of television may be rankled by the way in which I locate the history of new television so far outside of the history of television. I have defended this claim in more depth in Martin Shuster, *New Television: The Aesthetics and Politics of a Genre* (Chicago: University of Chicago, 2017). Here, let me just add that I do not mean at all to deny the importance of earlier television history, only to suggest that—because of the aesthetic qualities of new television—they cannot be located solely within the history of television. For more on the (extra-televisual) novelty of this sort of television, see Ted Nannicelli, *Appreciating the Art of Television: A Philosophical Perspective* (London: Routledge, 2016); Jason Mittell, *Complex TV: The Poetics of Contemporary Television Storytelling* (New York: New York University Press, 2015); Alan Sepinwall, *The Revolution Was Televised: The Cops, Crooks, Slingers, and Slayers Who Changed TV Drama Forever* (New York: Simon & Schuster, 2013). In this context, see also note 55.

6. Disposable or consumable works can also be interpreted, and, of course, I realize that even though created by Joey Soloway, *Transparent* is actualized by a team, and we cannot subscribe to an auteur theory of composition. My point is only to suggest that we view *Transparent* as a unified work of art, as if it has a unified intention. For more on all of this, see Shuster, *New Television*, 1–13, 50–85.

7. For the relationship between *Transparent*'s form as a sitcom and queerness, see Maria San Filippo, "*Transparent* Family Values: Unmasking Sitcom Myths of Gender, Sex(uality), and Money," in *The Sitcom Reader: America Re-viewed, Still Skewed*, eds. Mary Dalton and Laura Linder (Buffalo, NY: SUNY Press, 2016), 305–318.

8. For more on media specificity see Sarah Cardwell, "Television amongst Friends: Medium, Art, Media," *Critical Studies in Television: An International Journal of Television Studies* 9, no. 3 (2014): 6–21; Noël Carroll, "Medium Specificity Arguments and the Self-Consciously Invented Arts: Film, Video, and Photography," in *Theorizing the Moving Image* (Cambridge: Cambridge University Press, 1996), 127–153; "Forget the Medium!," in *Engaging the Moving Image* (New Haven, CT: Yale University Press, 1996), 1–9; Diarmuid Costello, "On the Very Idea of a 'Specific' Medium: Michael Fried and Stanley Cavell on Painting and Photography as Arts," *Critical Inquiry* 34, no. 2 (2008): 274–312. For media specificity in relation to television, see chapter 1 of Shuster, *New Television*.

9. John Dewey, *Art as Experience* (New York: Penguin, 1934), 207.

10. Stanley Cavell, *The World Viewed: Reflections on the Ontology of Film* (Cambridge: Harvard University Press, 1979), 31.

11. Shuster, *New Television*, 30–49.

12. Consider thinkers as diverse as Walter Benjamin, Robert Warshow, Stanley Cavell, and Gilles Deleuze.

13. Robert Warshow, *The Immediate Experience: Movies, Comics, Theatre, and Other Aspects of Popular Culture* (Cambridge: Harvard University Press, 2001), xxxviii. Emphasis added.

14. Stanley Cavell, *Pursuits of Happiness: The Hollywood Comedy of Remarriage* (Cambridge: Harvard University Press, 1981), 41. Emphasis added.

15. Marshall Berman, *All That is Solid Melts into Air: The Experience of Modernity* (New York: Simon and Schuster, 1983).

16. Hannah Arendt, "What is Authority?", in *Between Past and Future: Eight Exercises in Political Thought* (New York: Penguin, 2006), 91–141.

17   Robert B. Pippin, *Modernism as a Philosophical Problem: On the Dissatisfaction of European High Culture*, 2nd ed. (Oxford: Blackwell, 1999).
18   J. M. Bernstein, *Adorno: Disenchantment and Ethics* (Cambridge: Cambridge University Press, 2001), 1–136; Max Weber, "Science as Vocation," in *From Max Weber: Essays in Sociology*, eds. H. H. Gerth and C. Wright Mills (London: Routledge, 1948), 129–159.
19   Hannah Arendt, *The Origins of Totalitarianism* (London: André Deutsch, 1986), 123–305; Aimé Césaire, *Discourse on Colonialism*, trans. Joan Pinkbaum (New York: Monthly Review Press, 2000).
20   Walter Benjamin, "The Work of Art in the Age of Its Technological Reproducibility," in *Selected Writings*, eds. Howard Eiland and Michael W. Jennings, vol. 4 (Cambridge: Harvard University Press, 2006), 251–284; "Experience and Poverty," in *Selected Writings*, eds. Howard Eiland and Michael W. Jennings, vol. 2 (Cambridge: Harvard University Press, 2002), 2: 731–736; Guy Debord, *Comments on the Society of the Spectacle*, trans. Malcolm Imrie (London: Verso, 1990).
21   Frantz Fanon, *Black Skin, White Masks*, trans. Richard Philcox (New York: Grove Press, 2008).
22   Martin Shuster, "Language and Loneliness: Arendt, Cavell, and Modernity," *International Journal of Philosophical Studies* 20, no. 4 (2012), 473–497.
23   György Lukács, *The Theory of the Novel*, trans. Anna Bostock (London: Merlin, 1971).
24   Gilles Deleuze, *Cinema 2: The Time-Image*, trans. Hugh Tomlinson and Barbara Habberjam (Minneapolis: University of Minnesota Press, 1989), 5.
25   Cavell, *The World Viewed*, 4–5. Emphasis added.
26   Shuster, *New Television*, 41–47. See also Martin Shuster, "New Television and Film," in *The Routledge Companion to Historical Theory*, ed. Chiel van der Akker (London: Routledge, 2021), 446–461.
27   Deborah L. Jaramillo, "Rescuing Television from 'The Cinematic': The Perils of Dismissing Television Style," in *Television Aesthetics and Style*, eds. Jason Jacobs and Steven Peacock (London: Bloomsbury, 2013), 67–79; Brett Mills, "What Does It Mean to Call Television 'Cinematic'?" in *Television Aesthetics and Style*, eds. Jason Jacobs and Steven Peacock (London: Bloomsbury, 2013), 57–67.
28   Walter Benjamin, "The Storyteller: Observations on the Works of Nikolai Leskov," in *Selected Writings*, eds. Howard Eiland and Michael W. Jennings, vol. 3 (Cambridge: Harvard University Press, 2006), 143–167. This aspect of Benjamin is beautifully captured in Hannah Arendt, "Walter Benjamin: 1892–1940," in *Men in Dark Times* (New York: Harcourt, Brace & World, 1968), 153–207.
29   *Halacha* is a Hebrew term that denotes the entire corpus of Jewish law. The word literally comes from the root *halakh*, which means "to walk" or "to go." So, an approximation of the meaning of the word halacha is "the way [to go]." I mention this to highlight that, because this corpus is so varied—composed as it is of legal precepts, legends, folk tales, parables, philosophical treatises, surrealist tales, questions, debates, and so forth—it really in a way refers to the entire form of life that reflectively orients Judaism. Yerushalmi is thereby being playful here in saying that (obviously) formally, every people will have such a component to its form of life.
30   Yerushalmi, *Zakhor*, 113. Emphasis added.
31   Walter Benjamin, *Gesammelte Schriften*, vol. 2, series 3, eds. Rolf Tiedemann and Hermann Schweppenhäuser (Frankfurt am Main: Suhrkamp, 1977), 1282. Emphasis added.
32   Walter Benjamin, *The Arcades Project* (Cambridge: Harvard University Press, 1999), 388–389. Emphasis added.

33 Benjamin, "On the Concept of History," in *Selected Writings*, eds. Howard Eiland and Michael W. Jennings, vol. 4 (Cambridge: Harvard University Press, 2006), 390.

34 Martin Shuster, "The Ordinariness and Absence of the World: Cavell's Ontology of the Screen—*Reading The World Viewed*," *MLN* 130, no. 5 (2015): 1067–1099.

35 Robert Warshow, "The Gangster as Tragic Hero," in *The Immediate Experience: Movies, Comics, Theatre, and Other Aspects of Popular Culture, Enlarged Edition* (Cambridge: Harvard University Press, 2001), 97–105; "The Legacy of the 30's," in *The Immediate Experience: Movies, Comics, Theatre, and Other Aspects of Popular Culture, Enlarged Edition* (Cambridge: Harvard University Press, 2001), 3–19; "Movie Chronicle: The Westerner" in *The Immediate Experience: Movies, Comics, Theatre, and Other Aspects of Popular Culture, Enlarged Edition* (Cambridge: Harvard University Press, 2001), 105–124; Robert B. Pippin, *Hollywood Westerns and American Myth: The Importance of Howard Hawks and John Ford for Political Philosophy* (New Haven, CT: Yale University Press, 2010); Jonathan Munby, *Public Enemies, Public Heroes: Screening the Gangster from Little Caesar to Touch of Evil* (Chicago: University of Chicago Press, 2009); Eugene Rosow, *Born to Lose: The Gangster Film in America* (Oxford: Oxford University Press, 1978).

36 An earlier reviewer for this chapter wrote that "I don't see what Shuster is going for on this point. Yes, obviously the HOC shot mimics a meeting between Trump and Putin, but I don't see how this political allusion organizes our very understanding of the historical office of the U.S. presidency." This query, however, completely reverses the directionality in question here: *House of Cards* is not mimicking a meeting between Trump and Putin, rather the opposite. *House of Cards predates* the meeting between Trump and Putin (the episode aired well before Trump was president). Real life thereby appears to visually (if not conceptually) mimic television. My point here, in response to this earlier reviewer, is the same as throughout this chapter: that, as many from John Dewey to Cornelius Castoriadis have noted, art does not simply mimic reality but is also, or alternatively, *constitutive* of reality.

37 Thanks to Sandra Laugier for this important point. See Sandra Laugier, "Amour, marriage et KGB," *Libération* (2015), March 27. The same is true of new television, see Martin Shuster, "'Dig If You Will the Picture . . .': New Television, Myth, *Black Monday* and the 1980s," *Revue internationale de philosophie* 76, no. 3 (2022): 105–119.

38 My sense of all of these shows and films is that they above all respond to the economic realities and aporias that emerge in this period, most notably, for example, the specter of Communism (then in the form of the Cold War, now in the form of the collapse of leftist thought in the face of the Cold War) and the rise of neoliberalism (in the form of Reaganism and Thatcherism).

39 My analysis on this point is based on and follows the way in which it is expertly made in Joshua Louis Moss, "'The Woman Thing and the Jew Thing': Transsexuality, Transcomedy, and the Legacy of Subversive Jewishness in Transparent," in *From Shtetl to Stardom: Jews and Hollywood*, eds. Michael Renov and Vincent Brook (West Lafayette, IN: Purdue University Press), 73–98.

40 Vincent Brook, *Something Ain't Kosher Here: The Rise of the "Jewish" Sitcom* (New Brunswick, NJ: Rutgers University Press, 2003).

41 The terms are Joey Soloway's: "I like to call it fun-comfortable or vulnerable or fun-vulnerable or funerable." See "Amazon Finds Comedy in Reality with 'I Love Dick,' 'Catastrophe,'" *Reuters*, May 5, 2017. https://www.reuters.com/article/us-television-amazon/amazon-finds-comedy-in-reality-with-i-love-dick-catastrophe-idUSKBN18201J.

42 Compare to Moss, 76. And given that Joey Soloway's own gender fluidity has gained public attention, this impact is perhaps enhanced by discussions of Soloway's shifting identity. See https://www.theguardian.com/tv-and-radio/2017/may/21/transparents-jill-soloway-the-words-male-and-female-describe-who-we-used-to-be.

43 Talal Asad, "Thinking about Agency and Pain," in *Formations of the Secular: Christianity, Islam, Modernity* (Palo Alto, CA: Stanford University Press, 2003), 85.

44 This is one way to understand the thrust of Richard Rorty's stress on the power of literature, with the caveat that film and television have even more power in this domain than literature. See Richard Rorty, *Contingency, Irony, and Solidarity* (Cambridge: Cambridge University, 1989). For a related theme, see Judith Butler, *Precarious Life: The Powers of Mourning and Violence* (London: Verso, 2006).

45 Because he has been invoked throughout this essay, it is an interesting biographical point that Walter Benjamin briefly lived at Hirschfeld's institute (which had five patient/guest rooms). On this point, see Ralf Dose, *Magnus Hirschfeld: The Origins of the Gay Liberation Movement* (New York: New York University Press, 2014). There is also here the more serious issue of the connection between "gender purity" and "racial purity" in Nazi thought (which I cannot take up here but which continues into contemporary white supremacist ideology). On this point, see the concise piece by Joni Alizah Cohen, "The Eradication of 'Talmudic Abstractions': Anti-Semitism, Transmisogyny and the National Socialist Project," *Verso Books Blog Post,* December 19, 2018, . https://www.versobooks.com/blogs/4188-the-eradication-of-talmudic-abstractions-anti-semitism-transmisogyny-and-the-national-socialist-project?fbclid=IwAR0jtLaQTLQbSaO7706vtWZARgvwTpRGswC2N8hx2-nI4ymuMUkZ8C7DSO0.

46 Emmanuel Levinas, *Otherwise than Being: Or, Beyond Essence* (Pittsburgh: Duquesne University Press, 1981).

47 There is here a deep connection—but also important differences—to the way in which Benjamin inherits and modifies Proust's notion of *involuntary memory*. I cannot develop this point, but, for Benjamin's understanding of this notion and its connection to film, refer the reader to Miriam Bratu Hansen, *Cinema and Experience: Siegfried Kracauer, Walter Benjamin, and Theodor W. Adorno* (Los Angeles: University of California Press, 2012), 111. For the notion in Proust, see especially the various discussions in Joshua Landy, *Philosophy as Fiction: Self, Deception, and Knowledge in Proust* (Oxford: Oxford University Press, 2009).

48 *Transparent*, Season 2, episode 4, "Cherry Blossoms," Amazon Prime Video, December 11, 2015. Although the science here is not quite accurate (epigenetic inheritance is not inheritance of changes in DNA; rather, epigenetic markers affect the processes by which genes do or do not produce proteins), there are important studies on the transgenerational inheritance of trauma, including influential studies of Holocaust survivors and their children. In other words, Ari could have referenced research about the very community of Jewish survivors who are depicted in *Transparent*. See Rachel Yehuda et al., "Vulnerability to Posttramautic Stress Disorder in Adult Offspring of Holocaust Survivors," *American Journal of Psychiatry*, 155, no. 9 (1998): 1163–1171; Rachel Yehuda and Linda M. Bierer, "The Relevance of Epigenetics to PTSD: Implications for the DSM-V," *Journal of Traumatic Stress* 22, no. 5 (2009): 427–434.

49 For a powerful meditation on epigenetics and its usefulness in studying genocide, see Ada Jaarsma, "Epigenetics and the Molecular Memory of Genocide," in *Logics of Genocide: The Structures of Violence and the Contemporary World*, eds. Anne O'Byrne and Martin Shuster (Bloomington: Indiana University Press, forthcoming).

50 A history, again, almost in verification of Benjamin's intuitions about film, that has been seriously addressed by a film: *Paragraph 175*. Written by Sharon Wood. Directed by Robert Epstein and Jeffrey Friedman. Telling Pictures, 1999. 76 min.
51 Benjamin, "On the Concept of History," 391.
52 Wittgenstein noted, "nothing is more important for understanding the concepts we have than constructing fictitious ones." See Ludwig Wittgenstein, *Culture and Value*, eds. G. H. von Wright and Heikki Nyman, trans. Peter Winch (Oxford: Blackwell, 1980), 74. Incidentally, for the power I have in mind, note how *Transparent* was able to continue its artistic, historical, and ethical pursuits even without the presence of its lead, Jeffrey Tambor, who, after sexual harassment accusations, left the show.
53 John Gibson, "Narrative and the Literary Imagination," in *Narrative, Philosophy, and Life*, ed. Allen Speight (New York: Springer, 2015), 149.
54 Kathleen Lennon, "Re-Enchanting the World: The Role of Imagination in Perception," *Philosophy* 85, no. 3 (2010): 387.
55 Important questions and possible sites of connection arise here between *Transparent* and broader trends in how television relates to queerness. Part of this question touches on the issues flagged in note 7, but part has to do with situating *Transparent* amidst the broader questions surrounding the temporality of television, whether in new television or in reality TV (and possibly the two are exact inverses of each other). For more on this broader project, see Amy Villarejo, *Ethereal Queer: Television, Historicity, and Desire* (Durham, NC: Duke University Press, 2014).
56 Yerushalmi, *Zakhor*, 101.

Part 2
Performing Judaism and Jewish Identity

5
Dancing Out the Torah

Ritual, Bodies, and Transitions in *Transparent*

JODI EICHLER-LEVINE

Transparent takes place in a world abundant in ritual. The series' power lies in the ways it revivifies the ability of ritual to mediate the relationships of human bodies to the community around them. From young Ari's exuberant barefoot living room dance of her (canceled) bat mitzvah Torah portion to the impromptu rites of a trip to Israel, ritual provides a window into the turbulent beauty of the extended Pfefferman family's Jewish bodies. From 2014 to 2019, *Transparent* responded to and amplified the changes that feminist, queer, and trans Jews have wrought in their ever-evolving tradition.[1] But does the show queer—or trans—Judaism?

It does. But it does even more than that. Over four seasons and a musical finale, *Transparent* alters Jewish ritual through transness and queerness while subverting American rites through Jewishness. Max Strassfeld and Robyn Henderson-Espinoza argue that "the specificity of 'becoming trans' manifests a more general 'trans-becoming.'"[2] Both trans theory and religious ritual ask us to grapple with liminality. *Transparent*'s representations of ritual offer an unending becoming—a religious world that is trans, queer, and Jewish.[3]

This chapter examines a selection of the show's ritual moments, with a focus on Ari and Maura, in four sections: reinhabiting Jewish ritual; inventing new

Jewish moments; exploring feminist spirituality movements; and unmasking "secular" rituals. After "setting the table" with some terms, the chapter moves from the most familiar rite—lighting candles for Sabbath—to the most unusual: a Jewish riff on the airport ritual of security theater. Each of the chapter's main sections also corresponds to a biblical trope. Along the way, I add some reflections on what it means to use *Transparent* as a heuristic for thinking about Jewish rituals and the religious sensorium in twenty-first-century America.[4]

Setting a Queered Table for Jewish Rituals

Transparent emerged at a time of ongoing ritual ferment in American Jewish history. Those rituals are always changing. On an academic level, numerous theories of ritual have emerged from cultural anthropology and religious studies, with many cues taken from performance studies—theatricality and embodiment are crucial for understanding ritual. This makes interpreting performances of ritual that are quite literally cinematic performances a layered endeavor.[5] For our purposes, the historic changes in American Jewish rituals that have taken place since the 1970s are particularly salient. Indeed, the time period from the 1960s to the 1980s that gave us the widespread growth of the bat mitzvah, the first ordained women rabbis and cantors, and the rise of feminist ritual is what made *Transparent* possible. Without that history, there would be no Rabbi Raquel, no Ari's bat mitzvah to cancel, and no improvised seder (ritual Passover meal) on a cruise ship.[6]

The turn of the twenty-first century provides us with an explosion of feminist, queer, and trans approaches to religion that have opened up new avenues of both practice and theory. In both Jewish and non-Jewish settings, "queering" religion has become a way of thinking about not just the increased inclusion of LGBTQ adherents in religious settings, but also how recasting rituals from differently gendered and sexed vantage points changes them, re-rendering these practices for all Jews.[7] This includes rethinking an embodied Jewishness from a trans perspective. These literal and metaphorical spaces evoke startlingly transformative kinds of betweenness. As Noach Dzmura writes: "Reminiscent of Shalom Aleichem's iconic rooftop location for a fiddle player, a perch atop the mechitzah is easily recognizable as a quintessentially Jewish location. For many transgender persons, the middle ground represented by the space above the mechitzah is not the final destination, but an unavoidable ambiguity that results from 'being in transition.' For others, the space in between male and female is the goal; ambiguity becomes *haimish* (like home)."[8] Transing Jewish religion means many things, from ceremonies that explicitly address trans experience (for example, a visit to the *mikvah*, or ritual bath, to demarcate part of one's gender transition), to something subtler, a means of either blurring the gender binaries that have been inscribed on some Jewish rituals or of re-visioning them through a new, more fluid lens.

Transparent depicts ritual actions among almost all of its core characters. This chapter focuses on Maura, the trans parent of the title who comes out in her sixties, and her youngest child Ari, who trade off experiences of altering their gender performance and dabbling in Jewish tradition. It centers the depictions of these two characters because at some point in the series, both identify as something other than cisgender. Both Maura and Ari's actions echo a phenomenon that Vanessa Ochs describes: they draw from "the Jewish ritual toolbox."[9] They perform Jewishness by drawing upon familiar tools—practices already present in traditional Jewish rituals, such as dipping foods or saying blessings—and using them in new ways. Many characters are ritual novices who gradually become "ritual experts."[10] *Transparent* both reflects and enacts an innovative moment in an increasingly postdenominational American Judaism.

In the four sections below, we can see examples of how the boundaries of Jewish and secular rituals are expanding in the twenty-first century. *Transparent*'s ritual performances encapsulate the emotionally stirring ways that Jews of many genders are becoming ritual innovators in the early twenty-first century. It is both an artifact and catalyst of this fluid moment in the history of Jewish Americans.

Lech L'cha: Reinhabiting Jewish Rituals and Dancing Out the Torah

Transparent asks us to think about what it is like to reinhabit Jewish ritual in changing bodies. In a poignant scene from season 1, episode 6, "The Wilderness," Maura quite touchingly takes on the role of lighting the Sabbath candles on Friday night, which was classically considered a women's commandment. At first, she almost burns her fingers and stumbles over the tune, singing the notes of the Hanukkah blessing instead, but she continues, waving her hands toward her face in circles. In doing so, Maura becomes a matriarch of her family, briefly displacing her ex-wife, Shelley, who is absent from the scene. In this sense, *Transparent* maintains traditional, normative Jewish gender roles. Yet watching an adult woman learning how to light the Sabbath candles disrupts the fluidity of how this ritual is typically represented on film, accentuating its impact. At the same time, it is possible that Maura's trans-ness is not the factor that causes her to stumble over the blessing; rather, it could also be the fact that like most of the Pfeffermans—and like many American Jews—she is simply unfamiliar with the ritual; she is creaky and out of practice. Both of these readings can coalesce. What is most important is the fact that here, the celluloid depiction reminds us that ritual both on and off the screen truly is performed; bodies have motions to learn, and they falter in their gestures; synapses and vocal cords must recall the tunes. Maura inhabits a liminal space of somatic transition at this temporal threshold between the work week and the Sabbath.

Later in season 1—but earlier in time—young Ari Pfefferman cancels her bat mitzvah. In episode 8, "Best New Girl," we see the events of the would-have-been

1994 bat mitzvah weekend unfold. Abandoned by her parents and then her siblings, Ari lounges on the living room couch, clad in cutoff shorts and a soccer jersey. A catering employee arrives at the home with the drinks for the now-canceled event. She asks Ari how she got away with canceling the whole thing. "I didn't think I could memorize it all, so I told them I didn't believe in God and they canceled it," Ari answers. "Never understood how kids get up in front of all those people and sing," the young woman replies, taking a seat.

But Ari has, in fact, memorized her Torah portion. Lying on her back, she quietly chants, "V'yomer adonai al Avram" (in English, "And God said to Abraham") and "Lech l'cha" (in English, "Go forth.") *Leave*. Ari's Torah portion revolves around one of the central commands—and turning points—of Genesis.[11] Jews trace their lineage to a figure who leaves behind all that he has known, to a symbol of crossing and motion. What is most crucial, though, is how Ari recites this *parasha* (portion). She chants a few words on the couch, very quietly, as if in secret.

And then, something extraordinary happens. Ari stands up on the couch, her long brown curls streaming behind her, and she dances out her Torah portion. As she chants the verses, she stands tall, raising her arms like a ballerina. Her voice rises, and she leaps to the coffee table, toes pointed outward, as she finishes the verses. God tells Abraham that he will increase his offspring, that he will be a great nation among nations. A child has become an adult.

Many things about this scene are astounding. Unmoored from the text—from the typical location of a Torah reading, before a sacred scroll that must be carefully handled and placed, fixed, on a table—Ari can dance. She can twirl; she can soar. At times, the sharp drama of her movements evokes a Russian kazatsky; it also suggests her burgeoning sexual awareness and power over her audience. It is unusual enough to see the chanting of the Torah depicted onscreen.[12] It is even more unusual to see it chanted by a barefoot adolescent as she jumps and spins.

This opens new ways for us to imagine Jewish ritual. The scene, like the episode as a whole, encapsulates what it is to be a woman figuring out her body—or, in Ari's case, trying to figure it out and eventually realizing that she may not be comfortable in the gender ascribed to that body at birth. It represents a delicate dialectic between childhood and adulthood. Ari is dressed not in the poofy organza or sequined lace of a typical 1990s bat mitzvah girl but in mildly boyish casual wear, telegraphing her future gender ambiguity. Yet even without a DJ, a cake, or an uncomfortable synagogue service, the episode marks a clear transition from childhood to adulthood.

Like Abraham, Ari goes forth, to the beach and on a strange journey with an older man who works in the fields. Ari revivifies the bat mitzvah as a day of going forth on her own two feet, however confusing that journey might be. Her dancing ruptures filmic stereotypes of bar and bat mitzvahs, including those depicted in *Transparent*'s opening credit sequence. Dancing bodies, "have the potential to issue a dynamic challenge to static and repressive notions."[13] Ari's dance is indeed a challenge. It unsettles norms surrounding the ritual of Torah chanting, which requires a community, a strong sense of intention from the reader, an idealized sublimation of self, technical skills, and a great deal of rehearsal. As Jeffrey Summit writes, "I am hard-pressed to identify another cultural or religious performance that requires flanking experts to publicly correct the performer, and for the performer to accurately repeat the corrected section before being allowed to continue with the performance."[14] As she ends her chant with a flourish and a deep bow, Ari unveils the stark theatricality of chant. She needs no rabbi or cantor or family at her side, though we sense a bit of regret from her. She is woman (for now). Hear her chant.

Young Ari's performance queers the traditional practice of chanting Torah, celebrating its spirit while unbinding it from its usual anchors. As Melissa M. Wilcox demonstrated, the strategic use of religious individualism is a hallmark of queer spiritual experience. Ari's bat mitzvah evinces this kind of move, remaining tethered to the trope of the chant (in its musical modes) and to the trope of going forth on a literary level while transforming a communal ritual that normally requires a quorum of ten Jews into an intimate exchange with an audience of one. Ari's experience maps well onto Wilcox's analysis of "everyday *sacralogies*," which Wilcox describes as "individual understandings of the sacred," with themes of "nebulousness and mystery, immanence, limitation, love, and the female divine."[15] She resembles many of the women "seekers" Wilcox describes, in a pattern of embodied questing. In this early example, Ari has her own performative riff on a traditional practice. Over the course of the series, she also invents new Jewish rituals, explores not-so-Jewish rituals, and imbues everyday actions with forms of sacred questing. Her next ritual experiment will further trans Judaism by creating something new and even more liberatory.

Exodus on the Love Boat: Inventing a New Jewish Ritual

As an adult, Ari remains attached to Jewish rituals while further expanding their boundaries. In the final episode of season 3, "Exciting and New," Ari and Maura conduct an impromptu ritual that marks a turning point in Maura's transition process. Maura has learned that because of a heart issue, she cannot undergo gender confirmation surgery. She stands sadly on the deck of a cruise ship, clad in cruise casual pants and a flowered shirt, clutching a bag containing Spanx and other shapewear. Maura explains all of this to Ari, who is confused, thinking that the absence of surgery impedes transition. What now? Does this mean Maura will not transition? Maura tells Ari: "I've already transitioned, I'm trans, I'm just—this is me. This is it." Ari asks if they can say a prayer. The dialogue continues:

ARI Face the ocean and raise your arms. Great mystery. Goddess. Let us mark this moment to say goodbye to these tight, terrible Spanx.

MAURA Goodbye tight, terrible Spanx!
ARI Deliver us from feeling bunched up in the ass—
MAURA Dayenu!
ARI And restricted and confined! Let us just be! Set us free!
MAURA Set us—
BOTH FREE!!!

They stand before the ocean, arms raised, hands clutched. There is a beat. At the exact moment we expect them to send the Spanx flying, Ari stops. "Let's not actually do this," she says. The Spanx might hurt the marine life. Instead, she kisses the Spanx like a prayer book before placing them in a garbage bin.

This ritual uses familiar Jewish gestures in a new context. It is a ritual speech act that does something new, enacting a reality that simultaneously affirms Maura's gender identity and subverts contemporary American strictures around femininity. Like many ritual performances, it denotes a new moment in its performer's life cycle. Like many Jewish prayers, it opens by addressing the divine. The act of symbolically casting out an object echoes the Rosh Hashanah tradition of *tashlich*, wherein people toss bread into bodies of water, signifying the casting out of one's sins during a season of repentance. It uses the Hebrew language of the Passover ritual meal—*dayenu* (it is enough)—and performs Jewish sorts of blessings, sanctifying the messiness of this painful moment in Maura's journey.

The casting out of the Spanx mirrors ritual developments taking place among trans Jews today. Joy Ladin writes about saying the *shehechiyanu*, a prayer for being brought to a particular time, before ingesting her estrogen pills.[16] Through the websites Trans-Torah, Ritualwell, and other resources, one can find the scripts for ceremonies specific to trans experience. S. J. Crasnow's ethnographic work details transformations of the traditional mikvah and other innovations that "allow trans Jews to fill the inclusion or affirmation gap themselves by constructing queer/trans Jewish ritual, liturgy, hermeneutics, and communities."[17] *Transparent*'s casting out of the Spanx speaks powerfully of both grief and celebration for the never-simple process of transition and the subtleties that it entails. By marking this turning point in the development of Maura's identity, *Transparent* resists popular media emphases on dramatic physical transformations.

The Spanx ritual also highlights the complexities of "transition." What do you do about rituals that are supposed to mark closure when transition is not understood as a before and after but as an ongoing, fluid process—an act of becoming that is renewed each day? Ari and Maura's ritual constitutes a combination of both "reinterpretive" and "transformative" approaches.[18] Crasnow discusses how queer uses of the mikvah open "novel possibilities for reinterpreting the trans body outside the framework of contamination" in a way that allows for "affirmation."[19] The in betweenness and imperfection of this moment coincide with the idea of "process" invoked by many ritualists; Max Strassfeld, for example, describes "the idea of a gender transition as a process without a clear-cut beginning or ending."[20]

Season 3 contains threads of Passover, exodus, and the idea of a messianic age. At the season's close, deliverance comes in the form of recognizing that Maura's feminized gender performance is one that reaches toward a "queer horizon"—evoked by the literal one glimpsed in the distance from the deck of the ship.[21] It is not subject to the straitjacket of one curvaceously slender female body ideal. Though Maura had hoped to undergo gender confirmation surgery, when that avenue is closed, she realizes that it represented a limiting form to which she need not conform in order to transition.

Bemidbar: Goddess Spirituality in the Wilderness

These first examples are interpretations that work off of recognizably Jewish gestures and practices. *Transparent* also draws from non-Jewish sources, then plays on them in Jewish modes. The show evinces a complex attitude towards post-1970s feminist ritual. Sometimes earnest, sometimes snarky, often playfully irreverent, it provides us with a multivalent depiction of polyglot women's spirituality movements.

This is particularly evident in season 2, episode 9, "Man on the Land," in which Maura, Sarah, and Ari attend Idyllwild, a loosely veiled stand-in for the Michigan Womyn's Music Festival. The episode is both a celebration and a sobering assessment of such events. It has some appropriately humorous send-ups of the location, including mentions of a tampon-making workshop and jokes about vegan cuisine. In a nod toward what will become her spiritual-seeking arc in season 3, Sarah declares: "I'm gonna find some awe here, some fucking awe." "Man on the Land," as an episode, is many things—a Dionysian escapade, a loving but irreverent critique of New Age spirituality, a reflection on the controversies surrounding the presence of transwomen in dedicated women's spaces, and a continuation of the season's journey into the family's past. Sarah wants to find some "awe," suggesting something ineffable, but the tangible touch of bodies is an inescapable reality. She ends up deeply grounded in her own embodied desires, discovering the BDSM section of the festival. Maura cannot escape from the less mutable qualities of her body, fearful once she learns of the festival's "woman born woman" policy. Ultimately, she leaves the gathering in the middle of the night, yelling, "Man on the land!" And Ari, stumbling through the same dark woods, sees a horrific vision of books on fire and a different moment of physical expulsion in her family's past—a raid on the Institute for Sexual Science in 1933 Berlin and her Grandma Rose watching as her older sister Gittel—née Gershon—is dragged away by the Nazis. Bodies matter—and bodies are subject to vulnerability, persecution, and violence.

With one hand, Soloway gives us free-range ritual innovation—providing luminous interview quotes in which they discuss "the goddess" and postpatriarchal Judaism—and with another they taketh away, providing us the hysterical scene in which Sarah considers a visit to a "shaman" at Idyllwild, a woman who introduces herself in a nasal New Yawk accent as "Ashley, or, as I'm better known, Crying Bear."[22] In this send-up of feminist New Age cultural appropriation, Ashley offers visitors to her tent a chance to "mourn your murdered femininity." One minute we are rocking it out with the Indigo Girls, caught up in the collective effervescence of that moment, and the next, we are laughing our heads off as Sarah is awkwardly "anointed." Then, seeing an alluring dominatrix walk by, she deadpans that she has the wrong tent.

Historically, feminist spirituality movements encompass a broad range of practices and beliefs. They emerged prominently in the United States and the United Kingdom in the 1970s. Leaders both within and outside of mainstream religious traditions attempted to recreate traditions around goddesses and the feminine divine that they argued had been lost after the rise of monotheistic world traditions.[23] Fittingly, California was a particularly rich ground for these types of spirituality, including the Dianic wiccan movement surrounding Z. Budapest and related communities founded by Starhawk, who has familial connections with Judaism.[24] Culturally, feminist spirituality movements and the women's music scene have many overlaps, including homosociality, resonance with environmentalism, and the celebration of female bodies. For Jewish women, engagement with goddess rituals has been a fraught endeavor, in part because of internal Jewish anti-pagan traditions and in part because some Jewish women have encountered anti-Jewish sentiment among practitioners of feminist spirituality movements, who may sometimes blame Jews for the stamping out of ancient goddess worship and women-centered ritual.[25]

Ari resembles what Melissa Raphael calls Jewish feminists who celebrate the goddess within an alternative Jewish community.[26] Even though "Man on the Land" is a send-up of feminist spirituality, its conclusion gives us a painful spiritual vision, a ritualized performance that is the inverse of the raucous Weimar dance scenes from the opening of season 2. As the players from the original dance scene are violently dragged off by Nazis, Ari steps into the vision; she clasps the hand of her grandmother Rose—who is played by Emily Robinson, the same actress who portrays teenage Ari—and she meets the gaze of her transgender great-aunt Gittel, who is about to be deported and, presumably, killed. Dancing has been turned into death, joy into mourning. The ritual abandon of Idyllwild has given way to a more interior sort of cathartic experience for Ari. If, at the time of her bat mitzvah, she went forth for the first time, here she has stumbled deeper into the woods, into the unknown of the wilderness. The episode evokes the Hebrew word *bemidbar*, which translates as either "in the wilderness" or "in the desert" and is the Hebrew name for the book of Numbers. The wilderness as a space of separation and transition—a crucible in which either an individual or an entire people may be forged—comes forth as part of both goddess spirituality and Jewish textual tradition.

Natural spaces can also be the site of Jewish brushes against the divine. Julia Watts Belser writes about how nature figured in her childhood encounters with what would become, for her, religion: "I met my God unexpectedly, as a teenager one sunny afternoon, leaning out over a balcony rail... I recall the wind, crisp and bright against my face, the feel of my own body discovering center, stumbling into joy. *She* was none of this and all of that: the Presence that flooded through me, the press of the stones in my hand, the strange, sudden wideness of the sky."[27] Watts Belser argues for a trans understanding of God/dess, a "thealogy" that is nonbinary and fluid in its approach to gender. In season 4, *Transparent* moves from the wilderness of seasons 1 and 2 and the narrow ocean straits of season 3 to the queerest of Jewish spaces and soundscapes: the land of Israel, set to the tune of *Jesus Christ Superstar*.

Jesus Christ, Queer Jewish Superstar

We pivot now to a different kind of seeking journey in season 4, The Pfeffermans Go to Israel. The uncanny rituals of this moment in the series can best be explored through their linkage with a different biblical personage: namely, the figure of Jesus. Season 4 is, at heart, one about unpacking binaries, something that it does in ways that are both heavy-handed and subtle. More obvious moments of boundary crossing come in examples like Ari traversing geopolitical borders to visit Ramallah and breaking a Jewish ritual boundary by crossing over to the men's side of the *mechitzah* at the Western Wall. What I most want to explore here, though, is the less obvious way that ritual behavior in borderland spaces transmits meaning by reading Ari and Maura's trip through security theater in episode 2, "Groin Anomaly." Examining this scene with an eye toward religion helps us to think through both Ari's character and the transness of *Transparent*'s rituals. Just as Ari's first season Torah dance challenges Jewish norms, Ari and Maura's marijuana-laced trip through LAX airport defies the empty American ritual of security theater.

Airports, a fraught space where infinite kinds of bodies meet, evoke ritual and performance in a wide variety of ways. As Simone Browne writes, "At the airport, the traveler is incited to speak the truth through rites and rituals."[28] In the car on their way to LAX, Maura is nervous, quietly singing "Everything's Alright" from *Jesus Christ Superstar*. Ari gives her a marijuana-laced gummy bear to calm her. In the next scene, with "The Temple" track from *Superstar* blaring, we see the accoutrements of TSA land in stark cuts. Stylish black shoes placed neatly into a plastic bin; pilgrims awaiting their turn; the blue-gloved hand of a TSA employee; Maura's colorful toes on the cold institutional floor. Ultimately, the camera pans up toward the glass rooftop and the light streaming through it, following Maura's tripped-out gaze.

Then there is a dramatic moment of separation between mother ("Moppa") and child. After a pointed look at Maura, Ari, lit brightly, faces away and steps forward, glowing. She raises her arms, and then, as the shot reverses, we see her from Maura's view—from the back—as we hear a jet engine and see her rising upward in a kind of heavenly surrender. We do not see any security apparatus. In dreamy slow motion, Ari floats up, arms still lifted, walking toward a cluster of black-hatted Orthodox men, whose arms raise too, as if they are lifting her—among them but even higher—perhaps prefiguring her covert move across to the men's side of the Western Wall.

Then it is Maura's turn. The music hits a key change and skews into a frenetic mode. She enters the plastic tube of the body scanner, and a female TSA agent indicates that she should raise her arms; she does, in a moment that is partially in accord with the disciplined security state but partially, in the way she tips her head back, a kind of surrender.

Then, the music shifts again to the moment in the song where Jesus charges in and overturns the money lenders' tables. The driving beat stops. In a high shriek, he wails: "M-y-y-y temple should be a house of prayer. But you have made it a den of thieves!" Maura has now emerged from the scanner. As Jesus sings his lines, Maura sees Ari sitting in a chair—past the security boundary—tying her shoes. For a blink and a clever edit, Ari is a child, and Maura's face softens; we are catapulted into the way she remembers her daughter. Maura's mouth, opened in greeting toward Ari, briefly syncs with Jesus's shriek; she waves, a vulnerable, excited wave, the kind one uses to gesture toward a five-year-old on the swings.

On the soundtrack, Jesus commands, "Get out! Get out!" Then the music stops; the marijuana high is over; and the TSA agent tells Maura they will have to pat her down. She has a groin anomaly. Tragicomic dialogue regarding who should pat her down—a male or female employee—ensues as Ali whips out her phone to record. We are back to reality of the most appalling kind. As the music revs back in with the cries of the needy in the Temple—"See my eyes I can hardly see, see me stand I can hardly walk"—Maura spreads her arms wide and declares: "If you want me to be a man to pat me down, I'll be a man. If you want me to be a woman, I'll be a woman. If you want me to be a fucking chicken, I'll be a chicken!" The episode closes as she submits to the long arm of the state.

The point of ritualized security theater is in its show: it looks like it is enacting strong boundaries. It is also intended to produce docile patriots in how it does literal and symbolic violence to many kinds of bodies.[29] It is fitting that here, Maura becomes identified with the figure of Jesus. Susannah Heschel argues that "Jesus . . . functions as a kind of theological transvestite, calling into question the constructions of Christianity and Judaism and destabilizing the boundaries between them."[30] Just as Jesus's indeterminate position between the two traditions reveals their "fictive" initial construction, Maura's sacrificial positioning of her groin anomaly simultaneously unveils the vacuity of security theater and the fluidity of gender. The hyperbolic, comic example of the chicken puts it over the top. The fact is that it does not matter who pats Maura down because the security process is merely a performance of enacting boundaries rather than a necessary process of safeguarding people. Crucified by the indignity of this treatment, Maura invokes a more plastic body, one that could transcend not just gender but species. And she also subverts TSA land by violating another one of its central dictates: no jokes.[31]

Transparent and the Queer Boundaries of Bodies and Rituals

In *Transparent,* the notion of performance—long a theoretical staple in thinking about both gender and ritual—comes together with literal performances on a screen, streamed intimately to our televisions, tablets, and phones. Barbara Kirshenblatt-Gimblett writes that performed Jewish texts are "embedded in densely textured social worlds. They do not move telepathically between minds, but interpersonally in space and time, under particular conditions, and in physically coded and embodied ways—dramatically."[32] In turning toward these "sensuous histories," Kirshenblatt-Gimblett asks us: "What are the boundaries of the Jewish body, in all its variations, and where might such a question lead?"

Transparent powerfully transes Jewish rituals and "jews" secular rites.[33] *Transparent*'s world of porousness between God and Goddess, between male and female, gay and straight, and between screen and off-screen refuses boundaries in a generative and resistant manner. In season 1, the queerness of Torah reading, this uncanny practice of performing an ancient text out loud in a contemporary body, is made evident in the intimate unfoldings of Ari's living room dance. In season 3's casting out of the Spanx, the goddess emanates into an amalgamated Passover tashlich, mixing deities and holidays in reaching toward a horizon of queer Jewish futurity.

"Jewing" secular ritual is, perhaps, harder to grasp, but it is crucial. It is present in season 2's "Man on the Land," not just in the invocation of goddesses and drum circles, but in the ways that the family's Jewishness clings to them in the wilderness: as Ari wanders, lantern in hand, into her vision of the past, we hear the jingle of bells on her feet, and see that she is wearing medieval Jew shoes. Finally, in season 4, "Groin Anomaly" reminds us that there is no space for the nonbinary—for the trans, the gender-queer, or the gender fluid—in security theater. There is also no safe space there for the dark, the foreign, or the Other. Maura as a transwoman cannot queer that space; such significations are not legible. She can, however, "jew" it, through the likeliest and unlikeliest figure of all. Of course, it had to be Jesus. Maura as Jesus reveals security theater as the ritual drama it has always been. As Jesus, besieged, Maura can most fully display the brokenness and pain of contemporary America. She signifies as a Jewish Jesus—one in the Temple, in tension with his own people—and, especially, as a comic one. Her submission comes with Broadway music and humor, two hallmarks of the American Jewish experience.

Perhaps it was inevitable, then, that this would be the form through which the characters reached their dénouement. In 2019, *Transparent* returned with a one-off musical finale. After Maura dies, offscreen, the principal characters gather to process their grief. Ritual abounds—not just death ritual, but also a hint of a wedding and, finally, an impromptu "bart mitzvah" (combining "bar" [son] and "bat" [daughter]). Ari reads Lech L'cha in the backyard of Maura's former home, before the crowd that had gathered for the post-funeral meal. This time, they are not dancing—at least, not at first.

Broadway is the seam at which Jewish ritual meets popular culture, where, through the performance of "theatrical liberalism," Ashkenazi Jews (some of them queer) took their musical modes, their immigrant fiddles, and pianos hefted through the windows of apartments and helped create an American art form.[34] The final song, "Joyocaust!", erases the boundaries between Jewish ritual and the rituals of theater. As Ari finishes chanting the Torah portion, their mother, Shelley, bursts into applause, which does not conform to typical deportment after a reading. When chastised by Rabbi Raquel, Shelly bursts into song: "We Jews got a painful history/That we choose to convey in minor keys/And we say never to forget the pain/Never to forget the shame/So our songs they always sound the same," she intones against the wail of a klezmer clarinet. But one verse later, as she switches to her indecent proposal—"We need a Joyocaust!"—the jazz hands appear. The entire gathering busts out of the backyard and into the woods—bemidbar. Suddenly, everyone is garbed in bright colors, and characters from every season join the revelry.

Intercut with the final minute of this carnivalesque catharsis, we glimpse a return to the Sabbath candles. For a few seconds, we see the interior family home, which has been left to Davina, a non-Jewish trans woman. It is the near future. She is surrounded by formerly homeless trans teenagers, setting out takeout barbecue. Ari enters with challah and leads them in the prayer over glowing candles. Shabbat is open to all, Jew and non-Jew, masculine, feminine, and genderqueer. The candles endure.

Thus, the song that proudly declares "Hell yeah! We crossed that line!" in its irreverence toward the Holocaust simultaneously places one of the most traditional Jewish rituals as the button on the entire series, but with a nonbinary candle lighter and a non-Jewish chosen family reinhabiting the Pfefferman family home. Five years of depictions that strain against the limits of Jewish bodies take us into the nuanced ways that ritual, as a form of social interaction, both links and separates us.[35] However dysfunctional, the Pfeffermans' expansive love—of Torah and goddess, of Indigo Girls and *Jesus Christ Superstar*—is displayed and cemented in the rituals of their porous, morphable bodies. As Ari lights the candles, the lost tribe of non-Jews now dwelling at the Pfefferman homestead overcomes suffering by making a new home out of the emotional ashes.[36] What could be more queerly Jewish than that?

Notes

1. These groups of Jews (and non-Jews)—"feminist," "trans," and "queer"—do, of course, often overlap. I separate them here to reflect the diverse range of theoretical perspectives—sometimes closely connected, sometimes divergent—that informed my thinking over the long genesis of this essay. From media coverage, I suspect a wide range of theorists and activists informed the show's creators as well. On this history and some differences between trans theory and queer theory, see Susan Stryker, "Transgender Theory: Queer Theory's Evil Twin," *GLQ: A Journal of Lesbian and Gay Studies* 10, no. 2 (2004): 212–215; Susan Stryker, "(De)Subjugated Knowledges: An Introduction to Transgender Studies," in *The Transgender Studies Reader*, eds. Susan Stryker and Stephen Whittle (New York: Routledge, 2006), 1–18.
2. Max Strassfeld and Robyn Henderson-Espinoza, "Introduction: Mapping Trans Studies in Religion," *TSQ: Transgender Studies Quarterly* 6, no. 3 (August 2019): 292.
3. Both "trans" and "queer"—as verbs and adjectives—are appropriate when describing the show's contributions. The two main characters I discuss in this essay both identify as trans by the end of the show's run. They also inhabit a variety of sexualities throughout the show, although that is less of a focus in this piece. Some trans theorists, reacting in part to transphobia and trans exclusion from earlier generations of gay and lesbian activists and scholars, reject being included under the umbrella term "queer" (or being the oft-overlooked "T" in LGBTQ+). However, I would argue that for *Transparent*, both terms are relevant—not just in terms of the characters' identities but also in terms of different valences we can draw out from them. The mutability of gender identity in both ritual and trans theory draws me towards the verb "to trans;" yet queer theory, with its evocations of making that which is familiar uncanny and the possibilities of new horizons and new forms of family, is also deeply relevant for understanding *Transparent*'s world. As a result, I use both terms at various points throughout this essay.
4. The author wishes to thank a variety of scholars whose insights strengthened this essay in both direct comments and workshop conversations, including Brett Krutzsch, Lila Corwin Berman, Samira Mehta, Lesleigh Cushing, Anthony Petro, Nora Rubel, Melissa M. Wilcox, and a host of others I may have forgotten. It also benefited greatly from anonymous outside readers for Rutgers University Press. This piece emerged from its original presentation and the conversations at the *Transparent* Symposium at the University of Rochester in December 2016. Any faults, of course, remain my own.
5. For two helpful recent essays, see Ronald Gribes, "Ritual," and Ann Pellegrini, "Movement," in *Key Terms in Material Religion*, ed. S. Brent Plate (New York: Bloomsbury Academic, 2015), 153–160, 173–178. On the nuanced nature of mediating Jewishness on and off the screen (among other technologies), see especially Jeffrey Shandler, *Jews, God, and Videotape: Religion and Media in America* (New York: New York University Press, 2009), 4, 8–10, 230–282.
6. For a concise overview of many of these changes, see Riv-Ellen Prell, ed., *Women Remaking American Judaism* (Detroit: Wayne State University Press, 2007); Pamela S. Nadell, "A Bright New Constellation: Feminism and American Judaism," in *The Columbia History of Jews and Judaism in America*, ed. Marc Lee Raphael (New York: Columbia University Press, 2008), 385–405.
7. Two of the more influential edited volumes in this area are David Shneer and Caryn Aviv, eds., *Queer Jews* (New York: Routledge, 2002) and Daniel Boyarin, Daniel

Itzkovitz, and Ann Pellegrini, eds., *Queer Theory and the Jewish Question* (New York: Columbia University Press, 2003).
8   Noach Dzmura, ed., *Balancing on the Mechitza: Transgender in Jewish Community* (Berkeley, CA: North Atlantic Books, 2010), xviii. A *mechitza* is the physical barrier—sometimes a low railing, sometimes a high lattice wall or a curtain—that separates the men's and women's sides in those Jewish prayer spaces that are divided by sex.
9   Vanessa Ochs, *Inventing Jewish Ritual* (Philadelphia: Jewish Publication Society, 2007), 5–7.
10 Susan Starr Sered, *Women as Ritual Experts: The Religious Lives of Elderly Women in Jerusalem* (New York: Oxford University Press, 1992).
11 The passage in full can be found in Genesis 12.
12 A few examples include mainly scenes of bar mitzvah, such as those depicted in *A Serious Man* (2009) and *Keeping Up with the Steins* (2006). *A Serious Man.* Joel and Ethan Cohen (2009, Universal City, California: Focus Features), Apple TV+. *Keeping Up with the Steins.* Scott Marshall (2006, Los Angeles, California: Miramax Pictures), Amazon Prime.
13 Rebecca Rossen, "Jews on View: Spectacle, Degradation, and Jewish Corporeality in Contemporary Dance and Performance," *Theater Journal* 64, no. 1 (March 2012): 61.
14 Jeffrey Summit, *Singing God's Words: The Performance of God's Words in Contemporary Judaism* (New York: Oxford University Press, 2016), 162.
15 Melissa M. Wilcox, *Queer Women and Religious Individualism* (Bloomington: Indiana University Press, 2009), 168.
16 Joy Ladin, *Through the Door of Life: A Jewish Journey Between Genders* (Madison: University of Wisconsin Press, 2013), 3.
17 S. J. Crasnow, "On Transition: Normative Judaism and Trans Innovation," *Journal of Contemporary Religion* 32, no. 3 (September 2017): 406.
18 Crasnow, "On Transition," 405.
19 Crasnow, "On Transition," 409.
20 Crasnow, "On Transition," 412.
21 José Muñoz, *Cruising Utopia: The Then and Now of Queer Futurity* (New York: New York University Press, 2009), 19–32.
22 Soloway speaks about the goddess and the divine feminine during a 2016 speech at the Toronto Film Festival. Joey Soloway, "Joey Soloway on the Female Gaze: Master Class: TIFF 2016), *Tiff Originals*. YouTube. https://www.youtube.com/watch?v=pnBvppooD9I (accessed January 19, 2024).
23 Cynthia Eller, *Living in the Lap of the Goddess: The Feminist Spirituality Movement in America* (New York: Crossroad, 1995).
24 Melissa Raphael, "Goddess Religion, Postmodern Jewish Feminism, and the Complexity of Alternative Religious Identities," *Nova Religio* 1, no. 2 (April 1998): 198–215.
25 Judith Plaskow, *The Coming of Lilith: Essays on Feminism, Judaism, and Sexual Ethics, 1972–2003* (Boston: Beacon Press, 2005), 110–113.
26 Raphael, "Goddess Religion," 199.
27 Julia Watts Belser, "Transing God/dess: Notes from the Borderlands," in Dzmura, *Balancing on the Mechitzah*, 235. (emphasis original).
28 Simone Browne, *Dark Matters: On the Surveillance of Blackness* (Durham, NC: Duke University Press, 2015), 145.
29 Jasbir K. Puar and Amit S. Rai, "Monster, Terrorist, Fag: The War on Terrorism and the Production of Docile Patriots," *Social Text* 20, no. 3 (Fall 2002): 117–148.

30. Susannah Heschel, "Jesus as Theological Transvestite," in *Judaism Since Gender*, eds. Miriam Peswkowitz and Laura Levitt (New York: Routledge, 1997), 188–199.
31. Browne, *Dark Matters*, 146.
32. Barbara Kirshenblatt-Gimblett, "The Corporeal Turn," *Jewish Quarterly Review* 95, no. 3 (2005): 458–459.
33. Here I use "jews" in a theoretical verbal sense, suggesting how Jewishness, like transness, is a productive category of analysis.
34. Andrea Most, *Theatrical Liberalism: Jews and Popular Entertainment in America* (New York: New York University Press, 2013).
35. Clifford Geertz, *The Interpretation of Cultures* (New York: Basic Books, 1973), 168.
36. See Thomas Tweed, *Crossing and Dwelling: A Theory of Religion* (Cambridge: Harvard University Press, 2007), where he focuses on religion as a process of making homes and confronting suffering.

6

From *Oy* to *Hineni*

Language and Transition
in *Transparent*

SARAH BUNIN BENOR

While many films and television shows have depicted aspects of Judaism—a Jewish wedding, a menorah lighting, a Yom Kippur service—*Transparent* depicts all of these and dozens of other Jewish rituals and cultural practices.[1] Many of the Jewish aspects of *Transparent* relate to the show's primary theme: transition. We see a corpse prepared ritually for burial, a funeral, and a *shiva* (gathering with the mourning family). The main character, Maura, ritually casts away sins by tossing pieces of challah into a river. Rabbi Raquel preaches about Israelites wandering through the desert toward the promised land. And, as I have discussed elsewhere, characters immerse in an actual mikveh and several symbolic mikvehs.[2]

Another aspect of Jewishness is distinctive language, which manifests in America primarily in the use of Hebrew and Yiddish words within English conversations.[3] *Transparent* expertly uses language to depict individuals' transitions in Jewish identification, as well as the communal transition of American Jews from primarily ethnically oriented to primarily spiritually/religiously oriented. The series, which explores connections among Jewishness, gender, and sexuality, also highlights the role of language in individuals' transitions from male-identified to female-identified and straight to queer.[4]

This chapter analyzes *Transparent*'s use of language in depicting these transitions. In some cases, the presentation of Jewish, transgender, and queer identities is coded, offering different levels of meaning to viewers with different prior knowledge of these communities. Even for viewers who do not catch the coded language, the series demonstrates the importance of language in Jewish and queer identities and individual and communal transitions, as well as the intersections of Jewishness and queerness.

Communal Transition of American Jews

During Maura and Shelly's marriage, their Jewishness primarily involves having Jewish friends and partners, a personal connection to the Holocaust, and concerns about antisemitism. They participate in several nonreligious cultural practices associated with Jews. They have a standing order at Canter's Deli, and when they clean out their houses, they donate items to the "Hadassah League." Their relationship to religiosity is strained. When they cut ties with Maura's sister Bryna, they stop participating in Passover Seders. In a flashback, Maura discusses her doubts about the existence of God. Shelly goes to synagogue on Yom Kippur, but she flirts with a man during the serious Al Chet prayer and expresses discomfort with Judaism's "so many rules." Like many in their generation, Maura and Shelly experience Jewishness as more of an ethnic or communal category than a spiritual or religious one.

Initially, Jewishness plays a minimal role in the lives of their adult children. Sarah, Josh, and Ari do not have many Jewish friends, and most of their significant others are not Jewish. But all of that changes when Rabbi Raquel enters their lives. Josh has a serious relationship with Raquel and learns about her spiritual practices, including regular prayer. Ari asks Raquel about traditional Jewish death and mourning rituals, and she castigates her parents for having allowed her to cancel her bat mitzvah, claiming that she might have found God useful. She brings ritual to Pfefferman family gatherings, and by the series finale, she announces her intent to become a rabbi. Sarah and her (non-Jewish) wife light Shabbat candles and briefly instate a no cell phone rule at Friday night dinner (after reading about it in *Real Simple*). On Yom Kippur, Sarah does *teshuva* (repentance), asking her ex-wife for forgiveness. She becomes involved in Raquel's synagogue and organizes a *Havdalah* (concluding Shabbat) event. She talks about looking for "awe" and "finding my spiritual mojo." Even Josh embraces religious practices like saying the Mourners' *Kaddish* and symbolically marrying Raquel under a *tallit*. For the Pfefferman children, Jewishness is more of a religious and spiritual identity than an ethnic one.

These generational differences are reflected in language. The parents use Yiddish words within English, and the children use few Yiddish words but use some Hebrew words that their parents do not. Maura says, for example, *keppie* (head), *shaitel* (wig), *goyishe* (non-Jewish-seeming), *l'chaim* (to life), and *nisht ahere nisht aher* (an English-influenced version of the Yiddish phrase *nisht ahin, nisht aher*—neither here nor there). Shelly uses dozens of Yiddishisms, including *oy* (oh), *sha* (shush), *pish* (pee), *bashert* (predestined), *mishegoss* (craziness), *gey avek* (go away), *gotenyu* (oh my God), *alta kakers* (old shitters), *fakakta* (screwed up), and *farshtunkena* (stinking). She also uses Yiddish-influenced intonation (e.g., "He's a *macher* [high tone] at the temple [high tone]; he could have done something [high tone], and he didn't do it [low tone]") and some New York pronunciations (e.g., "harrible"), despite having grown up in Southern California.[5] Her language has led some viewers to criticize her character as exaggerated, as performing a kind of Jewish drag or "Jewface."[6] I agree with this critique; although some American Jewish women do speak with all of these linguistic features, they tend to be a generation older than Shelly and have grown up in the New York area.

All five Pfeffermans speak with a highly engaged discourse style, characteristic of New York Jews, involving overlapping turns and argumentation as sociability.[7] However, in contrast to their parents, Sarah, Josh, and Ari hardly use any Yiddishisms. There are a few exceptions: they refer to their great-aunt as Tanta Gittel, and Josh talks about Raquel's yarmulke and repeats a phrase his friend uses: "a diamond *moyel*" (circumciser). Aside from *tanta*, these words refer to specifically Jewish referents and do not have common English equivalents, in contrast to Maura and Shelly's Yiddish words, which could have been said in English. However, when Sarah and Ari become interested in Judaism, they use some Hebrew words that their parents do not. Sarah calls the Jewish event she plans *Tacos con Torah* and then *Hineni* (a biblical motif meaning "I am here"; see below). Ari talks about *Torah* and *Shechinah* (divine presence) and eventually learns to comfortably recite Hebrew blessings. These uses of Hebrew are characteristic of religiosity among contemporary non-Orthodox American Jews.

The older generation's use of Yiddishisms sometimes highlights the (increasingly fluid but still extant) boundaries between Jews and non-Jews. When Josh's biological son Colton, who is growing up in a Christian family, recites a predinner prayer "in Jesus' name," Josh says, "We're Jewish, man, we don't do that," and Maura responds simply with a Yiddish phrase: "Oy gevalt!" ("Oh no!"). This phrase not only expresses Maura's negative evaluation of a Christian prayer at her home but also draws the audience's attention to the differences between the Jewish Pfefferman family and their Christian relative. Similarly, at Maura's seventieth birthday party, when Shelly's Jewish boyfriend, Buzzy, congratulates Maura on her decision to pursue gender confirmation surgery with the phrase *Trog gezuntaheit*, the divide between the Jewish and non-Jewish guests is highlighted. Maura's non-Jewish transgender friend Davina, slightly agitated, says, "Was that Latin? What did he say? I don't know what he said." Maura explains with a smile, "It means in Yiddish, 'Wear it in good health.'" Shelly joins in, adding, "Wear it well." Three older Jews, Buzzy, Maura, and Shelly, bond over a Yiddish phrase, while their non-Jewish peer is excluded. Sarah, Josh, and Ari do not participate in this moment, but neither do they request translation. A minute earlier, Davina highlighted her insider status in the transgender community—she corrected Shelly for her inappropriate use of the term "sex change"—and now she bemoans her outsider status with regard to the Jewish community, especially its older members and their liberal use of Yiddishisms.

Jewish-non-Jewish boundaries are also on display in two Shabbat candle-lighting scenes involving Hebrew blessings. In the first, in season 1, Sarah invites Maura to light candles at Shabbat dinner. Davina offers to help, but Sarah declines, saying that this is traditionally the role of the mother of the house. Maura adds, "And you have to be chosen," emphasizing her understanding of the boundary between Jews and non-Jews. The second candle-lighting scene, at the end of the season finale, involves Ari leading the ritual as five characters—not identified as Jews—participate by standing around the table and circling their hands as Ari does. These five characters are three racially diverse queer and transgender teens from the LGBTQ center where Maura volunteered, as well as two LGBTQ center employees, Davina and Elizah (a Black transgender woman that Maura tried to help in season 3). In these two scenes, both Maura and Ari recite the candle-lighting blessing, sharing the Hebrew ritual with their non-Jewish friends. However, for the younger generation, the boundaries are more porous, the rituals more welcoming.[8] Judaism is something to share beyond the Jewish community, not just for Ari, but for *Transparent*'s creators, who have introduced a broad audience to many aspects of Jewish ritual.

The linguistic divide between the generations in *Transparent* reflects a real-life phenomenon. A 2008 survey found that older Jews are more likely than younger Jews to use Yiddish words like *naches* (pride) and *macher* (big shot), which are associated with an ethnic orientation, and younger Jews are more likely to use textual Hebrew words like *drash* (sermon, textual interpretation) and *chas v'shalom* (God forbid), which are associated with a religious orientation (see figure 6.1).[9] *Transparent* taps into these linguistic trends in its portrayal of Jews from two generations.

This linguistic phenomenon is part of a broader trend among American Jews away from ethnic identification and toward an understanding of Jewishness as primarily a religious identity. In the first half of the twentieth century, Jewishness was mainly an ethnic identity except among Reform Jews.[10] However, "it was religion and not ethnicity that provided the cloak under which American Jews presented themselves to the public," because "America was far more hospitable to immigrant groups that insisted on differentiating themselves religiously than to immigrant groups that insisted on differentiating themselves ethnically."[11] By the late twentieth century, this cloak became the primary garb. Quantitative research found that "younger Jews are just as religiously committed, God-oriented, and ritually observant as their elders. However, ... younger Jews are considerably less ethnically identified than their elders."[12] Recent national studies of American Jews have found that these trends continue today. Younger Jews are just as likely as older Jews to attend Jewish religious services at

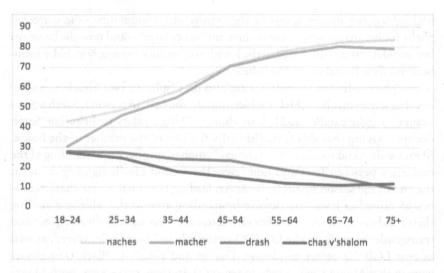

FIGURE 6.1 Age trends: reported use of Yiddish and Hebrew words among Jews who grew up in the United States speaking English.

least monthly, participate in a Passover Seder, and keep kosher. But they are less likely to have mostly Jewish friends, marry other Jews, donate to Jewish organizations, and feel attached to Israel—all characteristics that do not necessarily involve religiosity.[13]

Although we can separate various "ethnic" and "religious" markers in sociological analysis, it is important to note that ethnicity and religion have always been and remain tightly intertwined. The most religiously oriented Jews are most likely to participate in "ethnically" oriented activities, such as having mostly Jewish friends and eating distinctive foods. The group that has maintained spoken Yiddish to the greatest extent is Hasidic Jews, a community that is also strictly religious. Even very secular Jews tend to partake in some religious rituals, such as Passover Seders and Jewish burials. In addition, the terminology is controversial: many young Jewish adults today feel uncomfortable referring to their Jewishness as a "religious" or "ethnic" identity, preferring the term "tradition" for the aspects of Jewishness that they embrace.[14] Finally, ethnic manifestations of Jewishness vary significantly depending on individuals' ancestral origins. The Pfeffermans' immigrant ancestors spoke Yiddish, but many other American Jews descend from immigrants who spoke German, Ladino (Judeo-Spanish), Judeo-Arabic, and other languages. More recent immigrant groups, such as Persian, Russian, and Israeli Jews, maintain more of their ancestral languages, distinctive foods, and other ethnic markers. Despite these caveats, the general trend among American Jews is away from Jewishness as an ethnic category, and most Yiddishisms are decreasing, while Hebraisms, as well as

Yiddishisms in the religious domain (e.g., *shul*, *bentsh*), are increasing.[15] The older and younger Pfeffermans' language use is in line with this trend.

At the end of *Transparent*'s musical finale, the series underscores the importance of both religious observance and ethnic identification. Shelly leads the entire cast in "Joyocaust," a musical number that emphasizes joy in the face of Jews' collective pain regarding the Holocaust, "crossing the line" of tastefulness, as the lyrics declare. In line with Shelly's character, the song includes several Yiddish words, such as *shvitz* and *meshugas*. The song is sandwiched between two religious rituals involving Hebrew: Ari chanting their "bart mitzvah" Torah portion and the candle-lighting scene with Ari and non-Jewish characters. This finale highlights the continuing importance of Yiddish and Hebrew—and of ethnicity and religiosity—in contemporary American Jewish communities. And it demonstrates the porous communal boundaries, as non-Jewish characters observe and participate.

The distinctive linguistic features of Jewish characters are not limited to Yiddish and Hebrew words. In the photography session at Sarah and Tammy's wedding (figure 6.2), the Pfeffermans talk over each other, in stark contrast to the Cashmans' quiet decorum. It takes almost two minutes for the Pfeffermans to prepare for their photo, and most of the family members speak loudly, often multiple people simultaneously. After the photographer says, "Everybody say 'Cindy Lou'" (a reference to *How the Grinch Stole Christmas*), Shelly offers an alternative: "How 'bout a Jewish reference?" The photographer says in a whiny voice, "I want a little wine." Shelly complains, "A little pejorative," and Maura agrees: "A little antisemitic, but that's fine." Then on Shelly's suggestion they say, "Hanukkah." Over a minute later, when they are still trying to get the perfect shot, Maura walks out because the photographer calls her "Sir." Then, the (larger) Cashman family manages to gather and pose in less than half a minute—without

FIGURE 6.2 *Transparent*. "Kina Hora," Season 2:1. Written by Joey Soloway, directed by Joey Soloway, November 30, 2015.

drama. The photographer quickly captures his desired image and praises the Cashmans: "Ah, you're beautiful." This scene can be read as a comment on the Pfefferman family being roiled with drama, but it can also be seen as portraying Jews' higher-engagement discourse style. It also highlights the older generation—Shelly and Maura—using language to insist on Jewish particularism even in a non-particularistic context. Scenes like these depict how non-Jews are increasingly part of American Jews' families and friendship circles, and they emphasize the lingering contrasts between Jews and non-Jews, especially in the older generation.

Distinctive Jewish language has long been a theme in artistic representations of Jews—both by Jews and by others.[16] *Transparent* portrays Jewish language unapologetically and in (mostly) noncomedic ways. Even when non-Jewish characters encounter and comment on Jewish language, there does not seem to be an underlying critique or anxiety surrounding the use of Yiddish and Hebrew words. This reflects a broader acceptance of Jews in early twenty-first century America, which exists alongside increasing antisemitism in certain circles.

Individual Transitions

Another type of transition depicted in *Transparent* is the individual identity shift. Although many characters undergo such shifts, this chapter focuses on three: Maura's gender transition, Ari becoming a queer feminist scholar, and Sarah's increasing engagement with Judaism. All three of these transitions involve the characters changing aspects of their language and other characters assisting in their process of language learning.

To help make sense of these transitions and the accompanying language, we turn to research in linguistic anthropology on "language socialization."[17] Many scholars have analyzed how children and adults are socialized to use language in a certain way, and through that language use, they are socialized to be part of a community. When adults take on a new identity, such as training for a profession, acquiring a hobby, or undergoing religious conversion or intensification, they may not have to learn a whole new language, but they likely feel pressure to learn specialized terminology and other linguistic conventions.[18] Language socialization can involve overt teaching, imitation, making mistakes, and being corrected. Although scholarship on language socialization is based on observation of real-life interactions, these phenomena can also be found in works of fiction. In *Transparent*, the portrayal of language socialization sheds light on individual transitions in gender, sexuality, and Jewishness.

As Maura transitions from male-presenting to female-presenting, she encounters new terminology. Maura tries—unsuccessfully—to imitate her transgender friend Shea by using slang like "Yass, queen!" as Shea coaches her on pronunciation and intonation. Davina introduces Maura to phrases like "regendered photos." Davina's boyfriend, Sal, coaches Maura on the rationales she should recite to get the doctor's note required to undergo gender-affirmation surgery: "I hate my penis. I'm a woman trapped in a man's body. You know, I'm not gonna be happy unless I get tits."

These scenes demonstrate the importance of language in gender transitions, as well as the role of interaction in individuals learning the language of their new community. The scene with Sal highlights for Maura and the audience the gatekeeping associated with transgender medical care: she must produce a coherent narrative using particular language to access the care she desires. Shea and Maura's use of "yass" demonstrates the influence of African American English on transgender English, likely spread by the performative language of drag queens, especially RuPaul,[19] thereby highlighting the whiteness of most characters in *Transparent*.

The language learning extends beyond Maura to her relatives, friends, and others she encounters, as they are socialized to speak appropriately to her and about her. Sometimes this learning is assisted by Maura's corrections when people refer to her with masculine pronouns. For example, when Shelly is complaining agitatedly that her children have not visited enough as she is caring for her dying husband, she points to Maura and says, "He's the only one who comes." Maura corrects her: "She." Shortly thereafter, Shelly says, "He came over to be with me." Maura, still calm, corrects her once more: "She, I'm- I'm a she. I'm a woman." After a short pause, Shelly says, "*She* takes care of me." After multiple interactions of language socialization, Shelly finally uses the appropriate pronoun for her transgender ex-spouse. Maura also corrects how her children address her. Soon after she comes out to them as transgender, they begin calling her Moppa, a combination of Mom and Poppa. Later Maura asks them to call her Mom instead. Through overt corrections and requests, she is socializing those around her to use the proper names, pronouns, and terms of address in line with her new self-presentation.

Other times, Maura's friends and acquaintances correct others on her behalf. One of these language socializers is Elizah, a young transgender woman Maura has just met. A clerk asks Elizah, "Do you need me to call the police on this man? Is he bothering you?" Elizah responds, "Hey, it's not he. Does she look like a 'he' to you?" Some instances of correction are less direct. Maura's sister, Bryna, asks Maura's girlfriend, Vicki, "Don't you ever worry about him getting botched surgery?" Vicki responds, "Oh her? Yeah, I worry a lot. But if I've told her once I've told her 10,000 times—she's perfect the way she is." Rather than interrupt the flow of the conversation and offer a potentially offensive, overt correction, as Elizah does, Vicki chooses to embed her correction of Bryna's gender pronoun within continuing conversation.[20] She proceeds to use five female gender pronouns in her response, reminding Bryna multiple times how Maura prefers to be called. Sometimes the process of language socialization for people who interact with transgender folks can be long and protracted, especially among those who are reluctant to accept the transgender person's new self-presentation.

Name corrections are a motif in *Transparent* and not just for transgender characters. Cantor Duvid and Rabbi Raquel both correct people's pronunciations of the name of Duvid's daughter, sometimes to Idit and sometimes to Idith. When the Pfeffermans take a cruise, Maura says to a cruise staff member, "It's a lovely boat." He corrects her: "Ship, we call it a ship." Maura asks, with genuine curiosity, "What's the difference?" The response: "It's a matter of respect." Maura is convinced: "A matter of respect. Okay, I get that." That evening, Maura corrects Ari when she calls it a boat: "It's not a boat. It's a ship. You have to say 'ship'. You can't misgender the ship." Maura explicitly connects the misnaming of ships with the inaccurate gender identifications that she often experiences. The word "misgender" is technically inaccurate, as "boat" and "ship" are not gendered words (despite the convention of referring to boats and ships "she"). But it highlights the centrality of Maura's experiences of being misgendered, a lens through which she views even things unrelated to gender. This can be seen as an instance of "hyper-accommodation," a sociolinguistic term for newcomers going overboard in their use of the language of their new community.[21]

Ari also exhibits hyper-accommodation in her process of language socialization. She begins to identify as a queer feminist, spending time with a lesbian poet/professor and eventually training to become a gender studies scholar. She begins to use new words like "intersectionality"—appropriate for a series that highlights intersections among Jewishness, gender, and sexuality.[22] Maura notices Ari's increasing use of academic terminology in a conversation about the tables in the dining room: Ari says, "It's just been in this iteration for the last day because of the party." Maura calls attention to Ari's linguistic change: "Did you say iteration?"

Another instance of hyper-accommodation is Ari's use of the word "heteronormative" in a tense conversation with her girlfriend, Syd, after Ari cheats on her:

ARI What if we could just talk about it, process it together, maybe even get turned on by it?
SYD Okay, so what, you're into like polyamory now?
ARI No, I'm just saying, what if we didn't have the sort of knee-jerk heteronormative—
SYD Listen to yourself. Listen to yourself. You've been queer for like 30 seconds. Jesus.

Ari continues the conversation: "What is being queer if not questioning everything?" This can be seen as a coded allusion, which only some viewers will recognize, to the Jewish practice of asking many questions. Through metalinguistic conversation (talk about language—in this case not only about the word "heteronormative" but also about the linguistic practice of questioning), this scene highlights the connections between queer and Jewish identities, as Ari experiences them.

FIGURE 6.3 *Transparent.* "The Book of Life," Season 2:7. Written by Joey Soloway and Ethan Kuperberg, directed by Jim Frohna, December 11, 2015.

Ari's process of language socialization is primarily about becoming a queer, feminist scholar, but she also transitions to intensified Jewish study and observance. At the break fast she and Syd host, Ari presides over the premeal ritual (figure 6.3), explaining, "I've just started sort of investigating and wondering about my Jewishness." She asks for help with the Hebrew blessing over bagels, and several of the guests join together for *Hamotzi.* When Ari says, "Happy Yom Kippur," an unidentified male-sounding voice—perhaps Buzzy or Syd's father—corrects her overtly: "You don't say 'Happy Yom Kippur'—you say 'Gut Yontif!'" In these scenes, Ari and others are participating in three common practices of language socialization: hyper-accommodation (in this case using a holiday greeting that more experienced community members would not), asking for help, and correcting mistakes.

Ari brings together her interests in Jewishness and gender in her academic research, including learning about "Jew shoes," shoes with bells that Jewish women in medieval Arab lands were required to wear.[23] Soaking in a hot tub with Leslie, her future advisor and lover, Ari says, "I have this notion that there is something connected with the woman thing and the Jew thing." After offering a ridiculous analogy ("It's like phallus is to crucifix and vagina is to Holocaust"), she proceeds to link her research interests with her family's rifts, which she feels are based on inherited trauma. Ari's braiding of these disparate strands culminates in a powerful, dream-like sequence that connects the past with the present. Walking through the forest at a women's festival wearing Jew shoes, Ari happens upon a campfire, which turns out to be the 1933 Nazi book burning at Magnus Hirschfeld's Institute for Sexual Science.[24] Ari holds the hand of her (then young) Grandma Rose—played by the same actress who plays thirteen-year-old Ali—watching in horror as Nazis capture Rose's "transvestite" sibling Gershon/Gittel. After both scenes, Ari has sexual encounters with Leslie, expressing her desire to be socialized into academic and queer identities and connecting those with her Jewishness. Like language, sex and scholarship are among the tools Ari uses to perform her identities.

Ari's Jewish and gender transitions converge in the series finale when they come out as nonbinary and change their name from Ali to Ari (which their aunt Bryna identifies as the Hebrew word for lion). Ari leads their siblings in reciting the Mourner's Kaddish as their parent is cremated—another instance of the transition motif and quite a contrast to Ari's inability to lead Hamotzi in season 2. The theme of Lech Lecha, the Torah portion from Ari's canceled bat mitzvah, appears throughout this musical episode, including in a poster on the street, the recurring song "Run From Your Father's House," the many images of characters walking (or dancing), and Ari chanting the Hebrew words of Lech Lecha and explaining that it emphasizes leaving your father's house and charting your own path. Ari's path is influenced by Maura's transitions in Jewishness and gender but also diverges in that Ari embraces nonbinary gender and religious engagement with the divine. We see the intersection of Ari's Jewishness and gender not only in their "bart mitzvah" but also in their donning a yarmulke and walking to the men's side of the Western Wall in Jerusalem.

Ari's older sister, Sarah, is also socialized to use more distinctively Jewish language as she intensifies her Jewish engagement. Speaking to Rabbi Raquel and Cantor Duvid, Sarah explains her idea for a Jewish Tacos con Torah event in a school gym rather than at Raquel's synagogue:

SARAH And then right in the center, we have the—the Torah box right here.
RAQUEL It's the ark.
SARAH The ark! That's right.

Raquel is socializing Sarah to use the proper Jewish terminology (the English "ark," rather than the Hebrew *aron*, which would be less likely in a non-Orthodox context like this).

Duvid then comes to a realization regarding Sarah's proposed event:

DUVID Oh, my God, Raquel. This is *Shevet achim gam yachad* [siblings dwelling together].
SARAH *Sheve- shevet*? What?
DUVID Raquel had this idea in school for a temple without walls. *Shevet achim gam yachad*. This is her idea.
SARAH Wait a second. Wait. You had this idea.
RAQUEL I had so many big stupid ideas in seminary. This is—
SARAH It's not a stupid idea. It's a great idea. It's a stupid name, but it's a great idea.

When Duvid recites this Hebrew phrase (which Jewishly knowledgeable viewers will recognize as a quote from Psalms that is also part of "Hinei ma tov," a popular Jewish song), Sarah asks about it. Duvid repeats it but does not translate or explain. When Sarah criticizes the idea to use this Hebrew phrase as a name for a temple without walls, she is socializing Raquel and Duvid regarding the linguistic preferences of the "hipster Jews" (Sarah's phrase) that they hope to attract to their event. Although she does not say so explicitly, she likely feels that a four-word Hebrew phrase with two [ch] sounds is too "Jewy" for such a community.

A minute later, Sarah decides on a name for the event, based on a child's utterance. Duvid calls out to his daughter, Idit, in biblical Hebrew:

DUVID Idit! *Ayech*? [Where are you?]
IDIT *Hineni, Aba. Hineni.* [Here I am, Dad. Here I am.]
SARAH Hineni—what is that? That's so cute.
RAQUEL That means "here I am" in biblical Hebrew.
SARAH I love Hebrew. It's so great. Hineni. Hin—Here I am.
RAQUEL Yeah, she speaks—
SARAH Hineni. Hineni. Here I am. Yes. That's the name of it. The name of it. That's the name. That's the name of the event. Or the, the, the ceremony. Hineni. Here I am.

Raquel—with the help of Duvid and Idit—teaches Sarah a new Hebrew word, highlighting for both Sarah and the audience the importance of Hebrew in Jewish life. Sarah's statement "I love Hebrew" demonstrates that she has been socialized to hold positive opinions about the Jewish sacred language. And her attraction to a single ancient Hebrew word as a Jewish event name aligns with several new real-life organizations geared primarily toward hip, young, Jewish adults, such as *Ikar* (essence), *Kavana* (intention), and *Romemu* (exalt). Hineni is the name of a few real-life Jewish groups that attract similar crowds, including Esther Jungreis's Orthodox outreach organization founded in the 1970s and a program in St. Paul, Minnesota, that specializes in "adult Jewish learning" and "contemplative practice."[25] *Transparent*'s creator, Joey Soloway, may have been exposed to such trends through their participation in Reboot, a network of "Jewishly unconnected cultural creatives."[26] In fact, influenced by their Reboot experiences, Soloway and some other Rebooters founded a Jewish community organization, East Side Jews, in Los Angeles around the time *Transparent* was created. Many Rebooters, including Soloway, were also involved in creating a Jewish community called Nefesh ("soul," another one-word Hebrew name), founded in 2014 by Rabbi Susan Goldberg, the rabbinic consultant for *Transparent* and rabbi in residence for East Side Jews. Sarah's Hineni program in season 3, episode 5 resembles events of East Side Jews and Nefesh, and some of the Nefesh musicians performed in that scene.

The word *hineni* represents not only Sarah's increasing engagement with Judaism but also a biblical motif. At several pivotal moments in the Bible, God calls characters, and they respond, "Hineni!" Examples include God commanding Abraham to sacrifice his son (Genesis 22:1), God visiting Israel (Jacob) in his dream and instructing him to go to Egypt (Genesis 46:2), and God calling Moses from the burning bush to lead the exodus (Exodus 3:4). This motif also appears later in *Transparent*, in season 4, when Maura, taking a brief walk alone in the Israeli desert, encounters a feminine young adult version of herself. Young Maura accuses contemporary Maura of having abandoned her years ago. We see a flashback to Maura, then a young father, looking sadly at her newborn baby in a hospital incubator, as the dialogue continues:

MAURA I had—I had to choose. God was making me choose.
YOUNG MAURA Just because you hear God's voice doesn't mean it's God's voice.
   Look at you. You're here, and Ali's alive.
MAURA We *are* here. I'm *here*. I'm here.

As a young parent, Maura felt a divine pressure to choose between accepting her femininity and enabling her baby to survive, but she currently feels a divine call to accept her femininity. Her response, "I'm here" (English for *hineni*), can be read as her accepting God's call at a pivotal moment, just as the biblical characters did—in that very desert. Thus, for viewers with inside knowledge, the biblical hineni motif connects Sarah's socialization to Jewish life with Maura's acceptance of her gender identity.

The hineni motif also highlights self-presentation. When characters say, "I'm here," or "hineni," they are emphasizing *Transparent*'s theme of transitions in identification that lead to more accurate and comfortable presentations of self in Jewishness, sexuality, and gender. The series effectively makes a collective statement of pride: *hinenu* (we are here)—we transgender, queer, and Jewish people are here and are proud to present ourselves to the public. Hence the title of this chapter, "From *Oy* to *Hineni*." This represents not only the communal transition from Yiddish to Hebrew but also individuals' transitions from discomfort with their identities to proud self-presentation.

Conclusion

Language socialization involves learning not only new ways of speaking but also the ideologies that those linguistic features represent. In *Transparent*, those ideologies include the connection to Eastern European Jewish communities among Maura and Shelly's generation of American-born Eastern Ashkenazi Jews, the increasing importance of Jewish spirituality among some in their children's generation, and the importance of sensitive language to and about transgender people. The characters in the show are socialized to be aware of—and perhaps embrace—these ideologies, and so are *Transparent*'s audiences.

Language socialization also reminds us of the importance of community and interaction in individuals' identities. Transitions can be personal and internal, and individuals can learn language on their own by reading books, searching the internet, and watching videos. But, as the chapter's examples demonstrate, so much of language learning happens through interaction, especially questions, corrections, and other metalinguistic comments. Interaction is crucial in how characters experience their transitions and how they are socialized to use language associated with their new identities.

Transparent has garnered critical acclaim, including multiple awards. Part of this success is likely based on the impressive production values and the universal themes of family relationships and individual transformation. But, through distinctive language, *Transparent* also presents very particular themes that might seem to be of interest primarily among Jewish, transgender, and queer communities. Whether or not viewers are part of these communities, *Transparent* sends the message that these three identities—and their histories and current issues—are deeply intertwined. And as audiences watch characters undergo processes of language socialization, they, too, are socialized to understand some of the distinctive language of Jewish, transgender, and queer Americans.

Acknowledgments

Thank you to Nora Rubel, Brett Krutzsch, and the anonymous reviewers for providing helpful comments and to Claire Sufrin for organizing the AJS panel that springboarded this research. Thanks also to Joey Soloway and the *Transparent* team for producing such a rich work of art.

Notes

1. *Transparent*'s overt portrayal of Jewishness is part of a trend of increasing Jewish representation in American sitcoms and other cultural products, starting in the late 1980s. See Vincent Brook, *Something Ain't Kosher Here: The Rise of the "Jewish" Sitcom* (New Brunswick, NJ: Rutgers University Press, 2003). Several have written about *Transparent*'s Jewish practices and themes, including Debra Nussbaum Cohen, "How Jill Soloway Created 'Transparent'—the Jewiest Show Ever," *Forward*, October 21, 2014. https://forward.com/culture/207407/how-jill-soloway-created-transparent-the-jewiest/; Josh Lambert, "Pfefferman Family Matters," *Tablet*, December 7, 2015, http://www.tabletmag.com/scroll/195620/pfefferman-family-matters; Jonathan Freedman, "'Transparent': A Guide for the Perplexed," *Los Angeles Review of Books*, April 10, 2016, https://lareviewofbooks.org/article/transparent-a-guide-for-the-perplexed/.
2. Sarah Bunin Benor, "Have You Noticed These Images in 'Transparent'?" *Lilith*, February 29, 2016, http://lilith.org/blog/2016/02/have-you-noticed-these-images-in-transparent/.
3. Sarah Bunin Benor, "Do American Jews Speak a 'Jewish Language'? A Model of Jewish Linguistic Distinctiveness," *Jewish Quarterly Review* 99, no. 2 (2009): 230–269.

4   The growing body of scholarship on queer and trans language investigates individuals' voice quality, pitch, phonology, grammar, and lexicon, as well as ideologies among queer and trans folks and others about how individuals speak or should speak. This scholarship emphasizes individuals' acts of linguistic creativity, bricolage (performing a unique style using resources from multiple sources), and activism, the importance of intersectional analysis, and the social construction and non-binary nature of gender and sexuality—all themes that are found in *Transparent*. See, for example, Anna Livia and Kira Hall, eds., *Queerly Phrased: Language, Gender, and Sexuality* (New York: Oxford University Press, 1997); Don Kulick, "Transgender and Language: A Review of the Literature and Suggestions for the Future," *GLQ* 5, no. 4 (1999): 605–622; Lal Zimman, Jenny Davis, and Joshua Raclaw, eds., *Queer Excursions: Retheorizing Binaries in Language, Gender, and Sexuality* (Oxford: Oxford University Press, 2014); Lal Zimman, "Gender as Stylistic Bricolage: Transmasculine Voices and the Relationship between Fundamental Frequency and /s/," *Language in Society* 46, no. 3 (2017): 339–370; Lal Zimman, "Transgender Language Reform: Some Challenges and Strategies for Promoting Trans-Affirming, Gender-Inclusive Language," *Journal of Language and Discrimination* 1, no. 1 (2017): 84–105; Lia Litosseliti, "Language, Gender, and Sexuality: Reflections on the Field's Ongoing Critical Engagement with the Sociopolitical Landscape," in *The Routledge Handbook of Language, Gender, and Sexuality*, eds. Jo Angouri and Judith Baxter (London: Routledge, 2021), 323–338.

5   For discussion of how these linguistic features are distributed among Americans, see Sarah Bunin Benor, "*Mensch*, *Bentsh*, and *Balagan*: Variation in the American Jewish Linguistic Repertoire," *Language and Communication* 31, no. 2 (2011): 141–154. For analysis of Yiddish-influenced English in comedy, see Sarah Bunin Benor, "Pastrami, Verklempt, and Tshootspa: Non-Jews' Use of Jewish Language in the United States," in *American Jewish Year Book 2020*, eds. Arnold Dashefsky and Ira M. Sheskin (Cham, Switzerland: Springer, 2022): 3–69.

6   Diana Clarke and Saul Noam Zaritt, "Yiddish on Transparent: A Talk with Jill Soloway and Micah Fitzerman-Blue," *In Geveb*, March 2016, https://ingeveb.org/blog/yiddish-on-transparent.

7   Deborah Tannen, "New York Jewish Conversational Style," *International Journal of the Sociology of Language* 30 (1981): 133–149; Deborah Schiffrin, "Jewish Argument as Sociability," *Language in Society* 13, no. 3 (1984): 311–335. See also Benor, "*Mensch, Bentsh,* and *Balagan*."

8   On increasingly porous boundaries in American Jewish life, see Robert Mnookin, *The Jewish American Paradox: Embracing Choice in a Changing World* (New York: Public Affairs, 2018).

9   Data is from the 2008 Survey of American Jewish Language and Identity. See Benor, "*Mensch, Bentsh,* and *Balagan*," and Sarah Bunin Benor and Steven M. Cohen, "Talking Jewish: The 'Ethnic English' of American Jews," in *Ethnicity and Beyond: Theories and Dilemmas of Jewish Group Demarcation: Studies in Contemporary Jewry*, vol. 25, ed. Eli Lederhendler (Oxford: Oxford University Press, 2011), 62–78.

10 Charles Liebman, "Unraveling the Ethnoreligious Package," in *Contemporary Jewries: Convergence and Divergence*, eds. Eliezer Ben Rafael, Yosef Gorni, and Yaacov Roi (Leiden: Brill, 2003), 143–150.

11 Liebman, "Unraveling," 144.

12 Steven M. Cohen, "Religious Stability and Ethnic Decline: Emerging Patterns of Jewish Identity in the United States" (New York: JCCA, 1998), 2–3. https://www.bjpa.org/content/upload/bjpa/c__w/Religious%20Stability%20and%20Ethnic%20Decline.pdf.

13. Luis Lugo et al., "A Portrait of Jewish Americans: Findings from a Pew Research Center Survey of US Jews" (Washington, DC: Pew Research Institute, 2013). https://www.pewresearch.org/religion/2013/10/01/jewish-american-beliefs-attitudes-culture-survey/.
14. Ari Y. Kelman et al., "Traditional Judaism: The Conceptualization of Jewishness in the Lives of American Jewish Post-Boomers," *Jewish Social Studies* 23, no. 1 (2017): 134–167.
15. Sarah Bunin Benor, "How Synagogues Became *Shuls*: The Boomerang Effect in Yiddish-Influenced English, 1895–2010," in *Germanic Heritage Languages in North America*, eds. Janne Bondi Johannessen and Joseph Salmons (Amsterdam: John Benjamins, 2015), 217–233.
16. Sander Gilman, *Jewish Self-Hatred: Anti-Semitism and the Hidden Language of the Jews* (Baltimore: Johns Hopkins University Press, 1986); Sander Gilman, *The Jew's Body* (New York: Routledge, 2013); Hana Wirth-Nesher, *Call It English* (Princeton, NJ: Princeton University Press, 2008). See also Benor, "Pastrami, Verklempt, and Tshootspa."
17. Bambi Schieffelin and Elinor Ochs, *Language Socialization Across Cultures* (Cambridge: Cambridge University Press, 1986); Alessandro Duranti, Elinor Ochs, and Bambi B. Schieffelin, eds., *The Handbook of Language Socialization* (Malden, MA: Wiley-Blackwell: 2011).
18. Elizabeth Mertz, *The Language of Law School: Learning to "Think Like a Lawyer"* (Oxford: Oxford University Press, 2007); Lanita Jacobs-Huey, *From the Kitchen to the Parlor: Language and Becoming in African American Women's Hair Care* (Oxford: Oxford University Press, 2006); Sarah Bunin Benor, *Becoming Frum: How Newcomers Learn the Language and Culture of Orthodox Judaism* (New Brunswick, NJ: Rutgers University Press, 2012).
19. See Rusty Barrett, "Indexing Polyphonous Identity in the Speech of African-American Drag Queens," in *Reinventing Identities: The Gendered Self in Discourse*, eds. Mary Bucholtz, A. C. Liang, and Laurel A. Sutton (Oxford: Oxford University Press, 1999), 313–30; Stephen L. Mann, "Drag Queens' Use of Language and the Performance of Blurred Gendered and Racial Identities," *Journal of Homosexuality* 58, nos. 6–7 (2011): 793–811.
20. Gail Jefferson, "On Exposed and Embedded Correction in Conversation," in *Talk and Social Organisation*, eds. Graham Button and J.R.E. Lee (Clevedon, U.K.: Multilingual Matters, 1987), 86–100. See also Benor, *Becoming Frum*.
21. Malcah Yaeger-Dror, "Introduction," *Language and Communication* 12, nos. 3–4 (1992): 181–193. See also Benor, *Becoming Frum*.
22. This use of "intersectionality," an academic term coined by an African American feminist scholar to analyze the intersections of racism and sexism, highlights the question of race and the predominance of whiteness in *Transparent*. Kimberlé Williams Crenshaw, "Mapping the Margins: Intersectionality, Identity Politics, and Violence Against Women of Color," in *The Public Nature of Private Violence*, eds. Martha Albertson Fineman and Rixanne Mykitiuk (New York: Routledge, 1994), 93–118.
23. Freedman, "'Transparent.'"
24. See Lambert, "Pfefferman Family Matters," on the relationship between Jewishness and sexuality and the importance of the Hirschfeld scenes.
25. Hineni. https://www.ttsp.org/hineni/
26. Cohen, "How Jill Soloway."

7

Pfefferman's Complaint

Transparent and the Tenacity of Jewish Familial Stereotypes

JARROD TANNY

"It's not you. My father is my mother right now, and in my head I'm basically afraid I'm never gonna get a hard-on again,"[1] bemoans Josh Pfefferman during his failed sexual encounter with Rabbi Raquel in *Transparent*'s first season. Although the show focuses on the difficulties transgender people face, the series contains elements of a typical twentieth-century Jewish cultural production, particularly in its use of familial stereotypes, which can be seen most clearly in the character of Josh Pfefferman and his relationship with Shelly, his birth mother. Josh is a twenty-first-century incarnation of the archetypal diasporic Jewish male: driven by an insatiable hypersexuality yet incapable of meaningful intimacy, self-absorbed and torn between an inferiority complex and raw egotism, and, most significantly, emasculated since childhood by a smothering, domineering, guilt-inducing Jewish mother. Philp Roth was among the first to introduce the dysfunctional diasporic Jew and his overbearing mother into American literature in his classic novel *Portnoy's Complaint*, and the image was further developed and inculcated into mass consciousness through the comedy of Woody Allen, Jerry Seinfeld, and others. Although Josh's frailties are apparent in the first three seasons of *Transparent*, they are made blatant during the fourth season. This occurs because of the Pfeffermans' family trip to Israel, where their American

Jewishness is juxtaposed to the normative Israeli, the tough Jew who has negated his exilic condition through state-building, war, and male cultural codes. Although Josh wants to believe his sexual dysfunction with Raquel is because his erstwhile father has transitioned to a woman (and, accordingly, because he has "acquired" a second mother), the roots of his problem lie in his lineage—what Yiddish speakers call their *yichus*—the heritage of the stereotypical diasporic Jew; his transphobic confession to Rabbi Raquel cloaks the actual source of his impotence.

But the Pfefferman family pilgrimage to Zion is also where *Transparent* transcends what may be called the Portnoy template, with Israel serving as the catalyst for Josh and Shelly's personal growth and the reparation of their troubled relationship. Against the backdrop of the Jewish state, they begin the mending process, and the Jewish mother and son return to America prepared to own their damaged heritage and move forward. In this sense, *Transparent*'s exploitation of Jewish stereotypes is neither hackneyed nor superfluous. Although not as obvious as its negation of the antiquated male-female gender binary through characters such as Maura and Ari, *Transparent* brings the Jewish family—all of its members—into the twenty-first century by forcing the Pfeffermans to confront the ghosts of their pasts in a radically transformed present.

In the twenty-first century, Jewish TV is now everywhere. *Transparent* led the way through its pioneering yet subtle rendering of American Jews and their relentless quest to find meaning in the identities, collective memory, and Judaic rituals they inherited with ambivalence.

But in other respects, *Transparent* remains anchored to an earlier period in American Jewish entertainment. Its writers make liberal use of twentieth-century Jewish stereotypes and cultural tropes, discursive embellishments that often come across as outmoded and superfluous. This is most apparent in its depiction of Shelly Pfefferman. "Shelly," writes Sara Ivry in *Tablet*, "is portrayed more as a cartoon than any other character . . . she fussbudgets around like a Jewish mother caricature," in stark contrast to the psychological depth and multifaceted personalities of the rest of the Pfefferman clan.[2]

The Jewish mother has been a prominent archetype in American culture since the 1960s, first made famous with Mike Nichols and Elaine May's 1960 comedy sketch, "Mother and Son," Bruce Jay Friedman's 1964 novel *A Mother's Kisses*, Dan Greenburg's 1964 satirical instruction manual *How to be a Jewish Mother*, and, most notably, Philip Roth's 1969 novel *Portnoy's Complaint*.[3] In the following decades, it found its way into film, such as Woody Allen's 1989 short *Oedipus Wrecks*, in which the main character's mother disappears during a magic show and ends up surrealistically hovering in the sky above New York, where she continues to badger her son over trivialities in front of a million Manhattanites.[4] Most recently, the Jewish mother has surfaced on TV, featured on shows like *The Nanny*, *Friends*, and *The Big Bang Theory*. According to Joyce Antler, "Comedy is in large part responsible for making the negative Jewish mother stereotype so pervasive and disproportionately popular."[5] It is "Jewish comic shtick" that "has an immediate payoff, calling forth an automatic response that makes spectators laugh at this 'insider' humor."[6] "Because of its persistence and versatility," Antler maintains, the Jewish mother image became "the dominant Jewish American stereotype."[7]

On *Transparent*, Shelly Pfefferman is marked as the Jewish mother through her discourse and body language. She regularly embellishes her speech with Yiddish inflections. She repeats certain phrases in the form of questions, structures sentences with a Yiddishized syntax, and waves her arms in a manner (somewhat absurdly) reminiscent of Tevye the Dairyman from *Fidler on the Roof*. In the first season's second episode, after Ari inquires about the doctor's diagnosis of Shelly's ailing husband, Shelly retorts in a singsong voice: "The doctor! The doctor! What does the doctor say? I should write a song, 'What Does the Doctor Saaaayyy!'"[8] Although Yiddish ceased to be the spoken language for the vast majority of secular American Jews by the mid-twentieth century, such flourishes are still used in popular culture to mark a character as Jewish, making Yiddish "a semiotic system, in which its signifiers might be inflections, melodies, gestures, or objects, more than (or even instead of) words," as Jeffrey Shandler puts it.[9]

In keeping with stereotype, Shelly routinely berates her family for ignoring her, for mocking her, and for treating her like dirt. In the third season finale, she airs her grievances to Maura and their two daughters during an impromptu Passover Seder:

SHELLY I am not at home in this family. You ridicule me. You bond with each other behind my back. You roll your eyes at me.
ARI We do not roll our eyes [Ari rolls her eyes].
SHELLY You just did it. You just did it.
MAURA [TO ARI] SHE'S RIGHT, YOU ROLL YOUR EYES.
SHELLY [TO MAURA] Thank you, once for sticking up for me.[10]

However, it is their son, Josh, who bears the brunt of Shelly's rebukes, particularly in the fourth season after Shelly decides to move in with Josh without asking him. When he accuses her of never listening, of violating his boundaries, she retorts: "Why do you hate me so much?

. . . Stop being so mean to me!" Although Josh insists that he is merely trying to help, she rejects his response, and, hyperventilating, Shelly ostentatiously storms out of the room and proclaims that she will be spending the night at a hotel. But such antics are merely for show, and Josh later discovers his mother sleeping in the car. Mistakenly thinking she is dead, Josh panics, wakes her up, and with a gut-wrenching "Oy, oy, oy, oy, oy, my back, oy," Shelly gets up and reconciles with her beloved son.[11]

Josh must endure the weight of Shelly more than his siblings because the Jewish mother always exists in a symbiotic yet toxic relationship with the Jewish son. Simultaneously adulated and denigrated, the Jewish son is imagined as a perfect being who can never live up to the mother's expected perfection. "What was it with these Jewish parents?" laments Philip Roth's Alexander Portnoy in a tirade directed far more at his omnipresent mother than his emasculated father: "They were able to make us little Jewish boys believe ourselves to be princes on the one hand . . . geniuses and brilliant like nobody has ever been brilliant and beautiful before in the history of childhood—saviors and sheer perfection on the one hand, and such bumbling, incompetent, thoughtless, helpless, selfish, evil little shits, little *ingrates*, on the other!"[12]

Much like Mother Portnoy, Shelly extols the virtues of her precious progeny. She claims to always be thinking about his future, how to marry him off to a nice Jewish woman. This is Shelly's first impulse when she meets Rabbi Raquel—"far too attractive for a lady Rabbi!" she proclaims—who pays Shelly a visit to minister to her dying husband, Ed. "My Joshy is not married," she interjects, apparently forgetting that the rabbi is there for Ed. "Maybe you two could meet; he's gorgeous, absolutely gorgeous—how old are you?"[13]

Although Josh and Raquel hit it off on their own terms and have an intense but tumultuous relationship during the first and second seasons, Shelly continues to see their coupling and prospective marriage as an extension of herself. Her joy upon learning that they are dating—"Oh my God, are you fucking the rabbi? . . . You're fucking the rabbi!"[14]—is mild compared to the way she gushes and kvells upon learning that Josh got Raquel pregnant: "What do you mean she's pregnant? . . . What do you mean, we're gonna have a baby? . . . We're pregnant! . . . The Rabbi! . . . With my baby!"[15]

Any future child of the archetypal Jewish man is by definition a child of his Jewish mother because in her eyes, the adult son always remains a child. Shelly's infantilization of Josh is graphically displayed after she moves in with him and encroaches upon his privacy. "Tushy! Joshy! Tush! Tush-nush! Hungry! J-Joshy?" Shelly's voice echoes throughout the house as Josh is in bed, reading, annoyed at the disturbance and the creeping realization that she is about to barge in.

SHELLY Oh, there you are! Did you hear me calling you?
JOSH Yeah, I heard you. All the neighbors heard you.
SHELLY Oh, stop it. Why didn't you answer me?
JOSH Because, Mom, I'm trying to keep it chill in here, okay?

Shelly fails to take the hint and climbs onto his bed and proceeds to fawn over him, "Oouh, are you tired puppy?"[16] What had previously been a psychologically claustrophobic relationship for Josh has taken on a physical dimension, and Shelly remains unnervingly at his side for most of the fourth season.

The Jewish male's suffocation is a common trope in modern Jewish culture and in antisemitic discourse. It is defined as a sickness, inherited from the mother who serves as the conveyer of an insular and out-of-step Jewishness in a world dominated by WASPs. It manifests itself through anxiety, effeminacy, and sexual deviance.[17] According to Sander Gilman, it is viewed, in part, as a product of the Jew's circumcision, which in Europe came to be seen as symbolic castration and a source of trauma.[18] For Ritchie Robertson, this feminized Jew is marked as lacking the self-control of the "martial Aryan" and is "sensually self-indulgent."[19] Although these stereotypes emerged and gestated in nineteenth-century Europe, they subsequently found their way into twentieth-century American culture.[20] This is why Alexander Portnoy is "cunt crazy,"[21] and when he is not chasing shiksas (non-Jewish women), his hypersexuality induces him to masturbate incessantly. Yet Portnoy suffers from periodic impotence, lives in perpetual fear of syphilis and castration, and fails to establish meaningful relationships with women. Portnoy recognizes that there is a deep, dark connection between his mother, his Jewishness, and his sexuality. And he is not alone. It is also true with Sheldon Mills in Woody Allen's *Oedipus Wrecks*, Howard Wolowitz on *The Big Bang Theory*, and numerous other Jewish men who have appeared in literature, film, and TV since World War II.[22] They are deviants in a world of civilized, normative Christians because of their cultural heritage, their yichus.

Although he is handsome and ostensibly a lady's man, Josh Pfefferman's life is true to stereotype. The self-confidence he projects through his numerous romances and sexual relationships masks his insecurity and anguish. In the first episode, we learn of his ongoing relationship with Rita, his childhood nanny. Josh grew up believing that his teenage sexual escapades with Rita were an act of conquest, a badge of honor, and a testament to his virility. But his friends and siblings see things otherwise, and they eventually convince him that he was a victim of child molestation. This fuels a growing sense of anxiety over his sexuality, for which he holds his parents responsible, accusing his mother of "paying Rita to distract me with her tits" while she and Maura pursued their selfish interests.[23] Josh's trauma is compounded upon learning that the person who raised him as his father has come out as a woman, and the result is impotence during his first romantic encounter with Raquel. He believes his masculinity has been undermined by his parents and by Rita, whom he sees as their surrogate. Rita's subsequent suicide only makes matters worse, and her ghost haunts him at inopportune moments, including while masturbating. Rita appears on his bed and accuses Josh of dishonestly playing the victim:

RITA I can tell you what's wrong with you. You're other-justified.
JOSH What?
RITA Oh, you need to be liked, approved of. You know, real men grow out of that.
JOSH Just—

RITA Real men know how to be alone.
JOSH Fuck.
RITA With their own thoughts. Hey, you want some help with that?
JOSH No.
RITA Look at me. Look at me. Look at me.
JOSH No, I'm fine.
RITA You sure?
JOSH Yeah.
RITA Okay.

[Josh is now in bed, still trying to masturbate]

RITA [laughing] You're sure you don't want my help?
JOSH Fuck. Fuck![24]

Frustrated and flaccid, Josh admits defeat. He is unable to overcome the damage wrought on his psyche and his manhood, and, at the end of the fourth season, he joins a support group for sex addicts and accepts someone as his sponsor.

Unlike Alexander Portnoy, who came of age in the shadow of the Holocaust and the decimation of the proverbial old-world shtetl (a small, Jewish eastern European community), Josh never explicitly attributes his neuroses and sexual deviance to his Jewishness. He has an awareness of Jewish stereotypes, yet he treats them more as something to ponder rather than to take seriously. In one episode, he asks his sister Sarah if "Jews . . . [are] . . . more anxious than the average person, or do I just notice it 'cause I know more Jews?"[25] When we first see the three Pfefferman children together in the series pilot, they ridicule their Jewish lineage, discussing all the Jewish women their father (who had yet to come out to them) has dated:

ARI Haven't, like, the last six [women] been named Marcy?
JOSH Two.
SARAH Yeah, Goldberg, Kaplan.
JOSH Two Marcys.
SARAH Goldberg, Kaplan.
JOSH Marcy Fitzelfinerheinstein.
ARI Rubenstein, or what was that one? Ru-Rubishnowitzshitzlitz.
JOSH Ridinkle.
SARAH Marcy Kristallnacht [stressing the "ch"].
JOSH Belsenberger?
SARAH Kristallna-ch-t.[26]

Jewishness is reduced to a set of unintelligible family names, with allusions to Nazi Germany thrown in to underscore its presence yet irrelevance to three thirty-something adults in twenty-first-century Los Angeles. In another episode, when Maura picks up a fire iron intending to smash portions of the family home out of disgust with the unwanted, unappealing, and sterile renovations done in an earlier season, Josh sardonically quips that "we should call somebody... Jewish men don't do demo."[27] Maura calmly turns to her son and declares that "I am a Jewish woman Joshy, and Jewish women do whatever the fuck they want." Maura's response is a testament to her self-confidence and her right to live openly as a transgender woman after nearly seven decades of feeling unjustly trapped in a man's body. But it is also an ironic affirmation of the stereotypically brash Jewish mother. Paradoxically, Maura's appropriation of Jewish misogyny allows her to assert her womanhood. In making the case for the fluidity of gender boundaries, *Transparent*'s writers imply that Jewishness is inherited, reified, and perhaps indelible.

Josh also seems to be breaking with the Portnoy template in pursuing a stable, committed relationship with Rabbi Raquel. To be sure, when viewers first meet Josh, he is depicted as a serial seducer of the proverbial shiksa, a stereotyped rite of passage for the Jewish male, who, to quote Alexander Portnoy, does not "seem to stick my dick up these girls, as much as I stick it up their backgrounds—as though through fucking, I will discover America."[28] But Josh is not merely attracted to Raquel, a Jewish woman who has dedicated her life to the preservation and propagation of Judaism; he admits to being aroused by her Jewishness:

JOSH When you came in, I kind of thought you were gonna have the yarmulke on. Is that ridiculous?
RAQUEL It's not stapled. I don't staple it on my head.... I didn't want to throw you off with too much Jewiness on a first date.
JOSH I just want to sneak a peek. Just like a little bit. Can I? [He takes the yarmulke out of her bag and amorously examines it.] Oh, my God. Look at this. Okay, I'm gonna do this. [He puts it on her head.][29]

Raquel's protestations notwithstanding, Josh insists that her yarmulke is sexy. They proceed to kiss and attempt to make love. Unlike Portnoy, Josh is repulsed neither by Judaism nor the idea of conjugally binding himself to its continuity.[30]

Although Josh and Raquel's subsequent marital engagement ends in failure, ostensibly because of her miscarriage, Josh's history of promiscuity, and his seeming inability to function as her (much wanted) mature life partner, their Jewishness casts a shadow over their turbulent relationship. Raquel is certain that Josh's impotence during their first sexual encounter is her fault and not the product of Josh's confessed transphobia. "I have a fear," she tells him, "my mentor talked about how sometimes rabbis, anybody, like, priests, people just project their—all their God shit on you. So I'm just like a walking yarmulke; you can't ever get a hard-on in front of me."[31] Such fears are later put to rest, and Raquel's accidental pregnancy is met with joy. But the specter of the Holocaust and the uncertainty of Jewish continuity is manifest as the relationship fizzles out. Without permission (and to Raquel's horror), Shelly announces Josh's impending fatherhood while dancing the hora at Sarah's wedding. It is a scene that is fraught with symbolism: the Pfefferman wedding horah is interspersed with a flashback to a raucous dance party in Weimar Germany, where Maura Pfefferman's aunt Gittel is shown frolicking, celebrating life and blissfully oblivious to the violent fate awaiting her.[32] And just as Jewish continuity was snuffed out in Nazi Germany, Josh will have no Jewish offspring in America; Raquel miscarries and leaves Josh, who announces the sad news at the Yom Kippur break-the-fast dinner. Shelly immediately bursts into tears and blames herself, because "I was drunk at the wedding, and I told everybody to celebrate it; I brought out the evil eye. I killed the baby."[33] Without having eaten, Josh abandons the gathering and goes grocery shopping, where he gives into temptation and breaks his fast by gorging on a package of ham before reaching the cash register. Josh may not be a devout Jew, and his engagement with Judaic ritual is perfunctory at best, but his consumption of non-kosher food following Yom Kippur reflects a yearning to escape his life, which he now suspects is deeply intertwined with his Jewish ancestry, family, and sexuality.

Josh's inability to sire a Jewish child is underscored with brutal irony because he had in fact inadvertently fathered a baby with Rita. After an adolescent Josh had impregnated his nanny, the Pfefferman parents, now aware of their son's illicit affair, ensured that the delivery occurred in secret and that the baby was put up for adoption. Josh only learns of his son, Colton, at the end of the first season while visiting Rita from Kansas, where Colton lives with his adopted family. Colton is in many respects the stereotypical goy (non-Jew, generally White Christian) of Jewish humor, and he is everything Josh is not. He is muscular with chiseled features, well-mannered and soft-spoken, successful with women yet modest about his conquests, firmly in control of his life, and proud of his Christian piety. "Oh, my god, are you sure that he's one of us? He doesn't look like one of us," asks one of Shelly's relatives during Sarah's wedding. "We had the DNA test; he's Joshy's," insists Shelly, adding that his "build comes from Rita's father; he was a Norwegian shot-putter, apparently."[34]

If the extended Pfefferman clan views Colton as an alien in their midst, the young female musicians whom Josh manages see things differently. Salivating over his masculinity, they admire his beauty during a pool party where Josh is more than happy to assert his pride in having fathered this brawny shirtless man on display, whose prominent crucifix pendant accentuates his otherness:

MUSICIAN 1 Damn!
MUSICIAN 2 Look at him, yeah!
MUSICIAN 1 Your son is built! Yes!
JOSH Yeah, that's my seed! That's a good wholesome kid over there.

MUSICIAN 1 Hello!
JOSH That is grade-A grass-fed beef.³⁵

Where Alexander Portnoy envies his goyish counterparts because they are free of the anxiety, alienation, and sexual dysfunction that plagues the diasporic Jew, Josh sees his goyish son as living proof that the negative attributes of his inherited Jewishness are not necessarily transmittable, and, it should follow, not indelible.

But to be like the goys, one must also become a Christian, and Colton comes to the Pfeffermans with his Christianity. When he sits down to eat dinner with the family for the first time, a distraught Colton says, "I usually do a prayer before every meal." Josh brushes this off, insisting (rather ironically for a man dating a rabbi) that "we're Jewish man, we don't do that." Colton is their guest, however, and he is granted permission to say, "Thank you, Heavenly Father, for this food, this great day, these lovely people. In Jesus's name we pray." Josh remains indifferent, and Maura responds to the invocation of Jesus with an "oy gevalt" ("good grief" in Yiddish),³⁶ but this is just the beginning, and Josh's budding relationship with Colton—who later asks if he can call him dad—ultimately leads him to Christianity's doorstep. Josh sees Colton as his progeny, and, accordingly, a Jew by descent, an idea that is shattered when Colton's family comes to visit. When Colton's father, who is a pastor with a mid-sized congregation and a weekly TV show, learns that Raquel is a rabbi, he steers the conversation to Judaism, amicably but with a touch of Christian conceit:

COLTON Raquel's a rabbi.
RAQUEL Yes, but I do not have a TV show.
COLTON'S FATHER You know, we love the Jewish people. Have the utmost respect for them.
RACHEL Good [followed by a painful silence].
COLTON'S FATHER Jesus was a Jew.
RACHEL He was.
MAURA We're Jewish.
COLTON'S MOTHER Oh. All of you are Jewish?
JOSH Yeah.
COLTON'S MOTHER Oh.
JOSH Colton's Jewish. Well, some Reform people would say he's Jewish.
COLTON'S MOTHER [Laughing hysterically] No, he isn't, no. You're not, sweetie. Uh no, you're not.
COLTON [Interrupting] Uh, I didn't even, I haven't even showed you my room yet.³⁷

And after learning Raquel is pregnant with Josh's child, the pastor and his wife tell Colton that he cannot stay in Los Angeles living in a disorderly (and decidedly un-Christian) household consisting of an unwed pregnant rabbi and a transgender matriarch. Colton must immediately return to Kansas with them, lest he be conscripted into the Pfeffermans' deviance, which apparently goes hand in hand with their Jewishness.

But Colton's departure does not lead to a severance between him and Josh, and Josh is drawn deeper into Colton's Christian world when he travels to Kansas to deliver some of Rita's ashes to him. Colton is now a budding preacher and, attending one of his services, a forlorn Josh is swayed by Colton's earnest message of hope, forgiveness, and renewal:

> Jesus watches over us. His Holy Father created the heavens and the Earth and all of mankind in His own image. And that's why He cares about us even when we've lost our way. And the way we find our way back to Him, no matter how far we've strayed, is to come to the Lord in prayer.... Heavenly Father, we ask You to lift up all of God's children and guide us in Your ways. I wanna take this moment right now to ask if there's anyone out here today who might not be saved yet but wants to know Jesus as their personal Lord and Savior.... Would anyone here like to renounce Satan and accept Jesus into their heart? Who wants to have their burdens lifted from them? Who wants to be free?[38]

With the congregants cheering him on, Josh rises and approaches the pulpit, and, when Colton asks if "you accept Jesus as your Lord and Savior," Josh responds affirmatively. Josh comes away from church feeling reinvigorated. With his anxiety assuaged and his depression alleviated, he decides to buy a house and move to Colton's bucolic town. But Colton does not want Josh to stay in Kansas, and he asks him to leave. He understands that Josh has not sincerely embraced Christianity—that his renunciation of Satan and acceptance of Jesus was an impulsive move to ease his conscience and sense of guilt over his failed relationships and Rita's death and that the road to salvation requires far more commitment and faith than merely getting up in church and assenting to the words of a cleric. Although Josh is heartbroken, he accepts Colton's reasoning, and, accompanied by Ari who flew to Kansas to "rescue" her brother, he returns to Los Angeles and the misery he left behind.

Josh's relationship with Colton may be viewed through the same lens as his relationship with Raquel. They are both imagined opportunities to escape from his burdens, to reverse the anguish of his upbringing, raised by an oppressive Jewish mother, a father whose transition initially freaks him out, and a surrogate parent who sexually violated him. As the first three seasons progress and he endures failure after failure, his mental health deteriorates. When Shelly moves in with him at the start of the fourth season, he is completely reduced to the stereotyped smothered Jewish boy, a captive in a diasporic prison with his mother as his judge and jailer, who will never abandon her precious "Oy-ya-yoy... squidgy pudgy boy."[39] While Ari jokingly wonders if "you two are spooning" in bed at night,[40] Josh is not laughing because he is following in the footsteps of Alexander Portnoy, who found himself "living in the middle of a Jewish joke....

only it ain't no joke!"[41] And much like the narrative of *Portnoy's Complaint*, the climax of Josh's sickly diasporic oppression does not transpire in the Diaspora, but in Israel, the Jewish homeland that is supposed to heal through love of land, militarism, hypermasculinity, and Judaic pride.[42]

Since the emergence of Zionism and the subsequent birth of Israel, the envisioned Jewish state was intended to be the negation of the Diaspora, an opportunity to overturn the Jewish exilic condition that had rendered a (primarily European) stateless Jewish community weak, cowardly, sickly, alienated, and, in the end, exterminated. Although American Jews were spared the decimation unleashed against their European cousins and have flourished in a land of immigrants, they remain haunted by a collective memory of expulsion, pogroms, and Holocaust. Accordingly, Zion has persisted as an alternative in Jewish consciousness, an imagined path to power, freedom, and communal health that is routinely juxtaposed to American Jewry's alleged egotism, selfishness, materialism, and false sense of security in a land of Christian dominance. Landing in Israel, Alexander Portnoy is captivated by the sheer novelty he encounters: "I am in a Jewish country, everybody is Jewish..... Jewish graffiti! The *flag* is Jewish.... Faces like my own face! ... the faces of Eastern Europe, but only a stone's throw from Africa! Hey, here *we're* the WASPs!"[43] For Portnoy, the Israelis are living proof that his inherited Jewish affliction may be curable, and he sets out to cure himself by basking in this sea of Jews and by making love to a healthy, emancipated Israeli woman. Unlike Portnoy, Josh Pfefferman does not consciously travel to Israel on a journey of liberation; he is asked to come (along with his family, including his mother) by Maura to meet their extended Israeli family. But the Israelis he meets play a similar role to those in *Portnoy's Complaint*: they are a mirror through which he encounters and must reckon with the stubborn tenacity of his Jewish exilic condition.

During the Pfeffermans' first meal with their Israeli relatives, Josh is simultaneously marked as a sexual predator, a Jewish child, and a member of a family with deviant gender practices:

SARAH Don't hit on your aunt.
JOSH You don't hit on our aunt.
SARAH No, you don't hit on our aunt.
JOSH Nobody can have sex with any of those people here. Let's just, like, lay down the rules.
SARAH [referring to Josh] He gets into everything, so don't go too close—
JOSH Mom and I are [living] on the east side in Silver Lake right now.
ISRAELI MAN Oh, you live with your mom? That's good. Good boy.
SHELLY He is a good boy.
ARI I must be the bad girl.
ISRAELI MAN They say in Hebrew, you only have one mother.
SARAH We have more than one.

JOSH We kind of have more than one.
SARAH We have two.
ISRAELI MAN Oh, no. Oh, yeah, that's right. I'm so sorry.⁴⁴

Notwithstanding the Israelis' apparent obliviousness to the existence of queer families, the extended Pfefferman clan laughs at this amusing banter in what turns out to be an unexpected and, at least initially, delightful family reunion. And the L.A. Pfeffermans accept their hosts' offer to go on a private bus tour, complete with guides and security, of the Jewish people's ancestral homeland.

Where Alexander Portnoy believes that sexual intercourse with an Israeli woman is his path to liberation, Josh Pfefferman seeks freedom from imagined effeminacy and transphobia by learning how to fire a gun from Nitzan, their brawny security guard. At first he approaches the proffered weapon with curiosity, awe, and self-effacing humor:

JOSH Is the gun loaded?
NITZAN Of course, it's loaded. It's a gun.
JOSH I just didn't know if it was just to scare people off, or, I don't know, I don't know what—
NITZAN It is to scare people off.
JOSH Is that semiautomatic? What is it? Automatic? What's—what's the situation?
NITZAN It's called a Baby Desert Eagle.
JOSH Oh, Baby Desert Eagle.
NITZAN You know this kind?
JOSH No, I don't know that one, but, uh, the Toddler Desert Eagle is, um, I know that one. That one's a that's a that's a good one. It's a little bigger.

Nitzan casually removes the gun from its holster, twirls it, and offers it to Josh. After staring at it intensely, Josh refuses to take it. Nitzan continues to ponder Josh and mockingly asks, "So you're not packing heat?" And, as if underscoring the tremendous cultural gulf between the weak diasporic Jew and the liberated, martial, empowered Israeli, Josh quips that "my weapon of choice is self-loathing." But Josh's curiosity gets the better of him, and, after observing that "everybody seems real patriotic, and you got a whole country of people who know how to shoot a gun," Nitzan instructs the bus driver to pull over, and announces, "We need to stop for five minutes . . . Joshy needs to do pee pee."⁴⁵

And just as Alexander Portnoy's quest to transcend his oppression results in impotence and humiliation in front of an Israeli soldier he tries to seduce, Josh's encounter with a deadly weapon ends in disaster, in a scene replete with sexual overtones, familial strife, and humor. Leading Josh off the road into the desert, Nitzan takes out his gun and fires it into the rocky landscape. Startled, Josh leaps into the air, rams his fingers into his ears, and asks why there are "no earmuffs." Nitzan retorts, "Dude, you have too much estrogen around you." Handing Josh the gun, Nitzan asks, "What hand [do] you masturbate with?" Somewhat sheepishly, Josh says with both. "Okay," replies Nitzan, "hold it with both." Taking the gun, Josh's confidence is restored. "Fuckin' A," he exclaims with enthusiasm. "Let's shoot a gun . . . Let's do this shit!" Josh successfully fires the weapon, but he is momentarily dazed, and, disoriented with ringing ears, he turns around, gun still in hand, and aims it right at his mother. Shelly erupts with terror: "You pointed the gun right at me!" she cries out. "You tried to kill me!" Meanwhile, the normally unflappable Nitzan explodes in disbelief and tells Josh, "You don't do a pirouette with a gun like this; what are you, crazy?" Chaos ensues, and the Pfeffermans descend into a family squabble, with Shelly insisting that her kids hate her, that she only wants them to be happy, that she has in fact ruined them and now they want to kill her, and that being a mother is nothing but a burden and a source of anxiety.[46]

Although Josh's failure to negate his diasporic Jewishness nearly ends in accidental matricide, *Transparent*'s narrative subsequently shifts from the Portnoy template, and, unlike Roth's protagonist, Josh returns to America having healed in part. After the shooting, Shelly reveals that she was molested by a teacher as a child, and keeping it a secret for decades severely damaged her ability to function—as a wife, a mother, and a woman. This revelation forces her family to start taking her problems seriously. Josh breaks down but comes to accept that she needs him as much as he needs her and that he will always be there for her. The mother-child bond is restored in a touching scene at the Dead Sea, where Josh carries a petrified Shelly into the water and allows her to lie, nestled in his arms, floating in the curative waters.[47] And in the season finale, Josh is shown entering the airport arm-in-arm with Shelly.[48] Israel has restored their relationship and has given Josh clarity; he goes home with new insight into his issues, and, feeling a glimmer of hope, he joins a sex addict support group, prepared to face up to his demons. Israel may not have fixed Josh, but it set him on a path toward reparation. His turbulent confrontation with his mother and its aftermath were instrumental in making this happen.

Although Shelly and Josh Pfefferman are the latest in a long list of Jewish mother-son pairings in American culture, they transcend the caricatured portrayals of their predecessors. To be sure, their individual character traits and their relationship exude the all-too-familiar stereotypes. Given *Transparent*'s progressive focus, it may seem odd that its writers have made such frequent use of a Jewish cultural trope whose origins lie in an era known for its heteronormativity and sexism. But such archetypes can play a constructive role beyond the elicitation of laughter. Their troubled relationship helps bring the members of a disoriented and often ungrounded family closer together. This is made most apparent during their trip to Israel, where Josh's yearning to negate his onerous heritage triggers a potentially fatal accident and then a quarrel, one that forces the Pfeffermans to confront their problems. The often-oppressive Jewish mother-son pairing is ironically the catalyst for personal growth and familial bonding. The Pfeffermans—all of them—are navigating their way through a confusing, frightening, yet exciting twenty-first-century, a time and place where inherited axioms of gender, sexuality, and religion no longer hold true, but one in which the ghosts of their Jewish past and the burdens they bequeathed are still present.

Notes

1 *Transparent*, Season 1, Episode 8, "Symbolic Exemplar," Amazon Prime Video, September 26, 2014.
2 Sara Ivry, "*Transparent*," *Tablet*, Sara Ivry, "*Transparent* is the Most Jewish TV Show in a While—and it's Great," *Tablet Magazine*, October 1, 2014, https://www.tabletmag.com/sections/news/articles/transparent-is-the-most-jewish-tv-show-in-a-while-and-its-great
3 Mike Nichols and Elaine May, "Mother and Son," Track 4 on *An Evening with Mike Nichols and Elaine May*, Mercury, MG-20865, 1964, LP; Bruce Jay Friedman, *A Mother's Kisses* (New York: Simon and Schuster, 1964); Dan Greenburg, *How to Be a Jewish Mother: A Very Lovely Training Manual* (Los Angeles: Price, Stern, Sloan, 1964); Philip Roth, *Portnoy's Complaint* (New York: Vintage International, 1994).
4 "Oedipus Wrecks," directed by Woody Allen, in *New York Stories* (1989). Allen, Woody, director, "Odeipus Wrecks," in *New York Stories*. Touchstone Pictures, 1989.
5 Joyce Antler, *You Never Call! You Never Write! A History of the Jewish Mother* (New York: Oxford University Press, 2007), 5.
6 Antler, *You Never Call!*, 252.
7 Antler, *You Never Call!*, 10.
8 *Transparent*, "The Letting Go." The use of "should" (in the sense of "ought to") in an ironic tone is a direct borrowing from Yiddish. See Lillian Mermin Feinsilver, *The Taste of Yiddish* (South Brunswick, NJ: Thomas Yoseloff, 1970), 338–339.
9 Jeffrey Shandler, *Adventures in Yiddishland: Postvernacular Language and Culture* (Berkeley: University of California Press, 2006), 195.
10 *Transparent*, Season 3, Episode 10, "Exciting and New,Amazon Prime Video, September 23, 2016.
11 *Transparent*, Season 4, Episode 3, "Pinkwashing Machine," Amazon Prime Video, September 21, 2017.
12 Roth, *Portnoy's Complaint*, 119. Emphasis in the original.
13 *Transparent*, Season 1, Episode 5, "Wedge," Amazon Prime Video, September 26, 2014.
14 *Transparent*, Season 1, Episode 9, "Looking Up," Amazon Prime Video, September 26, 2014.
15 *Transparent*, Season 2, Episode 1, "Kina Hora," Amazon Prime Video, November 30, 2015.
16 *Transparent*, Season 4, Episode 1, "Standing Order," Amazon Prime Video, September 21, 2017.
17 See Sander Gilman, *The Jew's Body* (New York: Routledge, 1991); Bryan Cheyette and Laura Marcus, eds., *Modernity, Culture and "the Jew"* (Stanford: Stanford University Press, 1998); Norman L. Kleeblatt, ed., *Too Jewish? Challenging Traditional Jewish Identities* (New Brunswick, NJ: Rutgers University Press, 1996).

18. Gilman, *The Jew's Body*, 80.
19. Richie Robertson, "Historicizing Weininger: The Nineteenth-Century German Image of the Feminized Jew," in Cheyette and Marcus, *Modernity*, 32.
20. See "The Mouse That Never Roars: Jewish Masculinity on American Television," in Kleeblatt, *Too Jewish?*, 23–39; Susan A. Glenn, "The Vogue of Jewish Self-Hatred in Post: World War II America," *Jewish Social Studies* 12, no. 3 (Spring-Summer, 2006): 95–136.
21. Roth, *Portnoy's Complaint*, 78.
22. *The Big Bang Theory* ran on CBS from 2007 to 2019.
23. *Transparent*, Season 1, Episode 5, "Wedge," Amazon Prime Video, September 26, 2014.
24. *Transparent*, Season 4, Episode 3, "Cool Guy," Amazon Prime Video, September 21, 2017.
25. *Transparent*, Season 1, Episode 5, "Wedge," Amazon Prime Video, September 26, 2014.
26. *Transparent*, Season 1, Episode 1, "Pilot," Amazon Prime Video, February 6, 2014.
27. *Transparent*, Season 3, Episode 5, "Oh Holy Night," Amazon Prime Video, September 23, 2016.
28. Roth, *Portnoy's Complaint*, 235.
29. *Transparent*, Season 1, Episode 8, "Symbolic Exemplar," Amazon Prime Video, September 26, 2014.
30. Since 2018, there has been an explosive debate surrounding "Jewish continuity" and the possible misuse of data collected to police communal boundaries. "Most troubling about the data-driven mode of Jewish continuity conversations," write Kate Rosenblatt, Lila Corwin Berman, and Ronit Stahl, "are its patriarchal, misogynistic, and anachronist assumptions about what is good for the Jews. We learn that single women, queer people, unwed parents, and childless individuals or couples are all problems. And we learn that the Jewish community, should it want to survive, must step into the role of calling out and regulating those problems." See Kate Rosenblatt, Lila Corwin Berman, and Ronit Stahl, "How Jewish Academia Created A #MeToo Disaster," *Forward*, July 19, 2018, https://forward.com/opinion/406240/how-jewish-academia-created-a-metoo-disaster/. Although the specter of Jewish continuity looms over Alexander Portnoy and Josh Pfefferman, each responds to it differently. Whereas Portnoy avowedly rejects Jewish continuity (yet ironically demands that his non-Jewish girlfriend converts), Josh embraces it through his relationships with Rabbi Raquel and (perhaps more notably given that he is a devout Christian and the child of gentile mother) his son Colton.
31. *Transparent*, "Symbolic Exemplar."
32. *Transparent*, Season 2, Episode 1, "Kina Hora," Amazon Prime Video, November 30, 2015.
33. *Transparent*, Season 2, Episode 7, "The Book of Life," Amazon Prime Video, December 11, 2015.
34. *Transparent*, Season 2, Episode 1, "Kina Hora," Amazon Prime Video, November 30, 2015.
35. *Transparent*, Season 2, Episode 2, "Flicky-Flicky Thump-Thump," Amazon Prime Video, December 11, 2015.
36. *Transparent*, Season 1, Episode 10, "Why Do We Cover the Mirrors?" Amazon Prime Video, September 26, 2014.
37. *Transparent*, Season 2, Episode 5, "Mee-Maw," Amazon Prime Video, December 11, 2015.

38 *Transparent*, Season 3, Episode 7, "Life Sucks and Then You Die," Amazon Prime Video, September 23, 2016.
39 *Transparent*, "Standing Order."
40 *Transparent*, "Standing Order."
41 Roth, *Portnoy's Complaint*, 37. Emphasis in the original.
42 This essay does not address *Transparent*'s musicale finale (nominally known as season 5), which aired on September 27, 2019, as there were no significant developments in Josh and Shelly's relationship and their personal growth.
43 Roth, *Portnoy's Complaint*, 253–254. Emphasis in the original.
44 *Transparent*, Season 4, Episode 6, "I Never Promised You a Promised Land," Amazon Prime Video, September 21, 2017.
45 *Transparent*, Season 4, Episode 8, "Desert Eagle," Amazon Prime Video, September 21, 2017.
46 *Transparent*, Season 4, Episode 8, "Desert Eagle," Amazon Prime Video, September 21, 2017.
47 *Transparent*, Season 4, Episode 9, "They Is on the Way," Amazon Prime Video, September 21, 2017.
48 *Transparent*, Season 4, Episode 10, "House Call," Amazon Prime Video, September 21, 2017.

8

The Gentile, the Demonic, and Collapsing Binaries in *Transparent*

SHAUL MAGID

Transparent was one of the most celebrated, and brilliant, television series in recent times. It was also arguably the most "Jewish" show ever made for television. Jews, and Jewishness, have always been ubiquitous in American film and later television, beginning with Al Jolson in *The Jazz Singer*, the first talkie that was produced in 1927. Jonathan Freedman in his *Klezmer America* offers a brief analysis of three film versions of *The Jazz Singer*, the last starring Neil Diamond in 1980, as refracting the experience of Jews in America, from the tension of adaptation to the celebration of assimilation, from the Lower East Side to Los Angeles.[1]

Transparent picks up where Neil Diamond's move to Los Angeles in *The Jazz Singer* left off thirty-five years earlier. In the Diamond version of *The Jazz Singer*, the protagonist moves to Los Angeles to further his musical career, but it took a while for the city to find its Jewish sea legs. Much of the subsequent American Jewish television still centered on the East Coast, perhaps the latest iteration being the short-lived antics of Ilana and Abby in *Broad City*. Yet establishing *The Jazz Singer* in Los Angeles was in some way a marker of the transition of Jewish life from the Northeast to the West Coast. The Pfeffermans represent another iteration of that transition.

Other Jewish shows from television's early period include *The Goldbergs* (1949–1957), *Bridget Loves Bernie* (the first television show about intermarriage, 1972–1973), and, of course, *Seinfeld* (1989–1998) and *Curb Your Enthusiasm* (2000 to the present). All but *Curb Your Enthusiasm* took place in New York. I have excluded shows or films about the Holocaust, which deserve separate analysis (although, interestingly, the only sitcom about the Holocaust was *Hogans Heroes*, which ran from 1965 to 1971 and was not about Jews at all). Spielberg's film *The Fabelmans* (2022) also takes place on the West Coast.

In most cases, the depiction of Jews and Jewish families in American film and television is about how America views the Jews or how Jews try to struggle with their separate identity in a country inviting them to assimilate (this is captured with some complexity in the original *The Jazz Singer* and *The Goldbergs*).[2] These Jewish shows, along with Woody Allen's movies, offer the viewer a window into the American Jew and their idiosyncrasies, neuroses, and attempts to become an integral part of, and yet still distinct from, American society. The Jewish shows in television and film are largely about the Jewish foibles, and successes, of becoming American while remaining Jewish. They teach America about its Jews.[3] The innovation *Transparent* brings to the table is the lens of the "trans"—a category of viewing the Jew in transition and how the Jew views the Other through those transitions, as well as how the Jew engages in various acts of "transitioning" though acculturation, assimilation, and self-loathing. It addresses the renewed acquisition of Jewishness that has also been transformed into something beyond any recognized normative framework. In that sense, Los Angeles is the perfect venue for the show, a city of cultural transitioning that offers the Jew a different kind of experience than the East Coast, where Jewishness remains tethered in some ways to normative tradition, traditional or liberal, even as it may have rejected both.[4]

As I understand it, *Transparent*, in its post-assimilationist narcissism, is brilliantly doing something different from its predecessors. It is not a depiction of how the world views the Jews but how a Jewish family views the world, and in doing so, it suggests that full assimilation has not, perhaps cannot, uproot the tribalism deeply embedded in the fully integrated Jewish psyche. The Pfefferman family is Jewish not because they *want* to be, but because they cannot free themselves of the integrated/marginal status they inherited—a status that emerges in various guises such as affluent and Jewish West Los Angeles, the Holocaust, sexual identity, and Israel. Everything about them is Jewish, even when they are trying not to be—perhaps more so when they are not trying to be. This in fact lies at the very heart of their narcissism, partly affirming Freud's assessment of Jews in *Moses and Monotheism*, which Robert Paul, interpreting Freud, writes "is a collective obsessional neurosis, namely Judaism itself."[5] That such an assimilated tribalism does not produce a healthy solidarity is not surprising. In fact, its vacuity tortures its subjects. And it is here where religion enters, both Christianity and Judaism because the goy is, for the American Jew, Christianity. Formally the term means non-Jew, or gentile, but in American society it is also a label for Christian, which is the dominant culture. From the Jewish gaze of the Pfeffermans, Christianity is silly in its simplicity, but Judaism becomes neurotic and, as I read it, ultimately demonic in its complexity. Judaism is the Jewishness the Pfeffermans never really try. This chapter, therefore, focuses on the depiction of the demonic in *Transparent*—both how the Jews take on demonic valences and how the non-Jew, the goy, is demonized as well. The chapter also tackles how the goy serves as a lens through which the emasculated Jews of *Transparent* deconstruct and then reinvent themselves again and again.

As the show unfolds, each of the Pfeffermans tries their hand at Judaism, and in each case, they seem to screw it up or Judaism itself seems to reject them. Sarah "finds religion," and her request for synagogue board membership is denied; Josh dates the rabbi, and she leaves him; Shelly, Maura's estranged wife, hooks up with Buzz, the synagogue macher, who turns out to be a crook.

Because I argue that *Transparent* is really about how the Pfeffermans as Jews see the gentile world, I offer a reading of the role of the non-Jew in this nationally acclaimed series, specifically the Christian, but also the Palestinian, the gentile who appears in season 4 and in some way plays the role of the Jew; the Palestinian is also the only gentile who evokes sympathy from any of the Pfeffermans, that is, Ari, who finally finds the kinship that has alluded her. There are essentially four prominent non-Jewish personalities at play in the first three seasons of *Transparent*: Colton, Josh's long-lost son raised by evangelicals brings Christianity—and not just the non-Jew but real, demonstrable, Christianity—into the belly of the assimilated Jewish family beast by saying grace at a Pfefferman meal, ending the first season with Maura exasperatingly uttering, "Oy" (which perhaps presents a double entendre with "goy"); Tammy, Sarah's lover, who gets jilted by her at their wedding and returns to hold up a mirror to the Pfeffermans then, in a drunken tirade (stereotypical gentile behavior from the Jewish gaze), justifiably calls them "monsters"; Len, the hapless gentile ex-husband of Sarah, whom the audience does not actually know is not Jewish until the third season when he defines himself as "Jewcurious" (itself a take on the more well-known term "bicurious") at a Havdalah ceremony that Sarah organizes at the synagogue;[6] and finally, Leslie, Ari's lover and gender studies professor, has a breakout moment when she gets into a fight with synagogue volunteers after refusing to drink coffee manufactured in Israel, representing the intersectionality of gender politics and the Boycott Divest Sanction (BDS) movement. Leslie then walks outside and falls into a construction pit, injuring her leg, an apt biblical coda for messing with Israel, the sacred god of American Jewry. The pit, perhaps gesturing to the gaping hole that swallows the biblical Korah, teaches Leslie a lesson: be careful when you criticize Israel. But Leslie is a tough second-wave lesbian feminist; she does not give up easily.

She leaves Ari and then publishes a humiliating poem about her in *The New Yorker*. Right after Ari reads it, she decides to go with Maura to Israel. Her lesbian, gender-critical world has rejected her. She finds her Jewish soul.

Each of the non-Jewish characters in *Transparent* embodies a certain non-Jewish stereotype in the Jewish imagination. Colton is buff and sincere, Tammy is a thin, blonde, attractive woman (in profane Yiddish parlance, a classic *shiksa*), Len is a Jew-passer, a gentile who passes as a Jew, and Leslie is a classic, "goyish" radical atheist.

Colton's Christianity looms large in at least two seasons—he becomes the embodiment of the goy from the assimilated American Jewish gaze, square-jawed with a romanesque body always adorned with a cross, a gentle soul whose pollyannaish ways confuse the neurotic and self-absorbed Pfeffermans. Colton is the only one, except perhaps for the male cantor Duvid (a Jew of color and the only non-Ashkenazi character seen in an L.A. community full of Mizrahi Jews) who arrives late in the third season, for whom religion is really about belief. Apart from Rabbi Raquel (whose Jewish devotion becomes more complicated as the show progresses), Duvid is seemingly the only uncomplicated Jew in the show whose faith is never really tested: he speaks with his daughter in biblical terms and not in modern Hebrew, and his naivete seems boundless; it is that sincerity that underscores the Jewish sense of neurosis that dominates the Pfeffermans' world. Duvid is the Jewish Colton.

Colton is conspicuous even in his absence—from the moment he rejects the Pfeffermans' home to return to his Midwestern evangelical family in the second season, to his initial embrace and subsequent rejection of Josh's facile conversion to Christianity in the third season, to throwing Josh back into the Jewishness he cannot fully enter and yet cannot seem to escape. Josh tried to find love in Christianity, but the church refused to solve his Jewish problem of self-loathing. Josh's Jewishness made him anathema to Christianity. The gentile cannot stand such Jewish neurosis, even under the guise of sincerity—or Christianity.

In almost every case that a gentile character enters into the assimilated Jewish orbit of the Pfefferman family, they are expelled, and when the Pfeffermans enter into the gentile world, they are rejected. Even Vicki, Maura's devoted lover, is shut out when she refuses to support Maura's childhood hatred of her sister. Almost all the Pfeffermans' partners are non-Jews except for Shelly, Maura's wife; Syd Feldman, who dates Ari for a short time; and Rabbi Raquel, who dates Josh, making for not such an atypical American Jewish family. Each one becomes entrapped in the pretense of acceptance into the family only to be irrationally spun out of its orbit (the case of Sarah and Tammy is the most obvious). This is all counterintuitive to what we might think of this assimilated Jewish experiment. Is it not really all about Jewish integration?

Sarah's non-Jewish husband, Len, is tossed aside only to reenter her sexual orbit through the three-way erotic escapades that include Lila, a young Israeli woman they meet in Los Angeles and whose neurotic Israeli mother we meet in a West Bank settlement when the family travels to Israel. The Pfeffermans have no problem intermarrying in principle—why should they—they just cannot seem to pull it off. The critique here is not about assimilation and/as erasure but assimilation's failure in its success, not inspiring a return to any recognizable identity, except perhaps in Ari's discovery of the family secret in the Holocaust where her Great-Uncle Gershon is murdered not because he is a Jew but because he is trans. Rather, I would argue they fail in that they are consistently unable to take the gentile and his or her world seriously. And why should they? It is an interesting instantiation of a minority that acts like a majority, a piercing comment on the demise of American Jewish victimhood. Now the Jews are only victims to themselves.

In most cases, the gentile characters' reactions to their rejection by the Jews have a point. Colton is right about Josh's feigned conversion, Tammy is right about the Pfeffermans' monstrous tendencies, and Leslie is right when she challenges the liberal Jewish reflexive defense of Israel by people ignorant of the conflict. The gentiles continually show the Pfeffermans their Jewishness is facile, in all its inconsistencies. But it is Jewish nonetheless.

The problem with the vapid, post-assimilated Jewishness in this series is that the Jew begins to consume herself. And it is here where religion plays a crucial role and where *Transparent* makes its most lasting contribution, at least as far as Judaism goes. The demonic that threatens the Jew in *Transparent* is not the gentile (or the Nazis in the Holocaust memory sequence). The gentile is mostly a mere plaything, discarded when the Pfefferman in question loses interest. The demonic enters as Judaism itself. First, Buzz, whose gentle and generous demeanor and leadership role in the synagogue yields a much more pernicious and dark character, a deceitful liar and thief who takes advantage of the hapless Shelly. The demonic really emerges more prominently in Sarah, who slowly morphs into a devilish figure, a Los Angeles Lilith, over the course of season 3. One can see it in her smile, in her laugh, and in the darkness around her eyes. She can only be sexually satisfied through domination. And it is in this transformation to demon that she discovers her Judaism, only to ruin the lives of her benefactors, Rabbi Raquel and Cantor Duvid.

Sarah serves largely as the series' anti-Christ, convincing Rabbi Raquel to assuage her loneliness by seducing the hapless, eligible Duvid, an act that contributes to the very rupture of Raquel's faith already damaged by her failed relationship with Sarah's brother, Josh. And it is not insignificant that the conversation between Sarah and Raquel about seducing Duvid happens on synagogue grounds while preparing for a Jewish ritual event. But in a way, Sarah's demonic nature is an iteration of the entire Pfefferman family; it is only Sarah who succumbs fully to the mixture of narcissism and religion that attacks the faith they have all abandoned. Her application to become a member of the synagogue is rejected by the synagogue board because she has "dark energy," and then she proceeds to unleash it on one of the only anchors of identity assimilated Jews have left—the suburban synagogue and its female rabbi. Even though many, perhaps most, twenty-first-century American Jews are not members of a synagogue, the synagogue they do not attend still serves for many as an identity marker, even—or precisely—in their absence.

So why should we care about this sometimes obnoxious and often exasperating depiction of the American Jew? This multilayered and multimedia text only *seems* to understand Judaism in a superficial way. It may actually understand the role of Judaism for assimilated American Jews in a much more nuanced way than we first think. For most characters, the Jewish textual tradition is obsolete (books are rarely opened), even for the rabbi and cantor. Israel is hardly mentioned except in a facile manner (until season 4 where it takes center stage), and the Holocaust is ubiquitous as a memory in Ari's imagination, mostly about gender and sexual variance. *Transparent* portrays a Jewishness, and Judaism, ostensibly open to the world but in reality, the Pfeffermans' Judaism functions almost like a secular enclave that has no real understanding, or justification, of its existence. The Pfeffermans' collective life teeters on the edge of society in its focus on transgender identity but is wholly conventional in its self-understanding, or lack thereof, of its Jewishness.

What comes through is that as liberal and assimilated as Jews have become in America, they still cannot bear the intrusion of the gentile. Colton still evokes an "oy," and Tammy exits as a drunken goy. Leslie turns into an enemy because she is progressive and anti-Israel. She then turns into a real enemy in her humiliating portrait of Ari in a *New Yorker* poem. As Jewish viewers, we look at all this antipathy with horror, yet this is the mirror its creators have constructed for us to view ourselves. The Pfeffermans are not the typical American Jewish family, but they are not too far from it, particularly when we see how they are viewed by their Israeli family in season 4. As Sarah notes of their newfound family in Israel (the children of Maura's long-lost father who abandoned the family) at a communal dinner overlooking the Mediterranean Sea, "They're just like us—only better." But are they? We will see.

As we move to the fourth season, the bridge figure in the entire series becomes Ari, who holds the family's Holocaust secret and seems to understand the intersectionality of gender and religious politics. She wants her Jewishness, not to destroy Judaism like her sister, Sarah, or to love it like Raquel, but mostly to understand her sexuality. In her lives, the only hope is that post-assimilated Jewishness can be more than neurotic, affluent, narcissistic, bourgeois enclavism. She is the last hope that Freud was wrong about the Jews. Tammy picks up the pieces of her broken soul after Sarah breaks her heart and then laughs when Sarah tries out her Judaism by asking for forgiveness through confession before Yom Kippur. The gentile shows the Jew that Judaism cannot be that easy. Colton preaches salvation in Jesus, and Leslie sees the Jews as fake progressives stuck in an Israel mania they cannot think themselves out of. Ari knows Leslie is probably right, but she has to see for herself.

Unbeknownst to the writers, season 4 turned out to be the penultimate season. If the first three seasons played with the binary of Jew and gentile, and problematized the binary of male and female, the overarching frame of season 4 is the deconstruction of binaries. The Pfeffermans' exposure to Israel, which is also a newly discovered exposure to "Jews" and "Judaism" through Israel, makes those binaries untenable. In some way, they become the gentile Jews, dancing to *Jesus Christ Superstar* as their tour bus climbs the Judean hills to Jerusalem, the path Jesus walked.

The depiction of Israel is full of hopeless and unworkable binaries: religious and secular, Jew and gentile (Palestinian), man and woman (most prominent at the Western Wall), Maura's father Moshe's secular Israeli children, and the Pfeffermans, the American-assimilated family. Israel is a society of binaries. It is stuck in them. Israel needs these binaries to survive and yet wants to find a way out because Israel is suffocating because of them. Israel was supposed to bring the Jews together, which in some way it did. And then they began consuming one another. Israel wants to transcend the binaries that make Israel possible, and so a Tel Aviv university department invites Maura to speak about her transgender identity. The secular Tel Aviv audience views Maura as a kind of savior. Yet what she discovers is a sad salvation; she discovers that her father Moshe, who abandoned her long ago, had escaped to Israel to become a wealthy air conditioner salesman. Here the Israel/Diaspora binary also collapses. As much as Israel might be a homeland for the Jews it is also, in Moshe, a refuge for Jews running away from their broken lives and shattered families.

In their meeting, Maura's father explains that he came to Israel not as a Zionist but because he saw Israel as a land of opportunity, the place where he could make his fortune (much the way Jews in Europe saw America). And he succeeds. But Moshe's *aliyah* (immigration to Israel) is even more complex. Unlike many European Jews, Moshe is not running away from antisemitism; he runs to Israel to escape his abusive Jewish in-laws and start a new life. Moshe does not run away to Israel to escape the goyim; he runs away to escape the Jews.

The Pfeffermans' Israeli family is nice enough, but when they speak in Hebrew about the Pfeffermans right in front of them, you see they view them as the Other; the Pfeffermans come to Israel to find out that their own family perceives them as quaint Jewish gentiles. Are Moshe's Israeli children any better than the Pfeffermans? I do not think so; they are just as arrogant. But their Jewishness is not in crisis.

And in the background of the whole trip, Jesus is the center, the very embodiment of Jew and gentile. *Jesus Christ Superstar* is the soundtrack of the Pfeffermans' journey. And Jesus is, at least symbolically, the breaker of binaries ("there is no longer Jew or Greek; there is no longer master or slave; there is no longer male and female"; Galatians 3:28). Jesus overturns the money changers, breaking the class binary. And Ari's growing Jesus persona reaches a crescendo when she walks into the men's section at the Kotel, or the Western Wall, the great blasphemous act precisely where Jesus stood and similarly staked his claim, challenging the authority of the Pharisees and temple priesthood. Jesus, here, is a sexually ambivalent or queer-assimilated American Jew looking for an answer to her alienated status. Perfect.

As season 4 unfolds, Ari becomes the center of the Pfefferman family and the major protagonist. She comes to Israel with the most to gain and the most to lose. After her breakup with Leslie, dispensing herself of the gentile, she is the only one who really has nothing to go back to. It is Ari who discovers the other voice—the other piece of the binary that is left out. Here in the midst of the broken Jew-gentile binary, or its reversal (the Pfeffermans as the Jewish gentiles), we are introduced to another kind of gentile. Not the wild drunken goy (Tammy) or the pious Christian (Colton), but the generous and loving Lyfe, a Black activist who introduces Ari to the great challenge of the Israeli Jew: the Palestinian, the gentile who lives under the barrel of the Jewish gun. We should have been aware that something was wrong with the Palestinian scenes right away: they were too normal, too perfect, too happy, almost utopian. The Palestinians were the perfect gentiles, even better than the Jews. They were oppressed, but they could experience real joy. And they were optimistic and not neurotic. But we are getting ahead of ourselves.

The Palestinians in the edenic collective village Ari visits were not like the gentiles in Los Angeles. They welcome Ari as one of their own. Lyfe allows Ari to reassess her sexuality with no strings attached. Ari has finally discovered herself in the embrace of these Palestinian friends, not the gruff and obnoxious Israelis in the market or the Hasidim who knock her over at Ben Gurion Airport, and not Lila's mother who lives in a settlement whose chaos in trying to cook food for her guests almost burns down her own apartment. Ari becomes a Jew by joining the cause against the Israeli occupation. Her Jewishness stands in opposition to the Jew. The gentile finally redeems her Jewishness.

But then we see it was all an illusion. There were no Palestinian friends; it was some fantasy concocted from her meeting with Lyfe. When she returns to her Palestinian friends after her family departs, she discovers a long-abandoned village. She then realizes why she never saw her male Palestinian friend who drove her to the checkpoint and then disappeared. He did not exist. None of them did. The only gentiles that were worth anything never existed; they were all figments of Ari's imagination. And then like Jesus, she is abandoned (the Dead Sea scene with her alone is brilliantly baptismal). She sits under a makeshift shelter, forlorn like Jonah sitting under the gourd, and realizes her error. Then she must understand how it has changed her. Is she trans? Is she Jewish? What might that mean? How can she be Jewish without her Palestinian "family"? After fooling herself about her Palestinian friends, she does not know anything. Is she close to insanity? Or enlightenment? A total personality breakdown. "Jesus Christ. Superstar. Do you think you are what they say you are?"

Predictably, in her fully embodied demonic self, Sarah seems untouched by her Israeli experience. She still plays the role of seducer and destroyer, sexually insatiable. She cannot see beyond her body enough to absorb Israel; it does not mean anything to her, and the only things that really mattered were delivering the gift to Lila's mother and making sure Len did not leave her for Lila. That was the purpose of the trip for her. And when she forgets to buy Lila a gift from Israel, she just buys one in a Judaica shop in Los Angeles. Israel. Los Angeles. It really does not matter, does it?

In the end, the trip to Israel seemed only to be transformative for Ari. Maura's ex-wife, Shelly, found herself later in improvisation. Josh finds peace in sex-addiction therapy when he finally, after Israel, is able to let go of the binary that disabled him from liberating himself from his gentile childhood lover, the mother of Colton, who abused him as an adolescent and who committed suicide in an earlier season. Josh finally embraces her memory, and her power immediately diminishes. The demon is rendered powerless through love, which is very "goyish." Maura goes back to negotiating and deconstructing the binary of now being a heterosexual transgender woman. Ari is left alone. For her, the binary within herself collapsed.

Season 4, and Israel, is the provocative centerfold of *Transparent*. It exposes the Pfeffermans in a way that makes them feel just uncomfortable enough. And it is no accident that the soundtrack for the whole season is not the overture to Otto Preminger's *Exodus* but the rock opera *Jesus Christ Superstar*. Everything gets revealed and overturned. The Pfeffermans are like Jesus: Jew and gentile, Jew as gentile. The Pfeffermans cannot remain in Israel; for them it is a strange land. In Israel, they are the gentile and the Jew combined in a way that does not work. They need the land of Los Angeles where they can live quietly as Jews while the gentile world lurks just beyond them, close enough to enjoy and distant enough to be safe.

And Ari, poor Ari, carries everything in her fertile imagination, including the Holocaust secret and her Palestinian fantasy. The fate of all the other Pfeffermans is predictable, but hers is not. Ari has crossed over; she can never return to where she was; she was "without a home."

In some way *Transparent* may be the twenty-first-century Jewish *All in the Family* written in a brilliant—and Jewish—fashion, where dark humor just yields more darkness. The disturbing, annoying, and frustrating tropes and characters belie a nuanced understanding of the Jewish condition for those who have succeeded in America largely through white privilege and abandoned religion but who cannot quite seem to abandon their Jewishness. Maura Pfefferman is Archie Bunker: Archie, the pathetic American everyman, like a gentile Tevya the Milkman—simple, prejudiced, and mostly well-meaning and of average intelligence (remember the creators of *All in the Family* were Jews). Maura is a tragic American Jew: a professor tortured, confused, privileged, and overeducated. The Jews have finally made it in America, as Neil Diamond sang in the title song of his version of *The Jazz Singer*. It is now not only about how America sees the Jews but also about how the Jews see America. In the words of Bob Dylan, a Jew who knows how binaries crumble, who stared down Jesus and faced his demonic self, "How does it feel, to be without a home, like a complete unknown, like a rolling stone?"

Notes

1. Jonathan Freedman, *Klezmer America: Jewishness, Ethnicity, Modernity* (New York: Columbia University Press, 2008).
2. On the career of Gertrude Berg, the creator and star of *The Goldbergs*, see *Yoo-Hoo, Mrs. Goldberg*, directed by Aviva Kempner, 2009, New York, Docurama.
3. See, for example, Jeffrey Shandler's *Jews, God, and Videotape: Religion and Media in America* (New York: New York University Press, 2009). On Jews in popular American media more generally, see David Kaufman, *Jewhooing the Sixties: American Celebrity and Jewish Identity* (Waltham, MA: Brandies University Press, 2012); J. Hoberman and Jeffrey Shandler, eds., *Entertaining America: Jews, Movies and Broadcasting* (Princeton, NJ: Princeton University Press, 2003).
4. On "trans" as a lens to (re) envision Jewishness, see Max Strassfeld, *Trans Talmud: Androgynes and Eunuchs in Rabbinic Literature* (Los Angeles and Berkeley: University of California Press, 2022). Specific to *Transparent*, see Slava Greenberg, "Run from your Parent's House: Transfeminism and Abraham's Blessing," *Feminist Studies in Religion* 37, no. 2 (2021): 25–41.
5. Robert Paul, *Moses and Civilization: The Meaning behind Freud's Myth* (New Haven, CT: Yale University Press, 1996), 3. On a psychoanalytic view of Jews and Zionism, see Jaqueline Rose, *The Question of Zion* (Princeton, NJ: Princeton University Press, 2007).
6. Jewcurious is an interesting term, one that puts into relief that the Pfeffermans are not really "goycurious" (even though they live in a gentile society); an exception is in the case of Ari's ostensible encounter with the Palestinians in Israel/Palestine in season 4. On "bicurious," see Elizabeth Morgan and Elisabeth Morgan Thompson, "Young Women's Sexual Experiences within Same-Sex Friendships," *Journal of Bisexuality* 6, no. 3 (2006): 7–34.

Part 3

Transgressing and Queering Gender

9

Nostalgia, Queer Time, and the Ethnic in *Transparent*

JENNIFER GLASER

Transparent was always rooted in an engagement with the past. From the show's opening credits, a montage of images from 1990s bar mitzvahs and mid-century drag performances, to the extensive focus on individual characters' pasts via flashback during season 1, the series has been characterized by a commitment to history. However, it was not until season 2 that *Transparent* began to transcend its focus on the proximate history of its family of protagonists to focus on the more distant past and the ways both intergenerational trauma and an imagined utopian queerness had been passed down through the Pfefferman clan and American Jewish culture writ large. *Transparent*'s return to Weimar Berlin and the famous Institute for Sexual Science of Magnus Hirschfeld is laden with nostalgia for the anything-goes space of the clinic, which exists in a perennial state of *before* (before the Holocaust, before America, before gender). This queer rewriting of the past—and the central place of nostalgia within it—allowed the show's creator and its writers and actors to imagine a new future, one in which the queer past can provide the tools for dissent within the present at the same time that it underscores the limits of nostalgia in representation.

The late scholar Svetlana Boym, in her influential work *The Future of Nostalgia* (2001), differentiated between what she called "restorative" and "reflective" nostalgia. The former, which she associated with "recent national and religious revivals" "knows two main plots—the return to origins and the conspiracy."[1] In contrast, she writes, "Reflective nostalgia does not follow a single plot but explores ways of inhabiting many places at once and imagining different time zones."[2] She continues, "At best, it can present an ethical and creative challenge, not merely a pretext for midnight melancholies. If restorative nostalgia ends up reconstructing emblems and rituals of home and homeland in an attempt to conquer and specialize time, reflective nostalgia cherishes shattered fragments of memory and demoralizes space. Restorative nostalgia takes itself dead seriously."[3] Nostalgias dedicated to buttressing nationalist and ethnocentric filiations are, by definition, affective states that admit no possibility for cheekiness or self-reflection. According to Boym, "Reflective nostalgia, on the other hand, can be ironic and humorous. It reveals that longing and critical thinking are not opposed to one another, just as affective memories do not absolve one from compassion, judgment, or critical reflection."[4]

Boym's formulation of reflective nostalgia is particularly useful when thinking about *Transparent* because the series is invested both in "inhabiting many places at once and imagining different time zones" and doing so via irony and humor.[5] Moreover, the show, which stages an ironic return to Israel in its fourth season, takes the "demoralizing" of space as a core value, alongside the idea that longing need not be coextensive with fixed origins or racial essentialism.

Transparent is deeply invested in imagining a diasporic and queer-inflected Jewishness that can dip into nostalgia without trading on it for nationalist purposes. The following chapter, therefore, gestures at how the series succeeds and fails (perhaps productively fails) at this task while pointing out a missing piece in Boym's binary distinction between reflective and restorative forms of nostalgia. As the controversies swirling around Jeffrey Tambor, the actor who played the central character in the series, have illustrated, self-consciously reflective nostalgia cannot always avoid dipping into the well of restorative nostalgia and the forms of racial, ethnic, and gender chauvinism at its heart.

Although Maura Pfefferman is the show's central protagonist and the trans parent of the show's title, Joey Soloway and the show's other creators, which include a number of trans and queer writers and artists, are also profoundly invested in the transformations that are occurring in the lives of her children and in the wider culture they inhabit, particularly around issues of gender and sexuality.[6] The series' investment in gender and sexuality is informed not only by the types of nostalgia Boym described but by something akin to the backward-oriented glance that Heather Love notes in her celebrated work on melancholy and queer theory, *Feeling Backward: Loss and the Politics of Queer History*. In this iconic work, Love simultaneously empathizes with and critiqued the emphasis queer critics have placed on narratives of progress as a means of counteracting the dire social messages so often conveyed by the dominant culture to queer individuals. Love writes that

> Although many queer critics take exception to the idea of a linear, triumphalist view of history, we are in practice deeply committed to the notion of progress; despite our reservations, we just cannot stop dreaming of a better life for queer people. Such utopian desires are at the heart of the collective project of queer studies and integral to the history of gay and lesbian identity. Still, the critical compulsion to fix—at least imaginatively—the problems of queer life has made it difficult to fully engage with such difficulties. Critics find themselves in an odd position: we are not sure if we should explore the link between homosexuality and loss, or set about proving that it does not exist.[7]

Love's project made an elegant case for the importance of "feeling backward" in modern(ist) literary prose, even as it maintains the larger genealogical project of queer studies. Love's work recuperates the power of melancholy, loss, and bitterness, some of the "ugly feelings," to paraphrase Sian Ngai, that constitute queer writing and the experiences of many queer writers in a hostile world. Although Love's own work is not necessarily nostalgic in a classic sense, it does, like some of the strongest work explored by Boym, cast a delicate, self-critical eye backward at the contested origins of queer literary and cultural history. Critic Tamara de Szegheo Lang extends this argument by suggesting that nostalgia—and particularly the sort of reflective nostalgia favored by Boym—plays a constitutive role in queer popular culture and its imagination of a space for queer subjectivity.[8]

What makes *Transparent* a unique document in the history of nostalgia articulated by Lang, Love, Boym, and others is its complex interweaving of ethnicity, national (or transnational) identity, and queerness into a critical model of engagement with the past. As we will discuss, the series also illuminates some of the generative continuities and discontinuities between queer and trans theory and temporality. *Transparent* is characterized by a pervasive nostalgia. In its first season, this longing for the past centers on Los Angeles and an idea of pregentrification Los Angeles that is often explicitly marked as Jewish. The culture of Jewish food and the egalitarian synagogue, with Rabbi Raquel at its helm, becomes central to the show's early narrative arc. Season 1's action also focuses on nostalgia for an imagined past, particularly if we think of nostalgia etymologically as a longing for home. The Pfefferman house was (and remains) a key character in *Transparent*, as do the children's competing interests to get and transform the memory-haunted, but now economically valuable, family abode. One of the central conflicts of season 1, which threw into relief Maura's gender transition and lack of interest in continuing to play the role of family patriarch, was Josh's desire to keep the home as it is—to capitalize upon its mid-century retro credentials and aura of masculine authenticity versus the attempts by Tammy, his sister

Sarah's partner, to update the home. Tammy's renovation proves a move associated not just with her role as an interior designer but also with her perceived narcissism and vacuity. Not incidentally, when Sarah and Tammy's relationship falls apart in season 2, Sarah is portrayed as coming out from under her partner's spell to realize that she has ruined her family home by modernizing it. One of *Transparent*'s greatest early successes comes from showing the failure of this attempt to recreate the nuclear family unit by restoring the home.[9]

The form of the series, too, is nostalgic. *Transparent* has foregrounded intertextuality and citationality from its first moments. Trans artist and series consultant Rhys Ernst (and, sometimes, his artistic collaborator, Zackary Drucker) designed each season's opening credits with an eye to that year's themes and to locating the show in trans history.[10] The first season's opening credits roll over a sepia-toned backdrop of what looks like a series of amateur home videos but are actually a combination of clips from the 1968 documentary *The Queen* about a New York City drag pageant and scenes from bar mitzvahs culled from friends and the internet.[11] As Stephen Vider puts it, "Taken together, the clips could be the introduction to a gender studies course: What does it mean for the bar mitzvah boy to 'become a man,' and the drag queen to 'become a woman?'"[12] These clips are significant because they overtly mix the series' preoccupations with Jewishness and queerness and because they manifest an interest in various kinds of queer temporality—from the developmental gender transitions Vider identifies (the rituals that "make" or "unmake" one as a man or a woman) to the queer/trans genealogy that it allows the show to trace. This move is continuous with that of many queer artists and critics. As Love suggests, many contemporary queer critics and artists have seen it as their job to recover or recreate a queer history that can redress the erasure of queer experience in official narratives of the past.[13]

This kind of historical and temporal reimagining—a form of "queer time"—is central to queer theory and experience. As Jack Halberstam suggests in their pivotal work, *In a Queer Time and Place: Transgender Bodies, Subcultural Lives*, "Queer subcultures produce alternative temporalities by allowing participants to believe that their futures can be imagined according to logics that lie outside those paradigmatic markers of life experience—namely, birth, marriage, reproduction, and death."[14] Halberstam notes that the theory of queer time emerges in part from the crisis in temporality occasioned by the AIDS epidemic, a crisis, both literal and epistemic, that affected not only white men, the most visible victims of the disease, but also "those lives lived in the shadow of the epidemic, the lives of women, transgenders, and queers who partake of this temporal shift in less obvious ways."[15]

The Pfefferman clan inhabits queer time not only because of *Transparent*'s focus on the experiences of those normally-left-out-of-official narratives (queer or otherwise) but also because their preoccupations mirror those of the show's many creators—artists who are often marginalized by mainstream aesthetic and cultural representation. Halberstam contends that "queer time is the term for those specific models of temporality that emerge within postmodernism once one leaves the temporal frames of bourgeois reproduction and family, longevity, risk/safety, and inheritance."[16] All of the characters on *Transparent* navigate these central concerns and search for ways to live outside conventional models of kinship, safety, history, and risk.[17]

In Elizabeth Freeman's *Time Binds: Queer Temporalities, Queer Histories*, she further articulates a link between queer time and a particular relationship to the historical past. The artists she treats live in queer time because they "engage the temporal politics of deconstruction (through as an antirepresentational strategy of delay, detour, and deferral) to arrive at a different modality for living historically, or putting the past into meaningful and transformative relation to the present."[18] The idea that queer representation can make a "meaningful and transformative" intervention in the present by looking at history differently is central to Freeman's concept of the radical nature of queer time. It is also fundamental to the world of *Transparent*, as well as to recent trans theory that has sought to further imagine trans interventions into temporality. Recent works that explore trans temporality as related to, but not entirely continuous with, queer time include Trish Salah's work on "afterwardness" in trans representation and Jenny Sunden's work on transition.[19] Sunden suggests that "a focus on transition as a continuous, unresolved open-ended process enables an understanding of gender as parallel and overlapping temporalities."[20]

The opening credits are not the only place where the show's creators manifest an interest in queer time and how the past might inform the present. From the beginning, the world of *Transparent* has been constructed as a series of narratives of return. Lengthy flashbacks are the primary device through which characters are developed. In season 1, in a series of competing flashbacks, daughter Ari, the show's moral center and an avatar of Soloway themself, revisits the scene of their failed bat mitzvah, while Maura recalls her trip to a secret retreat for people who "cross-dress" during the same weekend. Although the bat mitzvah/retreat weekend took place in the none-too-distant past—the 1990s—it appears to take place outside of conventional time, in a fairy tale temporality where Maura can openly live as a woman and have an affair with an accepting female partner.[21] These interrupted rituals of normative gender identification are accompanied, during the first season, by a soundtrack of nostalgic hits, most notably Jim Croce's "Operator," a song that brings out the Pfefferman children's longing for a childhood that never quite existed as they had imagined.

Season 2 focuses on another, even more potent form of nostalgia, this one a look backward that marries queer and Jewish aesthetics to reclaim the stories of the voiceless dead. At the center of the season, I would argue, is a strategic use of nostalgia to reimagine (or to quote Boym, "reflect on") American ethnicity from a queer and feminist perspective. In the iconic 1986 book *Beyond Ethnicity*, Werner Sollors situates "the ethnic" at the center of America's symbolic imaginary.[22] Ethnicity, he contends, is another way of marking the dialectic between consent and descent relations at the heart of U.S. identity. To illustrate the significance of this move between consent and descent, Sollors looks to the omnipresent representation of the marriage plot in American (ethnic) fiction of the nineteenth and twentieth centuries. In turn-of-the-century works like Abraham Cahan's *Yekl* (1896) or Charles Chesnutt's "The Wife of His Youth" (1898), men bent on asserting their Americanness and their (comparative) whiteness are haunted by the return of the repressed in the form of the more ethnically or racially marked wives they had thought they had left behind. This plotline continues to resound in American representations of ethnicity. I remark upon Sollors' reformulation of the marriage plot because I think *Transparent* makes a twenty-first-century queer and feminist intervention into this narrative strategy. In *Transparent*, Soloway explores some of the same issues that Cahan and Chesnutt did, but they do so by recovering and re-narrating the story of the wife and family, as well as the secret history, left behind when a man (in this case, Maura's grandfather) attempts to leave his family to forge a new identity in America. This leave-taking provides an ironic shadow history for Maura's own, later transition—and her leaving of masculinity itself behind. At the same time, it emphasizes one of the pitfalls of the series and, perhaps, of American (and American Jewish) culture: the inability to completely avoid a nostalgic relationship with the patriarchy—what trans writer Jordy Rosenberg has called "the daddy dialectic."[23]

Given this focus on gender and the marriage plot, season 2 of *Transparent* begins, appropriately, with a wedding—the glamorous, all-white Palm Springs nuptials of Sarah Pfefferman and Tammy Cashman, the woman for whom Sarah left her male partner, Len, in season 1. The first images of the season are comical, a series of staged family wedding photographs that function as a burlesque of the Pfeffermans' characteristic Jewish dysfunction as contrasted to the smiling, blonde, and sun-kissed WASPish-ness of the Cashman clan. As the wedding progresses, Sarah looks increasingly uncomfortable, her eyebrows too dark, her makeup running, her brow covered in sweat. It is clear that her marriage will not be a successful one and that something of her (racialized) otherness is melting through the carefully maintained façade of the white wedding. As the rest of the self-involved Pfefferman family parties at the wedding venue, Sarah hides in the bathroom, weeping. The episode culminates in a dramatic and hallucinogenic dancing to "Hava Nagila."

As that traditional wedding song plays, the scene suddenly strays, through the wildly dancing body of the Pfefferman cousin labeled a "strange boy" by his aunt Maura, from the sunny California present to Berlin in 1933 and the sexology clinic of Magnus Hirschfeld, whose pioneering work on homosexuality and gender dysphoria (as well as his Jewishness) made him an enemy of the Nazi regime.[24] In 1897, Hirschfeld cofounded the Scientific Humanitarian Committee, a group that is commonly identified as the first organization to explicitly advocate for the rights of homosexual individuals. His Institute for Sexual Science, founded in 1919, was also the first of its kind. The prehistory of trans studies can be found in Hirschfeld's coinage of the term "transvestite" to connote a broad spectrum of nonbinary gender identifications.[25] In *The Transvestites* (1910), the famed sexologist differentiated between homosexuality and transvestitism, which he closely aligned with what would later be called transgender identity.[26] Although Hirschfeld focused mainly on cross-dressing in his analysis, he was quick to point out the difference between transvestitism and fetishism, depathologizing transvestitism and focusing instead on the idea of "sexual intermediaries" who exist somewhere between male and female on the gender spectrum.[27] As Susan Stryker puts it, Hirschfeld's concept of "sexual intermediaries" posited "the idea that every human being represented a unique combination of sex characteristics, secondary sex-linked traits, erotic preferences, psychological inclinations, and culturally acquired habits and practices."[28] But *Transparent* is less concerned with Hirschfeld's ideas than with their reception and the biographical details that surrounded his Institute for Sexual Science and its destruction by Nazis in Berlin in 1933. In the world of *Transparent*, Hirschfeld is a figure who melds Jewishness and queerness and opens a space for the natal myth of the Pfeffermans.

This myth is explicitly linked to Hirschfeld. As we learn throughout the season, Maura is not the first trans person in her family. Her mother's sibling, known alternately as Gittel or Gershon, played by trans actor Hari Nef, was also trans—at a time when such an identity was even more a matter of life and death than it is for Maura. The first episode of season 2, called "Kina Hora," a play both on the Jewish phrase used to ward off the evil eye and on the dancing of the hora that marks the peak of the wedding celebration, becomes a means to meditate on how the past structures the present, functioning simultaneously as a curse and as a potential blueprint for freedom. Nef's character haunts the periphery of the wedding, intruding into the present life of the family as the episode ends.

Tammy and Sarah's failed wedding is, as Rabbi Raquel points out, like all weddings, "a ritual, a pageant, like a very expensive play."[29] But it is not the only unsuccessful union in the Pfefferman universe. In season 2's fourth episode, "The Cherry Blossoms," we are again taken into the family's past. Maura's mother, then a young girl, visits her sister Gittel at Hirschfeld's institute, one of the few places Gittel feels secure to appear as a woman, to ask for money so that she and their mother can go to America to pursue their absent father/husband. Maura and her sister later experience something similar when their father, Moshe, leaves the family, eventually moving to Israel and becoming the air conditioning king of Tel Aviv, as we learn in season 4. These serial paternal abandonments, along with the return of the world of Magnus Hirschfeld as a sort of queer utopia, become a way to think about both the need to destroy patriarchy and the difficulty of forging new identities in its wake. The representation of Hirschfeld's clinic as a place friendly to sexual minorities also offers, in a more extended manner than the series' opening credits, a method for constructing a trans history that encompasses both triumph and tragedy. The clinic is portrayed as a utopian space where queer—and particularly trans—people can feel at home, but it is clear to the viewer that this space will not last.[30]

Season 2 continues in this vein, mingling Berlin with America, queerness with Jewishness, familial with gender identity, and celebration with mourning. *Transparent* intersperses scenes of the Pfeffermans' obscured past as Jews in Nazi-occupied Germany with moments that highlight the family's complicated negotiations with genealogy and kinship in the present. Brother Josh, often called Joshie, portrayed as something of a man-boy due to his long and complicated sexual relationship with the predatory Rita, endeavors to create a family with Rabbi Raquel. His attempts are undermined both by Raquel's miscarriage (and his infantile response to it) and his insistence on integrating his teenage son, Colton, into the family he is creating/recreating in his family's old house. Josh's inability to understand or move beyond his past—Rita's gray area sexual abuse of him, her pregnancy, their late-life rediscovery of the son they gave up for adoption, and his continuing connection to his former babysitter—is portrayed as an echo of the woes experienced by the other members of the family, as well as Maura's thwarted desire to rewrite her past.[31] Near the end of episode 5 of the season, "Mee-maw," Maura looks at friend Davina's childhood photographs, which she has had adapted to better reflect her experience of gender, and thinks longingly of her own wish to have had a history as Maura to draw upon in her current life.

Especially alongside the season's focus on Weimar Berlin, this scene of Maura wishing for a representation of her own experience of (personal) history as a trans woman evokes a deeply Jewish desire to recover the past—particularly in the form of the lost archive of pre-Holocaust European life. This is a common move in contemporary Jewish aesthetics. In Art Spiegelman's iconic *Maus*, Art seeks to recover the absent history of the Holocaust, as well as the story of his parents and lost family members, by finding and painstakingly recreating experience through visual media, including photographs.[32] A similar emphasis on the archive of pre-Holocaust Jewish life recurs in narratives as varied as the novels of Jonathan Safran Foer and Michael Chabon and the visual art of Shimon Attie.[33]

Jewish recovery—or, rather, Jewish nostalgia—is at the heart of *Transparent*, alongside nostalgia for an imagined, and often inaccessible, queer past. The radicalism of its vision is as much in its imagination of American Jewish identity as in its portrayal of gender. In the same spirit that *Esquire* labeled *Transparent*, "the most Jewish show on television,"[34] critic Joshua Louis Moss argues that "the Jewishness of the Pfeffermans plays a critical role in the successful integration of gender and genre fluidity within the text."[35] In *Transparent*, Eastern and Central Europe (Ashkenazi culture) and Israel function as the twin poles of Jewish life, with urban America as a mediating force between the two. As Moss suggests, the Jewishness of *Transparent* is not incidental to its larger exploration of themes relating to gender, sexuality, and national identity. He writes, "In invoking the familiar (wacky TV Jews) to examine previously unseen screen subject matter (complex gender fluidity without obvious resolution), the show produces an uncanny tension between form and representation that echoes its thematic engagement with the fluidity of problematic concepts such as diaspora and queerness. Transgender identity becomes safer when performed by screen Jews, the privileged avatars of historical televisual transgression."[36] The show's marriage of gender and ethnic "historical televisual transgression" makes it safer for mainstream viewers, as Moss suggests. But it also provides a more radical critique of the Jewish family—first and foremost through the dysfunctional parental dyad of Maura and Shelly Pfefferman, played by Jeffrey Tambor and Judith Light, avowedly Jewish actors, both of whom—as characters—are defined by inarticulable traumas, personal and historical. Early on in Maura's transition, her children struggle with what to call her, eventually settling on "Moppa," an amalgam of mama and papa that recalls both the show's Old World commitments and its preoccupation with the relationship between parents and their children as life-defining. The simultaneous need—and impossibility—to get beyond one's parents is at the center of the show's exploration of Jewish identity and queerness.

Seasons 1 and 2 focus primarily on Maura's transition, and season 3 brings Shelly, the stereotypical Jewish mother, beyond caricature and further into the story. Shelly's triumphant cruise ship performance at the end of season 3—her singing of Alannis Morrissette's "Hand In My Pocket" borrowing from a long tradition of Jewish women divas and stage performers, heralds her own coming-out narrative. In season 4, Shelly admits to her children the foundational nature of sexual abuse in her own fragile personality and its role in her relationship with the young Maura and her secrets during a family trip to Israel. The fact that this admission takes place in Israel feels significant, as the family members all come to Israel burdened with their own ideas about the nation and its natal role in Jewish identity.

In season 4, *Transparent* shows the link between nostalgia, ethnic chauvinism, and the possibility of creating a more equitable future. Set in Israel, season 4 allows all the characters to continue their negotiation of ethnicity and gender. Maura's unselfconscious support of Israel collides with its self-representation as a paragon of machismo and patriarchal Judaism. Israel as identified with masculinity is a recurrent theme in the series. In one episode, Joshie loses control of a gun he is pressured to shoot by the hypermasculine Israeli bodyguard who works for Maura's father, Moshe. In another episode, Ari experiences firsthand the perils of the occupation when they return from a farm run by Palestinian activists in Gaza, as well as the problems of pinkwashing, Israel's use of its image as friendly to gay life to pave over other forms of oppression in which it takes part. Sarah and her husband, Len, meet their girlfriend's mother and get a crash course in ultraright wing Israeli politics.

The death of the father is a theme throughout the season, reflecting a preoccupation that occurs throughout the series. Maura's pretransition name, Mort, etymologically emphasizes the proximity and importance of death and (failed) mourning in *Transparent*.[37] In season 4, when Maura journeys to Israel to give a paper, she finds out that her purportedly dead father, Moshe Pfefferman, is alive and well with a healthy new Israeli family in Tel Aviv. Here, Israel becomes the place in which a Jewish man can remake himself away from the fetters of his importuning family and the pathology/decadence he imagines them to possess. When the American Pfeffermans meet the Israeli Pfeffermans, the viewer is reminded of the commonplace assumption that Israel embodies health to the Diaspora's sickness. This point is complicated in fascinating ways by the fact that season 4 was shot not in Israel but in California after Soloway agreed with critics of Israel that it was wrong to patronize the nation as long as the occupation persisted.

Despite the show's politically progressive appraisal of Israel during season 4 and its search for queer origins and kinship in the world of Hirschfeld's clinic in season 2, *Transparent*'s queer, Jewish space is not necessarily a utopian one. In the introduction to the *Transgender Studies Reader*, Susan Stryker writes that since the 1990s, "academic attention to transgender issues has shifted over the span of those ten years from the field of abnormal psychology, which imagined transgender phenomena as expressions of mental illness, and from the field of literary criticism, which was fascinated with representations of cross-dressing that it fancied to be merely symbolic, into fields that concern themselves with the day-to-day workings of the material world. *Transgender* moved from the clinics to the streets over the course of that decade, and from representation to reality."[38]

Stryker's overview of the field of trans studies prompts several questions about the successes and failures of *Transparent*. Does *Transparent*'s focus on the story of Weimar Berlin and Magnus Hirschfeld's famous institute end up doing the retrogressive work of returning the trans experience to the "clinics" from which scholars and activists have worked so hard to escape? Is it part and parcel of the series' overall refusal to foreground trans experience in the show—a move best emblematized by the often criticized fact that its central character, Maura, was played by a cisgender actor? Is there something inherently patriarchal about nostalgia and its desire for return that *Transparent* cannot ultimately get beyond? Moreover, does the series' focus on epigenetics, the inheritance of trauma via DNA, re-racialize or essentialize Jewishness in problematic ways?

Transparent has long been plagued by criticisms of both its inauthenticity and its appropriative tactics. Early critics focused on the fact that the series depicted the trials of a "trans parent" but did so without significant participation from either trans actors or writers. Although the show's creators addressed this criticism and hired more trans actors, writers, and producers for season 2, the series continued to garner criticism for its casting of Tambor, who was, not incidentally, let go from the show after its fourth season due to accusations of sexual harassment by his former assistant, a trans woman and a trans actor on the show.

In addition to its criticism of Israel, season 4 provides a critique of gender binaries. The focus of the series moves from Maura's experience as a trans woman to Ari's growing realization that they are a nonbinary person. This move maps onto a subterranean theme in the series—the move from vertical to horizontal relationships as models for kinship. As Halberstam notes, queer studies has long been engaged in issues of inheritance and legacy and the larger project of reimagining kinship outside a system that privileges heteronormative and heteropatriarchal transmission and filiation. In *Transparent*, the less hierarchical sibling relationship replaces the parents as foundational to the emotional life of the family.

In ways both intentional and unintentional, the use of nostalgia in the series points, in the end, not to a fetishization of hierarchy and return but toward a revaluation of the Diaspora as a site from which to critique settler consciousness in all its forms. Season 4 of the series takes place in Israel, but, significantly, the show chose not to film there, refusing the model of futurity offered by the Jewish state and instead choosing to map Israel onto California and the mediating force of Jewish urban America. Even in Israel, the Pfeffermans are in America and an America haunted by loss. *Transparent*'s insistence on maintaining this narrative of loss is what makes it a paragon of critical queer consciousness and a bulwark against the sort of restorative nostalgia that makes us long for the violent certainties of men and their nations. Perhaps it is for this reason—among others—that the show's creators chose to end it on a note of impermanence and irresolution. After Tambor's firing from the show, rather than film a fifth season, *Transparent*'s finale aired as a movie-length musical that featured the entire cast mourning Maura, who is portrayed as having died after the end of season 4. The finale has been criticized for its at times confusing melding of pathos and camp, particularly its exhortation to stage a "Joyocaust!" to rival the lugubrious nature of Jewish history and memorialization. But in its very ambivalence, the finale staged the central drama at the heart of the series: how to erase the patriarchal structures of the past while continuing to live in its shadow.

Notes

1. Svetlana Boym, *The Future of Nostalgia* (New York: Basic Books, 2001), xviii.
2. Boym, *The Future of Nostalgia*, xviii.
3. Boym, *The Future of Nostalgia*, 49.
4. Boym, *The Future of Nostalgia*, 49.
5. Boym, *The Future of Nostalgia*, xviii.
6. The blueprint for *Transparent* comes from Joey Soloway's own experience with their parent's gender transition, as well as their and their sister's own complicated relationship to gender. Seasons 2 and 3 are in part about Ali's relationship with celebrated lesbian poet Leslie, a thinly veiled stand-in for Eileen Myles, Soloway's partner at the time.

7. Heather Love, *Feeling Back: Loss and the Politics of Queer History* (Cambridge: Harvard University Press, 2009), 3–4.
8. Tamara de Szegheo Lang, "The Demand to Progress: Critical Nostalgia in LGBTQ Cultural Memory," *Journal of Lesbian Studies* 19, no. 2 (2015): 230–248.
9. In later seasons, the home remains largely empty, rented out to eccentric AirBNB guests, while Maura and her friend Davina are consigned to a basement apartment beneath the house.
10. Stephen Vider, "Why Is an Obscure 1968 Documentary in the Opening Credits of *Transparent*?" *Slate*, October 23, 2014, https://slate.com/human-interest/2014/10/transparents-opening-credits-are-a-lesson-in-the-history-of-gender.html.
11. Vider, "Why Is an Obscure 1968 Documentary."
12. Vider, "Why Is an Obscure 1968 Documentary."
13. Heather Love, Feeling Backward: Loss and the Politics of Queer History (Cambridge: Harvard University Press, 2007).
14. Jack Halberstam, *In a Queer Time and Place: Transgender Bodies, Subcultural Lives* (New York: New York University Press, 2005), 2.
15. Halberstam, *In a Queer Time and Place*, 3.
16. Halberstam, *In a Queer Time and Place*, 6.
17. See Jack Halbertstam, *Trans*: A Quick and Quirky Account of Gender Variability* (Berkeley: University of California Press, 2018. Halberstam writes admiringly of *Transparent* as a rare form of trans representation that does not try to trivialize or universalize trans life, 97-99.
18. Elizabeth Freeman, *Time Binds: Queer Temporalities, Queer Histories* (Durham, NC: Duke University Press, 2010), xvi.
19. Trish Salah, "'Time Isn't After Us': Some Tiresian Durations," *Somatechnics* 7, no. 1 (2017): 16–33.
20. Jenny Sunden, "Temporalities of Transition: Trans-Temporal Femininity in a Human Musical Automaton," *Somatechnics* 5, no. 2 (2015): 199.
21. Maura's liberating experience at the retreat is also one of many moments in *Transparent* where the show takes on the complicated relationship between transvestitism and trans identity.
22. Werner Sollors, *Beyond Ethnicity* (Oxford: Oxford University Press, 1986).
23. Jordy Rosenberg, "The Daddy Dialectic," *Los Angeles Review of Books*, March 11, 2018, https://lareviewofbooks.org/article/the-daddy-dialectic.
24. The cousin's body is both queer and a reminder of the importance of bodies to the universe of the series.
25. Susan Stryker, *Transgender History* (New York: Seal Press, 2008), 17.
26. Stryker, *Transgender History*, 16-17.
27. Stryker, *Transgender History*, 39.
28. Stryker, *Transgender History*, 39; Stryker points out that Hirschfeld was also a "pioneering advocate" for trans rights, advocating for trans individuals with the police and hiring trans people to work in his clinic.
29. Many critics have noted the centrality of ritual in season 2 of the series.
30. Susan Stryker also wrote that Hirschfeld was revolutionary in his employment of trans people in his clinic, but he employed most of them in relatively menial positions.
31. Rita's later suicide does little to erase her presence. She is portrayed as a ghost haunting Joshie, as Gittel haunts the Pfeffermans.
32. It is not by accident that photographs are so central to Marianne Hirsch's theorization of post-memory and its role in *Maus* and postwar representation more generally or to Spiegelman's description of constructing *Maus* in *MetaMaus*.

33 Memory and memorialization are also central to the project of many scholars of the Holocaust—from James Young's interest in the ethics of memory to David Roskies' and Samuel Kassow's interest in the recovery of Holocaust archives made by the Warsaw ghetto collective *Oyneg Shabbos* and Michael Rothberg's exploration of the power of comparison in memorialization.
34 Eric Thurm. "*Transparent* Is the Most Jewish Show on Television," *Esquire*, October 16, 2016, https://www.esquire.com/entertainment/tv/a49295/judaism-on-transparent-jill-soloway/.
35 Joshua Louis Moss, "The Woman Thing and the Jew Thing: Transsexuality, Transcomedy, and the Legacy of Subversive Jewishness in Transparent," in *From Shtetl to Stardom: Jews and Hollywood*, eds. Michael Renov and Vincent Brook (Lafayette, IN: Purdue University Press, 2016), 76.
36 Moss, "The Woman Thing," 76.
37 It is significant, too, that the process of using the pretransition name of a trans person is commonly called deadnaming for the violence it does in conjuring the often painful past.
38 Susan Stryker, "Introduction," *Transgender Studies Reader* (New York: Routledge, 2006), 4.

10

Don't All Have Your Family

The Critique of Religion
in *Transparent*

KATHRYN LOFTON

The history of religions has a poor record of avoiding the reproduction of colonial violence in its work of classification and interpretation. Understanding trans experience should not create more violence toward trans people. How do we begin interpretive work about gender and religion without repeating abusive patterns? Susannah Cornwall, a Christian theologian who has attended to gender and sexuality, reminds us that whatever we do, we should not make this about the individuals whose personhood pulls us into the conversation: "Transgendered people who are simply trying to get by should in no way have to bear the responsibility of 'solving' it on behalf of everyone else," she writes.[1]

Thinking about trans life requires new concepts, new vocabularies, and new organizational structures for decided topics.[2] Incorporating transgender perspectives into our scholarly world will not keep our thinking life the same. If the academy truly reckons with trans life, it will change the academy, challenging the "ongoing processes of cisgendering reality" in which social authorities erase evidence of transgender existence from their worldviews and define transgender existence as problematic or other.[3] *Transparent* focuses on persons who express two identities—transgender and Jewish—that have been, throughout history, at significant risk of interpretive harm. I flag at the ethical outset that critique cannot happen without risk.

In what follows, I identify a form of family religion in *Transparent*.[4] I do so to explore the limits of queer expressivity in the biological family that religion often abets.[5] From the beginning, *Transparent* tells us it is about sexual need, first, and Jewish identity, second. The first episode presents its characters through a series of erotic chords: Sarah flirts with an old girlfriend outside their kids' school; Josh tells Ari that he does not "fuck" his new girlfriend but "makes love" to her. The episode is bracketed by vaguely forbidden sexual encounters, whether it is Sarah's infidelity with her ex, Josh's return to (who we later find out is) his childhood babysitter, Rita, for an evening tryst, or Ari's masochistic encounter with a personal trainer. The first episode introduces the Pfefferman children as a series of unresolved sexual actors seeking energetic resolution through encounters outside the frame of monogamy or legibility. Within this erotic frame, the central scene of the pilot is a meal shared by the three Pfefferman children with the person they think of as their father. As they meet in the driveway before entering the family home, Josh sees the takeout Sarah has brought and replies: "I just got a boner in my tummy." This statement launches the conjunction between food and sex that thrums throughout *Transparent*, a show that returns to scenes of orgiastic epicurean experience to link the wandering Pfeffermans. (see figure 10.1)

The dinner scene also first introduces the Pfeffermans as Jews. As the children approach their father's door, they try to remember which "Marcy" he was currently dating and then list a series of possible last names for her: "Goldberg," nominates one, "Kaplan," says another; "Fitzel-feiner-hein-stein," chimes in a third. As they eat voraciously, their father explains their messiness with a genetic

FIGURE 10.1 *Transparent*. "The Pilot," Season 1:1. Written by Joey Soloway, directed by Joey Soloway, August 27, 2014.

callback: "We come from shtetl people." Eating baby back ribs, discussing whether their father has cancer, this is a family united in a profane communion: they are a family, they are not *frum* (religiously observant of Jewish law). Whether or not they are, exactly, a *Jewish* family is a backseat question for much of what unfolds in the series.[6]

At the center of that debate is the gender identity of their patriarch and the connected sexual and gender journeys of the main cast. In the first episode, Maura's trans identity is not revealed to the family. The viewers of *Transparent* know it, but its central family does not. In the privacy of the once-upon family home, in a phone conversation with an unseen friend, and in the space of the Los Angeles LGBT Center trans support group we, the viewers, see Maura as she is: a female-identified person. The viewer formally meets Maura through the support group, a secular form of ecumenical commons that links differently raced and classed people united through their marginalized struggles. The challenge for Maura in the first episode is that of bringing who she is in the support group to her family. The members of the support group, perhaps like the viewing audience, recognize the difficulty. Being your actual self in your natal family seems the hardest thing to do, harder maybe than figuring out who you are.

I want to pause here to remark on my language choices in what follows. Throughout this essay, I observe how *Transparent* poses questions about patriarchy. I ask what it means for the family to lose its cismale patriarch; I ask whether Maura remains a patriarch, even after she comes out as a woman. Can a woman-identified person be a patriarch? bell hooks famously declared: "Patriarchy has no gender."[7] Like hooks, I see patriarchy as an ideological practice, and so it is possible to read patriarchic practice onto Maura: the show depicts her wielding authority, money, and power in a way that subordinates other women-identified persons. We see these acts of subordination when we observe Maura interrupting female religious leadership, when she uses her wealth to compel her family to make certain choices, and when she continues to expect deference for being the family's leader, a headship derived from her much-examined place in the family tree. Being female does not make someone a feminist. Watching *Transparent*, the viewer participates in the process by which one family—and one set of cast and crew members for the show itself—figure out a variety of feminist dilemmas.[8] Like the society in which *Transparent* emerged, that figuring out is stumbling and not without interpretive harm. This chapter focuses on what family the Pfeffermans have as they wrestle with Maura's gender and the resultant sexual feeling and spiritual awakenings her gender produces in her children.

This is where the tension of religion in *Transparent* plays out most: not in the question of whether it is okay to have a father who is woman-identified but what kind of family remains from that realization. It is not coincidental but necessary that the Pfefferman family identifies as Jewish: what is a Jewish family without a father? How far queered by trans life can a family be and still be a family, still be a Jewish family, *still be*? It is impossible to answer these questions without thinking about the normal against which trans life is interpreted.[9] Indeed, scholarship on transgender experience has focused as much on understanding cisnormativity as it has on transgender people. Cisnormativity, the ideology that all people should interpret their gender identity as congruent with the sex they were assigned by society, disallows transgender experience.[10] Religion has been a critical tool of cisnormativity, insofar as many religious systems are male-dominated systems that rely upon an initial cisnormative separation of people into men who lead and women who follow.[11] People who promote and enforce cisgender realities—consciously or otherwise—often also rely upon these assumptions to maintain patriarchal patterns that subordinate noncisgender people to cisgender ones.[12] Queer theory has been an essential space to think about these acts of subordination and about the role of noncisgender experience.

Although there is little work in the study of religion on noncisgender people, there has been work applying queer theory to religious studies. The work only reiterates the sense that those two words—queer and religious—are, finally, uncomfortably paired.[13] There is plenty of evidence that there are queer things to observe about rituals or theologies and that there are self-identified queer people who locate themselves in particular religions.[14] The traditions of Judaism continue to wrestle specifically with homosexuality, transgender experience, and gendered leadership, resolving in a variety of legal positions, political practices, and ritual transformations.[15] *Transparent* does not portray such denominational history or the work of rabbinical councils. Rather, it returns, inexorably, to the family frame as the space of primary religious interpretation. And the biological family—one of the defining units of religions—is hard to queer. What *Transparent* suggests is that the critique of religion—insofar as it is often also a critique of the patriarchal family—is one way to queer freedom, inside families and out.

Family as Religion

Halfway through the first season of the show, Maura, who is now out to her family as transgender, describes her gender transition to her youngest child, saying, "Some people say it runs in the blood."[16] The "it" is not so obvious: Is it gender confusion? Is it the ennui that seems to seep throughout the family? A pearl ring passed between the siblings in one episode is fodder for speculation about whether it was handed over by an aunt who was in line at Treblinka—is that "it"?[17] Thinking through the family and its blood inheritance is a key motif of the show. Ari seems arrested especially by genealogical thought, at one point invoking a study that suggests genetic changes that stem from the trauma suffered by Holocaust survivors can be passed on to their children.[18] Through its use of flashbacks to Weimar Germany and mid-twentieth-century California, *Transparent* concurs with epigenetic arguments that one person's life experience can affect subsequent generations. To be in a family is to be subject to a manifold inheritance.

In the history of its English language usage, "family" usually means one of two things: a group of descendants of a common progenitor or a group of persons who form a household. The latter suggests a bond forged for reasons of material contingency; the former depends on notions, explicit or inferred, of blood relation.[19] Either way one defines it, family is a claim of differentiating dependency: this "us" exists in part by how it distinguishes itself from all the other "they." Religions have described how families are constituted as a specific unit relative to a whole—how, for example, a particular family can be understood as Jewish. Within Judaism, one feature of family reproduction has been matrilineal descent—a child of a Jewish mother is Jewish, regardless of the father's lineage, but the child of a non-Jewish mother is not Jewish. Differentiating who is and is not a Jew is not a simple matter, yet time and again this feature of Jewish law is invoked, even outside of Orthodox communities.[20] Tradition suggests that a Jewish family needs a Jewish mother to be Jewish.

What kind of father does Judaism need? Jewish law suggests that the father is obligated to circumcise his son, to redeem him if he is the firstborn, to teach him the Torah, to find him a wife, and to teach him a trade.[21] Michael Satlow, a historian of ancient Judaism, argues that such pedagogical masculinity is not a simple occupation. "For the rabbis," he writes, "being a man means using that uniquely male trait, self-restraint, in the pursuit of the divine through Torah study ... manhood was an acquired status that was always at risk and was thus consistently a focus of anxiety."[22] Put baldly, according to *halakha* (Jewish law), the mother gives genetic assurance of Jewish identity, the father tactical education in the practice of identity. To be sure, by the time we meet the Pfeffermans, Jews have contested virtually every element of traditional law. Perhaps most dramatically for family matters, on March 15, 1983, the Central Conference of American Rabbis (CCAR), the Reform movement's body of rabbis, passed a resolution on patrilineal descent entitled *The Status of Children of Mixed Marriages*. The CCAR resolution stated that it accepted the Jewish identity of children of Jewish fathers and non-Jewish mothers under certain circumstances: "If the parents ... will make a declaration to the rabbi that it is their intention to raise the child as a Jew, the child may, for the sake of impressive formality, be recorded in the Cradle-Roll of the religious school and thus be considered converted." For the CCAR, a child can be raised Jewish even if not born Jewish. The rule to maintain is that the family is Jewish.[23]

Trans Religion

Gender-variant persons are frequently marked within religious traditions as figures who serve a critical maintenance role. For example, the Qadesh, the gender variant priests and priestesses of the Canaanite goddess Athirat, known as the "holy or consecrated one," were the faithful companions of the goddess and her consort; they maintained temple grounds, sacred groves, and made ritual objects.[24] Wendy Doniger's work on androgynes in India emphasizes the mixed representational matrix those figures embody, including distortions of the male-female relationship and tensions of equality and inequality. The true mythical androgyne is equally male and female. "Dangling before us," Doniger writes, is "the sweet promise of equality and balance, symbiosis and mutuality," but "the androgyne, under closer analysis, often furnishes bitter testimony to conflict and aggression, tension and disequilibrium between female and male and between the human and the divine."[25] The Talmud contains references to an androgynos (a person with male and female organs), a *tumtum* (someone with hidden or underdeveloped genitalia), a *eylonit* (a masculine woman), and a *saris* (a feminine man). The Talmud recognizes that sex organs do not determine gender identity. Many religious traditions include gender variant individuals who possess special ritual significance. Gender variant shamans, for example, might serve as ritual guides in entering a trance state and practicing divination and healing.[26] Of course, androgynes and trans persons are not the same; few shamans could be productively described as transgender. What I want to highlight is that these figures are not only described as dissenting from established gender norms but also as separated from established genetic familial connections. Most gender variant figures live on the margins of a given sectarian community, in the temple, or at the outer limits of town. Their physical sequester does not lessen their communal necessity.[27]

What came first, the religious need for gender variant persons to do certain kinds of temple rites or the existence of gender nonconforming persons who needed a location in temple cultures that prescribe gender dimorphism? What is clear is that gender variant persons in most societies have found spaces to serve religious systems and not be exiled by them. Yet contemporary religious denominations in the United States have been less clear about emplacing trans persons. According to a recent study by the Pew Research Center, most Christians—63 percent—in the United States say that whether someone is a man or a woman is determined by their sex at birth. Among religious "nones"— those who identify as atheist, agnostic, or "nothing in particular"—about six in ten, or 62 percent, say that they think a person's gender is not necessarily determined by the sex they are assigned at birth.[28] This would suggest that being Christian makes it difficult to recognize trans life as real, but for people who are religiously "nothing in particular," being trans is not necessarily false. Neither seems a great vantage from which to be trans: in one, the trans person is trapped in a hospital label, and in the other, the trans person is received with a shrugging "maybe." Bee Scherer, a scholar of religion and gender, writes, "Challenging the spiritual phallus, LGBTIQ perceived, identifying, and/or expressing individuals are often becoming the prime targets of religious hatred."[29] Results of the 2015 U.S. Transgender Survey suggest that trans people are aware of the ambivalent place they have in organized religion. Sixty-six percent of trans survey respondents said they had been part of a faith community at some point in their lives; of that 66 percent, 39 percent reported that they left those communities specifically because they felt they were, or would be, religiously rejected for being trans.[30] This data suggests that only part of the religious world is safe for trans people. Other parts of that world do not agree they even exist.

Religion in *Transparent*

Transparent occupies a present world in which being trans is increasingly normalized, but the memory of its danger—and the danger, generally, of being self-realized in a conformist world—is still felt through family memory. Religion is a portal for this tango between past and present, although the Pfeffermans are not disposed toward their Jewishness or Judaism in any simple way. When Sarah recommends bringing the rabbi over to help them think through their stepfather's end of life, their mother, Shelly, says, "What, we're like religious Jews?"[31] There is a resistance among the Pfeffermans to identifying as religious, even as they liberally use religion to think about their changed family.

For viewers, the most obvious way the characters' Jewishness is evinced is through the language choices of its main characters. Shelly hears something from one of her children and says, "I wouldn't believe a word your father said. Nothing, not a word, nada, ninca, nein, necht." Maura has a medical event, and she tells the EMT who picks her up, "I'm Jewish, please take me to Cedars Sinai."[32] (As it happens, they do not, shuttling her to a county hospital that misgenders her and gets her last name wrong, suggesting that outside the frame of Jewish care, Maura will be illegible not only as a Jew but also as trans.) (see figure 10.2) These Jewish words and references are not merely phrases tossed out to show the

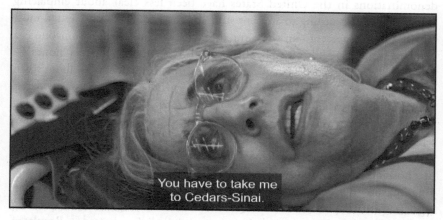

FIGURE 10.2 *Transparent*. "Eliza," Season 3:1. Written by Joey Soloway and Ethan Kuperberg, directed by Jim Frohna, September 23, 2016.

vestigial presence of immigrant grandparents. There is also a story of Jewishness that unfolds in them, one in which the Pfeffermans are playing a bit of discursive drag. This notion of Jewishness as performance is made literal in a scene in which Maura, experimenting with her emerging feminine look, tries on a wig. She rejects it, saying that when wearing it she felt like she was wearing a sheitel, a wig some married Orthodox Jewish women use to cover their natural hair. Maura thereby rejects, while simultaneously invoking, the association of her trans identity with orthodoxy. The sheitel is, in any case, a complex gesture: hair to cover hair. In some Hasidic groups, the fear that people might mistake the fake hair for real hair causes some women to wear a scarf or a hat over the sheitel to avoid any confusion. With Maura trying on and rejecting a wig as a path to gender expression, *Transparent* gives viewers a rich motif to ponder here, assuming they can access the reference.[33]

Although the Pfeffermans use terms that suggest a confidence in their Jewishness, there is also considerable confusion about Judaism. At her stepfather's shiva, Ari says, "I know so little about Judaism it's sad."[34] At their Yom Kippur celebration, Ari asks, "Does anybody know the blessing?"[35] At a Shabbat dinner, Maura puts a regular Shabbat prayer to a Hanukah tune, and when this is pointed out, she self-describes the group of gathered family as "semi-chosen."[36] Jewish rites are a fumbling space for the Pfeffermans, and as they confront the question of trans identity, there are no ritually expert trans figures to curate the unease. Instead, a cisfemale rabbi, Raquel Fein, enters the scene. When Raquel is introduced, it is in a moment where their stepfather has gone missing, and the person they called "Papa" has become "Moppa." Josh pleads to Raquel, "Please, please, I'm sorry. Will you please help us, please?" The Pfeffermans seem to ask Judaism itself for an assist. "I'll try," Raquel responds.[37] As a person and a rabbi, Raquel represents a Jewish leader, a conscientious person, and someone with the capacity for wellness, consideration, and vulnerability—traits the Pfeffermans distinctly lack. But in front of the Pfefferman fumbling, Raquel herself gets nervous. She becomes concerned about what Jewishness does to sexual strength, worrying to Josh that her yarmulke diminishes her sex appeal. He seems to like the yarmulke as a possible kink accessory, but she turns out to be on to something. Josh loses his erection with her, claiming that it is because "his father is his mother."[38] The viewer senses, though, that it is more: it is her goodness, manifest in her religious role, that makes her a less erotic partner for him.

The shadow of Maura's gender affects each of the Pfefferman children in their sexual expression. Josh's relationship with Raquel becomes the strongest testimony to this. Their romantic relationship bridges the first and second seasons and is defined by dramatic personal revelations and promises, only to conclude with Raquel leaving Gittel's ring on their bed after her miscarriage and, more critically, her realization that Josh cannot fully "man up," either sexually or ethically. Here Raquel discovers the limit to her compassion.

Raquel frequently appears as a limit for the Pfeffermans, setting boundaries against their seemingly boundless need to take and manipulate what they need, contrasting her clarity about the good against their messy ambivalence. In one climactic scene where Raquel confronts Sarah about her shallow use of Jewish tradition, Raquel screams, "I don't give a shit if Moshiach himself is coming." When Sarah replies, "Who's Moshiach?" Raquel supplies, "He's the Messiah. He's the fucking Messiah."[39]

Despite Pfefferman fumbling around form, the show depicts ritual as supplying rectitude amid everyday chaos. One episode's opening scene shows Raquel visiting the *mikveh* (ritual bath) and does so with visual reverence.[40] Another episode opens with Ed, their stepfather, being dressed in a plain, white traditional burial shroud to prepare him to stand before God in judgment.[41] In one lengthy sequence, Josh sits in synagogue during the Viddui, a confession prayer recited just before Yom Kippur and repeated many times throughout the holiday. He and Raquel have just broken up. During the Viddui, worshipers gently beat themselves on the chest for each transgression listed. This action is addressed to the heart, which is ultimately responsible for sins of greed, lust, and anger.[42] We watch Josh pound his chest from the pews, and Raquel pound hers on the stage; they are communicating their relationship through this ritual.

This borrowing of religious intensity for family drama is elaborated by the series, which does not show the Pfeffermans in obedience to Judaism as much as picking up religion only to drop it, returning only to leave, time and again. In *Transparent*, Judaism is a scrim against which the Pfeffermans' struggles are contrasted, and their wandering needs are occasionally articulated. We watch as Shelly uses the synagogue as the starter space for her one-woman show.[43] We watch as Sarah and Tammy use Shabbat as a frame to fulfill a *Real Simple* recommendation for familial "unplugging."[44] We see how Maura decides to insert the mourner's prayer into the Havdalah, the prayer that ends the Sabbath, usurping Raquel's religious authority in a kind of thoughtless patriarchy.[45] These instances show how Judaism provides an effective toolkit for the Pfeffermans to maximize their individual feelings, not an investment in a tradition to uphold a social whole no matter their experiences.

Internal to the show, there are critics of this use of religion. When Josh converts to Christianity, Ari remarks, "It's not a bit," in other words, it is not a performance designed for spectatorship.[46] As Maura interrupts with the Kaddish, Raquel tries to intercede but is bulldozed by Maura. Later, Raquel gets an opportunity to bark back at the spiritually steamrolling Pfeffermans. "It's not spirituality!" she screams to Sarah. "Can you clarify for me really fast what spirituality is for you, Sarah? I can tell you what it's not. It's not changing your mind whenever you feel like it. It's not following your bliss. It's not finding yourself by crawling through your belly button and out your own asshole and calling it a journey."[47] Here Raquel offers a strong voice of resistance to the mutable Pfeffermans, who seem to trade partners and grab ritual power whenever it suits them but do not seem able to show up regularly for anything or anyone. All options seem fair game to the Pfeffermans who commit to no religion. We watch as Josh converts to his son's Christianity after his son's moving sermon, but the born-again moment does not last long.[48] In the show, religion emerges as a commitment incompatible with the Pfefferman phobia of regularity. Others can adhere to a liturgical rule or a scriptural narrative structure. The Pfeffermans cannot decide which commitments will hurt them further and which ones might make them feel free.

The Problem and the Possibility of Religion

All of this might suggest that *Transparent* is positively disposed toward religion and critically disposed toward the Pfefferman family. This is not quite right. For one thing, a TV series relies on the watchable intrigue of characters that cannot simply be bad or good. Viewers return to see which way they will go and with what mistakes and possibilities. Even more, though, *Transparent* does have a negative assessment of religion: it has a critique of Judaism as an extension of the patriarchy. Lurking in the background of the show is some sense that the representative men of Judaism—fathers, brothers, husbands, rabbis—are a part of why it is so hard to be a Pfefferman. Sarah says that she chooses to avoid engaging rabbis because it is "mostly guys with beards that creep me out."[49] In a flashback, we see Gittel drinking with her sister, Rose. Gittel says, "L'Chaim" as she lifts her glass, and Rose says, "No, don't do that. It makes me think of Dad."[50] The viewer is meant to consider how thinking about Jewish expressions brings fathers to mind. According to the show, this is not a great recollection to have.

In American culture, the Jewish mother is a powerful emblem, discussed with acuity in this volume. In the longer history and practice of Judaism, patriarchs abide. Whether we consider the original biblical patriarchs of Abraham, Isaac, and Jacob, or the role of descendants recognizably linked to the twelve tribes of Israel, or the rabbis who formed the voices gathered in Mishnaic literature and the Talmud, the early history of what becomes Judaism is defined by patronymic and paternalistic authority. *Transparent* shows a contemporary Jewish family without any yeshiva students or Orthodox rabbis, but it is still a world mindful of this gendered aspect of Judaism within the positive power of their Jewishness. When Ari and Maura arrive in Israel, they are overwhelmed with positive spirit. "Do you feel that?" They fall to their knees, and marvel, "Israel." The show will not tolerate such sentiment for long, though, and we quickly see two Haredi men brazenly brush past them, pushing Maura over. Ari says, "Oh, hey, fuck." Maura says, "Excuse us," and Ari reiterates, "Excuse us."[51] (see figure 10.3) But the tradition incarnated by those figures moves on. Observing the gender segregation at the Wailing Wall, Ari remarks, "It's fucking bullshit, this divide." And Sarah shrugs, saying, "It's tradition."[52]

FIGURE 10.3 *Transparent*. "Pinkwashing Machine." Season 4:2. Written by Joey Soloway and Our Lady J, directed by Allison Liddi-Brown, September 22, 2017.

Ari rejects this tradition and becomes a vocal agitator on the dangerous classificatory distinctions it imposes. "Arabs and Jews, blacks and whites, men and women, fucking binary, everywhere you look, screwing things up."[53] She looks at the Wailing Wall and sees that the women's side is somber and prayerful, but the male side is homosocial and joyous. At the end of the episode, she dons a kippah and joins the male side.[54] The joy she seizes upon—that good feeling that Judaism can create and that the Pfeffermans have grabbed for through their Shabbat and Havdalah services—is something secular life does not easily supply. As Ari will later remark about Israel and Palestine: "There have been moments here where I have felt more like myself than I ever have. And I need to feel more of that."[55] Something about being in the middle of the messy religious and political space of Israel/Palestine allows Ari to find internal resolve. She finds something settled within the unsettled space of border settlements and conflict.

In an earlier episode, the show draws a parallel between the Israelites' journey from slavery in Egypt to freedom and the journey of individuals to their truer identity. Raquel reminds us that the Israelites wandered a distance equivalent to that between Los Angeles and Mexico; she reminds us that Moses did not make it to Israel; and she reminds us it took them forty years to go a relatively short way. Why does it take so long? Because—as the Bible tells us—the Israelites had to shed their enslaved ways. As Baruch Spinoza wrote in the seventeenth century, "They were not in any way to make laws wisely or organize a government in a collegial manner among themselves; for they were all of rude intelligence and down-trodden by the miseries of slavery."[56] The Israelites could not get to the Promised Land until they had changed from being enslaved persons to being free people. And, indeed, many would not make it—the Bible suggests only those born in the wilderness could see the Promised Land. It is so hard to change, and so rare, that sometimes we need generations to pass before we are ready for the next stage of development. We need to realize, too, that there is no salvation out there. There is just us, as ourselves, making our way. Raquel ends the episode: "What if you had to be your own Messiah? Then what?"[57]

Some religions suggest that gender nonconformity is the result of a sinful past. Thai Buddhist authors view trans persons as individuals who are born with a disability as a direct consequence of their past sins.[58] *Transparent* wagers, through Ari, that being on the outside of norms, being unlike all the rest, is the sign that one has figured out the sinful past and become realized as holiness. "What if that otherness were the Messiah?" Ari asks her girlfriend. Her girlfriend replies: "You sound nuts."[59] But Ari here joins a body of queer theory that argues similarly, albeit with a proviso. As Max Strassfeld writes, "If intersex and disabled bodies are natural, and stand as instantiations of the diversity of God's creation, then they are naturalized by being 'born queer.'" This is a problem, however, Strassfeld says, because then "a subtle hierarchy is enacted, between queer bodies that are born queer and those that acquire queerness later in life."[60] *Transparent* is trying to figure out how to make being trans something natural to behold—that we do not run from or fear—while not devising new hierarchies in which Maura's trans female clarity is superior to Ari's gender nonconforming emergence simply because it is, well, clear.

This is not an easy dance to do. I am attracted to the study of religion in part because the word "religion" often summarizes an effort to make things clear while itself being a pretty queer thing. Scholarly work sometimes tries too hard to make things clear when this weirdness, this queer, is the thing we also want to guard through sensitive description. For example, queer studies has long been understood as antiheteronormative (against the assumptions of heterosexuality) to such an extent that it becomes a new vehemence, a homonormativity that can be blind toward "other modes of queer difference."[61] Religious studies has fallen prey, too, to such dichotomies, sometimes affirming a clarity of piety and negating the messiness of indiscriminate spiritual borrowing. In its criticisms of modern spirituality as a dilution of religious seriousness, religious studies can sound like Raquel yelling at Sarah, wishing for more tradition in modern spiritual meandering.

Recall that when she was a girl, Ari canceled her bat mitzvah. She did so in part because of typical adolescent resistance to norms, religious and otherwise. But the episode depicts her receiving support because Maura wanted to do something else the weekend of her party—attend a cross-dressing camp. For me, this is a brilliant conjunction in *Transparent*: the person understood as father seeks freedom from the role the world has assigned her, namely the role of the father teaching Torah to their child. Maura wants to be out of that assigned instructional role. She wants to be another self, one unaccountable to those patriarchic Jewish responsibilities. Not coincidentally, the parsha (chapters of scripture) that Ari was supposed to have read for her bat mitzvah is Lech Lekha (literally, "Go you"), which begins with Genesis 12 in which Abram (later called Abraham) is exhorted to leave his father's house and go to an unknown place. *Transparent* suggests that there is a price to pay no matter what you choose—a price for not going forth and for going forth. Life does not get easier simply because you have found it necessary to change.⁶²

In *Transparent*, the family continues to be together, to cling to one another, despite the many reasons they might need to go forth. As Sarah remarks, "Family is gross but it's important."⁶³ It is important, though perhaps not for the reasons Sarah thinks. One of the most poignant exchanges in the series occurs when Maura's friend and trans mentor, Davina, reacts negatively to advice Maura gives her about her partner. Davina is the only person of color on the show and the trans figure whose backstory of abuse and suffering is depicted powerfully through flashbacks. Maura's trans story is one of white privilege and family inheritance. Davina's is one of poverty and struggle to survive. When Maura inserts herself into choices Davina made with romantic relationships, Davina's fury rises up at Maura's privilege: "My god. Who do you think you're talking to? I'm going to tell you one thing: mind your own goddam business. You have no right. We don't all have your family. We don't all have your money."⁶⁴ (see figure 10.4) *We don't all have your family*. Here Davina seems to suggest that there is something deeply cisnormative about what Maura has, and what she assumes—how she has privileges in her premise that most queer people have not been able to assume. Family and money, family and religion, identity and security—for many trans persons, these are scarce objects. Families reject them, and they face more economic discrimination than economic opportunity. We may live, as of this writing, in a time when this demographic prediction is changing, but we cannot run too fast into that hopeful future without acknowledging that being not of the norm has left people houseless, wandering, and sometimes in a perpetual desert of illegibility.

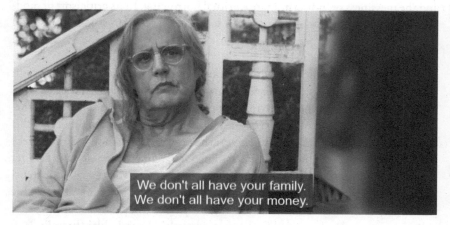

FIGURE 10.4 *Transparent*. "The Book of Life," Season 2:7. Written by Joey Soloway and Ethan Kuperberg, directed by Jim Frohna, December 11, 2015.

We can make this seem romantic. In a reflection on queer life, Jonathan Kemp succinctly observed that "Queer, if it names anything, names a critical impulse that can never, must never, settle."[65] But we also must acknowledge that being outside the family, much less outside religion, is a place of hardship. I look here at *Transparent* to illuminate how much we seem to need religion still to explain our concept of family and how much our families are the conceptual thrall that secures us within broader social chaos. If we want a world more inclusive of real difference, we must ask how we get to the place of expressiveness that Ari attains, a place described well by scholar Nikki Young: "What if the intersection of religion and queer studies resides in each one's capacity to foster human pursuits of freedom? What if they both give us new ways to think about how our liberation is tied up with the destruction and dismantling of oppressive orderings of the world as well as ways that we allow ourselves to fit into others' narratives of our lives?"[66]

I, therefore, conclude by asking if we have done enough to disassemble the frame of family to rethink its "oppressive orderings." *Transparent*, as a show, needs the family to return but also aches for it to split apart, to fall apart as their togetherness is shown to be a part of their common but individual suffering. Trans life changes the terms of relation, inviting us to imagine worlds where family order has no assumptive hierarchy. Such a world seems far away. Yet it is one story that *Transparent* presses us to imagine. In a world without patriarchy, there would be different families, different religion, and maybe, just maybe, more freedom to "go you" into the unpredictable desert of queer making.

Notes

1. Susannah Cornwall, "Apophasis and Ambiguity: 'Unknowingness' of Transgender," in *Trans/formations*, eds. Lisa Isherwood and Marcella Althaus-Reid (London: SCM Press, 2009), 29.
2. For an excellent overview of the current state of writing on transgender experience generally on trans religious experience specifically, see J. E. Sumerau, Lain A. B. Mathers, and Ryan T. Cragun, "Incorporating Transgender Experience toward a More Inclusive Gender Lens in the Sociology of Religion," *Sociology of Religion* 79, no. 4 (2018): 425–448.
3. J. E. Sumerau, Ryan T. Cragun, and Lain A. B. Mathers, "Contemporary Religion and the Cisgendering of Reality," *Social Currents* 3, no. 3 (216): 293–311; Lain A. B. Mathers, "Bathrooms, Boundaries, and Emotional Burdens: Cisgendering Interactions through the Interpretation of Transgender Experience," *Symbolic Interaction* 40 (2017): 295–316; Carla A. Pfeffer, "'I Don't Like Passing as a Straight Woman': Queer Negotiations of Identity and Social Group Membership," *American Journal of Sociology* 120, no. 1 (2014): 1–44.
4. This argument relies on the assertion that objects of popular culture offer a space where some of the strongest theorizing about religion occurs. For other examples of this assumption, see R. Laurence Moore, *Selling God: American Religion in the Marketplace of Culture* (New York: Oxford University Press, 1994); Leigh Eric Schmidt's *Consumer Rites: The Buying and Selling of American Holidays* (Princeton, NJ: Princeton University Press, 1995); David Chidester, *Authentic Fakes: Religion*

and *American Popular Culture* (Berkeley: University of California Press, 2005); David Feltmate, *Drawn to the Gods: Religion and Humor in The Simpsons, South Park, and Family Guy* (New York: New York University Press, 2017).

5   Although at times the terms "queer" and "trans" can seem synonymous, they are not. In this essay, the latter is an identity, and the former is a posture of resistance.

6   *Transparent*, Season 1, episode 1, "Pilot," Amazon Prime Video, February 6, 2014.

7   bell hooks, *Teaching Critical Thinking: Practical Wisdom* (New York: Routledge, 2010), 170.

8   Although I do not focus on backstage aspects of *Transparent*, it is impossible to watch the show without considering the politics of sex and gender, of harassment and deadnaming, and of authorial license and individual aggrandizement that haunt its creator, Joey Soloway, and its star Jeffrey Tambor. Marcy Cook, "Why *Transparent* Has Lost the Trust of the Trans Community," *The Mary Sue*, February 4, 2015, https://www.themarysue.com/transparent-trust/; Spencer Kornhaber, "The *Transparent* Allegations and the 'Politicized' Workplace," *Atlantic*, November 21, 2017, https://www.theatlantic.com/entertainment/archive/2017/11/jeffrey-tambor-transparent-allegations-politicized/546368/.

9   When I ask if a Jewish family can exist without a father, readers may feel I here obscure the fight for lesbian legibility in Jewish congregations. As a lesbian-identified person, I recognize and benefit from such denominational battles. Observing popular culture, it is indisputable that lesbian families remain a minority report in Judaism and beyond. Seeing a lesbian family, Jewish or not, in American television is rarer than seeing a gay family, a Hindu family, or a Muslim family. For those interested in the history of lesbian ordination in American Judaism, an excellent starting point is Rebecca Trachtenberg Alpert, *Lesbian Rabbis: The First Generation* (New Brunswick, NJ: Rutgers University Press, 2001).

10 Laurel Westbrook and Kristen Schilt, "Doing Gender, Determining Gender: Transgender People, Gender Panics, and the Maintenance of the Sex/Gender/Sexuality System," *Gender & Society* 28, no. 1 (2014): 32–57.

11 Bernadette Barton, *Pray the Gay Away: The Extraordinary Lives of Bible Belt Gays* (New York: New York University Press, 2012).

12 Julia Serano, *Whipping Girl: A Transsexual Woman on Sexism and the Scapegoating of Femininity* (Emeryville, CA: Seal Press, 2007).

13 For an elaboration on this point, see Kathryn Lofton, "Everything Queer?" in *Queer Christianities: Lived Religion in Transgressive Forms*, eds. Kathleen Talvacchia, Mark Larrimore, and Michael Pettinger (New York: New York University Press, 2014), 195–204.

14 Representative works include Melissa M. Wilcox, *Queer Women and Religious Individualism* (Bloomington: Indiana University Press, 2009); Anthony M. Petro, "Beyond Accountability: The Queer Archive of Catholic Sexual Abuse," *Radical History Review* 2015, no. 122 (2015): 160–176; Kathleen T. Talvacchia, Michael F. Pettinger, and Mark Larrimore, eds. *Queer Christianities: Lived Religion in Transgressive Forms* (New York: New York University Press, 2015).

15 This essay focuses on the concept of family in religion without offering detailed account of how Judaism particularly has engaged queer politics and transgender identity. For a theoretical reflection on these themes, see Daniel Boyarin, Daniel Itzkovitz, and Ann Pellegrini, eds., *Queer Theory and the Jewish Question* (New York: Columbia University Press, 2003). For a documentary revision of the tradition, see Noam Siena, *A Rainbow Thread: Anthology of Queer Jewish Texts from the First Century to 1969* (Wynnewood, PA: Print-O-Craft Press, 2019). For a sample

interpretation by a rabbinical council, see Rabbinical Assembly of Conservative Rabbis, "Resolution Affirming the Rights of Transgender and Gender Non-Conforming People," April 6, 2016, https://www.rabbinicalassembly.org/story/resolution-affirming-rights-transgender-and-gender-non-conforming-people.

16 *Transparent*, Season 1, episode 6, "Wilderness," Amazon Prime Video, September 26, 2014.

17 *Transparent*, Season 1, episode 2, "Letting Go," Amazon Prime Video, September 26, 2014. Later we discover the route of the ring to America via immigrants from Germany who had melted it in chocolate.

18 *Transparent*, Season 2, episode 4, "Cherry Blossoms," Amazon Prime Video, December 11, 2015.

19 On the problem of blood and genetic evidence for relation, see Arthur Daemmrich, "The Evidence Does Not Speak for Itself: Expert Witnesses and the Organization of DNA-Typing Companies," *Social Studies of Science* 28, nos. 5–6 (October 1998): 741–772; Jenny Reardon, "The Human Genome Diversity Project: A Case Study in Coproduction," *Social Studies of Science* 31, no. 3 (June 2001): 357–388.

20 Shaye J. D. Cohen, *The Beginnings of Jewishness: Boundaries, Varieties, Uncertainties* (Berkeley: University of California Press, 2001).

21 Talmud, *Kiddushin* 29a.

22 Michael L. Satlow, "'Try to Be a Man': The Rabbinic Construction of Masculinity," *The Harvard Theological Review* 89, no. 1 (1996): 20.

23 This 1983 resolution made it also possible for male same-gender couples to raise their children as Jews. This long preceded the recognition of same-sex unions. In 1996 and 1997, the CCAR and the Union for Reform Judaism, respectively, adopted resolutions in support of civil marriage for same-sex couples; in 2000, the CCAR gave its full support to Reform rabbis who choose to officiate same-sex marriages.

24 Randy P. Conner, David Hatfield Sparks, and Mariya Sparks, "Qadesh," in *Cassell's Encyclopedia of Queer Myth, Symbol, and Spirit* (London: Cassell, 1997), 274.

25 Wendy Doniger O'Flaherty, *Women, Androgynes, and Other Mythical Beasts* (Chicago: University of Chicago Press, 1980), 334.

26 Randy P. Conner, David Hatfield Sparks, and Mariya Sparks, "Shamanism," in *Cassell's Encyclopedia of Queer Myth, Symbol, and Spirit* (London: Cassell, 1997), 28.

27 Gurvinder Kalra, "Hijras: The Unique Transgender Culture of India," *International Journal of Culture and Mental Health* 5, no. 2 (2011): ; Serena Nanda, *Neither Man nor Woman: The Hjras of India* (Belmont, CA: Wadsworth Publishing Company, 1990); Jennifer Ung Loh, "Representation, Visibility, Legibility: The 'Queer' Subject in Contemporary India," *Queer/Religion* 14, no. 2 (2017), https://sfonline.barnard.edu/representation-visibility-legibility-the-queer-subject-in-contemporary-india/2/.

28 Gregory A. Smith, "Views of Transgender Issues Divide Along Religious Lines," Pew Research Center, November 27, 2017, http://www.pewresearch.org/fact-tank/2017/11/27/views-of-transgender-issues-divide-along-religious-lines/.

29 Bee Scherer, "*Queer* thinking Religion: Queering Religious Paradigms," *Queer/Religion* 14, no. 2 (2017), https://sfonline.barnard.edu/queerthinking-religion-queering-religious-paradigms/

30 2015 U.S. Transgender Survey, National Center for Transgender Equality (December 2016), 49, 64, 76, https://transequality.org/sites/default/files/docs/usts/USTS-Full-Report-Dec17.pdf.

31 *Transparent*, Season 1, episode 9, "Looking Up," Amazon Prime Video, September 26, 2014.

32 *Transparent*, Season 3, episode 1, "Elizah," Amazon Prime Video, September 23, 2016.
33 *Transparent*, Season 1, episode 4, "Moppa," Amazon Prime Video, September 26, 2014.
34 *Transparent*, Season 1, episode 10, "Why Do We Cover the Mirrors?" Amazon Prime Video, September 26, 2014.
35 *Transparent*, Season 2, episode 7, "The Book of Life," Amazon Prime Video, December 11, 2015.
36 *Transparent*, "Wilderness."
37 *Transparent*, Season 1, episode 5, "Wedge," Amazon Prime Video, September 26, 2014.
38 *Transparent*, Season 1, episode 7, "Symbolic Exemplar," Amazon Prime Video, September 26, 2014.
39 *Transparent*, Season 3, episode 7, "Life Sucks and Then You Die," Amazon Prime Video, September 23, 2016.
40 *Transparent*, Season 3, episode 9, "Off the Grid," Amazon Prime Video, September 23, 2016.
41 *Transparent*, "Why Do We Cover the Mirrors?"
42 *Transparent*, "The Book of Life."
43 *Transparent*, Season 3, episode 2, "When the Battle Is Over," Amazon Prime Video, September 23, 2016.
44 *Transparent*, "Wilderness."
45 *Transparent*, Season 3, episode 5, "Oh Holy Night," Amazon Prime Video, September 23, 2016.
46 *Transparent*, "Off the Grid."
47 *Transparent*, "Life Sucks and Then You Die."
48 *Transparent*, "Life Sucks and Then You Die."
49 *Transparent*, "Cherry Blossoms.".
50 *Transparent*, "The Book of Life."
51 *Transparent*, Season 3, episode 3, "Pinkwashing Machine," Amazon Prime Video, September 21, 2017.
52 *Transparent*, Season 4, episode 6, "I Never Promised You a Promised Land," Amazon Prime Video, September 23, 2016.
53 *Transparent*, "I Never Promised You."
54 *Transparent*, "I Never Promised You."
55 *Transparent*, Season 4, episode 10, "House Call," Amazon Prime Video, September 23, 2016.
56 Baruch Spinoza, *Theological-Political Treatise* (Cambridge: Cambridge University Press, 2012), 74.
57 *Transparent*, Season 3, episode 1, "Elizah," Amazon Prime Video, September 23, 2016.
58 Peter A. Jackson, "Thai Research on Male Homosexuality and Transgenderism and the Cultural Limits of Foucaultian Analysis," *Journal of the History of Sexuality* 8, no. 1 (July 1997): 52–85.
59 *Transparent*, "Off the Grid."
60 Max Strassfeld, "'You and I Have Bodies That Make People Pray': Queer Bodies and Religion," *Queer/Religion* 14, no. 2 (2017), https://sfonline.barnard.edu/you-and-i-have-bodies-that-make-people-pray-queer-bodies-and-religion/.
61 Susan Stryker, "(De)subjugated Knowledges: An Introduction to Transgender Studies," in *The Transgender Studies Reader*, eds. Susan Stryker and Stephen Whittle (New York and London: Routledge, 2006), 7.

62 *Transparent*, Season 1, episode 8, "Best New Girl," Amazon Prime Video, September 26, 2014.
63 *Transparent*, Season 4, episode 1, "Standing Order," Amazon Prime Video, September 21, 2017.
64 *Transparent*, "The Book of Life."
65 Jonathan Kemp, "Queer Past, Queer Present, Queer Future," *Graduate Journal of Social Science* 6, no. 1 (2009): 3–21.
66 Nikki Young, "Queer Studies and Religion: Methodologies of Freedom," *Queer/Religion* 14, no. 2 (2017), https://sfonline.barnard.edu/queer-studies-and-religion-methodologies-of-freedom/.

11

From Beautiful Rabbi to Queer *Kohenet*

Gender and Judaism in and beyond *Transparent*

SHARI RABIN

In episode 7 of *Transparent*'s second season, Rabbi Raquel Fein leads Yom Kippur services in front of her L.A. congregation. Immediately before the service, she explained to her ex-almost-fiancé Josh Pfefferman that they were indeed over. Now she stands in white, a symbol of purification but also the same dress she wore to officiate his sister's abortive lesbian interfaith wedding. The specter of their own hoped-for wedding comingles with their immediate context and its demand of repentance. As the cantor chants, she recites in English: "We have sinned against you willingly and unwillingly. And we have sinned against you by hardening our hearts" (see figure 11.1). Josh beats his chest harder and harder before fleeing from the synagogue, overwhelmed by the simultaneous ritual and personal admonishment.[1]

At first glance, Rabbi Raquel—a cisgender, heterosexual woman and a religious leader at that—seems counter to the show's focus on trans lives and queer possibilities. And yet the character of Rabbi Raquel brings the show's queer concerns into dialogue with an older set of conversations about gender, religion, and Jewish difference.

FIGURE 11.1 *Transparent*. Season 2:7. Rabbi Raquel leads Yom Kippur services after her break-up from Josh Pfefferman.

Over a century and a quarter ago, in 1890, another woman stood before a west coast crowd on the Day of Atonement: Rachel "Ray" Frank. Traveling in Spokane, Washington, on the High Holidays, she had asked a local Jew about services and was told that they would be organized if she agreed to speak. Preaching on that day launched Frank's celebrity, which revolved around her—rather mistaken—identity as "The First Woman Rabbi."² Retracing the territory from Rachel Frank to Raquel Fein and beyond, this chapter unearths the logics undergirding representations of Jewish women's religious leadership in American popular culture. The actual first woman rabbi, Regina Jonas, was ordained in 1935 in Germany before perishing in the Holocaust. The first woman rabbi in the United States, Sally Priesand, was ordained in the Reform movement in 1972, followed by Sandy Eisenberg Sasso in the Reconstructionist movement in 1974 and Amy Eilberg in the Conservative movement in 1983.³ In the new millennium, women's religious leadership has expanded in numbers and in pathways. From 2005 to 2023, the Kohenet Institute trained "Jewish women's spiritual leadership in an embodied, earth-honoring, and feminist mode," and in 2009, Yeshivat Maharat began training women for positions of formal, paid leadership in Orthodox congregations.⁴

Since Rachel Frank, Jews in Hollywood and elsewhere also entered into American popular culture, both as creators and subjects.⁵ Eventually, women even reemerged in popular culture as potential Jewish religious leaders. Despite their different historical contexts, various women rabbis embody persistent assumptions about female power, likeability, and Jewish difference. The beautiful rabbi is not only accepted but also beloved because of her ability to soothe amidst social, economic, and cultural disjuncture. She represents an ancient tradition but espouses liberal religious values; she is an unmarried authority figure, and yet she is a conventionally attractive romantic object who advocates for heteronormative family life. Under the cover of inclusion, the beautiful rabbi models disciplined performances of both liberal religion and normative white femininity. With the character of Raquel, *Transparent* gives us a "beautiful rabbi," but the show also complicates, critiques, and ultimately moves beyond her, offering a radical new vision of Judaism, gender, and American society.[7]

Rachel Frank in the 1890s

Rachel Frank was born in California in 1861 to parents that she described as "orthodox Jews of liberal mind." They settled in Oakland, "the Brooklyn of San Francisco," where Frank eventually taught Sunday school at the First Hebrew Congregation, founded in 1875.[6] Although she would eventually spend a semester studying at the Hebrew Union College, she was never ordained as a rabbi. Yet soon after her Yom Kippur debut in Spokane, Ray began speaking to large crowds of Jews and non-Jews around the country. Her success was remarkable, and it came in part because in a time when immigrant Jews and the "new woman" were unsettling the status quo, she elaborated an acceptable image of Jewishness and white womanhood.[7]

The first Jewish communities in California were established in the early 1850s, in the aftermath of the Gold Rush, and the first rabbis soon followed, arriving in San Francisco in 1854 and Los Angeles in 1862. In those cities and in mining towns filled with largely male populations of diverse backgrounds, Jews contributed to a religious environment that was remarkably eclectic. Jews and others regularly crossed denominational boundaries and eschewed dogmas and orthodoxies, including those restricting the roles of women.[8] As historian Jeanne Abrams has argued, for Jews and non-Jews, "newness loosened the constraints under which women lived in more established areas and offered them a variety of opportunities."[9] As Jews in the West and elsewhere worked to adapt Judaism to American life, including but not only through Reform Judaism, the highly gendered system of Jewish law was increasingly replaced with an emphasis on individual meaning and identity. Reformers argued that Jews were to be a "light unto the nations," and they affirmed women's equality in the synagogue, in theory if not always in practice.[10]

In this new context, rabbis, whose traditional role had been to interpret Jewish law, increasingly came to be seen as preachers and teachers of ethical wisdom as well as public representatives. In effect, the rabbinate—and Judaism itself—became detached from arcane Jewish texts that required extensive training to understand. Frank's preaching career was indebted to these new understandings of women and the rabbinate, and it centered on liberal messages of religious simplicity and universalism. She insisted that "all there is in Judaism is embodied in the ten tablets which the Lord gave unto Moses at Mount Sinai"[11] and that "there is only one religion, and the differences that exist are only differences in theologies."[12] This message—and the Reform Judaism of the day more broadly—sought to fit Judaism into Protestant-inflected understandings of "religion" as private, individual, and rooted in belief, eschewing if not altogether rejecting its public, communal, and legal dimensions.[13]

By the 1890s, Americans had lived through a series of economic depressions and transformations. In this Gilded Age, income inequality soared as masses of immigrants—including large numbers of Jews—entered the nation to work in factories, and a small number of robber barons amassed huge amounts of wealth. Against this backdrop, a range of new theories about human difference gained popularity. Jews came to be understood by many as a—usually undesirable—racial group, with opponents of immigration emphasizing their inherent poverty, political radicalism, or religious traditionalism. New forms of scientific knowledge and mass culture also fueled dramatic changes in American understandings of gender and sexuality. This was the era of the new woman, who gained access to higher education, the workforce, and public speaking, and of the invention of the homosexual. Both categories raised questions about traditional notions of gender and sexuality and led to widespread anxiety about "sexual anarchy."[14]

In this context, Frank's geographic locale and religious tradition created the possibility of a woman rabbi and shaped her message but also served as key aspects of her public image. Her lecture tours were accompanied by press reports that lavished praise upon her, written in a voice that was presumptively Protestant, white, and male. In 1896, the *New York Tribune* reported "Rachel Frank, of California, will stand preeminent, not only as a writer and lecturer of distinction, but as the only woman rabbi in America and as the 'inspired prophet' of the Jews of the Pacific Coast."[15] According to historian Catherine Brekus, "Throughout most of American history, female preaching has been characterized not by upward progress, but by discontinuity and reinvention;" this meant that female preaching and public speaking were not unheard of by the 1890s, but they were hardly the norm.[16] Nonetheless, as Frank gained attention, she was favorably compared to new Jewish immigrants. This was accomplished first by emphasizing her California roots, understood in contradistinction to the eastern urban centers where most immigrants resided. By contrast, the American, and more comfortably white, Frank "furnishes a splendid example of what the West can give in the way of education, refinement, and above all good sense."[17]

In describing a synagogue consecration in San Francisco, one journalist described Frank's appearance as "a very pleasing feature" in contrast to the Yiddish-speaking attendees, in part because it "has generally been alleged against the ultra-orthodox Jewish congregations[,] that they relegate women to the background and allow them no part in synagogal affairs."[18] Frank was deemed continuous with the "good" biblical prophetic tradition but discontinuous with the "bad" orthodoxy of the urban Jewish masses.

If Frank's womanhood was proof that Judaism could be recast in a more acceptable form, it also was potentially threatening. The most common image of the Jewish woman in western culture in the nineteenth century was that of the *belle juive*, the beautiful Jewess. Her roots lay in older medieval motifs and more recently in the characters of Shylock's daughter Jessica in Shakespeare's *Merchant of Venice* and of Rebecca in Sir Walter Scott's *Ivanhoe*. Although the belle juive was much more sympathetic than many depictions of Jewish men—which often focused on grotesque physicality, abnormal sexuality, and exploitative economic activity—in fin de siècle Europe, with the rise of racial thinking, this type began to take on shades of the femme fatale, dangerous and irredeemable, even through conversion.[19]

There were some echoes of this image in press accounts of Frank, which "converted" her by arguing that she was essentially Christian while focusing on her physical appearance. For instance, in 1897 the *Stockton Daily Record* praised her for possessing the "true spirit of Christianity, not in its ofttimes narrower sense, but in its broad and sublime interpretation."[20] At the same time, press accounts regularly lingered on her "dark brown Jewish eyes," her "narrow, dark, rapt face," and her "intensely dark hair."[21] Her "Jewish eyes" in particular echoed the racialized, beautiful Jewess image, and yet this symbol was defanged and domesticated by her religiosity and her conservative femininity. Frank spoke out against female suffrage and wrote, "I even do not aspire to the office of Rabbi; I could never be one [because] that is thoroughly masculine." Frank eventually married and abandoned her public career for life as a faculty wife at the University of Illinois.[22]

The 1890s were a time of dramatic change in American life. The rise of mass culture brought new understandings of race and gender to a wide audience faster than ever before, and emerging cultural logics came to be elaborated in specific instances of fame and infamy. Frank, then, is an early example of a Jewish woman who became a public figure, both as a result of her own talent and savvy and because of the voracious popular press and its understanding of what would sell. It is almost as if white Christian Americans wanted women rabbis before they existed because of the story they told about Jews—that they can be changed—and about America—that it accepts them, even as it occasions their transformation. Frank was a mirror that showed American society in a flattering light even as it reinforced the idea that there was a problem with most American Jews—and with many women.

The Twentieth Century, toward *Yentl* and Rabbi Ari

Frank's career burned bright but short, and although women would remain active in Jewish religious life, there was not a wave of celebrity female rabbis in her wake, either in real life or in popular culture.[23] There was, however, continued Jewish immigration to the United States and a flourishing of Jewish storytelling for an American audience, primarily by Yiddish-speaking writers and performers of Eastern European descent (there was also a smaller community of Ladino-speaking Jews who immigrated from the Ottoman Empire). Jewish women, when they were present in such work, were largely limited to narrow representations of the Jewish mother and the Jewish American princess, although that would begin to change in the 1980s.

Overwhelmingly situated in New York and centered on a binary between religious traditionalism and secular cosmopolitanism, these types were forged out of the women depicted in film and literature of the immigrant experience. The 1927 film *The Jazz Singer* is an early example of the former, the mother portrayed as "excessive, overprotective, neurotically anxious, and ever present."[24] In the conflict between her husband, an orthodox cantor, and her assimilated son, she is a mediating figure. Her maternal love—represented as a matter of excessive feeling—softens the religious scruples of her husband, but she does not challenge religious traditionalism itself. She urges her son to reenter the synagogue, and she remains in the women's gallery, a symbol of sentimental traditionalism. In the film's finale, she sits in the audience, smiling as her son serenades her with "My Mammy" in blackface, an expression of his complicated relationship with whiteness.[25]

The Independent immigrant daughter, on the other hand, birthed the Jewish American princess, who emerged in earnest in the postwar period of Jewish social mobility. Marked by her enthusiasm for consumption and her sexual passivity, the Jewish American princess is the inversion of the Jewish mother, "requiring everything," usually from her father or husband, "and giving nothing."[26] Riv-Ellen Prell argues, "In keeping Jews apart from the majority, the Mother endangered Jewish acculturation, while plunging Jews into the middle class and its desires, the Jewish American Princess tainted affluence."[27] The Jewish mother and the JAP were largely the creation of men, although Jewish women participated in their dissemination.[28] Jewish women also crafted their own image of the bawdy, sexually frank Jewess, usually in the more autonomous realm of comedy.[29]

Although Ray Frank had largely been forgotten, a version of the beautiful rabbi would reemerge in 1983 with Barbra Streisand's *Yentl*. By the postwar period, many children of Eastern European Jewish migrants had settled comfortably into the white middle class, with Jewish life centered on the suburban synagogue and Jewish community center. In the 1960s and 1970s, challenges to this status quo came from second-wave feminists, who pushed for greater egalitarianism within religious life, and from a rising tide of multiculturalism. Even as leaders worried about threats of intermarriage and assimilation, Jews fostered identities in relationship to representations of ethnic authenticity like the 1971 film *Fiddler on the Roof*.[30] Against this backdrop, Streisand, one of the most famous entertainers of the second half of the twentieth century, worked for years to have *Yentl* made; it was her directorial debut, earning her a Golden Globe for her work behind the camera.[31] In the film, the forty-something Streisand plays a seventeen-year-old Jewish girl in Eastern Europe in 1904 who feels stifled by a community in which it is understood that "the world of study belongs only to men." Yentl is not strictly a "beautiful rabbi"—indeed, becoming a rabbi per se is never mentioned, and she spends most of the film disguised as a man—but she nonetheless shares her soothing critique of unruly forms of religion and gender.[32]

At the beginning of the film, Yentl studies in secret, and when her father dies, she recites the mourner's prayer, despite being a woman; ultimately, though, it is only by posing as a man that she can participate in the highest form of Jewish life, learning in the yeshiva. Yentl embraces the religious texts and rules of traditional Judaism, but she also pushes against the rigidity of those rules, first by entering the yeshiva and then by pleading the case of Avigdor, who is unable to marry the woman he loves because of his brother's suicide. She pushes back against a hidebound community that refuses to reevaluate its interpretations of tradition, putting the letter above the spirit of the law. Like Rachel Frank before her, Yentl rejects legal rigidity for spiritual wisdom. She represents engagement with "authentic" Judaism but also critiques its less photogenic elements. At the end of the film, she leaves for America; only by leaving the backwardness of the old world can she hope to fulfill her ambitions.

Yentl challenges gender norms within her community, but she is hardly a feminist radical. She cross-dresses and engages in a same-sex marriage, but ultimately it is in service of heteronormative romance. Her love of Avigdor is reciprocated at the end of the film and her beauty is acknowledged, but because he is unwilling to accept her as a scholar, she leaves alone. *Yentl* gives us an ambitious Jewish woman protagonist who is passionately engaged in religious life, although her gender is something to be overcome and hidden rather than embraced. In some ways, she combines aspects of the Jewish mother and the JAP: she embraces and softens traditional Judaism but also nurtures personal ambitions.

The first women rabbis were portrayed on television in the 1980s and 1990s, performing rituals, offering advice, and even, on the L.A.-set *Platypus Man* and *The Larry Sanders Show*, becoming love interests.[33] Although Rachel Frank had been portrayed as physically attractive, and Yentl had engaged in romantic entanglements, here the sexual subtext was brought to the surface, a pattern that would be repeated in later representations. Indeed, this was the case of Rabbi Ari in Alan Ball's *Six Feet Under*, introduced in a 2002 episode written by Joey Soloway. Rabbi Ari is a short-lived character, appearing in only two episodes, and yet, she is significant as a precursor to Rabbi Raquel; twelve years before the premiere of *Transparent*, we have a show featuring a sympathetic woman rabbi, set in Los Angeles and combining aspects of the belle juive with religious authority.

Played by actress Molly Parker, Rabbi Ari encounters the Fisher family, owners and operators of a funeral home, as a source of comfort and, for main character Nate Fisher, an object of flirtation. Like earlier beautiful rabbis, Ari offers a universal and comforting message in times of stress: "I don't know what the Jewish answer is—I know what I try to do. I try to live my life every day in a way that honors God." Rabbi Ari's Judaism brings spiritual wisdom, but she is carefully distinguished from that which is undesirable in other Jews. The man being buried died of autoerotic asphyxiation and at his *shiva*, the obligatory gathering in the home of the mourners, Rabbi Ari and Nate watch a gimmicky male comic from the edge of the room, embodying her removal from excessive ethnic Jewishness.[34]

Rabbi Ari espouses both universalism and heteronormative family values against the backdrop of the dysfunctional Fisher family; specifically, she offers a contrast to Nate's partner, Brenda, who is sexually promiscuous and psychologically troubled. Nate is clearly attracted to Rabbi Ari and she almost reciprocates. She notes that he is not Jewish so it could not work out, although she also claims, "I have a bit of a messiah complex—saving the men." She chides him for marrying Brenda, who he admits is not his soul mate, but then reappears in a later episode to give them marriage counseling.[35] She praises marriage—although she is not married herself—and encourages Nate to consider his impending fatherhood a blessing. Through her universal message and her flirtation with Nate, Rabbi Ari almost fulfills the script of the belle juive who falls in love with, and even becomes, a Christian, although she stops short: when he puts his hand on hers, Rabbi Ari firmly removes it.

Although Rabbi Ari and Yentl's contexts differ, both would pave the way for Rabbi Raquel in Joey Soloway's *Transparent*.

Rabbi Raquel, Beautiful Rabbi?

Rabbi Raquel and *Transparent* are products of Soloway's professional trajectory as a writer in the twenty-first-century entertainment industry but also of their personal experiences with countercultural Judaism and contemporary feminism. Although Soloway grew up in a Jewish family in Chicago, they have told interviewers that they only became interested in Judaism after having children and attending a retreat sponsored by Reboot, an innovative L.A. Jewish organization that seeks to "rekindle connections and re-imagine Jewish lives full of meaning, creativity, and joy." Soloway founded East Side Jews, described on its website as "an irreverent, upstart, non-denominational collective of Jews." Rabbi Raquel was modeled in part on Rabbi Susan Goldberg, a Los Angeles-born rabbi who has served as the rabbi in residence for East Side Jews and as a consultant on the show.[36]

Raquel is arguably the most beloved character within the world of the show and among critics and viewers of *Transparent*. Writing in 2015, *New York Magazine*'s Devon Ivie argued, "With all the chaos that surrounds the Pfeffermans, there's one ray of sunshine: Rabbi Raquel."[37] Protestant theologian Kathryn Reklis agreed, "The most compelling—and least self-centered—character on the show is a young female rabbi who is actively engaged in ministry."[38] In many ways, Rabbi Raquel fits the pattern of the beautiful rabbi, espousing comforting forms of religious liberalism and normative femininity like Ray Frank and Rabbi Ari before her. She is a cisgender, heterosexual woman in a show filled with complex and shifting expressions of gender and sexuality. Although for the Pfeffermans Jewishness is best expressed in Holocaust references, Jewish jokes, and a standing order at Canter's delicatessen, Raquel offers an identifiably religious Judaism that is nevertheless universal and prophetic. She argues in one sermon, "You don't have to be Jewish to feel like you're running from something."[39] Raquel's sermons punctuate and even narrate episodes, linking Jewish texts to other characters' struggles. Season three begins with her voice: "Thoughts on Passover ... you will not be a slave anymore."[40] Even as she embraces both queer and Christian people—after all, she performs a lesbian interfaith wedding ceremony—Raquel herself is beloved because she is sexual but heteronormative, Jewish but identifiably religious.

In the pulpit, on her own, and in the eyes of the Pfeffermans, Raquel embodies both gender and religion as stable, safe, and apolitical. She does not only offer a comforting contrast to the chaos that surrounds her, however. An integral part of the cast rather than a flash-in-the-pan guest star, she also intersects with and parallels the Pfeffermans in important ways, recasting the beautiful rabbi in light of the show's concerns with gender performance, sexual identity, and families, both chosen and given. *Transparent*'s trans storytelling not only "subverts and fractures" familiar Jewish sitcom tropes, as Joshua Louis Moss argued, but also the beautiful rabbi.[41] In earlier iterations, heterosexuality served as an unfulfilled ideal. Yentl and Ari have romantic flirtations with men but ultimately remain single, and Ray Frank left public life when she married. The role of rabbi could not coexist with that of wife and mother. Raquel does not marry or bear a child in the course of the show's four seasons, but *Transparent* vividly depicts her struggles in pursuit of normative femininity, heterosexuality, and motherhood.

Raquel enters the world of *Transparent* in a pastoral role, but when she first enters Shelley Pfefferman's condo, the Jewish mother exclaims, "Look at you—a lady rabbi! You're far too attractive for a lady rabbi!"[42] Shelley tries to set her up with her son Josh, warning her that she might end up childless otherwise. In this instance, Raquel's femininity overpowers her rabbinic authority, but later on, Shelley will emphasize the latter, saying of Josh, "Look at him now. He's with a rabbi!"[43] Apart from Raquel, almost all of Josh's sexual relationships represent violations of social boundaries. Partners include his childhood babysitter, a young musician under his professional guidance, and close friends of both his sibling, Ari, and his parent, Maura. For him, Raquel represents "respectable" performances of gender and sexuality; indeed, one scholar has described Raquel as Josh's "mother/savior ... the parent figure that Mort/Maura was/is unable to fulfill."[44] Josh is often positioned below Raquel in the frame; almost the first thing he says to her, positioned on his knees looking up at her for guidance, is, "Will you please help us?"[45]

Yet from the beginning, Raquel's femininity is marked by anxious forms of embodiment. Her first real conversation with Josh takes place in an empty *mikveh*, or Jewish ritual bath, where they discuss her fears of waning fertility.[46] Raquel communicates what queer studies scholar Jack Halberstam has described as "a middle-class logic of reproductive temporality" that upholds "respectability and notions of the normal."[47] If her empty womb is one site of gendered anxiety, her religious attire is another. On their first date, they have a discussion about her yarmulke, the head covering traditionally worn by men. "Sexy," she says in a playful exchange, taking the yarmulke off. "Not sexy," she says as she replaces it on her head. In contrast to Maura's exuberant celebration of Jewish womanhood—she declares, "I am a Jewish woman, and Jewish women do whatever the fuck they want"[48]—Raquel fears that she is "just a walking yarmulke," too Jewish but also insufficiently feminine.[49]

Although her combination of femininity and religious authority prove attractive to those around her—Josh indicates that he is sexually aroused by her yarmulke—they continue to chafe in various ways. Eventually, Raquel becomes pregnant, and in season 2 moves with Josh into the Pfefferman family home. Between Sarah and Tammy's ill-fated wedding in episode 1 and Yom Kippur in episode 7, we never see Raquel outside of that space; she is most often shown cleaning and doing laundry and she rarely smiles, evoking Betty Friedan's classic critique of "the problem with no name" (see figure 11.2).[50] She is dissatisfied not only as a woman but also as a rabbi. She tells Josh that she feels uncomfortable becoming visibly pregnant in front of her congregation without making plans to wed, and after waiting for him to act, she proposes marriage. Josh becomes angry at her usurpation of his masculine role, exclaiming, "You don't

FIGURE 11.2 *Transparent*. Season 2:5. Josh holds the ring he expects Raquel to wear as she holds cleaning supplies.

trust me!"[51] As a rabbi she will be judged as an unwed mother, but as a woman she is judged for asserting agency to change this.

As Raquel and Josh endeavor to create a family, heterosexual partnership is a site of struggle, as is motherhood. Ultimately, Raquel miscarries, and when Josh is reluctant to try again, she leaves him.[52] In the interim, they are confronted with Colton, Josh's long-lost son with his childhood babysitter, Rita. Colton, a faithful Christian, moves into the Pfefferman home, but biology and cohabitation are not enough to make them a family. Raquel warns Josh that adopted kids are "performing all the time because they want to be kept"[53] and after a pool party says, "The one person I could not keep my eyes off of was Colton. Standing there all by himself. Cross necklace. I just want to protect him."[54] Raquel sympathizes with Colton as a people-pleaser and a person of faith. When Josh discovers Colton praying, he is deeply uncomfortable, but Raquel assures him, "You have a spiritual practice and I have one as well." Although Josh describes himself as "like a heathen up in this house," Raquel's legible form of Jewish religiosity gives her some common ground with Colton.[55]

Colton's Christianity proves more of a barrier than a bridge, however, adding to Raquel's unease about embracing him as her stepson. The otherness of Colton's Christian identity and the instability of her partnership with Josh come together when Colton's adoptive parents arrive. Josh tries to convince Raquel to wear a wedding ring in front of the conservative Christian mother and father, himself a pastor. She refuses, asking, "Why would you possibly care what they think of us?"[56] Raquel pointedly rejects the Christian gaze of which the beautiful rabbi was typically an object. Despite her liberal approach to Judaism, Raquel maintains a sense of Jewish particularism alongside a desire to create a biological family. The result is a rejection of Colton, whom she convinces Josh to send back to Kansas.[57]

In season 3, Josh's abrupt departure from Raquel's Yom Kippur service is paralleled and reversed when he responds to Colton's evangelical alter call in Kansas and—at least nominally—converts to Christianity. Here we see a reversal of the belle juive's Christianization. It is the man who converts to Christianity, although it is in desperate pursuit of male familial love rather than the outcome of romance and moral purity.[58] Familial and religious roles have become intertwined, as the fiancé who is a rabbi is replaced temporarily by a long-lost son who is a Christian preacher.

If Shelly thinks Raquel is "too pretty to be a rabbi," Josh's sister, Sarah, who contains elements of the Jewish American princess character, says, "I'm not usually into the rabbi thing because it's mostly dudes with beards that creep me out. But I don't know, you're cool."[59] She affirms the progressive vision of Judaism that the beautiful rabbi enables but in practice, her relationship with Raquel highlights the limitations of religious authority for a woman. On the surface, Sarah has what Raquel wants; she is a mother of two, although she has left her husband for a woman and eventually experiments with sadomasochism and polyamory.

Raquel performs Sarah's ill-fated second wedding, but her remarks appear in a surreal mashup, secondary to Sarah's emotional dysphoria. Sarah quickly regrets the marriage, and Raquel, her rabbi as well as her potential sister-in-law, has to admit that because she has not yet sent in the civil documents, the ceremony she has performed is not a binding authoritative ritual but "a very expensive play."[60] Sarah later does go to Raquel for help, asking, "How did you get to be so happy?" Raquel responds, "I'm as confused and complicated as any other person," then asks, "Can I just talk to you as a friend right now and not [as a rabbi]?"[61]

If her romance with Josh became a conduit to a potential parental relationship with Colton—a Christian preacher—Raquel's friendship with Sarah becomes a conduit to a potential romantic relationship with Duvid Ovadia, a cantor recently hired by her congregation. Duvid, who is played by Black actor Kobi Libii, illuminates the whiteness and Ashkenormativity shared by Raquel, the Pfeffermans, and indeed almost all representations of Jews in American popular culture. This is despite the fact that, according to studies that postdate the show but document long-simmering developments, Jews of color comprise an estimated 12 percent of the American Jewish community. The largest proportion of Jews of color—an estimated 42 percent—live in western states, including California, home to the Pfeffermans, Soloway, and Hollywood.[62]

Like Sarah, Duvid, a widower with a small child who knew Raquel in seminary, serves as a confidante; she opens up to him about the pain of her miscarriage and her growing doubts about God.[63] It is Duvid who encourages a reluctant Raquel to take on Sarah's new project, a community Havdalah service—for closing out the Sabbath—hosted at her children's school. The event goes well, but it spirals out of Raquel's control in ways small and large. Despite the Tacos con Torah concept, Sarah brings pupusas—a cultural insensitivity born of a clueless white liberalism—and Raquel finds herself in the same room as Josh on the day of his ex-lover's death. Although Raquel tries to stop her, Maura takes over the service in order to recite the prayer for mourners.[64]

Duvid cohosts the event, and Sarah encourages Raquel to sleep with him, although she initially demurs, deeming him to be "too sweet." Ultimately, they do have sex after an apparition of Sarah taunts her to do so. Their sexual encounter is an awkward one, with Duvid reverently asking, "May I touch your nipple? . . . Your areola is a relief map to every place you've been." Although initially presented as a plausible alternative to Josh—one who is also clergy and already a parent—Duvid quickly becomes a comedic figure, whose approaches to sex and to Judaism are depicted as excessively earnest. He has just returned from living in Israel, his daughter has a difficult-to-pronounce Hebrew name (Idit), and his yarmulke dwarfs Raquel's, signaling an eagerness for religious authenticity that differentiates him from the normative Judaism permeating *Transparent*. Duvid's presence implies a critique of white Ashkenormativity, but it is ultimately defanged by his devolution into a punchline.[65]

The stress of Raquel's relationships with Sarah and Duvid explodes during preparations for a community Passover Seder, a follow-up to the Havdalah event. Sarah offhandedly describes Raquel and Duvid as potential cult leaders and starts waxing poetic about her search for spirituality. Raquel screams at her: "It's not spirituality! . . . Can you clarify for me really quickly what spirituality is for you, Sarah? . . . Cuz I can tell you what it's not. It's not changing your mind whenever you feel like it. It's not following your bliss. It's not finding yourself by crawling through your belly button and out your own asshole and calling it a journey." If, in the domestic sphere, she drew the boundary of religious inclusion at the Christian Colton, in the professional sphere she now draws it at Sarah's cultic spirituality. Duvid tries to offer his own earnest definition of spirituality and Raquel yells at him, "Fuck you, Duvid . . . I'm not doing your shitty fucking seder."[66] In one fell swoop she ends these parallel gendered relationships—the gal pal and the hookup—and reasserts her authority and agency as a rabbi.

Raquel's relationships with Josh and Sarah show the strains of trying to simultaneously embody normative femininity and religious authority. The character of Ari, however, offers an alternative vision of gender, sexuality, and Judaism.[67] Apart from Maura, Ari is the Pfefferman with whom Raquel interacts the least, and yet their encounters are significant. At Ed's shiva, Ari asks her, "Why do we cover the mirrors?", a question that gives the episode its title. Raquel answers, "It's about being free from vanity, free from that extra layer of being seen." Ari responds, "I know so little about Judaism. It's sad." In response, they share their own knowledge of Josh's colorful sexual history, implying that he is a sex addict. The conversation leads to two fights—Ari asks Maura why their bat mitzvah was canceled, declaring, "That's our family religion—secrecy!" and Raquel confronts Josh before storming out of the shiva, asking, "How many [women] are there?"[68] One short conversation shakes Ari and Raquel so profoundly in part because of their similarities.

Ari and Josh are so close that at several times people note their resemblance to a romantic couple.[69] Ari is also unmarried, Jewish, and assigned female at birth, and, although we never see them inside the synagogue, they begin their own journey of Jewish exploration. Ari leads the Yom Kippur break fast in Raquel's place, pursues academic Jewish gender studies, and ultimately envisions fantastical flashbacks to Pfefferman family history in prewar Germany, where the first woman rabbi was ordained. After the Havdalah service that Raquel leads, they announce, "I did not expect to be so moved."[70]

Raquel struggles within the bounds of heterosexuality, but Ari's development is marked by a sexual transformation. Although they initially identify as a straight woman, they begin to pursue romantic relationships with women. They attend the Havdalah event with Leslie Mackinaw, a feminist poet who serves as a queer parental figure. During the event, Leslie, who is not Jewish, gets into a fight over BDS, the movement to Boycott, Divest from, and Sanction Israel in protest of its treatment of occupied Palestinians. Other attendees become upset at the incursion of the political into a space that has been designated as religious, and notably, although Raquel is leading the event, she is nowhere to be found.[71] Ari is angry that Leslie has started a fight and breaks up with her soon after the event, although the moment foreshadows their later immersion in Israel/Palestine. In season 4, Ari goes to Israel with the whole family, peeling off to visit friends in Palestine and ultimately staying on to continue their explorations of Jewish and queer identities.

Notably, Raquel is entirely absent from the fourth season and is thus contained within Los Angeles and outside of the political sphere. Her last appearance in the regular series shows her alone, going to a mikvah, where it is implied that she symbolically cleanses herself of the Pfeffermans.[72] As scholar Sarah Benor argues, the mikvah in *Transparent* is where "Judaism, femininity, sexuality, transparency, and transitions" intersect.[73] In a world of transgressive sexualities, gender transitions, and secular Jewishness, Raquel's heterosexuality, femininity, and Jewish authority attract the Pfeffermans and the audience, echoing Ray Frank and Rabbi Ari before her. But this beautiful rabbi deals with a miscarriage, failed relationships, depression, doubt, and anger. Raquel's interactions with the Pfeffermans lay bare the tensions inherent within the beautiful rabbi and her careful performances of religion and gender.

Beyond the Beautiful Rabbi

In the years that *Transparent* was on the air, a number of other TV shows included women rabbis as minor characters. These shows inserted the woman rabbi into new genres, namely the comedy, the musical comedy, and the dystopian drama, and they presented her outside of the frame of heterosexual romance as part of intergenerational, women-centered stories. Even as these shows raised new possibilities and meanings for the beautiful rabbi, *Transparent* itself returned in 2019, along with Rabbi Raquel. In its musical finale, *Transparent* not only critiqued the beautiful rabbi but moved beyond it, enacting yet another transition, this time to the figure of the queer kohenet.

Difficult People and *Crazy Ex-Girlfriend* are both shows created by, starring, and representing Jewish women over a decade younger than Joey Soloway: Julie Klausner and Rachel Bloom. Both shows revived the tradition of the bawdy Jewess and played with the stereotypes of both the Jewish American princess and the Jewish mother. In *Difficult People*, Julie Klausner is a bratty and misanthropic New York Jew desperate to make it in showbiz and constantly dealing with her narcissistic mother, played by Armenian American Andrea Martin. *Crazy Ex-Girlfriend* is about Rebecca Bunch, a high-powered New York lawyer who abruptly moves to West Covina, California, in pursuit of her summer camp boyfriend, the Filipino Catholic Josh Chan. A musical comedy, its songs include "JAP Rap Battle" and the melodramatic "Where's the Bathroom?" performed by Jewish actress Tovah Feldshuh as Rebecca's mother.[74]

In *Difficult People*, an unnamed woman rabbi appears briefly in two scenes to facilitate Julie's efforts to gain acceptance into a group of powerful show business Jews, itself a satire of Reboot, the group that spurred Soloway's interest in Judaism. Describing the group, she says, "I'm not a fan. It's less of a spiritual group than it is for high powered Jews in show business to network." Julie and her best friend, Billy, attend services to meet members of the group, and while Billy immediately leaves when she starts singing, Julie stays, ignoring the rabbi to express admiration for Lilith Feigenbaum, played by Jewish comedienne Sandra Bernhard, who she announces is "one of my all-time top ten female show runners, and since there are only three of you you're basically my top six." The cultural authority of Jewish women as creators and rabbis is dramatized, with the former clearly elevated above the latter in the mind of the self-centered protagonist.[75]

In the second season of *Crazy Ex-Girlfriend*, Rebecca brings Josh Chan, now her boyfriend, to a bar mitzvah in Scarsdale, where they meet Rabbi Shari, played by Italian American actress Patti Lupone. For Rebecca, the Jewishness of Scarsdale and the East are, "Dark. Sad." as opposed to, "West coast. Light. Happy." She tells Josh Chan, who has his own close relationship with a priest, "[Rabbi Shari is] not nice. She's a programmed robot who's trying to incept God into me all the time." A song-and-dance number breaks out called "Remember That We Suffered," skewering the role of melancholy and the Holocaust in Jewish life. Later the two women have a heart-to-heart, during which Rabbi Shari chastises Rebecca for refusing to take responsibility for her own happiness. Of Josh Chan she says, in some ways summarizing the message of the season, "That's not love my dear. That's fantasy, it's not real." Here, as in *Difficult People*, the woman rabbi is a fount of wisdom, although she is comically rejected by the misguided main character; also significant, each rabbi is located on the East Coast and closely linked with the Jewish Mother.[76]

In the second season of Hulu's *The Handmaid's Tale*, set in a dystopian theocracy called Gilead, a woman rabbi appears in an authoritarian Christian context as a sign of a lost world of pluralism and feminism. The middle-aged Sally (actress Deb Filler) appears in one episode as a resident of a toxic labor camp set up to punish unruly women. We learn that she has taken on the task of caring for the constant flow of dead bodies, reciting a prayer over them, and she is later called upon to officiate an impromptu deathbed wedding for an interracial couple. The ritual itself is not Jewish, although we hear her say, "Usually the seven blessings come next." Janine, the former handmaid who orchestrates the wedding, tells her friend Emily, "I told her that they're not Jewish, but she says that God doesn't care."

This intimate and affecting ritual between two women—occurring in the dark dormitory, in shades of brown—is not only a far cry from Rabbi Raquel's marriage of Tammy and Sarah in a glamorous outdoor ceremony in *Transparent* but also contrasted with another wedding earlier in the same episode of *The Handmaid's Tale*. This one is an impersonal mass wedding between men and anonymous girls, justified by words from Genesis and set in a formal event hall punctuated by bright whites, reds, and blues. In a dystopian Christian theocracy and surrounded by women, the rabbi becomes a countercultural facilitator of queer love, although she does it in secret and in one brief scene involving minor characters.[77] If in *Difficult People* and *Crazy Ex-Girlfriend* the woman rabbi is a rejected mentor, in *A Handmaid's Tale*, she becomes a radical activist and queer advocate.

In 2019, after accusations of sexual harassment on set by star Jeffrey Tambor, *Transparent* concluded its run with a movie centered on Maura's funeral. Ari offers to perform Maura's funeral, saying, "In Israel I became a priestess." They are almost certainly referring to the kohenet movement, which critiqued the rabbinic paradigm altogether, training women and nonbinary people in a form of Judaism influenced by "neo-paganism, Jewish mysticism, and Jewish feminist ritual, liturgy, and theology."[78] Ari elaborates on their new status: "Judaism is so binary. We need to change that."[79] Whereas Raquel struggled to balance rabbinic authority and heteronormative femininity, Ari rejects both while remaining committed to a Jewish religious framework.[80]

Despite Ari's offer to officiate and Josh's reluctance, Sarah takes them to Raquel at Camp Kohenet—literally, Camp Priestess—where she is the chaplain, preparing adolescent girls, as she says, "to greet the onset of their menses with a sense of wonder." This camp offers a vision of embodied Jewishness beyond the synagogue, hearkening on the one hand to the mikvah that is so closely associated with Raquel, and on the other hand, to the Idyllwild Wimmin's Music Festival, which Ari, Sarah, and Maura visited in an earlier season.[81] Camp Kohenet is a collective Jewish version of these spaces, where Raquel actively celebrates women's embodiment, including her own: whereas previously she struggled with her femininity, now she performs a confident, sexy dance number about confronting emotions. When Ari mentions they are thinking of becoming a rabbi, Raquel immediately responds "I think you would be a fantastic rabbi."[82]

Maura's funeral is performed by a male rent-a-rabbi who mispronounces their last name and speaks in a dull monotone. Maura's friend Davina gently nudges him offstage and begins singing, supplanting rabbinic authority with that of the trans chosen family. Ari will come to synthesize these Jewish and queer forms of community and authority. Josh later brings Raquel to Maura's shiva—a parade of friends and former lovers—in order to facilitate Ari's "bart mitzvah." The beautiful rabbi gives way to the queer kohenet as Raquel helps Ari become a Jewish adult (see figure 11.3). Wearing Maura's tallit and a yarmulke, Ari sings their Torah portion, Lech Lecha, and an English version, "Run from your father's house," a reference to Maura's decision to leave the family home to Davina but also perhaps to traditional Judaism itself.[83]

After the Torah reading, Shelly begins clapping and Raquel gently chastises her. "We don't clap after a Torah reading... there are a lot of rules about what we do when the Torah is out." Shelly, who earlier sang "Your boundary is my

FIGURE 11.3 *Transparent*. Season 5:1. Rabbi Raquel passes the torch to Ari, the priestess.

trigger," grumbles her dissatisfaction with the rules of traditional Judaism before transitioning into the final song, the exuberant "Joyocaust." Josh and Raquel dance with the rest, succumbing to a vision of Jewish life that is a multicolor, multiracial, multireligious, and multitemporal fantasia. Before returning to the shiva, Raquel and Josh had entered the camp's chapel and, with imagined relatives sitting in the pews, embraced under a prayer shawl—a symbolic wedding that indicates their joyous reunion as a couple. They have been granted a heteronormative happy ending, and yet they embrace the queerness of others, along with more expansive visions of gender, sexuality, and Judaism.[84]

The logics undergirding the representation of Rabbi Raquel have had considerable staying power for well over a century, holding up the woman rabbi as a sign of Judaism's transformation and America's openness. In its first four seasons, *Transparent* offered a more critical take, raising questions about the desirability of normative femininity and traditional Jewish authority. The new string of representations that followed Raquel retained her wisdom and likeability but further deviated from the beautiful rabbi, removing her from the realm of heteronormative romance. In the *Transparent* finale—itself a musical comedy—the beautiful rabbi is replaced altogether by a nonbinary priestess.

Conclusion

In 2017, as Joey Soloway was promoting the fourth season of *Transparent*, they came out as nonbinary, having two years earlier come out as queer.[85] These biographical developments solidify the connections between Soloway and the character of Ari in *Transparent*. The character's entrance into the priestesshood suggests the analogy between rabbi and show runner that Julie Klausner had raised in a comedic vein in *Difficult People*, arguably blurring the boundary between rabbi and showrunner, television and Torah as sources of spiritual authority and knowledge.

At the very least, this connection points to Soloway's serious interest in the conjunction of feminism and Judaism. The finale's last shot shows Ari lighting Sabbath candles in the Pfefferman home with Davina and the multireligious, multiracial chosen family of trans teens she has taken in. The queer kohenet combines a radically inclusive approach to religion with a transgressive performance of gender. In so doing, they not only work to change Judaism but to Judaize—and indeed revolutionize—American culture.

Notes

1 *Transparent*, Season 2, episode 7, "The Book of Life," Amazon Prime Video, December 11, 2015.
2 Ellen M. Umansky and Dianne Ashton, *Four Centuries of Jewish Women's Spirituality: A Sourcebook* (Hanover, NH: University Press of New England, 2009), 139; Shari Rabin, "'The Advent of a Western Jewess': Rachel Frank and Jewish Female Celebrity in 1890s America," *Nashim: A Journal of Jewish Women's Studies and Gender Issues* 22, no. 1 (2011): 111–135.
3 Pamela S. Nadell, *Women Who Would Be Rabbis: A History of Women's Ordination 1889–1985* (Boston: Beacon Press, 1999).
4 Jewish Women's Archive, "Kohenet: the Hebrew Priestess Institute, Launches its First Training Institute in Accord, NY," August 14, 2006, https://jwa.org/thisweek/aug/14/2006/kohenet-hebrew-priestess-institute; Pamela S. Nadell, "Rabbis in the United States," in *Jewish Women: A Comprehensive Historical Encyclopedia*, Jewish Women's Archive, accessed June 11, 2020, https://jwa.org/encyclopedia/article/rabbis-in-united-states.
5 Paul Buhle, *From the Lower East Side to Hollywood: Jews in American Popular Culture* (New York: Verso, 2004); Joyce Antler, ed. *Talking Back: Images of Jewish Women in American Popular Culture* (Hanover, NH: University Press of New England, 1998).
6 Letter to Rev. S. T. Willis, December 15, 1896, P-46, box 1, folder 5, Papers of Ray Frank Litman, Collection of the American Jewish Historical Society, New York (from here, PRFL).
7 "New Woman" was a term coined in the 1890s to refer to a type of woman understood to be taking advantage of expanded possibilities for economic, political, and sexual activity. Martha H. Patterson, *Beyond the Gibson Girl: Reimagining the American New Woman, 1895-1915* (Urbana and Chicago, IL: University of Illinois Press, 2005).
8 Laurie F. Maffly-Kipp, *Religion and Society in Frontier California* (New Haven, CT: Yale University Press, 1994); Rudolf Glanz, *The Jews of California: From the Discovery of Gold until 1880* (New York: Walden, 1960); Ava Fran Kahn, *Jewish Voices of the California Gold Rush: A Documentary History, 1849–1880* (Detroit: Wayne State University Press, 2002).
9 Jeanne Abrams, *Jewish Women Pioneering the West* (New York: New York University Press, 2006), 12
10 On American Jewish women and religion in the nineteenth century, see Karla Goldman, "Women in Reform Judaism: Between Rhetoric and Reality," in *Women Remaking American Judaism*, ed. Riv-Ellen Prell (Detroit: Wayne State University

Press, 2007), 109–114; Paula Hyman, *Gender and Assimilation in Modern Jewish History* (Seattle: University of Washington Press, 1995), 24–49; Nadell, *Women Who Would Be Rabbis*, 5–39; Ann Braude, "The Jewish Woman's Encounter with American Culture," in *Women and Religion in America, I: The Nineteenth Century*, eds. Rosemary Radford Ruether and Rosemary Skinner Keller (San Francisco: Harper & Row, 1981), 150–157.

11 Letter to Willis; see also "A Grand Reception," *Daily Nevada Tribune*, March 18, 1895, box 2, folder 4, Papers of Ray Frank Litman. On universalistic and liberal religion in the late nineteenth century, see Leigh Eric Schmidt, *Restless Souls: The Making of American Spirituality* (New York: HarperCollins, 2005), chapter 3.

12 *The Morning Oregonian*, October 14, 1895, box 2, PRFL.

13 Shari Rabin, "Working Jews: *Hazanim* and the Labor of Religion in Nineteenth-Century America," *Religion and American Culture: A Journal of Interpretation* 25, no. 2 (Summer 2015): 178–217; Leon Jick, *The Americanization of the Synagogue* (Hanover, NH: University Press of New England, 1976); Leora Batnitzky, *How Judaism Became a Religion: An Introduction to Modern Jewish Thought* (Princeton, NJ: Princeton University Press, 2011).

14 Elaine Showalter, *Sexual Anarchy: Gender and Culture at the Fin de Siecle* (New York: Bloomsbury, 1991); Beryl Satter, *Each Mind a Kingdom: American Women, Sexual Purity, and the New Thought Movement, 1875–1920* (Berkeley, CA: University of California Press, 2001); Gail Bederman, *Manliness and Civilization: A Cultural History of Gender and Race in the United States, 1880–1917* (Chicago: University of Chicago Press, 2008); George Chauncey, *Gay New York: Gender, Urban Culture, and the Making of the Gay Male World, 1890–1940* (New York: Basic Books, 1994); Todd Samuel Presner, *Muscular Judaism: The Jewish Body and the Politics of Regeneration* (New York: Routledge, 2007); Sander L. Gilman, *The Jew's Body* (New York: Routledge, 1991); Edgar Rosenberg, *From Shylock to Svengali: Jewish Stereotypes in English Fiction* (Stanford, CA: Stanford University Press, 1960); Regine Rosenthal, "Inventing the Other: Ambivalent Constructions of the Wandering Jew/ess in Nineteenth-Century American Literature," in *Representations of Jews through the Ages*, eds. Leonard Jay Greenspoon and Bryan F. Le Beau (Omaha, NE: Creighton University Press, 1996), 171–188; Harley Erdman, *Staging the Jew: The Performance of an American Ethnicity, 1860–1920* (New Brunswick, NJ: Rutgers University Press, 1997).

15 A Woman Rabbi Here," *New York Tribune*, November 15, 1896, p. a5.

16 Catherine Brekus, *Strangers and Pilgrims: Female Preaching in America* (Chapel Hill: University of North Carolina Press, 1998), 339.

17 "Newspaper Work for Women," *The [Spokane Falls] Spokesman*, September 23, 1890, box 2, scrapbook, PRFL.

18 "Consecration of a New Synagogue," box 2, scrapbook, PRFL.

19 Amy-Jill Levine, "A Jewess, More and/ or Less," in *Judaism Since Gender*, eds. Miriam Peskowitz and Laura Levitt (New York: Routledge, 1997), 149–157; Sander L. Gilman, *Love + Marriage = Death, and Other Essays on Representing Difference* (Stanford, CA: Stanford University Press, 1998), 65–90; Roberta Mock, *Jewish Women on Stage, Film, and Television* (New York: Palgrave Macmillan, 2007).

20 *Stockton Daily Record*, May 1897, box 2, scrapbook, PRFL.

21 "Work of a Woman Rabbi" (above, note 50); "A Woman in the Temple," *San Francisco Chronicle*, March 23, 1896, p. 26, box 2, PRFL.

22 Ray Frank Litman, sermon reprinted in Simon Litman, *Ray Frank Litman: A Memoir* (New York: American Jewish Historical Society, 1957), 36; Shari Rabin, "'The Advent of a Western Jewess.'"

23. Nadell, *Women Who Would be Rabbis*; Shuly Rubin Schwartz, *The Rabbi's Wife: The Rebbetzin in American Jewish Life* (New York: New York University Press, 2006).
24. Joyce Antler, ed. *Talking Back: Images of Jewish Women in American Popular Culture* (Hanover, NH: University Press of New England, 1998), 2.
25. *The Jazz Singer*, directed by Alan Crosland (Warner Brothers, 1927), https://www.amazon.com/Jazz-Singer-Al-Jolson/dp/B00KVWH04G; Michael Alexander, *Jazz Age Jews* (Princeton, NJ: Princeton University Press, 2001); Michael Rogin, *Blackface, White Noise: Jewish Immigrants in the Hollywood Melting Pot* (Berkeley, CA: University of California Press, 1996).
26. Riv-Ellen Prell, *Fighting to Become American: Assimilation and the Trouble between Jewish Women and Jewish Men* (Boston: Beacon Press, 1999), 180.
27. Prell, *Fighting to Become American*, 243.
28. Donald Weber, "The Jewish-American World of Gertrude Berg: *The Goldbergs* on Radio and Television, 1930–1950," in Antler, *Talking Back*, 85–102. See also Prell, *Fighting to Become American*, 228–230.
29. Prell, *Fighting to Become American*, 302; Joyce Antler, "One Clove Away from a Pomander Ball: The Subversive Tradition of Jewish Female Comedians," *Studies in American Jewish Literature* 29 (2010): 123–138.
30. Rachel Kranson, *Ambivalent Embrace: Jewish Upward Mobility in Postwar America* (Chapel Hill: University of North Carolina Press, 2017); Hasia Diner, Shira Kohn, and Rachel Kranson, *A Jewish Feminine Mystique?: Jewish Women in Postwar America* (New Brunswick, NJ: Rutgers University Press, 2010); Matthew Frye Jacobson, *Roots Too* (Cambridge: Harvard University Press, 2006).
31. June Sochen, "From Sophie Tucker to Barbra Streisand: Jewish Women Entertainers as Reformers," and Felicia Herman, "The Way She *Really* Is: Images of Jews and Women in the Films of Barbra Streisand," in Antler, *Talking Back*, 68–84, 171–190; Marjorie Garber, "Category Crises: The Way of the Cross and the Jewish Star," in *Queer Theory and the Jewish Question*, eds. Daniel Boyarin, Daniel Itzkovitz, and Ann Pellegrini (New York: Columbia University Press, 2003), 19–40; Stacy Wolf, "Barbra's 'Funny Girl' Body," in *Queer Theory and the Jewish Question*, eds. Daniel Boyarin, Daniel Itzkovitz, and Ann Pellegrini (New York: Columbia University Press, 2003), 246–265; Barbra Streisand, *My Name is Barbra* (New York: Penguin, 2023), 506–600.
32. *Yentl*, directed by Barbra Streisand (United Artists, 1983), https://play.max.com/movie/17c95173-4fcd-4268-8e62-108693eeec6d.
33. Jonathan Pearl and Judith Pearl, *The Chosen Image: Television's Portrayal of Jewish Themes and Characters* (Jefferson, NC: McFarland, 1999), 91.
34. *Six Feet Under*, Season 2, episode 7, "Back to the Garden," HBO, April 14, 2002.
35. *Six Feet Under*, Season 2, episode 7, "Back to the Garden," HBO, April 14, 2002; see also *Six Feet Under*, Season 2, episode 11, "The Liar and the Whore," HBO, May 12, 2002.
36. Gordon Haber, "Her Beachfront Home in Heaven," *Forward*, January 1, 2012, https://forward.com/articles/148658/her-beachfront-home-in-heaven/; "About," Reboot, accessed February 5, 2018, http://www.rebooters.net/about-us/; "East Side Jews," *SIJCC*, accessed February 5, 2018, https://sijcc.net/east-side-jews; "Our Clergy," Wilshire Boulevard Temple, accessed February 5, 2018, https://www.wbtla.org/pages/the-temple-pages/our-clergy.
37. Devon Ivie, "*Transparent*'s Kathryn Hahn on Raquel and Josh's Chemistry and How She Fits in with the Pfeffermans," *Vulture*, December 16, 2015, http://www.vulture.com/2015/12/transparent-kathryn-hahn-raquel-josh.html.
38. Kathryn Reklis, "On Media: Transparent Need," *Christian Century*, March 18, 2015, http://www.christiancentury.org/article/2015-03/transparent-need. In some

ways Soloway's treatment of Raquel is in keeping with contemporary Jewish cultural producers who, Jenny Caplan argues, "point [their] sharpest barbs at the [Jewish] community; at its secularity, its complacency, its materialism. But rabbis and rituals are treated more gently, and used to humanize a story, not as a punchline." Jennifer Caplan, "All Joking Aside: The Role of Religion in American Jewish Satire" (PhD diss., Syracuse University, 2015), 163.

39 *Transparent*, Season 3, episode 2, "When the Battle is Over," Amazon Prime Video, September 23, 2016.
40 *Transparent*, Season 3, episode 1, "Elizah," Amazon Prime Video, September 23, 2016.
41 Joshua Louis Moss, "'The Woman Thing and the Jew Thing': Transsexuality, Transcomedy, and the Legacy of Subversive Jewishness in *Transparent*," in *From Shtetl to Stardom: Jews and Hollywood*, eds. Michael Renov and Vincent Brook (West Lafayette, IN: Purdue University Press, 2017), 78.
42 *Transparent*, Season 1, episode 5, "Wedge," Amazon Prime Video, September 26, 2014.
43 *Transparent*, Season 2, episode 5, "Mee-Maw," Amazon Prime Video, December 11, 2015.
44 Moss, "'The Woman Thing,'" 84.
45 *Transparent*, Season 1, episode 5, "Wedge," Amazon Prime Video, September 26, 2014.
46 *Transparent*, Season 1, episode 6, "The Wilderness," Amazon Prime Video, September 26, 2014.
47 Jack Halberstam, *In a Queer Time and Place: Transgender Bodies, Subcultural Lives* (New York: New York University Press, 2005), 4.
48 *Transparent*, Season 3, episode 5, "Oh Holy Night," Amazon Prime Video, September 23, 2016.
49 *Transparent*, Season 1, episode 7, "The Symbolic Exemplar," Amazon Prime Video, September 26, 2014.
50 Betty Friedan, *The Feminine Mystique* (New York: Norton, 1973).
51 *Transparent*, Season 2, episode 3, "New World Coming," Amazon Prime Video, December 11, 2015.
52 *Transparent*, Season 2, episode 6, "Bulnerable," Amazon Prime Video, December 11, 2015.
53 *Transparent*, Season 2, episode 3, "New World Coming," Amazon Prime Video, December 11, 2015.
54 *Transparent*, Season 2, episode 2, "Flicky-Flicky Thump-Thump," Amazon Prime Video, December 11, 2015.
55 *Transparent*. "Cherry Blossoms." Season 2, episode 4, Amazon Prime Video, December 11, 2015.
56 *Transparent*, Season 2, episode 5, "Mee-Maw," Amazon Prime Video, December 11, 2015.
57 *Transparent*, Season 2, episode 5, "Mee-Maw," Amazon Prime Video, December 11, 2015.
58 *Transparent*, Season 3, episode 7, "Life Sucks and Then You Die," Amazon Prime Video, September 23, 2016.
59 *Transparent*, Season 2, episode 4, "Cherry Blossoms," Amazon Prime Video, December 11, 2015.
60 *Transparent*, Season 2, episode 1, "Kina Hora," Amazon Prime Video, December 11, 2015.

61 *Transparent*, Season 2, episode 2, "Flicky-Flicky Thump-Thump," Amazon Prime Video, December 11, 2015.
62 Ari Y. Kelman, Aaron Hahn Tapper, Izabel Fonseca, Aliya Saperstein, "Counting Inconsistencies: An Analysis of American Jewish Population Studies, with a Focus on Jews of Color: Methodological Appendix" *Jews of Color Field Building Initiative* (2019), accessed January 8, 2024, https://www.jewishdatabank.org/content/upload/bjdb/2019_Counting_Inconsistencies_Methodological_Appendix_Focus_on_Jews_of_Color.pdf; Tobin Belzer et al., "Beyond the Count: Perspectives and Lived Experiences of Jews of Color," *Jews of Color Initiative* (2021), accessed January 8, 2024, bit.ly/BeyondTheCount.
63 *Transparent*, Season 3, episode 3, "To Sardines and Back," Amazon Prime Video, September 23, 2016.
64 *Transparent*, Season 3, episode 5, "Oh Holy Night," Amazon Prime Video, September 23, 2016.
65 *Transparent*, Season 3, episode 7, "Life Sucks and Then You Die," Amazon Prime Video, September 23, 2016; *Transparen*,. Season 3, episode 4, "Just the Facts," Amazon Prime Video, September 23, 2016.
66 *Transparent*, Season 3, episode 6, "The Open Road," Amazon Prime Video, September 23, 2016.
67 The name Ari, chosen by the character in the show's musical finale, is used in this essay and this volume to refer to them throughout the course of the show.
68 *Transparent*, Season 1, episode 5, "Why Do We Cover the Mirrors?" Amazon Prime Video, September 26, 2014.
69 *Transparent*, Season 3, episode 9, "Off the Grid," Amazon Prime Video, September 23, 2016; *Transparent*, Season 3, episode 3, "To Sardines and Back," Amazon Prime Video, September 23, 2016.
70 *Transparent*, Season 3, episode 5, "Oh Holy Night," Amazon Prime Video, September 23, 2016.
71 *Transparent*, Season 3, episode 5, "Oh Holy Night," Amazon Prime Video, September 23, 2016.
72 *Transparent*, Season 3, episode 9, "Off the Grid," Amazon Prime Video, September 23, 2016.
73 Sarah Bunin Benor, "Have You Noticed Those Images in Transparent?" *Lilith*, February 29, 2016, accessed June 10, 2020, http://lilith.org/blog/2016/02/have-you-noticed-these-images-in-transparent/,.
74 See the special issue of *Journal of Modern Jewish Studies*, Jennifer Caplan "Thinking about *Crazy Ex-Girlfriend*," *Journal of Modern Jewish Studies* 19, no. 1 (2020): 1-5.
75 *Difficult People*. "Unplugged." Season 2, episode 1, Hulu, July 12, 2016.
76 *Crazy Ex-Girlfriend*, Season 2, episode 10, "Will Scarsdale Like Josh's Shayna Punim?" The CW, January 13, 2017.
77 *The Handmaid's Tale*, Season 2, episode 5, "Seeds," Hulu, May 16, 2018.
78 Cara Rock-Singer, "Prophetesses of the Body: American Jewish Women and the Politics of Embodied Knowledge (PhD diss., Columbia University, 2018), 22–23.
79 *Transparent*, Season 5, episode 1, "Musicale Finale," Amazon Prime Video, September 27, 2019.
80 Ari also challenges understandings of religion as inherently hostile to queer and trans people. Yvette Taylor and Ria Snowden, eds., *Queering Religion, Religious Queers* (New York: Routledge, 2014); Naomi Braine, "Queering Secular Jewish 'Culture(s),'" in *Queering Religion, Religious Queers*, eds. Yvette Taylor and Ria Snowden (New York: Routledge, 2014), 31–43; on the associations of Jews with

queerness, see Daniel Boyarin, Daniel Itzkovitz, and Ann Pellegrini, eds., *Queer Theory and the Jewish question* (New York: Columbia University Press, 2003).

81. *Transparent*, Season 2, episode 9, "Man on the Land," Amazon Prime Video, December 11, 2015.
82. *Transparent*, Season 5, episode 1, "Musicale Finale," Amazon Prime Video, September 27, 2019.
83. *Transparent*, Season 5, episode 1, "Musicale Finale," Amazon Prime Video, September 27, 2019.
84. *Transparent*, Season 5, episode 1, "Musicale Finale," Amazon Prime Video, September 27, 2019.
85. Hadley Freeman, "*Transparent*'s Jill Soloway: 'The Words Male and Female Describe Who We Used to Be,'" *Guardian*, May 21, 2017, https://www.theguardian.com/tv-and-radio/2017/may/21/transparents-jill-soloway-the-words-male-and-female-describe-who-we-used-to-be; Ariel Levy, "Dolls and Feelings," *New Yorker*, December 14, 2015, accessed January 8, 2024, https://www.newyorker.com/magazine/2015/12/14/dolls-and-feelings.

Part 4
Queering Jewish and Transgender History

Three Perspectives on *Transparent*'s Use of the Holocaust

Part 4

12

Queer Temporality in Trans Times

Connection and Belonging in *Transparent*'s Second Season

JOSHUA FALEK

As the flash clicks and the shutter closes, the opening scene of *Transparent*'s second season descends into utter chaos just prior to Sarah and Tammy's wedding.[1] Bickering over who to include in their family photo, the Pfeffermans simply cannot seem to agree on who should be in the frame. Repeatedly interrupting the photographer's staging by inviting relatives and friends alike, tensions reach a fever pitch as Ari sarcastically asks if "anybody else wants in?"[2] Unbeknownst to them, Ari's seemingly innocuous question actually acknowledges the spectral presence that follows the Pfeffermans throughout the season: the ghosts of the past that interrupt both the idealized stability of the family and of linear time.

To reckon with this relationship between linear time, familial structure, and sexuality, queer theorists have proliferated theories of "queer temporality" to explore both how time structures western definitions of sexuality and embodiment and how temporal analyses may reveal potentials for novelty, pleasure, and joy that appear as excess(ive) to "straight time."[3] Due to an innovative combination of casting, and visual and narrative techniques, scholars have previously argued that *Transparent* achieves and complicates theories of queer temporality. On the one hand, Linda M. Hess argues that *Transparent*'s portrayal of character development and focus on trans aging and nonlinear storytelling "queers" temporality.[4] On the other hand, Nicole Morse mines *Transparent*'s employment of double casting (or doubling)—when one actor plays multiple roles within the same performance—for trans and queer temporalities. Morse illustrates how doubling is so pervasive that by the end of season 2, only two of the main characters, Maura and Gittel, have not been doubled; instead "they nonetheless double each other metaphorically" in part producing "an alternative, nonlinear temporality in Transparent."[5]

In conversation with these authors, this chapter nuances earlier analyses of *Transparent*'s queer temporality through two interventions. First, this chapter evinces how pleasure is the scaffolding of *Transparent*'s putatively queer temporality. Although characters experience a range of emotions that may interface with queerness, I argue that pleasure comes to both represent and catalyze queer temporality in its capacity to push the characters, narratively and metaphorically, out of time. To do so, I employ erotohistoriography, an alternative historiographical practice developed by Elizabeth Freeman that endeavors to trace versatile moments of queer pleasure. For Freeman, "erotohistoriography indexes how queer relations complexly exceed the present. It insists that various queer social practices, especially those involving enjoyable bodily sensations, produce form(s) of time consciousness, even historical consciousness, that can intervene upon the material damage done in the name of development."[6]

Erotohistoriography may be conceived of as an alternative method of history, weaving threads of pleasure together for knowledge production. Through this process, erotohistoriography traces queer forms of kinship and affective investments. By searching for pleasure, erotohistoriography helps reveal *Transparent*'s reputed queerness, exposing different theoretical mobilizations of queer temporality.

Secondly, this chapter employs trans theories of time, alongside queer theories, to account for what Hess describes as the "concurrence of contradictory elements" that cannot be easily categorized as either invoking a distinct straight or queer temporality.[7] I argue that Julian Carter's "transitional time" better accounts for the contradictory minutiae of *Transparent*'s storytelling than do theories of queer temporality.[8] Therefore, this chapter engages with theories of affect, Judaism, television narrative, and trans embodiment to explore the role of pleasure in *Transparent*'s narrative structure and to illustrate the contingencies of different theories of queer temporality, including those of Carla Freccero, Jack Halberstam, and Heather Love. The chapter begins by demonstrating how Jewish ritual and history are imagined as the progenitors of queerness, building to an analysis of the penultimate episode of season 2 when the Pfeffermans finally face their Weimar relatives. I conclude by exploring how trans theory accounts for the series' contradictory portrayal of temporality and suggest that this contextualization of *Transparent*'s moments of queer temporality might elucidate the show's relevance for post-Holocaust media scholars.

Movement and Pleasure: Straight Failures to Backwards Progress

Throughout the first two-thirds of the show's second season, *Transparent*'s characters find pleasure through failing to attain or sustain the criteria of "chrononormativity." Coined by Elizabeth Freeman, chrononormativity characterizes the ways time/age-based assumptions of progress and productivity enact a normative standard against and through which subjects are disciplined and regulated.[9] These "hidden rhythms," similar to Pierre Bourdieu's *habitus*, disguise the compulsory by normalizing select livelihoods while penalizing those outside of these rhythms.[10] Chrononormativity is constituted both at the micro level of the schedule and the timetable—like a nine-to-five job—and at the macro level— through the ascription of specific productive and developmentalist narratives— such as the idealized age that one supposedly should marry, begin family planning, or expect to die. Chrononormativity subtends the idealized progression from monogamous partners, to having children, and then "saving for a well-earned retirement (think Cam and Mitch from ABC's *Modern Family*)."[11]

Freeman argues that chrononormativity disciplines individuals so that they embrace a narrative of generational development and familial coherence, as the coherence of the family promises the advancement of the population. As Jack Halberstam writes, "The deployment of the concept of family, whether in hetero- or homo-contexts, almost always introduces normative understandings of time and transmission from one generation to the next."[12] Given this inextricability of the nuclear family, heterosexuality, and chrononormativity, queerness thus names alternative temporal structures that reject such normative generational transmissions.

Reevaluating the Pfeffermans' photograph, queerness might index the incapacity of the family to be captured. Though seemingly banal, Freeman intimates a certain, conservative nature to the medium of photography in contrast to the freedom of video. Where one can play with meaning by rewinding or fast-forwarding a VHS tape, the photograph is instead characterized by a supposed stasis that ossifies meaning.[13] This unyielding quality renders the family photo, for Marianne Hirsch, "the primary" medium of familial "self-knowledge and representation".[14] If the family photo is thereby the predominant "means by which family memory would be continued and perpetuated,"[15] the Pfeffermans' failure to maintain familial distinction may intimate the queer impossibility of transmitting, representing, or containing their family. Fighting among one another, the family cannot simply stage their coherence let alone actualize it beyond the symbolic. For after all that hustle and bustle, the audience never even sees the photograph and remains unable to stabilize either the photograph or the family. This lack of photographic representation simply affirms the porous nature of the Pfeffermans, filled with relationships that cannot be entirely named or fleshed out. Incapable of simply staying still, settling, or agreeing upon what or who constitutes the family, or even representing the family, the photograph is symptomatic of a failure to enact the chrononormative regulation of familial bounds and transmission of familial memory. Thus, by denying the audience the satisfaction of the photograph's success, the series intimates the Pfeffermans' familial intransmissibility, both broadly in their incapacity to secure the boundaries of their family and specifically as a harbinger of the impending doom of Tammy and Sarah's marital bliss.

The photograph, too, is a telling depiction of the affective relationship that the Pfeffermans share with the normative. As they endeavor to take this picture, there is little pleasure to be found: it is a cringeworthy scene of frustration and anxiety. Though many may find trying to take a family photo to be annoying, for the Pfeffermans this public display of emotions also demonstrates how they bristle against the normative structure of the family. Instead, granting the frustration of this photographic endeavor, this scene serves as the audience's first insight into how the Pfeffermans may only find pleasure in excess of straight time. This excess is one of queer pleasure facilitated by familial permeability and instability. Thus, these pleasures of malleability, plasticity, or disorientation that cannot be captured by the photograph are also what constitutes Freeman's and *Transparent*'s queer temporality, as evidenced by the scene following Sarah and Tammy's wedding ceremony.

During the reception, Sarah flees to the bathroom upon realizing that her marriage to Tammy was a mistake. Confused by her sudden absence, Tammy shouts, "Where's my girl at?" while Simon, Sarah's cousin, dances the hora with the rest of the attendees (see figure 12.1). As Simon twirls joyfully beneath the camera, the audience is transported to the 1930s, where Simon or another character doubled by Bashir Naim, continues to dance with others at the Hirschfeld Institute for Sexual Science. Through Simon's bodily pleasure, the show shifts into magical realism. Here, pleasure is the needle pulling thread, sewing together

FIGURE 12.1 *Transparent*. Season 2:1. Simon's dance brings the Pfeffermans to relatives past.

a history that unites Simon, who is heavily queer-coded though described only as nerdy, with a historic trans and queer community. Eschewing identity as necessary for connection, pleasures from Jewish familial ritual and the sundering of marital chrononormativity create this vulnerability to temporal potential. The catastrophe of Sarah's wedding yields to a renewed openness to queerness that pushes Simon to new pleasures, to new times. It is not pain alone (or even Simon's own pain), but pleasure in the face of this pain, a pleasure in the pain of the incoherence of the nuclear family that is the operative mechanism through which *Transparent* queers temporality. In all three of the Pfefferman children's storylines, queerness occurs as and through pleasure in the failure to abide by normative standards.

At the beginning of season 2, the middle child, Josh, starts dating Rabbi Raquel to the great delight of his mother.[16] However, Raquel leaves him after he fails to support her through her miscarriage.[17] He does not truly face his failure until his ego is tested on Yom Kippur, as he is forced to look Raquel in the eye when she leads the prayer, Al Chet.[18] Capturing the graceful march of pulsing fists upon the chest, as is custom to Al Chet, the camerawork imbues the scene with tension.[19] As Josh struggles to cope with his profane reality at the sight/site of the holy, the momentum builds. Shots become shorter, fists faster, and the collective beat arhythmic until Josh can no longer stand still. Before the prayer ends, he flees out to the white steps of the synagogue.[20] His exit provides momentary relief, but he takes far more drastic steps after his mother becomes distraught upon hearing of his separation. Leaving soon after this confrontation, Josh embraces the childlike when he finds himself devastated in a market and breaks down, stuffing his face with bread and ham in the store before paying.[21]

Here, Josh takes pleasure in the collapse of his Judaism and his heterosexual relationship through food, declining the supposed politeness of the nice Jewish boy for spoiled, indulgent sustenance. According to Hess, this is just one example of how all three siblings engage in "age-inappropriate" behaviors, building throughout the season to question temporal structures and acting as "an illustration of 'immaturity and a refusal of adulthood.'"[22] These behaviors are further related to a sense of the inappropriate, as they have commonly been understood to signify queerness. As Heather Love explains, "Homosexuality is often seen as a result of a failure of maturation ... associated with narcissism and infantilism as well as with incomplete or failed gendering."[23] *Transparent*'s utilization of this backward trope reorients Josh from heteronormativity and discloses associations to other "ruined identities," such as Jewish masculinity.[24] As Ashkenazi Jewish men have often been stereotyped as weak and soft, Josh's meltdown connects him to historical lineages of failed Jewish genders, co-constituting stereotypes of frailty among both Jews and queer men.[25] Namely, Josh becomes representative of a form of developmental failure by embracing the disorienting pleasure of the forbidden (i.e., ham).

Central to Hess's analysis and to others who employ notions of development in arguments regarding queer temporality is the putative progressive quality of chrononormativity. By sidestepping or actively delaying what should appear as the future (for Josh, a child and a wife), Hess and others consider these fraught forms of kinship outside of the family structure to be a sign of what Halberstam has described as "the queer art of failure."[26] For Halberstam, failure offers a certain queerness because queer people are not only regularly thought to fail in regards to upholding the "good life" but also, failure is "something queers do and have always done exceptionally well."[27] Transgressing normative ideals of productivity, failure offers the potential for some to achieve respites from punitive modes of discipline and for certain potentials for pleasure.[28] Thus, swerving away from a life with Rabbi Raquel, Josh's breakdown is emblematic of a certain type of failure that offers pleasures previously forbidden (ham and a breakdown) from the blundering of both a properly heterosexual and properly Jewish masculinity. This is not to say that Josh is queer but that his failure could be categorized as reflecting Halberstam's theoretic, which idealizes queerness as offering an escape to the temporal discipline of everyday life.

Meanwhile, Ari and Sarah also depart from the "good life" as they reckon with pleasures assumed unruly and adevelopmental. Ari begins the season identifying as straight and single, but they quickly embrace their queerness and find a partner, only to leave that partner—due in part to reading queer and feminist theory—to explore nonmonogamy.[29] Although there is nothing more or less queer about polyamory, there is a specific backwardness about leaving one's partner because one is so enamored with queer theory. For within this scenario, a belief in the possibility of a theoretical utopia scaffolded by queer, polyamorous love reorients Ari away from both the immediate pleasures of heterosexuality and queerness for an assumedly deferred resolution. It is in this hope, what we may interpret as a childish optimism, that queerness operates even as it displaces Ari's love object. Queerness here functions not only as a failure to maintain heterosexuality but also as investments in objects that do not grant traditional pleasures (i.e., theory). That is, though distinct from the more immediate pleasures that Josh and Sarah embrace, Ari's desire is no less queer in its deferral of normative ground for mere potential itself.

Sarah begins the series married to Len, the father of her two children.[30] But by the end of season one, she is engaged to Tammy. All does not go as planned, and Sarah calls off the wedding before the reception is over—once again, a refusal of the normative lineage toward futurity and family.[31] She falls far from the heteronormative dream with Len, and the homonormative dream with Tammy, finding herself unbound by a need to be consumed, finally asking for her drug dealer to rape her without it hurting.[32] This is a jarring request that is both indicative of Sarah's fall from grace, but also, in her explicit ask for an act of sexual violence sans pain, Sarah articulates a desire for the pleasures of rough, masochistic, and violent sex that are seemingly incommensurable with the familial home (though which often are found within it nonetheless).

All three Pfefferman children engage in new bodily pleasures, "confront[ing] the idea of progress in terms of heteronormative markers of futurity and ... interrogat[ing] the logic of family."[33] Through this relationship between failure, pleasure, and backwardness, *Transparent* envisions specific connections between corporeality and temporality, wherein the failures of the characters to follow prescribed developmental pathways construct opportunities to explore divergent formations of sexuality and gender.

Moppa on the Land

Following these events, Ari, Sarah, and Maura head out on a road trip to the Idyllwild Wimmin's Music Festival, *Transparent*'s homage to the transphobic Michigan Womyn's Music Festival (or MichFest).[34] As the characters explore the grounds, the audience may feel unsettled due to the disjunction between the Pfeffermans' excitement and the strain on the viewer who may already know of MichFest's reputation. This uncanny feeling is compounded by the episode's complicated—loving, yet critical—portrayal of the aesthetics and politics of MichFest, and more broadly, the ostensibly passé status of these second-wave feminist music festivals typical from the 1970s to the 1990s with utopian and separatist ideals. Integrating both parodic and celebratory elements of the separatist movement, including white women acting as experts on indigeneity, women's folk music, "vagitarian" T-shirts, and mass nudity, Idyllwild engages with a political lesbian public, regarded by many as a distinct part of the second-wave—that is, the feminist—past.[35] This homage is further dated by the episode's premiere three months after the final MichFest.[36]

By embracing this eeriness within the almost-but-not-yet-gone, the episode also appears to "disorient and denaturalize historical chronology and straight time ... caution[ing] us against the idea of 'getting history right.'"[37] As political generations are perceived to cleanly progress past one another, this episode, as Freeman might describe, also disrupts the idealized notion of linear history. With the contemporary moment characterized as the "Transgender Tipping Point,"[38] or supposedly a moment when trans people will be fully seen as human with recognized civil rights, the attitudes of Idyllwild appear out of time,[39] and the Pfeffermans appear out of place.[40] As Emi Koyama writes, these festivals and their exclusionary policies revealed the faults of feminist organizing at that time, depending on a static definition of womanhood and providing influence for some of the rethinking that shaped the contemporary mainstream movement.[41] With trans people now presumably traveling upon teleological roads toward acceptance, where "progress is linear ... and there is no going back," this stereotyped, exclusionary attitude occurs as not simply anachronistic but as though it has incomprehensible ties to the past and the present.[42] Thus, by constructing both generations as concurrent, the episode harkens to a former call that cannot be currently answered, demonstrating a queerness apparent through the contact between "two historically distinct forms of womanhood."[43] *Transparent* complicates narrative by situating this episode within a festival that is not only now gone but hailed as having had a revolutionary potential that is no longer commensurable to contemporary politics. It connects the very failures of the family to the collective unanswered aspirations of the movement.

Shortly after the family separates at the festival, Maura finally learns of the festival's transphobic policies, and panic sets in: the camerawork increases in speed, the shots become shorter, and the pace echoes the frantic Al Chet.[44] Eventually, Maura and Ari find each other at Camp Sojourner, run by Leslie, Maura's former academic colleague, and Ari's potential new love interest.[45] Frustrated by the conversation between the women about trans-exclusive spaces, Maura rushes back to her campsite as Ari chases after her. While this occurs, Sarah engages in a BDSM bondage scene where she is lost at the borders of pain and pleasure. Her whimpers and yelps lead the way for Maura and Ari to lose themselves deeper in the woods, as the family faces dissolution over transmisogyny. The family appears here severed: Maura running off, Ari searching for her, and Sarah tied up.

As Ari continues to repeatedly scream, "Moppa," without any parent to be found, Sarah's moans are interspliced, mixing pleasure with discipline and loss. But Maura steals the scene, tearing down her campsite while repeatedly screaming, "Man on the land!" and transforming her anger into near song.[46] Playing with her fury, Maura takes pleasure in this destruction for it is a moment of self-articulation, abjection, and discovery. Rage such as Maura's, that has the power to deliver one to one's body, to speak one's body into becoming, and to create embodied novelty, has previously been described by Susan Stryker as "transgender rage."[47] For Stryker, transgender rage is that "bred by the necessity of existing in external circumstances that work against [her] survival."[48] Yet for Stryker, this rage also produces a unique temporality, where "in birthing my rage, my rage has rebirthed me."[49] Through this process of subjectivization, Stryker's transgender rage elucidates why the most spectacular and horrifying instance of shifting temporalities occurs following Maura's "giv[ing] voice to what had previously been silent."[50] Her rage cleaves a schism in the present that facilitates both a pleasure in campsite destruction and the potential to give birth to oneself, which occurs through the metaphorical doubling between Gittel and Maura. Recognizing these connections through erotohistoriography reveals pleasure's ability to structure disorientation and vice versa, suggesting certain relationships between self-shattering, pleasure, and temporality. The pleasure and danger[51] of self-articulation and queer sex not only saturate the scene but seem to offer the affective landscape to produce the season's most obvious temporal turmoil.

Witness

The scene continues: Maura dances, lifting her arms in the air until a sudden ringing of bells—Ari passes their great-grandmother along the path, whose "Jew shoes" ring out the temporal shifting from Maura's rightful rampage to the violence of Weimar Germany.[52] The drumbeat is suddenly replaced with a melancholic theme featured in the previous episode, "Kina Hora," and both timelines converge upon a singular location in a startling process.[53]

Watching Gittel and Rose, happy as can be in the Hirschfeld institute, the audience sees the soldiers approach through the windows.[54] Intriguingly, the characters' lack of awareness of their impending harm is itself doubled, as during the scene's shooting, the actors playing the Nazis were not introduced to the main cast so as to intimidate both cast and character.[55] This leaves the viewer watching the reunion of siblings past with relative(s) future, touching one another, as they witness Gittel's demise (see figure 12.2). Ari and Rose hold hands, taking flight through this intergenerational, familial, Jewish, and queer somatic gesture. Yet this touch is not only from one to another but from one to oneself—Emily Robinson, who plays Rose, actually doubles as young Ari—during season 1.[56] This doubling creates both an intimacy between Ari and Rose and Ari and their younger self, obscuring, muddying, and potentially queering the forms of kinship and subjectivity present. Queer failure to maintain heteronormativity does not always succeed in eschewing the family altogether but also may lead to different permutations of its formation and function. Here, *Transparent* masters melodrama, utilizing affect, pleasure, and danger as cause for event, as the logic for why Gittel and Rose appear upon a campground somewhere between there and now. This moment is not a

FIGURE 12.2 *Transparent*. Season 2:9. Ari and Rose hold hands, watching as Gittel faces Nazi violence.

manufactured prescriptive saviorism, wherein Ari can change the past; rather, they can only give witness to trans and queer Jews who faced Holocaust brutalities. Ari does not turn away from Gittel but instead stares on. They stand with the dead and with themself. Shattered between Leslie and Maura, Ari recuperates with(in) themself.

Carla Freccero theorizes about this form of witnessing as a queer spectrality, an ethical orientation toward the historical past that responds to the "politico-logic of trauma" through a patience to hear the past's call.[57] Freccero furnishes a case for using spectrality as an ethic for attending to the demands of the past while reminding that this "patience" can also function as "passivity," or the waiting for the arrival of specters.[58] By staying with the vulnerable, by refusing to turn away, but knowing they cannot do more than meet eyes, Ari and Rose perpetuate both this form of attendance and passivity. Ari engages a mode of "historical attentiveness that the living might have to attend to what is not present," as they join Rose in witnessing the end of one line in their family's lineage.[59] *Transparent* mobilizes a temporality that not only refuses normativity but actually complicates the very manner of subjectivity and Heather Love's demand to resist "the call of gay normalization [by] refusing to write off the most vulnerable, the least presentable, and all the dead."[60] So, this witnessing here acts as the key to a mode of being that does not turn away from the ugly but instead permits impression.

This act of witnessing is substantial, as it is a witnessing to what has been both historically erased through archival destruction—hidden histories—and cinematically erased for the viewer, as Gittel's screams are drowned out by the score and her very fate concealed as she is dragged off camera. Ari and Rose are two of the few people to bear witness to her story, but the characters' doubling further complicates the temporality, as it is unclear who is truly watching this scene. Is it Ari and themself imagining, Rose and herself remembering, or Ari and Rose together?[61] The casting choices are themselves witnesses to temporal troubles. In effect, one might consider that this reflects the doubling found within the art of *Transparent* consultant Zachary Drucker, whose use of the method, as Nicole Morse describes, is to make "transfeminine history visible."[62] This doubling of both Ari and Rose and Maura and Gittel allows the audience to see and feel such a transfeminine history even if Ari may not fully comprehend the touch of the self or to what they are a witness.

If this scene ensures the visibility of this history, it also renders the audience another witness to the transmisogyny always already constitutive of this history. As a witness, the audience is compelled to share in the ethical dilemma of what to do when one sees fascist violence—a question that could not be more relevant in the current political climate. Where the possibility for Ari to save Rose may be foreclosed, if I am to be generous, then perhaps the audience's witnessing might also articulate that witnessing is not enough. Queerness cannot save Rose, but others do not have to fall to her same fate. If at best a queer temporality can offer the potential to reflect upon this loss, indexing both its promise and its very real limits, then perhaps instead, might this queer spectrality offer an attunement to the past so that one may do more than witness in the present day but resist transphobia by whatever means necessary? Neither inherently revolutionary nor productive, witnessing is an act that can provide an orientation toward the present where the fight continues.[63]

All Tied Up

Following pleasure and affect, it is evident that *Transparent* diverges from a multitude of the normative "interlocking temporal schemes necessary for genealogies of descent" through backward impulses, witnessing, and spectrality.[64] This final section contends with how *Transparent* acts as a venue to consider how queer theories of temporality might further interface with trans studies and Holocaust studies. As illustrated throughout this chapter, queer theories of temporality often mobilize notions of development or delay. Yet as Julian Carter posits, queer theories that rely on "delay would seem particularly complex for trans-subjects."[65] Writing about a trans man, Carter points to how delaying a trans person at the childlike merely asks them to be interpellated incorrectly, for "arresting his development at that stage would foreclose his access to gay masculinity, not confirm it."[66] Instead of arrest, Carter suggests that trans subjects and temporalities might be similarly marked by a "return with a difference."[67] Thus, although the Pfefferman children access and even mark the narrative with queerness through developmental arrest, to argue as such regarding Maura would be to foreclose her from transition. To account for these contradictions, of both future orientations and narrative failures, Carter introduces a theory of "transitional time" to reckon with queer temporalities for trans studies and trans subjects; transitional time integrates "straight and queer temporalities.... enclosing the notion of queer time in a trans embrace."[68] Thus, Carter's theoretic provides the means to reckon with how queer and straight times are not merely a "concurrence of contradictory elements," as Hess writes, but come together themselves to form a transitional time.[69]

For Carter, transitional time diverges from queer theories of delay that "simultaneously shuts down the space for becoming-trans" and instead provides for alternative forms of temporality that may still offer progression yet "heighten the body's sensitivity, invaginating it so that it touches itself in several different moments at once."[70] Within this series, the entanglements of straight and queer times can perhaps most easily be glimpsed in regards to Hess's argument about inheritance. For Hess, because the episode following "Man on the Land" features flashbacks to Maura's birth and her parents' confusion about her in utero sex, Gittel's death putatively bequeaths transness to Maura, enacting a progressive logic of family and rebirth.[71] By deploying both the transgender rage wherein Maura gives birth to herself and the linearity of familial transness, *Transparent* plays with transitional time that does not delay Maura but instead permits a spaciousness for a multitude of temporalities. This is also seemingly the very point that Soloway and their collaborators are endeavoring to show through the season's consistent references to epigenetics and intergenerational trauma. Transitional time marks the form of inheritance that, like epigenetics, forms through permutation, "a return with a difference," wherein one is not delimited from development, but any such development is saturated by other forces.[72] Therefore, I want to suggest that *Transparent*'s second season acts through strands of queer and straight temporalities to form a transitional time.

Yet the inheritance of trauma and transness within this transitional time also reflects a trope of post-Holocaust media. Within what Hirsch describes as "postmemory" media, narratives frequently occur that feature "a structure of inter- and trans-generational transmission of traumatic knowledge... recall[ed]... at a generational remove."[73] Hirsch argues that in postmemory media, "gender and familiarity... absorb the shock, filter and diffuse the impact of trauma, diminish harm."[74] This characterization of postmemory media more fully explains why Gittel functions as Maura's double, or as Hess notes, her "heir," as the means through which Maura can live.[75] *Transparent* employs Gittel as the sponge for the trauma of both the Holocaust and transmisogyny; a future is impossible for Gittel but feasible for Maura through this transitional time, which again serves to question our ethical orientation to the past and the present.

This birth and death, the temporal touching, and the distortions of subjectivity between Rose and Ari are all characterized by Hirsch when she notes that postmemory media "actually reinforce[s] the living connection between past and present, between the generation of witnesses and survivors and the generation after."[76] Regarding this, then, as a form of inheritance does not necessarily destroy the potentiality for queerness, as it unites those like Ari and Rose and begets an attendance that would otherwise be lost. If anything, by reinforcing the "living" connection between what has been and what is, Hirsch envisions a queerness that similarly to Freeman would "propose other possibilities for living in relation to indeterminately past, present, and future others."[77]

Nevertheless, this connective tissue, no matter how queer, does once again require a reckoning with trans embodiment. For if, as Hess proposes, Maura inherits Gittel's transness, then *Transparent* accurately depicts "straight time" as marred or rather concomitant with transmisogyny. Here, inheritance and lineage are bequeathed through a violence that cannot be queered away. Thus, considering *Transparent* through the lens of queer temporality yields an opportunity to ask what queer means and who can be queered. Theories of developmentality that are carried from queer to trans theory must then address the divergent livelihoods of trans people, and the importance of Carter's theory cannot be overstated. Namely, when Hess writes that the series "*queers* aging and temporality," it is imperative to account, as Hess does, for whom?[78]

In effect, attending to postmemory media and transitional time provides a crucial addition to theorizations of *Transparent* by expanding how scholars have thought *Transparent* either within trans theories of temporality or as an example of post-Holocaust media. Capturing the spectral spirit central to *Transparent*'s narrative, Hirsch exemplifies how Jewish studies and queer theory might be just as porous as the Pfefferman family. *Transparent* provides an opportunity to explore the interstices of Judaism, trans embodiment, and theories of temporality, making the boundaries between witnesses, survivors, and familial generations permeable, amorphous, and, perhaps remarkably, queer.

Notes

1. *Transparent*, Season 2, Episode 1, "Kina Hora," Amazon Prime Video, November 30, 2015.
2. *Transparent*, "Kina Hora."
3. See, for example, Elizabeth Freeman, *Time Binds: Queer Temporalities, Queer Histories* (Durham, NC: Duke University Press, 2010); Jack Halberstam, *The Queer Art of Failure* (Durham, NC: Duke University Press, 2011); or the special issue from *GLQ* 13, no. 2–3 (June 2007), edited by Elizabeth Freeman.
4. Linda M. Hess, "My Whole Life I've Been Dressing up like a Man: Negotiations of Queer Aging and Queer Temporality in the TV Series Transparent," *European Journal of American Studies* 11, no. 3 (2017): 3.
5. Nicole Morse, "Seeing Double: Visibility, Alternative Temporality, and Transfeminine History in 'Transparent,'" *Jump Cut: A Review of Contemporary Media*, accessed January 9, 2024, https://www.ejumpcut.org/archive/jc57.2016/-MorseTransparent/index.html.
6. Freeman, *Time Binds*, 120.
7. Hess, "My Whole Life," 14.
8. Julian Carter, "Embracing Transition, or Dancing in the Folds of Time," in *The Transgender Studies Reader 2*, eds. Susan Stryker and Aren Z. Aizura (New York: Routledge, 2013), 139.
9. Freeman, *Time Binds*, 3.
10. Freeman, *Time Binds*, 3.
11. Matt Knutson, "Backtrack, Pause, Rewind, Reset: Queering Chrononormativity in Gaming," *Game Studies* 18, no. 3 (December 2018), http://gamestudies.org/1803/articles/knutson.
12. Halberstam, *The Queer Art of Failure*, 71.
13. Freeman, *Time Binds*, xviii.
14. Marianne Hirsch, "Introduction" in *The Familial Gaze*, ed. Marianne Hirsch (Hanover, NH: Dartmouth College, 1999), xvi.
15. Marianne Hirsch, "Introduction" in *The Familial Gaze*, ed. Marianne Hirsch (Hanover, NH: Dartmouth College, 1999), xvi.
16. *Transparent*, Season 1, Episode 9, "Looking Up," Amazon Prime Video, September 26 2015.
17. *Transparent*, Season 2, Episode 5, "Bulnerable," Amazon Prime Video, November 30 2015.
18. *Transparent*, Season 2, Episode 7, "The Book of Life," Amazon Prime Video, November 30 2015.

19 *Transparent*, "The Book of Life."
20 *Transparent*, "Bulnerable."
21 *Transparent*, "Bulnerable."
22 Hess, "My Whole Life," 9.
23 Heather Love, *Feeling Backward: Loss and the Politics of Queer History* (Cambridge: Harvard University Press, 2009), 2.
24 Love, *Feeling Backward*, 30.
25 Daniel Boyarin, *Unheroic Conduct: The Rise of Heterosexuality and the Invention of the Jewish Man* (Berkeley: University of California Press, 2000), 229.
26 Hess, "My Whole Life," 8–9.
27 Halberstam, *The Queer Art of Failure*, 3.
28 Halberstam, *The Queer Art of Failure*, 3.
29 *Transparent*, Season 1, Episode 7, "The Symbolic Exemplar," Amazon Prime Video, September 26, 2015.
30 *Transparent*, Season 1, Episode 1, "Pilot," Amazon Prime Video, September 26, 2015.
31 Hess, "My Whole Life," 10.
32 *Transparent*, "The Book of Life," 2015.
33 Hess, "My Whole Life," 10.
34 Emi Koyama, "Whose Feminism Is It Anyway?: The Unspoken Racism of the Trans Inclusion Debate," in *The Transgender Studies Reader*, ed. Susan Stryker and Stephen Whittle (New York: Routledge, 2006), 698–705.
35 Freeman, *Time Binds*, xxiii.
36 Trudy Ring, "This Year's Michigan Womyn's Music Festival Will Be the Last," *Advocate*, April 21, 2015. https://www.advocate.com/michfest/2015/04/21/years-michigan-womyns-music-festival-will-be-last.
37 Gunhild Borggreen and Rune Gade, *Performing Archives / Archives of Performance* (Copenhagen: Museum Tusculanum Press, University of Copenhagen, 2013), 459.
38 This is a reference to a 2014 *Time* article that proudly announced that trans rights had entered a new era of progress.
39 This essay was originally written in 2015, and so while Idyllwild may have felt out of place then, I hazard to guess that this notion of the tipping point could, too, feel out of place granting the violent assault on trans people and especially on trans visibility across the United States, Canada, United Kingdom, and many other countries. Nevertheless, in its representation of second wave music festivals, Idyllwild does still perform a sort of pastness.
40 Samantha Allen, "Whatever Happened to the Transgender Tipping Point?," *The Daily Beast*, March 31, 2017, sec. arts-and-culture, https://www.thedailybeast.com/articles/2017/03/31/whatever-happened-to-the-transgender-tipping-point.
41 Koyama, "Whose Feminism Is It Anyway?," 702.
42 Koyama, "Whose Feminism Is It Anyway?," 702.
43 Freeman, *Time Binds*, 70.
44 *Transparent*, "Man on the Land," 2015.
45 *Transparent*, Season 2, Episode 9, "Man on the Land," Amazon Prime Video, November 30, 2015.
46 *Transparent*, "Man on the Land," 2015.
47 Susan Stryker, "My Words to Victor Frankenstein above the Village of Chamounix: Performing Transgender Rage," in *The Transgender Studies Reader*, ed. Susan Stryker and Stephen Whittle (New York: Routledge, 2013), 248–249.
48 Stryker, "My Words," 249.
49 Stryker, "My Words," 252.

50 Harlan Weaver, "Monster Trans: Diffracting Affect, Reading Rage," *Somatechnics* 3, no. 2 (September 1, 2013): 298, https://doi.org/10.3366/soma.2013.0099.
51 Carole S. Vance, *Pleasure and Danger: Exploring Female Sexuality*, United Kingdom: Pandora, 1992).
52 *Transparent*, "Man on the Land," 2015.
53 *Transparent*, "Kina Hora." 2015.
54 *Transparent*, "Kina Hora," 2015.
55 David Naim, "Gendering the Holocaust" (presentation, *Transparent*: A Multidisciplinary Symposium, University of Rochester, Rochester, NY, December 2nd 2016.
56 *Transparent*, "Best New Girl," 2014; Morse too makes this point in their article "Seeing Double."
57 Carla Freccero, *Queer/Early/Modern* (Durham, NC: Duke University Press, 2006), 104.
58 Freccero, *Queer/Early/Modern*, 104.
59 Freccero, *Queer/Early/Modern*, 69.
60 Love, *Feeling Backward*, 30.
61 This paper was originally written prior to the airing of the fourth season where Ari reveals that they were not aware of Gittel.
62 Morse, "Seeing Double."
63 Though this does beg the question of what kind of an ethical orientation requires this violence in the first place as the antecedent to one's orientation.
64 Freeman, *Time Binds*, xxii.
65 Carter, "Embracing Transition," 139.
66 Carter, "Embracing Transition," 139.
67 Carter, "Embracing Transition," 139.
68 Carter, "Embracing Transition," 142.
69 Hess, "My Whole Life," 35.
70 Carter, "Embracing Transition," 142.
71 Hess, "My Whole Life," 13.
72 Carter, "Embracing Transition," 139.
73 Marianne Hirsch, "The Generation of Postmemory," *Poetics Today* 29, no. 1 (2008): 106.
74 Hirsch, "The Generation," 125.
75 Hess, "My Whole Life," 14.
76 Hirsch, "The Generation," 106.
77 Freeman, *Time Binds*, xxii.
78 Hess, "My Whole Life," 3.

13
Queering the Holocaust

Intersecting Jewish and Transgender Identities in *Transparent*

KERSTIN STEITZ

In *Transparent*, Joey Soloway uncovers and creates intersectionality between Jewish and transgender identities and histories on both the level of narrative and by practices of queering the narration. Soloway does so to show that Jewish and queer identities do not have to be distinct. Their queer Jewish retelling of the Holocaust in episodes 8 and 9 of season 2, entitled "Oscillate" and "Man on the Land," respectively, emphasizes that for the Pfefferman family and the broader communities it represents, the Holocaust is about Jewish and queerness at once.

These episodes trace Maura Pfefferman's family history and transgender history back to the German Jewish sexologist Magnus Hirschfeld (1868–1935). The National Socialists derogatively labeled Hirschfeld's research as "Jewish science," but in these episodes, Soloway proudly reclaims Hirschfeld as the first Jewish-identified trans activist. The fictional story of Gittel, Maura's transgender maternal aunt, and her deportation are embedded in the historical context of the Nazi's destruction of Hirschfeld's Institut für Sexualforschung, or Institute for Sexual Science, and the "homosexual" and "transvestite" community of 1933 Berlin.[1] The transgression of time and space in *Transparent* with this narrative to Weimar Berlin is interwoven into the present life of the

Pfefferman family through various flashbacks, which I argue serve as techniques of queering.

In this chapter, I focus on the second flashback in "Man on the Land" as a technique of queering, which is presented in the form of a parallel montage, and its specific functions and effects. I propose that the editing technique of parallel montage—alternating between flashbacks from the past to present events—reflects upon and creates intersectionality between Jewish and transgender intellectual and traumatic histories and identities. The parallel montage brings these categories in relation to one another and shows how they might intersect. In addition to employing the parallel montage structure, which creates intersectionality (suggesting similarities while simultaneously emphasizing differences between Maura and her aunt Gittel's experience as a Jewish transgender woman), Soloway also queers time on a structural level by means of flashbacks that converge with the present time at the end of the episode. In *Transparent*, Soloway revisits Jewish history and the Holocaust from a new queer perspective. Ultimately, Soloway rewrites history and actively shapes future discourses on Jewishness, queerness, and transness.

Legal scholar Kimberlé Williams Crenshaw introduced the term "intersectionality" in her 1989 essay "Demarginalizing the Intersection of Race and Sex: A Black Feminist Critique of Antidiscrimination Doctrine, Feminist Theory and Antiracist Politics" and elaborated on it two years later in "Mapping the Margins: Intersectionality, Identity Politics, Violence Against Women of Color."[2] She developed the concept based on her study of the marginalization of Black women in antidiscrimination law, which she observes fails to understand Black women's discrimination as both sexist and racist and instead considers them either as women, that is, white women, or as Black, that is, Black men, thereby erasing their difference to these groups as Black women: "Discrimination, like traffic through the intersection, may flow in one direction, and it may flow in another. If an accident happens in an intersection, it can be caused by cars traveling from any number of directions and, sometimes, from all of them. Similarly, if a Black woman is harmed because she is in the intersection, her injury could result from sex discrimination or race discrimination."[3]

Although the origins of Crenshaw's concept of intersectionality, a concept that has evolved in the past thirty years into "a method and a disruption, a heuristic and analytical tool,"[4] lie in Black feminism and critical race theory, it is intended to be and has been meaningfully applied to a variety of fields. Carbado et al. emphasized as much in the introduction to *Intersectionality: Mapping the Movements of a Theory*: "All intersectional moves are necessarily particularized and therefore provisional and incomplete. This is the sense in which a particularized intersectional analysis or formation is always a work-in-progress, functioning as a condition of possibility for agents to move intersectionality to other social contexts and group formations."[5] For example, before Soloway emphasized the intersectionality of Jewish and queer identities in *Transparent*, Jakobsen argued, in her famous polemically entitled text "Queers Are Like Jews, Aren't They? Analogy and Alliance Politics," in favor of the use of intersectionality over analogy because it allowed for the acknowledgment of similarities without erasing individual difference.[6] Jakobsen explained, "The queer-Jewish relation is historically grounded in and continues to work out of an attribution of complicity between the two specifically in antihomosexual and antisemitic discourses. One way to establish a more positive force to the analogy—one in which the queer-Jewish relation to difference is in play—is to recognize, and then resist, the constitution of their relation within a negative discourse."[7]

In the episode "Man on the Land," the show presents Maura as perceiving her "queer-Jewish" identity "within a negative discourse," which Soloway depicts in a complex and nuanced way, for example, by contrasting Maura's experience with the positively connoted queer Jewish sexologist Hirschfeld. Maura attends the Idyllwild Wimmin's Music Festival with Sarah and Ari. According to the fictional festival's policy in *Transparent*, only cisgender women, that is, biological women born with "a uterus and a vagina," are allowed to attend. Therefore, as a male-to-female transgender woman, Maura is not supposed to be present at the festival—a circumstance that neither her daughters nor she is aware of.[8]

After a heated debate with a group of feminists and Ari, in which all of them defend this policy by arguing that the exclusion of male-to-female transgender women is due to the male privilege they enjoyed before transitioning, Maura intends to leave. The scene of her frantically packing her belongings is interspersed with flashbacks to the destruction of Hirschfeld's institute by the National Socialists in 1933. These fragmentary flashbacks continue a crucial subplot that began in the previous episode, "Oscillate," as a cold-opening and isolated flashback. In that flashback, Gittel and her younger sister, Rose, explain to their mother, Yetta, why they refuse to leave Nazi Germany for the United States, arguing that Gittel has a good position at Hirschfeld's institute and feels protected by her trans activism.

Flashbacks are commonly used to signify memories in film. Turim defined the term flashback as "an image or a filmic segment that is understood as representing temporal occurrences anterior to those in the image that preceded it. The flashback concerns a representation of the past that intervenes within the present flow of the film narrative."[9] In the flashbacks, Hirschfeld's institute is presented in warm, bright colors as an almost utopian place for the 1933 Weimar Berlin of homosexuals and transgender individuals. In accordance with the actual institute, which Hirschfeld founded in 1919 and which offered a wide range of medical and counseling services around topics related to sexuality, Soloway depicts it in *Transparent* as a safe haven, providing this community with medical, psychological, intellectual, social, and cultural resources and opportunities. For example, "Oscillate" stages a variety show in which Gittel jumps happily on stage in a costume covering her genitals and breasts with leaves after successful gender confirmation surgery, followed by dancing, drinking, and intellectual conversations.

On the level of narration, I argue that the flashback functions here as queering because it is asynchronous. Evans explains the purposes and methodologies of queering history as follows: "A queered history questions claims to a singular, linear march of time and universal experience and points to the unconscious ways in which progressive narrative arcs often seep into our analyses. To queer the past is to view it skeptically, to pull apart its constitutive pieces and analyze them from a variety of perspectives, taking nothing for granted."[10] Queering history in these episodes of *Transparent* means revisiting the Holocaust from new perspectives to account for and retell histories from the perspective of LGBTQ individuals whose experiences of persecution during the Holocaust have been historically underrepresented. The practice of queering history requires, according to Elizabeth Freeman, the analysis of "points of resistance to ... temporal order." Freeman "track[s] the ways that nonsequential forms of time ... can also fold subjects into structures of belonging and duration that may be invisible to the historicist eye."[11] In addition to queering time structurally using flashbacks, Soloway goes back to 1933 Weimar Berlin, which marks a crucial point in modern German Jewish queer history. This time is personified by the historical figure of Magnus Hirschfeld. Hirschfeld's German Jewish identity, his sexual "disposition," as well as activism, point to intersectionality between these identity categories.[12]

In *Transparent*, Hirschfeld is staged sporting gray hair, a mustache, and round glasses amidst queer individuals in his institute.[13] Hirschfeld's research focus was homosexuality, which he considered a "third gender" (*drittes Geschlecht*), and sexual intermediacy.[14] He was the first person, as early as 1910 in his work *Die Transvestiten* (*Transvestites*), to coin the term "transvestite" for hetero- and homosexual cross-dressers, as well as for individuals whose gender assigned at birth did not match their gender identity.[15] Soloway proudly reclaims Hirschfeld in these flashbacks as the first Jewish trans activist.[16] From a medical and criminological perspective, according to Rainer Herrn, a German expert on Hirschfeld, cross-dressers were considered to be so-called "homosexuals," although this was not the case for every cross-dresser.[17] In *Transparent*, Yetta is prejudiced toward her trans-identifying daughter, Gittel. She neither understands the differences among cross-dressing, transgender, and homosexuality—"What is transvestite? That's like feygele, right?" and "Who is Magnus? Is he your gay lover?" she asks her daughters—nor accepts Gittel's transgender identity but calls her by her deadname, Gershom. *Feygele* is both a Yiddish term of endearment meaning little bird and a derogatory term for Jewish men to suggest that they have feminine qualities and are gay. Yetta's use is certainly derogatory and implies the common assumption in Weimar Germany that cross-dressers were gay. Male homosexuality was illegal according to paragraph 175 of the 1872 *Reichsstrafgesetz* (*RStG*; Criminal Code of the Reich) and also during National Socialism; it was not decriminalized in Germany until 1994. Hirschfeld sought to abolish paragraph 175.[18] Unlike male homosexuality, cross-dressing in public was not illegal in Weimar Berlin unless it was considered a "disorderly conduct," or *Erregung öffentlichen Ärgernisses* according to paragraph 183 *RStG*, or a "public nuisance" according to paragraph 360 *RStG*.[19] To protect the "transvestite" community in Berlin from the police and legal prosecution, Hirschfeld provided individuals with so-called "transvestite certificates," which indicated "that the bearer was known to the police and was not guilty of Unfug [nonsense] if apprehended while cross-dressing."[20] According to Herrn, under Nazism, fewer of these transvestite passes might have been issued, and consequently, many trans-identifying individuals might have lost their protection.[21] The transvestite certificates are also mentioned in *Transparent* when Gittel explains to her mother that Hirschfeld issued transvestite passes that allowed cross-dressing in public: "No one can arrest me. I am protected by the city." Gittel feels safer as a trans woman with a transvestite pass in Nazi Germany than her Jewish mother does. Her trust in her affiliation with Hirschfeld, his institute, and the community of other self-identifying transvestites, "who identified as members of the 'opposite sex'" as well as "homosexuals," gives her a greater sense of belonging and security than the visas her mother intends to get for each family member to join the father in the United States—an illusion, as it turns out, because Gittel is deported shortly thereafter in "Man on the Land."[22]

To reach wider acceptance and civil rights for homosexuals and transvestites in Weimar Berlin, Hirschfeld argued that it was natural that everyone was an "intermediate type" with feminine and masculine attributes.[23] Although Hirschfeld considered homosexuality as natural, he did conduct experiments to "cure" homosexuals of their sexual desires, for example, by implanting in homosexual men the testes of heterosexuals.[24] Hirschfeld's activism for civil rights for queer individuals seems to be closely connected to and informed by his confrontation with antisemitism. According to Ralf Dose, a science historian who cofounded the Magnus Hirschfeld Foundation in Berlin in 1982, Hirschfeld refused to consider the attributions "German" and "Jewish" as mutually exclusive binaries: "'The question: Where do you belong—what are you really? tortures me. If I frame the question as: 'Are you German—a Jew—or a world citizen?' then my answer is always 'world citizen' or 'all three.'"[25] This is consistent with Hirschfeld's theory that gender is not binary but a spectrum, although his theories also bear a certain essentialism because he assumed inherent male- and female-coded traits that can be found in the opposite gender. Hirschfeld applied his theories on gender and sexuality to race. In *Racism*, he proposed that race was a construct and sexuality was biological.[26]

Heike Bauer points to the "racialised reception" of Hirschfeld's work as Jewish science by antisemites and the National Socialists.[27] She emphasizes that Hirschfeld "himself neither responded directly to the antisemitism nor commented on his own Jewishness, but focused his efforts on the strengthening of sexual science."[28] According to Christina von Braun, the antisemitic and National

Socialist attribution of sexology as Jewish science was defamatory and closely connected to antisemitic sexual imagery.[29] Von Braun suggests that one reason why antisemitism discredited sexology as Jewish science was that its subject lends itself to defamation, especially in combination with Jewishness.[30]

Sander Gilman examined the antisemitic history and discourse of the feminization of Jewish men, which assumed that male Jews menstruated: "The idea of male menstruation is part of a Christian tradition of seeing the Jew as inherently, biologically different. From the late fourth-century *Adversus Judeaos* (*Against the Jews*) of the early church father St. John Chrysostom through the work of Thomas Cantipratanus, the thirteenth-century anatomist, the abnormal and abhorrent body of the Jew marked the implacable difference of Jewish males."[31]

Based on that discourse, the German Jewish sexologist Sigmund Freud, Wilhelm Fliess, and Hirschfeld continued to claim that male menstruation existed.[32] David Katz mentions that Hirschfeld used male menstruation as a basis to support his argument of "the existence of a continuum between male and female sexuality. He was also very interested in the phenomenon of the hermaphrodite, a male who menstruated, which played a large role in his work [*Sexualpathologie*]."[33] Freud and Fliess argued that male menstruation was connected to the nose and was not unique to male Jews but universal to all men:[34] "What once was a sign of difference (Jewish nose/Jewish menstruation) becomes a sign of universality (all males menstruate through the nose). Jews should therefore not be seen as different and inferior in their physical make-up, but rather as exemplars of a universal sign, a physical common law of periodicity in male bodies which in turn links all human beings, male and female."[35] Freud's argument of the universality of male menstruation also served the purpose of arguing for Jewish emancipation. Von Braun observes that the main difference between antisemitic Jewish sexual imagery and, for example, Hirschfeld's description of sexual intermediaries was their purpose: the former was defamatory toward Jews, and the latter established new notions of sexual and racial normalcy.

With *Transparent*, Soloway inserts themselves in this discourse and continues the work that Jewish sexologists began by reinterpreting antisemitic stereotypes about Jewish men for their own agenda in support of the transgender community. Instead of ascribing to and continuing with the negative antisemitic discourse of defaming Jewish men for menstruating, Soloway joins Jewishness and transgender identities in their Jewish transgender protagonist Maura, thereby attributing this discourse with new positive meaning, which is also a means of queering history. Likewise, in these episodes about Hirschfeld, Soloway reflects upon the Jewish history, origins, and discourses of sexology and proudly joins this tradition of Jewish sexology to contribute further to it. Although von Braun neutrally concludes that there are two distinct sexologies—a Jewish one and a Christian one—insofar as the religious thought traditions are contained in each, Soloway attributes new positive meaning to the antisemitic and Nazi ascription of Hirschfeld's science and sexology in general as Jewish science and proudly reclaims it—another significant dimension of queering.

The intersectionality between Jewish and queer traumatic histories is further reflected in *Transparent* in the presentation of the Nazi destruction of Hirschfeld's institute.[36] After establishing the historical context in the cold-opening flashback in "Oscillate," Soloway shows the destruction of the institute in fragmented flashbacks in "Man on the Land." Initially, Hirschfeld's institute is presented in bright colors, which not only signify these images as being from the past but also represent the institute's enlightened character. The peacefulness of the bright days of the institute in "Oscillate" gives way to fragmented flashbacks in its presentation in "Man on the Land." The sequence sets in with Amy Boman's melancholic song "Waiting" in the background. Rose is sitting in an armchair in a circle with Hirschfeld, Gittel, and Mendel, played by Luzer Twersky. Crucial in Soloway's staging of the institute is that they portray its members as both Jewish and queer. For example, Gittel toasts to "L'Chaim" and even the extra character Mendel has a Jewish name. Although it is not historically accurate that everyone who was affiliated with Hirschfeld's institute was Jewish, Soloway's directorial choice is crucial because it creates intersectionality between the Nazi destruction of the Jewish and queer communities, which certainly did overlap.

The wholesomeness of the institute ends abruptly when a mob of young, blond-haired men in white button-down shirts and black ties appears outside the institute's glass doors, tearing at the doors to force their entry inside. Some individuals inside the building run to the rescue, attempting to barricade the doors to prevent them from violently entering. With the start of the lyrics of Boman's "Waiting," the young men have forced their way inside Hirschfeld's library. What follows is chaos. The men outnumber the individuals present in the institute and encircle them. Everyone is separated, except for Rose and Gittel, who holds her little sister protectively in her arms. A German soldier wearing a Nazi uniform is shown smoking, coldly observing the disarray. The German students storm to the glass cabinets holding books—Hirschfeld had an extensive library with his own works and other relevant works on sexology—aggressively tearing them out of the cabinets while Gittel and others continue to resist, trying to save the works. Accompanied by photo flashes from the press, the students leave the scene with the books.

The fictional character Gittel is portrayed as a heroic resistance fighter in the forefront, wearing a bright red wrap dress, which evokes the image of the little girl in the red coat in Steven Spielberg's *Schindler's List*. All the while, Hirschfeld is presented in the background, not actively resisting but rather passive, possibly an allusion to the fact that he was not present during the destruction of his institute but in exile in Ascona, Switzerland.[37] More importantly, the focus on Gittel instead of on Hirschfeld indicates that he merely serves as the historical background, and it closely connects this historical narrative to the Pfeffermans' personal family history.

Hirschfeld's institute was indeed destroyed by one hundred physical education students on May 6, 1933. The destruction plans were announced in the daily newspaper *Berliner Lokalanzeiger* the morning of and took place from approximately 9:30 A.M. to noon.[38] According to the eyewitness report quoted in Günter Grau, the German National Socialist students who entered the institute emphasized that they did not want to confiscate Hirschfeld's books but that their plan was to destroy the institute and his legacy.[39] Because Hirschfeld was not present, they asked about his whereabouts and return date with the intention to murder him.[40] In *Transparent*, the destruction of the institute and the book burning take place on the same night and end with the Gittel's detention. The German National Socialist students burned Hirschfeld's books among many others on May 10, 1933, at the Berliner Opernplatz. No one was murdered or detained at this point, unlike in *Transparent* where Gittel is violently detained during the book burning following this scene.

Equally important as the content of this scene is its narrative form—how and in what context the destruction is presented. The destruction follows a linear narrative, but the editing technique of parallel montage creates interruptions in the 1933 sequence narration: flashbacks of the past alternate with images of the present. Turim defined this editing technique of parallel montage as "the cutting from one series of action in one space to another simultaneous series of actions in another space."[41] Parallel montage fulfills a variety of functions and has specific effects. In contrast to the flashback to 1933 Weimar Berlin in "Oscillate," in which the height of Hirschfeld's institute is shown in one consecutive scene to signify its wholesomeness and completeness, the narrative of destruction is presented in fragments, visualizing the destruction of the institute as a symbol for the mass murder of the LGBTQ community as well as its ongoing traumatic effects.

In addition to visualizing destruction, murder, loss, and trauma, the parallel montage brings these past images of Gittel's experience in 1933 Weimar Berlin in relation to Maura's present situation, thereby establishing complex connections between the characters and further suggesting the intersectionality between Jewish and transgender identities and their shared traumatic histories. At first glance, the parallel montage, alternating among Gittel, Maura, and Ari—who is searching for her mother in the dark—might suggest that Gittel's and Maura's experiences of discrimination based on their transgender identities are analogous, that Maura's experience of exclusion from the Idyllwild Wimmin's Music Festival is a repetition of her aunt Gittel's experience of Nazi persecution. Freedman argues that these scenes are not analogous but "rather, the point is that history—the historical experience of trauma—shapes the ways that people perceive events, understand their world even when that world is no longer suffused with an immediate threat."[42]

In agreement with Freedman's interpretation, I propose that the flashbacks in combination with the parallel montage suggest that it is Maura's subjective interpretation of the events, which she perceives as analogous to Gittel's persecution by the Nazis. A later flashback to Maura's childhood supports this interpretation when her maternal grandfather tries to prevent her from cross-dressing by evoking his daughter Gittel's murder by the Nazis as a cautionary tale of the consequences of cross-dressing. Rather than an analogy to and repetition of the past, this scene points to what Hirsch has termed "postmemory," which she defines as "a form of heteropathic memory in which the self and the other are more closely connected through familial or group relation—through an understanding of what it means to be Jewish or of African descent, for example"[43]—or, as in the case of Maura and Ari, what it means to be of transgender descent and transgender and Jewish. In combination with the parallel montage, the flashback of the destruction of the institute suggests subjective personal memory mediated through and in relation to Maura Pfefferman, influenced by the Pfefferman family history.[44] In the story of Gittel, the historical memory of Hirschfeld and the subjective family memory of their ancestor converge.

The parallel montage suggests that Maura conceives of her experience as analogous to that of her ancestor and that she traumatically reenacts the fate of her aunt as it was passed on by her family narrative; the mise-en-scène and transitions between shots, however, establish intersectionality between them. Maura is presented as a complex character, who has as much in common with her aunt as she does with the German National Socialists destroying Hirschfeld's institute. Her aggressive behavior in this scene—tearing down the tent, refusing help, using profane language, and even abusing the festival's safe phrase "Man on the Land"—appears equally analogous to that of the Nazis as to Gittel's victimization—and yet different from both. The episode's title "Man on the Land" equally applies to Maura—she facetiously refers to herself as such—as to the male students who invaded Hirschfeld's institute. A further analogy between her and the National Socialists might be suggested by the pan shot camera movement of her tearing the tent from the right of the screen to the left, which is followed by a cut to Hirschfeld's Institute (see figures 13.1 and 13.2). These events certainly share parallels; however, their similarities are not inherent but constructed through the editing technique of parallel montage.

Due to the ambivalences and the complexities, nothing in this scene can be read as analogous, although it may seem that way at first. The present is not a repetition of the past; everything appears to be similar yet is in fact simultaneously very different and much more nuanced and complex. Further, the double casting of several actors functions as a metaphor for this intersectionality. Soloway plays with analogy yet subtly refrains from a heavy-handed implementation because they are aware that it oversimplifies complexities and homogenizes experiences, thereby erasing difference. What Maura and her family in *Transparent* perceive as analogy is in fact intersectionality. By means of pointing to this intersectionality, Soloway is able to achieve another dimension of

FIGURE 13.1 *Transparent*. Season 2:9. Shot of Maura tearing aggressively on the tent in the present time of *Transparent*.

FIGURE 13.2 *Transparent*. Season 2:9. Flashback to the past: Magnus Hirschfeld in his institute. Gittel is shown in the background on the left.

queering in *Transparent*: to abstain from traditional and absolute categories and to instead embrace ambivalence and variation.

In the next scene, the parallel-montaged flashbacks are replaced by a merging of images of the Weimar past with the present at the Idyllwild Wimmin's Festival. As Ari continues walking in search of her mother, she nears a bonfire on which the National Socialists burn the books from Hirschfeld's library. When Ari enters the scene, the past and the present are no longer separate as in the previous flashbacks; here they merge, and Ari faces her late aunt Gittel. Despite this merging and Ari's presence in the past, she is distinctly separated from the historical events recreated in this scene. She is neither part of the action nor does anyone notice or interact with her, except for her grandmother, Rose, with whom she holds hands. From the margins, Ari silently witnesses the book burning and Gittel's deportation without intervention because she cannot change the course of history. Ari's presentation in this scene as holding her grandmother's hand indicates that she is not an eyewitness to these historical events but that her memory of the Nazi persecution of her aunt Gittel is—literally—second-hand memory, that is, postmemory, passed down by her ancestors. Simultaneously, the convergence of time and place points to the vividness of Ari's postmemory and trauma, as if this experience was not mediated through the stories of her eyewitness grandmother, the family narrative, and her own historical knowledge.

Similarly, like the parallel montage in the previous scene, the convergence in this scene, Ari's status as a secondary witness, and the absence of Maura in the book burning scene further support the interpretation that none of these flashbacks suggest analogy but that they point to and create the intersectionality between Maura's experience of discrimination and Gittel's deportation and eventual execution. The merging makes visible the effects of the National Socialist's destruction of Hirschfeld's institute and the Weimar LGBTQ community even more than eighty years later. Converging the past and the present emphasizes and, in conjunction with the melancholic music, mourns the irretrievable loss of an entire generation of LGBTQ people murdered by the National Socialists and the German LGBTQ community's civil rights advancements.

The merging is another way of queering the past; it allows a revisiting of the past from new perspectives in the present. Although this scene shows that Ari cannot change the course of history, its unique perspective on the "queer Holocaust" indicates that how historical events are remembered is subject to change. With the focus on Gittel's detention by the National Socialists, Soloway presents the Holocaust as the persecution of the transgender community. In *Transparent*, Gittel is detained because she is a transgender woman, not because she is Jewish (as indicated by the fact that her Jewish cisgender sister, Rose, is not detained). Instead, Rose survives the Holocaust because she is able to immigrate to the United States, where she eventually gives birth to a child she names Mort who then transitions to Maura. Rose's survival as a Jewish woman suggests by no means a hierarchy between Jewish and transgender Holocaust victims but instead highlights their intersectionality. Without Rose's survival and eyewitness report, there would neither be a first-hand memory of Gittel's detention nor a second generation after the Holocaust. She is the essential survivor who bears witness and commemorates. And although Jewish and queer communities, and transgender individuals in particular, share the experience of Nazi persecution, Soloway refrains from homogenizing their experiences by focusing on Gittel's deportation and thereby pointing to a diversity of experiences.

Herrn confirms this when he points out that although extensive research has been conducted on the Nazi response to male homosexuality, there has not been any systematic research on the persecution and experience of so-called "transvestites" during that time.[45] Because of the scarcity of historical sources and research on the topic—the institutions, networks, and publications of "transvestites" were destroyed—Herrn concluded from his analysis of police reports and trial protocols that the National Socialist regime represented a rupture for these individuals.[46]

Given the diversity of "transvestites" with regard to their gender and sexual identities, Herrn has suggested the plural term "transvestitisms" to do justice to the diversity in sexual and gender identities.[47] This distinction is crucial because the treatment and experience of these individual groups were different during the National Socialist regime. From a criminological perspective, cross-dressing was considered proof of homosexuality, a sexual orientation that was illegal for men, and the treatment and experiences of male homosexual cross-dressers were different from heterosexual cross-dressers.[48]

After 1933, transvestite certificates were still issued if the individual could prove their heterosexuality, for example, through marriage and children.[49] Yet psychiatrist Karl Bonhoeffer reported in 1941 that, after 1933, gender confirmation surgery could only be performed with the permission of state institutions, such as public health institutes, but this was not the case before.[50] In a footnote, Herrn mentions that there is no relevant information about how the National Socialists treated individuals who underwent gender confirmation surgery before 1933.[51] Given the complexity of the terminology "transvestitism," the dearth of historical resources, and the incompleteness of research, it is not surprising that Herrn's research does not particularly focus on the experience of Jewish transgender individuals, as *Transparent* imagines it. None of the resources Herrn examined mentions Jewishness. Based on the biographical information of the victims Herrn cites, they all appear to be non-Jews.

The absence of historical resources and research specifically on the experience of Jewish transgender individuals during the Holocaust might be due to several reasons: because transgender individuals were medically and criminologically considered homosexuals, they might have been persecuted as such by the Nazis, which erases their difference and distinct experience. Also, in concentration camps, Jews were forced to wear the yellow star to identify them, and male homosexuals wore the pink triangle. Jewish homosexuals had to wear an upward-pointing yellow triangle to show that they were Jewish and a downward pink triangle indicating their homosexuality. There were no specific signs for transgender individuals in concentration camps because it was not illegal, and, therefore, there is no specific identification for Jewish transgender individuals. It is also likely that Jewish transgender individuals were persecuted due to their Jewishness, as homosexuals, or as both. Because the National Socialists tried to erase difference with regard to race, gender, and sexuality, it is crucial to examine—and imagine—their intersectionality. Imagining a fictional character like Gittel creates the exact type of intersectionality the German National Socialists intended to erase and provokes viewers to distinguish experiences that are often subsumed under the predominant historical narratives and become acts of resistance.

With the fictional character Gittel, Soloway reminds their viewers not only that the experiences of Holocaust victims differ based on their intersectional identities, but consequently that these victims are remembered and commemorated differently. Jews and non-Jews alike primarily remember the Holocaust as a Jewish genocide. Transgender individuals are generally excluded from Holocaust memory and commemoration. In fact, there appears to be only one Holocaust memorial, which is in Tel Aviv, that also commemorates transgender people murdered by the Nazis, although it is not solely dedicated to them but to the entire LGBTQ community. The dedication reads: "'In memory of those persecuted by the Nazi regime for their sexual orientation and gender identity.'"[52]

By creating an intersectional character like Gittel and placing her in the historical context of the Holocaust, Soloway queers the Holocaust. They present it with a focus on the mass murder of an entire generation of transgender individuals, as well as their and Hirschfeld's legacy. Soloway precisely chose the Holocaust as an event that everyone is familiar with—especially American Jews—to highlight the intersectionality between the experiences of Jews and transgender individuals in the Holocaust and how they are remembered and commemorated today. This also allowed Soloway to uncover the long history of intersectionality of Jewish and transgender intellectual, political, and traumatic history. In so doing, Soloway erected a memorial in honor of the (Jewish) transgender community murdered by the National Socialists and opened the discussion to imagine other marginalized historical narratives.

Notes

1. Because the acronym LGBTQ did not exist during Hirschfeld's time, I use the historical terms "transvestites" and "homosexuals" based on Katie Sutton, "'We Too Deserve a Place in the Sun': The Politics of Transvestite Identity in Weimar Germany," *German Studies Review* 35, no. 2 (2012): 335–354.
2. Kimberlé Williams Crenshaw, "Demarginalizing the Intersection of Race and Sex: A Black Feminist Critique of Antidiscrimination Doctrine, Feminist Theory and Antiracist Politics," *University of Chicago Legal Forum* 1989, no. 1, art. 8, https://chicagounbound.uchicago.edu/uclf/vol1989/iss1/8; Kimberlé Williams Crenshaw, "Mapping the Margins: Intersectionality, Identity Politics, Violence Against Women of Color," in *The Public Nature of Private Violence*, eds. Martha Fineman and Rixanne Mykituik (New York: Routledge, 1994), 93–118. In this context, it should be noted that *Transparent* has been criticized for its whiteness and lack of racial diversity—a criticism Soloway attempts to address in season 3. Compared to the historic racialization of Jewishness in Nazi Germany, where Jews were considered a race and persecuted as such, the Jewishness of the Pfefferman family in contemporary Los Angeles has significantly less bearing on how others perceive them racially; largely, they are simply considered white.
3. Crenshaw, "Demarginalizing," 149.
4. Devon W. Carbado et al., Intersectionality: Mapping the Movements of a Theory, *Du Bois Review* 10, no. 2 (2013): 303–312. https://scholarship.law.columbia.edu/cgi/viewcontent.cgi?article=3783&context=faculty_scholarship.

5   Carbado et al., "Editorial Introduction," 304.
6   Janet R. Jakobsen, "Queers Are Like Jews, Aren't They? Analogy and Alliance Politics," in *Queer Theory and the Jewish Question*, eds. Daniel Boyarin, Daniel Itzovitz, and Ann Pellegrini (New York: Columbia University Press, 2003), 64–89.
7   Jakobsen, "Queers Are Like Jews," 73.
8   At the actual Michigan Womyn's Music Festival, the policy that excluded transgender women was only in effect for one year.
9   Maureen Turim, *Flashback in Film: Memory and History* (Abingdon, Oxfordshire: Routledge, 2015), 1–2.
10 Jennifer Evans, "Introduction: Why Queer German History?" *German History* 34, no. 3 (2016): 371.
11 Elizabeth Freeman, *Time Binds: Queer Temporalities, Queer Histories* (Durham, NC: Duke University Press, 2010), xi.
12 The terms "sexual orientation," "sexual identity," and "gender identity" did not exist yet. Hirschfeld used the term *Veranlagung* (disposition) to indicate the naturalness of homosexuality and transvestitism. See Sutton, "'We Too Deserve,'" 337 and 346.
13 Jonathan Freedman mentions that Soloway credits Robert Beachy's book *Gay Berlin* for the information about Hirschfeld. See Freedman, "A Guide for the Perplexed," *LA Review of Books*, April 10, 2016, https://dev.lareviewofbooks.org/contributor/jonathan-freedman; Robert Beachy, *Gay Berlin: Birthplace of a Modern Identity* (New York: Vintage, 2015).
14 Ralf Dose, *Magnus Hirschfeld: The Origins of the Gay Liberation Movement*, trans. Edward H. Willis (New York: Monthly Review Press, 2014), 71.
15 Dose, *Magnus Hirschfeld*, 72.
16 It should be noted that Soloway does not consider some of the problematic aspects of Hirschfeld's research that are also emphasized in Dose's Hirschfeld biography as well as in Beachy's *Gay Berlin*. For example, Dose criticizes his interest and engagement in eugenics. See Dose, *Magnus Hirschfeld*, 77.
17 Rainer Herrn, "In der heutigen Staatsführung kann es nicht angehen, daß sich Männer in Frauenkleidung frei auf der Straße bewegen. Über den Forschungsstand zum Transvestitismus in der NS-Zeit," in *Homosexuelle im Nationalsozialismus. Neue Forschungsperspektiven zu Lebenssituationen von lesbischen, schwulen, bi-, trans- und intersexuellen Menschen 1933 bis 1945*, ed. Michael Schwartz (München: Oldenburg Wissenschaftsverlag, De Gruyter, 2014), 103.
18 Dose, *Magnus Hirschfeld*, 73.
19 Dose, *Magnus Hirschfeld*, 72; Rainer Herrn, "Transvestitismus in der NS-Zeit—Ein Forschungsdesiderat," *Zeitschrift für Sexualforschung* 27, no. 4 (2013): 331.
20 Sutton, "'We Too Deserve,'" 337. See also Dose, *Magnus Hirschfeld*, 72.
21 Herrn, "In der heutigen Staatsführung," 104.
22 Sutton, "'We Too Deserve,'" 335.
23 Dose, *Magnus Hirschfeld*, 72.
24 Dose, *Magnus Hirschfeld*, 73. See also Beachy, *Gay Berlin*, 173.
25 Dose, *Magnus Hirschfeld*, 37.
26 Heike Bauer, "'Race,' Normativity and the History of Sexuality: Magnus Hirschfeld's Racism and the Early-Twentieth-Century Sexology," *Psychology & Sexuality* 1, no. 3 (September 2010): 246.
27 Bauer, "'Race,'" 240.
28 Bauer, "'Race,'" 244.
29 Christina von Braun, *Gibt es eine "jüdische" und eine "christliche" Sexualwissenschaft? Sexualität und Säkularisierung* (Wiener Vorlesungen im Rathaus, Band 110,

Herausgegeben für die Kulturabteilung der Stadt Wien von Hubert Christian Erhalt, Vortrag im alten Rathaus am 13 Mai 2004 (Wien: Picus Verlag, 2014), 17.

30 Von Braun, *Gibt es eine "jüdische" und eine "christliche" Sexualwissenschaft?*, 20.
31 Sander Gilman, "Whose Body Is It Anyway?: Hermaphrodites, Gays, and Jew in N.O. Body's Germany," in *Jewish Masculinities: German Jews, Gender, and History*, eds. Benjamin Maria Baader, Sharon Gillerman, and Paul Lerner (Bloomington: Indiana University Press, 2012), 147–148.
32 David S. Katz, "Shylock's Gender: Jewish Male Menstruation in Early Modern England," *The Review of English Studies* 50, no. 200 (1999): 455.
33 Katz, "Shylock's Gender," 456.
34 Katz, "Shylock's Gender," 456.
35 Katz, "Shylock's Gender," 457.
36 Another representation of the destruction of Hirschfeld's Institute is in Rosa von Praunheim's 1999 film biography *Magnus Hirschfeld: Der Einstein des Sex*.
37 Dose, *Magnus Hirschfeld*, 65.
38 Günter Grau, ed., *Homosexualität in der NS-Zeit: Dokumente einer Diskriminierung und Verfolgung* (Frankfurt am Main: Fischer Taschenbuch Verlag, 2004), 60–61.
39 Grau, *Homosexualität in der NS-Zeit*, 61.
40 Grau, *Homosexualität in der NS-Zeit*, 62.
41 Turim, *Flashback in Film*, 7.
42 Freedman, "A Guide."
43 Marianne Hirsch, *The Generation of Postmemory: Writing and Visual Culture After the Holocaust* (New York: Columbia University Press, 2012), 86.
44 Turim, *Flashback in Film*, 2.
45 Herrn, "Transvestitismus in der NS-Zeit," 331.
46 Herrn, "In der heutigen Staatsführung," 105.
47 Herrn, "Transvestitismus in der NS-Zeit," 367.
48 Herrn, "Transvestitismus in der NS-Zeit," 368.
49 Herrn, "Transvestitismus in der NS-Zeit," 368.
50 Herrn, "Transvestitismus in der NS-Zeit," 369.
51 Herrn, "Transvestitismus in der NS-Zeit," 360.
52 "Tel Aviv Unveils Memorial to Gay Holocaust Victims: Landmark is the first in Israel to Deal Universally with Jewish and non-Jewish Individuals Persecuted by the Nazis," *Times of Israel*, January 10, 2014, accessed January 24, 2018, http://www.timesofisrael.com/tel-aviv-unveils-memorial-to-gay-holocaust-victims/.

14

Making Jewishness Transparent and *Transparent* Jew-ish

MARILYN REIZBAUM

In season 3, episode 2 of *Transparent*, while observing Ari Pfefferman teaching a class in which she uses Jews in prewar Berlin as the lens on feminist dystopia and historical memory, her teacher/advisor/lover Leslie wonders what Jewishness and the Holocaust have to do with it. Apart from Leslie's need to diminish Ari—a seeming critique on the part of the show of power imbalance in romantic relationships—Leslie's inquiry poses a larger question about the series overall. However skeptical viewers may feel about Ari's incessant search for meaning, we may also be waiting for the truth to be revealed about *Transparent*. What is its thesis? What is, after all, *seen through*? What should be apparent is the connection the series establishes between Jewishness and transitioning, or with gender and sexuality more broadly. The connection, I argue, is presented problematically, both wittingly and unwittingly, as "intrinsic," mimicking a historical conflation between Jewishness and queer referenced by the program while eluding most of its critics.

In this chapter, I examine *Transparent*'s representation of the historical intersections among Jewishness, queer, and transgender through the concepts of chosenness, landedness, and deliverance. Each concept presents a challenge to the way categories of ethnicity, gender, and sexuality are constituted and thereby reveals a shifting terrain in an arena that may seek, however paradoxically, stability and authentic representation. I make the case that *Transparent* takes on the challenge and both participates and revels in the messiness of terms and positions.

Season 2, announced in its poster with an exhortation and/or promise to "get messy," traces back to 1930s Berlin and Magnus Hirschfeld's Institute for Sexual Science as a historical backdrop to the Pfefferman family (see figure 14.1); it is also a historical referent for transgender studies and for the interface between Jewishness and sexual deviance that was extant in Germany in this period and emblematized by Hirschfeld as a gay, Jewish sexologist who oversaw some of the earliest gender affirmation surgeries. This historical alignment suggests that the roots of this connection are deep, not whimsical. Channeling Sartre in *Anti-Semite and Jew*, Josh Lambert writes about the Pfeffermans, "Jews were crucial, ardent supporters of sexual science and minority rights throughout the 20th century, for many reasons; often because, being Jewish, they [the Pfeffermans] understand that persecution or prejudicial treatment of any minority is actually a threat against us all."[1] This familiar structure of empathy belies any substantive, no less a historically perceived intrinsic connection between Jews and "deviant" sex. Further, such an argument about the Pfeffermans' capacity for empathy resides on shaky ground. It is reminiscent of Ari's theory of intersectionality later in season 3, episode 6, in which all marginalized groups merge into a "holy other." Whereas Ari's first critical stretch between feminist dystopia and "asocials" in 1930s Berlin was imaginative, this later intersectional proposition (which she offers as a graduate thesis topic) is reductive; at least, it loses the historical specificity that undergirds Soloway's thesis about Jews and transgender lives, which is, the show proclaims, a historical phenomenon not a trend. Critics' obtuseness around this feature of *Transparent* corresponds somewhat to Leslie's patronizing dismissal: they love the show, but they do not see the vital historical connection between Jewishness and queerness, except, perhaps, in Ari's diffuse association of the holy others.

The inflection of the idea of "choice" informs this discussion throughout, such that it may perform both transitively and intransitively: to choose or be chosen, to have or be a choice. "Intrinsic" is a word that militates against choice; intrinsic and extrinsic in this way are affiliated, respectively, with limitation and liberation, though they might be inflected differently as natural (selection) and denatured, as constitutive of belonging on the one hand, and otherness, on the other. And such vagaries in these terms are particularly apt for the categories of ethnicity, gender, or sexuality, wherein, for example, gender transition seeks to "confirm" a gender identity by moving genders. Jewishness, too, historically has been difficult to delimit: religious or cultural designation, racial or ethnic, inborn or chosen, Jew or Jew-ish. What one critic calls the "prism of identity" when referring to the way *Transparent* places Jewishness, sexuality, and gender in contention, also becomes at times the prison of identity.[2] The chaos or unruliness of *Transparent* might be read as a marker of that nominal messiness, revolving

FIGURE 14.1 Promotional poster for *Transparent*'s second season. *Transparent* images provided by Amazon Content Services LLC.

around words that are both Jewishly and sexually inflected, chosenness, in particular, and its attendant aspect of feeling and/or desire.

The central tenet of Jews as a chosen people (by God) is a constant theme throughout the series. The central conflict expressed in the comic gloss on the idea of chosenness—"chosen for what?" as the Jewish joke goes—lines up with the "Jewish question," that is, the nineteenth and twentieth-century euphemistic "dilemma" regarding the status of Jews (what to do with the Jews?). Chosenness, which should confer privilege, becomes a mark of difference, making Jews historically subject to persecution. Therefore, the privilege of Jews is a vexed matter, one showcased by *Transparent*. "The Jewish Question," both in terms of what the series posits and also as historical referent, faces off with *trans*gender trouble, wherein "being born this way" or "no-choice" becomes the point of inflection. Ari is the character who most consciously brings these together by exploring trans identities through a Jewish lens.

The Split

Although critics and viewers have been piqued by *Transparent*, in both senses of that word, it is unclear why—if, as I argue, the intersection of the show's subjects is central—that connection has been so critically elusive. Some have been thrilled by its "Jewiness," a term often used by Soloway when referring to the show, and some about its presentation of transgender issues, but rarely both at the same time.[3] Those who are irritated or affronted are mostly piqued by a sense that justice is not being done or is underdone either to the Jews or to the transgender community.[4]

One focus for consternation had to do with the choice of a cisgender man—Jeffrey Tambor—to play Maura, the central transgender woman. Tambor was given a pass because of his laudable acting (until charges of sexual misconduct were brought against him and his resignation from the show); Soloway was mostly tolerated for their choice of Tambor due to the number of transgender and queer actors, producers, technicians, and writers hired for the show and their subsequent decision to produce a season 5 without Tambor. And Soloway themselves was transitioning, as were their trans politics. The question of "intrinsic" redounds upon these calls for authentic casting. In all this, Tambor's Jewishness has hardly been mentioned.

In her essay on the intersectionality in *Transparent*, Amy Villarejo is forgiving of the show's transgressions. She criticizes its racial politics while still thrilling at its representation of transgender identities. She smartly posits that "whiteness is being naturalized by Jewish cultural identity ... that it becomes an alibi for evacuating *Transparent*'s locale of black, and brown and yellow people." But when it comes to the show's handling of queer and transgender matters, Villarejo "still can't quite believe that a show like *Transparent* exists, much less succeeds as the critical and artistic force it has become."[5] The whiplash we experience in Villarejo's expression of appreciation is present even on the level of the sentence—"also," "however," "despite"—registering both pleasure and uneasiness. She continues:

> Despite my observations about its relentless whiteness, despite my observations about the liberties it takes with the historical record, and despite my own cringy reactions to Jill Soloway's memoir and bio-details, *Transparent* gives voice to marginalized people, battles stereotypes, and diversifies production. It presents that kind of visual storytelling that social justice advocates usually look for in documentary feature productions. It explores present-day social issues and hot-button cultural flashpoints using the best tools and talents in the industry.

Alisa Solomon writes about her partner's response to the opening of season 2—the wedding scene of Sarah and Tammy—that it is "not good for the Jews."[6] This is a Jewish meme that filters through literary and popular culture. The show is rich with Jewish memes. But what is it about this "messy," nonnormative family that is "not good for the Jews"? Solomon observes that "as the group arranged itself for the portrait, they squabble like noisy geese (an actual gaggle of which figures into later episodes)."[7] Included in the family portrait are Bianca, the Black daughter that Tammy adopted with her previous spouse; Maura, who is referred to by the photographer as "sir"; and the evangelical Colton, whom Josh fathered with his babysitter. Solomon also cites Ari's comment at the end of the "messy" lineup: "It's supposed to be family. Anyone else want in?" then continues with, "Ari's crack, muttered amid the mayhem, comes off as a throwaway line, but it neatly raises a question any viewer must ask about the lovers and youngsters attaching themselves to this entitled, competitive, relentlessly narcissistic, so very SoCal family: Why *would* anyone want in? The Pfeffermans' dysfunction is hilariously contrasted when the Cashmans efficiently and cheerfully line up for the other bride's family pic."[8] Of course, the other side's orderliness is also critiqued as Waspy and homogeneous, whereas the Pfeffermans display heterogeneity to a comical extreme, and are therefore difficult to organize into a picture of "family." Is that what is meant by the anxiety expressed in the reaction that this is "not good for the Jews," that is, that the Jewish is being diluted to the point of extinction? Perhaps, instead, the unruliness is a measure of a new kind of chosenness.

Solomon responds to their own questions about why the Pfeffermans must be so "relentlessly narcissistic"—or put another way, why we are "so eager to spend five hours in the Pfeffermans appalling presence"—by contending that Soloway "put Jewish stereotypes of loudness and pushiness on display as a way of suggesting that there is pleasure in those attributes, too, and in knowing their codes."[9] The family's imperfections or "failures" are an important part of Soloway's equation between Jews and trans subjectivities. Contravening her partner's fears,

Solomon concludes that Soloway renders the famous metric of "not good for the Jews" an anachronism.

It seems, however, that Solomon is at once saying, somewhat defensively, that what might be objectionable about these characters must finally accrue to their Jewiness, but in the show's presentation of gender, there is nothing to be sorry for. For example, in discussing the "binding agent ... that has to do with the show's sly use of its high octane Jewy-ness," Solomon argues that Soloway "melds the Jewish stance with the show's unrepentant queerness," as though to suggest that the Jew-ish needs to repent.[10] And if Jewiness is what is so central to the show, as Soloway said and others have repeated, then that, it would appear, is the core of disaffection (or pleasure). In fact, Soloway has reported that the vitriol aimed at the show on social media was more often laced with antisemitism than transphobia.[11] It appears that *Transparent* is "too Jewish," to bring another Jewish meme to mind, which is yet another measure. If "too Jewish" is bad, Solomon and Soloway respond with "Too bad."

Repeatedly within this emphatic critical response, the question of the Pfeffermans' narcissism, their privilege, and their excesses arises. The shift in Solomon's attitude toward the Jewish stereotypes that populate the series reflects an ambivalence within the series itself, which both critiques and finds a certain pleasure in the "too muchness" of the Pfeffermans, in Isaac Butler's formulation.[12] Sara Ahmed discusses queer pleasure by calling on Zizek's analysis of "the ambivalence of the investment in 'the other' as one 'who enjoys' and whose enjoyment exceeds the economies of investment and return." She argues that, equally, "others can be envied for their lack of enjoyment, for the authenticity of their suffering, their vulnerability, and their pain" and warns against the way in which such affect of either pleasure or pain may become a means of subject constitution, a form of property—"a feeling we have."[13] Might we think of Jewishness, or particularly the Pfeffermans' Jewishness, in these terms, characterized by an abundance of either pleasure or pain? On the other hand, the "surfeit of feeling" as a Jewish attribute, as we shall see, also attaches to the idea of choice as experiential knowledge and lines up in this sense with "transgender phenomena," which makes essential "the embodied experience of the speaking subject, who claims constative knowledge of the referent topic."[14] Feeling is knowing or being.

These splits in critical sentiment regarding the Jewish and transgender subjects in *Transparent* are reflective of the very same division that exists in historical considerations of Magnus Hirschfeld and his groundbreaking sexological work in the first part of the twentieth century. Scholars of Hirschfeld's work rarely pay more than lip service to his Jewish background and to the role it might have played in both his disposition to his subject and the reception of his work. Although fewer scholars focus on the Jewish aspect of his life and work, those who do have failed to consider these connections in any depth.[15] In the early twentieth-century German milieu in particular, more than in other European countries, Jews and homosexuals were seen as synonymous, exemplified by Hirschfeld himself, who identified as homosexual (though closeted) but was identified by others as Jewish. His theories about sex and gender were radical, but when the books were burned, famously in Berlin's opera square, it was an effigy of Hirschfeld with the caption "Jude" (German for "Jew") that was held up. The theories were condemned as intrinsically Jewish, like Freud's science.

Regardless of Soloway's intentions, their move to Hirschfeld as a historical backdrop for the show brings both a historical rationale and continuity to Maura's transition and the Jew-ish position. Soloway has been criticized for the liberties taken with this history—primarily, having Hirschfeld present at the Berlin institute when it was sacked in 1933. (He is also referred to in the scene as the Isaac Newton of sex, whereas the sobriquet that stuck involved that other physicist—the Jewish one—Einstein of Sex). But these do not seem to me egregious distortions. Hirschfeld is there to represent and voice a movement that was very much alive and active but has been relatively obscured. It could be argued that Soloway's move evacuates his erasure, thereby erasing the history. But I see the error as corrective, as it were, of the absence or removal of Hirschfeld, whose Jewishness kept him in exile from the institute and Germany and whose fate has kept him from a fuller appreciation by scholars; he died in Paris in 1935 at the age of 67. Much of his original work is listed as *verloren* (lost) in the Berlin libraries, a euphemism for destroyed. Much has been retrieved in copy or reconstructed, but not all. As a result, very little was translated or available until recent efforts to bring the complete work to light.

One major objection to Hirschfeld's theories of the sexual spectrum was to the alignment of homosexuality with femininity. Building on predecessor Karl Heinrich Ulrich's theories, Hirschfeld argued that homosexuality involved an internalization of the opposite gender—that is, that male homosexuals were effeminate and vice versa. There were groups of self-identifying homosexuals such as the Männerbund and "official" transvestites who insisted on presenting as cisgender (the "manly men" of Hans Blüher and Benedict Friedländer, both outspokenly antisemitic; Friedländer was of Jewish origin). We see this phenomenon represented in the Hirschfeld sequences in *Transparent* and in the flashback to Maura's first trip to the cross-dressing camp with her new friend Mark, played by Bradley Whitford, who also plays Hirschfeld. Mark, sitting in drag as "Marcie" at the camp, is horrified along with others at the idea of transitioning. They are *men* who cross-dress. This *weiblichkeit* (femininity) was the nub of the conflation between Jews and homosexuals; Jews were feminine in the racial science of the day, and therefore, too Jewish was too feminine (i.e., homosexual) and vice versa.

When recalling this moment at Camp Camellia (perfectly named after the consumptive Dumas courtesan), it is worth noting a small detail—the lie to Shelly, Maura's wife, about the subject of the conference she was ostensibly attending. Maura claims that there will be new information about Rosenberg's execution, and this speaks to the historical interface between Jewishness and political persecution; this lie acts as a kind of Jewish alibi, wherein the real transgression is the sexual one. As with the relationship between homosexuality and Jewishness, treason (in the form of Communism in this instance) is marked similarly, as intrinsic to Jewishness. It is worth noting, too, that Maura produces this alibi while taking the seemingly neutral, even "goyish" pseudonym Stephen Baker at the camp. (The name "Stephen" might be in homage to the main character in Radclyffe Hall's *The Well of Loneliness*, a 1928 novel about "sexual inversion," one term for trans in that period.)

Looking at Hirschfeld's theories and methodology of representation, we understand something about the phenomenon of transgender identity that is not reflected in the genuflections of critics who see that aspect as distinct and praiseworthy in Soloway's treatment. Hirschfeld disavowed dimorphism—the biological case of an absolute male or female—in favor of a sexual spectrum, but he recognized that one still had to contend with the ideal of binarism. This presents a paradox, as in the act of transitioning to achieve gender affirmation, using today's terminology, which is itself, of course, the proof of gender's instability. Hirschfeld's methodologies were accordingly playful, using photography, whose technical vagaries were then slowly becoming apparent to a science dependent on photography's evidentiary powers, to prove the case he wished to make about the sexual and gender spectrum.

In this photograph from Hirschfeld's extensive collection, most of which was lost, we see what Hirschfeld termed "metatropic" (technically, regressive) transvestites, which emphasized the gender they sought (see figure 14.2). Important here is the adherence to a gendered norm in dress and that Hirschfeld pasted a mustache onto the trans man in order to enhance the presentation.[16]

Hirschfeld insisted throughout his career on the right to present a desiring self. Yet it should be mentioned that Hirschfeld most always appeared as the scientist in a white coat or suit, a seemingly straight man in the midst of a variety of sexual and gender positions. Bradley Whitford plays Hirschfeld in this manner; it is an ingenious choice on the part of Soloway to have him double as the cross-dresser who insists on identifying as cisgender. In presenting in this way, Hirschfeld desires to achieve, one would presume, an image of neutrality and therefore respectability or even gentility. In other words, as radical and transformative as Hirschfeld's theories were, they were fraught with the troubled categories and history in which Hirschfeld worked.

The desiring self in *Transparent* is a dominant idea, productive, I argue, of transgender trouble, which we understand when we consider the interaction between Jew-ishness, which riffs on the historical idea of Jews as impure and at once "chosen," and the question/struggle of transgenderism's place in historical feminism. As Judith Butler writes in *Undoing Gender*, "The transsexual desire to become a man or a woman is not to be dismissed as a simple desire to conform to established identity categories.... It can be a pursuit of identity as

FIGURE 14.2 Die Frau ist ein femininer Mann, der Mann eine virile Frau mit angeklebtem Bart. [The woman is a feminine man, the man is a mannish woman, with taped on mustache.] Image courtesy of the Magnus Hirschfeld Institute in Berlin, Germany.

a transformative exercise, an example of desire itself as a transformative activity.... what is livable for some is unlivable for others.... The differences in position and desire set the limits to universalizability as an ethical reflex."[17] One of the more telling phrases in her formulation here is "simple desire," reminiscent of Hirschfeld's positions on the transformative desire of transvestism (a term he coined) and transsexuality as historical antecedents to Maura's transition, and by no means simple.

Feeling Landed

It is through this juncture of chosenness, impurity, and the feeling and/or desiring self that we might best appreciate the import of the very provocative scene at the Idyllwild Wimmin's Festival at the end of season 2.

The climactic montage collapses histories—bringing together Ari Pfefferman with her transgender descendant, Gershon/Gittel, and her grandmother, Rose, as her 1930s avatar; all are gathered around a bonfire, which had a moment before been the scene of a campfire discussion of feminist versus transgender rights, the upshot of which is an angry Maura leaving the camp. The departing Maura violently smashes up tents, declaring "This wo*man* is leaving this feminist fuckhole— thank you for your kindness and fuck you." This scene cuts to the violent destruction of the Hirschfeld institute and the removal of its inhabitants, including Gittel, all happening around the symbolic fire. The scene has been described as a harsh commentary on trans-exclusionary feminism, and it is difficult not to conclude that Soloway is equating Nazis with feminists of a certain brand. But I argue this is too simple a reading; no ideology as presented in the montage is pure, though ideology by definition is constituted as such. The fire at the conclusion reflects these convergent and at once competing histories of Jewishness and transgender identity or queer identity: the book burning, the ovens, the destruction of an institution, and a sexology that was submerged by the history that encompasses all these. I see here merging histories on a continuum, not metonymies, much like Hirschfeld's sexual spectrum. However justified Maura may seem about being excluded, she is also portrayed as obtuse about privilege rather than privileged by the scene. When Maura complains to the women around the campfire that her rights are being violated, she is confronted with making what might seem an impossible separation—the pain of the desiring or transitioning self is different from the privilege that as a man he enjoyed, Leslie remonstrates. These things are uncomfortably placed in contention, and the discomfort is key. The series worries whether "landing" is desirable at all, in that the festival's originary aim to valorize or give space to and ground women (land) is troubled by the transgender claim to identity—to land in the sense of arriving— and further complicated by the question of the chosen versus the intrinsic. The charge of "man on the land" aimed at Maura rehearses that contest by denying trans identity on the basis of a grievance about the denial of women, which here becomes a double entendre, transitive and intransitive (women who have been denied are now denying trans women).

In her essay on *Transparent*, Seymour argues that its "use of the transition narrative is reductive to the marginal ways in which transgender lives construct embodiment and belonging," in particular, in its use of the coming out narrative and "wrong body" rhetoric. Both imply an "obligation to unveil what no cisgender person must—a true identity."[18] Seymour cites Nael Bhanji's work on the transition narrative, where he "suggests that it is often framed as a hasty departure from 'the transgressive' and liminal, towards a place of identification and transgender embodiment—a homely space. His critique of this particular trope, inseparable from the themes of location, self actualisation and integration, lies its participation in liberal discourses of exclusion and inclusion."[19] I argue that Maura's seeming journey toward the "homely space" is constantly shifting in *Transparent*'s messy drama, though the feeling of being is consistently reaffirmed.

Seymour's critique of the way transgender lives are narrated is similar to the problem of representation of Jews in the media—the demands for authenticity, as with the questions about the "right" gender or body, are more than hard to meet; they are ill considered. A search for the authentic self characterizes Ari's exploration throughout the series. She is looking for the key, the trick, the formula and tries out epigenetics (the inheritance of trauma), Jewish ritual, academia (gender studies, in particular), and changing sexual orientation. Her desires and conclusions tend to cancel each other out, and viewers are left to wonder whether she is to be lauded for her searching or mocked for her piety. As her mother, Shelly, says of her at one point, "She can't land."

"Land" also raises the subject of the Jewish Diaspora and Zionism, with a similar problem of deliverance. As such, it ties in with the issue of gender confirmation that is presented in the Idyllwild Wimmin's Festival camp's refusal of "man on the land." This issue comes into focus in season 4, which begins with the family's journey to Israel. The landing is bumpy, to say the least, and Ari, who is transitioning, comes to identify with the Palestinian cause, as the just belonging (transgression as transition) whose right to the land makes political sense. The idyll she discovers in the West Bank activist camp deserts her at the conclusion of the season. It has been forcibly dismantled, and we are left with the feeling that needing to land is itself checked by the restricted or troubled access to home experienced by all the characters in their various pursuits of it (with the metonymy of checkpoint restrictions between Israel and the occupied territories and despite the privilege that Ari does experience in the Jewish homeland). The last image of the season takes place at a table outside of the Pfefferman Palisades palazzo, on the patio. If there is an arrival, it seems to be more to the family, which here includes Maura, her new boyfriend Donald, Davina, who has been living in the basement of the house, Shelly, and Josh. Any normative idea of family is repeatedly transgressed. Ari's comment in season 2, "Anyone else want in?", echoes throughout. The last line of the episode and the season, "Everything's all right," comes from the playbook of the season, transgressively, *Jesus Christ Superstar*; the line is countered with Maura's kvetch, "I think my neck went out." Apart from the typing hypochondria of Jewish pain, this utterance performs yet another double entendre: Maura has been sticking her neck out. When it comes to the double entendre of land, as verb and noun, perhaps the pun of "settling" becomes most apt; the Pfefferman circle are settlers not at home but *about* the location or idea of home.[20]

Deliverance

The concept of chosenness in a traditionally Jewish sense as privileged evolves through the seasons until it lines up with the categories of queer-ish and Jew-ish and correlates with the lesson about the distinction between privilege and pain that Maura receives at Idyllwild, finally arriving at the qualified "semi-chosen."[21] All continue to be part of the "swirl" (Maura uses this word to describe the shifts) of a messy enterprise. Still, although the Pfeffermans remain ungrounded, there is in the search a mystical key. In a scene from season 1, episode 6 ("The Wilderness"), Maura lights the candles at a Shabbat dinner over which she presides as mother and father, still in the early stages of transitioning. At the table are Sarah and her two children as well as Tammy, Bianca, and Davina. Davina's wish to participate in the candle lighting is rebuffed, as Sarah explains that it is the tradition that the "mother of the family" lights the candles: "And you have to be chosen," adds Maura, which elicits a laugh from the others at the table, in particular, Bianca. Her laughter would seem to register this dubious distinction, the absurdity of having insider status marked by one's performance of such a ritual, or she is laughing at the performer, whose chosenness is in doubt. When saying the prayer over the candles, Maura stumbles, not remembering the words and seeming to get the tune wrong. Sarah mockingly rescinds her chosen status based on this lapse, and Maura adds that she "once was chosen," and is now maybe "semi-chosen." The viewer has the sense that Maura and Sarah are shamed by both claiming and having to relinquish chosenness. Yet that part of the scene ends with a sense of wonder—the candles lit, the laughter subsided.

Chosenness is a concept that is also meant to signal solidarity. The question is begged: how can Maura and Sarah be Jewish when they cannot remember the prayer for Shabbat? I like the idea of semi-chosen, which corresponds to the "ish" case. I am reminded of David Ben Gurion's discussion with eminent Jewish scholar Gershom Scholem about Leopold Bloom, the Jew-ish protagonist of Joyce's *Ulysses*. It is a novel whose major preoccupation is the problem of homecoming. Scholem wondered (as have many Joyce scholars) how Bloom could be Jewish when he was not circumcised, had never had a bar mitzvah, and lacked other such distinguishing Jewish features. Ben Gurion purportedly responded by saying that if Bloom felt he was Jewish, then he was.[22] This, too, seems funny. In terms of its potential ramifications, why would one make such a claim—that is, choose to be Jewish? Moreover, such an understanding of what constitutes Jewishness seems comical coming from the first prime minister of the newly minted modern Israeli state. Chosenness becomes a *trans*-itive state; it is a feeling.[23]

Season 3, episode 3 ("To Sardines and Back") offers a mirror scene to the dinner in season 1 where the idea of being chosen has transitioned in just these terms of feeling. It is enacted rather than received. We are at Maura's seventieth birthday party, and present at the table on this occasion are all her children along with Shelly, Shelly's current partner, Buzzy, Davina, Shea (another of Maura's transgender friends), and Maura's girlfriend, Vicki, played by Angelica Houston. In the scene, Maura proposes a toast in which she expresses her gratitude to her biological family and her chosen family, prefaced by a seeming non sequitur regarding the family house: "I don't remember there being such high ceilings and such goyish lights." As an expression of defamiliarization, it is also one of "familalization," one might say, which garners a titter in response by those in the know about "goyish." So at the very moment that Maura makes the distinction between the privilege of chosenness and a desiring self—her Jewish family and her chosen family—she is asserting that privilege through a private/tribal language, a kind of Yiddish slang. At the same time, Maura is defamilializing the house by seeing something un-Jewish in it, a style chosen by her Jewish family. Later in this scene, though not in sequence, Maura announces her intention to transition medically, which is received differently by her Jewish family, her chosen family, and her girlfriend. Shelly asks whether that means she intends to have a sex change and is corrected by Davina—it is called "gender confirmation." Buzzy salutes Maura's decision with a Yiddish expression—"Trug Gesunteheit" (Wear it well)—which Maura must explain to the uninitiated. Davina asks, "Is that Latin? What does that mean?" Her ignorance of Yiddish corresponds to the language of transitioning that the family does not understand.

In response to Maura's initial toast, Shelly remarks, "I guess that makes us the not chosen family," regarding their children and herself. Though there has been an evolution in Maura's concept of her gender identity, Maura snaps back to the position of privilege, making her announcement to the assembled without having considered the "feelings" of the different parties. To choose registers here as a misstep, a blunt instrument; to be not chosen is a demotion in status for the Pfefferman family that is uncomfortable. Here as throughout, we struggle with a sense that Maura's choices (maybe Soloway's, too), past and present, have done, do, and will continue to do damage, where these collective and personal histories converge. The idea of choosing also applies to one's willingness to accommodate the mess—the whirlpool—within these constellations, a description Maura used in the first Shabbat scene in response to her son-in-law's distress over the changes that have taken place in his family and the choices that have been made. Both Jewish and transgender identities work along a spectrum of feeling and choice, sometimes intersecting, even when diverging as in the language of representation.

At the conclusion of her seventieth birthday toast, all raise their glasses and Maura says, "L'Chaim." This Hebrew salutation translates to "cheers" but literally means "to life" and has entered into the American vernacular. Most cultures toast to good health or happiness, and "L'Chaim" covers it but with more at stake. This has to do with the ironic historical consequences of chosenness, where life might literally be on the line.

In conclusion, I take up the Jewish kabbalistic idea of *gematria*, or Jewish numerology, which Soloway weaves through the series. One commonplace use of Jewish numerology among secular and religious Jews has to do with the number 18, the numerical value of the letters that spell life in Hebrew—*chai*, as in l'chaim. Charity is typically given in multiples of 18, for example. Soloway is interested in the mystical properties of numbers and the messianic undertow of cultural structures, including popular culture, all as delivery systems.

When Ari has her revelation about intersectionality as "the holy other" in season 3 during a nitrous trip at the dentist (who mystically appears to her again at the ruined idyll in Ramallah), she conflates a piece of American popular culture, the game show *Wheel of Fortune*, with the figure of gematria. The idea is that numerology works as a structuring device to represent overlapping ideas with a mystical aim of transformation or, for Ari, of arriving. Conveying her vision to Leslie, Ari asks, "What if this otherness made up of the sum of intersectional parts was the messiah?" Leslie yet again demeans her, and the viewer, too, may be similarly dubious about what sounds, in Leslie's words, "nuts." Significantly and punningly, it is a (home)stretch. Why this combined image of the mystical and the mundane, of the Kabbalah's and television's *Wheel of Fortune*? Soloway explains that the whole of season 3 is structured to correspond to a Passover Seder, which occurs in a makeshift way in the final episode of the season. Passover is, of course, the holiday of liberation and deliverance. But given the history of the Jews, it is an attenuated homecoming.

> So we started doing some research about the story of Elijah . . . and the story of Elijah's wheel, and realized that in this idea of what god looks like and the goddess, that the image of a circle that was like a spinning wheel actually had a lot more resonance in terms of trying to represent spirituality. . . . *Wheel of Fortune* seemed perfect. If you look closely, all the numbers on the wheel are multiples of 18 and 36, both of which are considered important and auspicious numbers in Judaism. They also continually pop up throughout the season as little Easter (er, Passover?) eggs."[24]

Jewiness, of which these numerological ticks are a part, provides a structuring principle in *Transparent*. On Ari's first nitrous trip of season 3 that produces the hallucinatory dream set in a *Wheel of Fortune* game, where Caitlyn Jenner and Ntozake Shange are on competing teams, Ari asks for a "J" to solve the puzzle. This hallucinatory sequence appears in the same episode as the seventieth birthday dinner, with its particular theme of deliverance. Soloway suggests certain investments in associations whose recurrence produces both an uncanny effect (like Freud)—some repetition compulsion—and a meaning created by and for the show that corresponds to what Freedman calls its "units of attention," suggestively its Talmudic parts, a structure of questions and answers.[25] This Talmudic mode is yet another Jewish meme, reflecting a perception of Jewishness as dynamic and studiously unsettled: but "why," the joke goes, "do Jews always answer a question with a question?" "Why not?" is the punchline. Some might interpret this as a refusal to land. For Soloway, that is the Jewishness of the transgender story.

Notes

1. Josh Lambert, "Pfefferman Family Matters: Why Is a Jewish Family at the Center of a Story about a Transgender Woman, in 'Transparent'?" *Tablet*, December 7, 2015, https://www.tabletmag.com/sections/news/articles/pfefferman-family-matters/.
2. Amy Villarejo, "Jewish, Queer-ish, Trans, and Completely Revolutionary: Jill Soloway's *Transparent* and the New Television," *Film Quarterly* 69, no. 4 (2016): 10–22. On page 14, Villarejo picks up on the "ish" idea as "important: "I think it's worth borrowing the meme of 'ish' from Glitterish because it is so right for *Transparent: it enfolds all that is Jewish-ish* and queer-ish and allows their qualities and characterizations to transform and transmute lovingly through the show's rich and thick audio-visual landscape." Glitterish is a girls' band that appears in *Transparent* and sings the Jim Croce song "Operator."
3. See Debra Nussbaum Cohen, "How Jill Soloway Created 'Transparent,'" *Forward*, October 21, 2014, https://forward.com/culture/207407/how-jill-soloway-created-transparent-the-jewiest/, where series creator and executive producer, Jill Soloway, said in an interview, "It's so Jewy. We got away with that much Jewiness? I can't believe it. Surprisingly today it's more controversial to be Jewy than trans." Robert Tobin does consider the connection in "*Transparent*: Healing the American Family through the German Discovery of Sex," January 4, 2016, http://pennpress.typepad.com/pennpresslog/2016/01/transparent-healing-the-american-family-through-the-german-discovery-of-sex.html.
4. Taffy Brodesser-Akner, "Can Jill Soloway do Justice to the Trans Movement?" *New York Times Magazine*, August 29, 2014, https://www.nytimes.com/2014/08/31/magazine/can-jill-soloway-do-justice-to-the-trans-movement.html/.
5. Villarejo, "Jewish, Queer-ish, Trans," 12–13, 21.
6. Alisa Solomon, "Jewy, Queer, Daring, and Political: Transparent Pushes Past Parody," *The Nation*, 2016, https://www.thenation.com/article/archive/jewy-queer-daring-and-political-transparent-pushes-past-parody/. A good example of the dictum "bad for the Jews" appears in Philip Roth, "The Conversion of the Jews," in *Goodbye Columbus* (Boston: Houghton Mifflin, 1959).
7. Solomon, "Jewy, Queer, Daring, and Political: Transparent Pushes Past Parody."
8. Solomon, "Jewy, Queer, Daring, and Political: Transparent Pushes Past Parody." The emphasis on "would" is in the original.
9. Solomon, "Jewy, Queer, Daring, and Political: Transparent Pushes Past Parody."
10. Solomon, "Jewy, Queer, Daring, and Political: Transparent Pushes Past Parody."
11. Cohen, "How Jill Soloway Created 'Transparent.'"

12 Isaac Butler, "*Transparent* is the Most Profoundly Jewish Show in TV History," *Slate*, September 27, 2017, https://slate.com/culture/2017/09/transparent-is-a-profoundly-jewish-tv-show.html/.
13 Sarah Ahmed, "Queer Feeling," in *Routledge Queer Studies Reader* (New York: Routledge, 2012), 435.
14 Butler references Mark Oppenheimer, "Jerry Seinfeld is Well, Jew-ish," *Tablet*, September 19, 2017, https://www.tabletmag.com/sections/news/articles/jerry-seinfeld-is-well-jew-ish/. Oppenheimer uses the expression a "surfeit of feeling" to describe a "Jewish sensibility, a way of seeing the world" (he is himself referencing Devorah Baum's book *Feeling Jewish* (New Haven: Yale University Press, 2017). Susan Stryker describes "transgender phenomena" in "(De) Subjugated Knowledges: An Introduction to Transgender Studies," in *The Transgender Studies Reader*, eds. Susan Stryker and Stephen Whittle (New York: Routledge, 2006), 12.
15 Exceptions are in the work of Heike Bauer, Rainer Herrn, and Ralf Dose.
16 Magnus Hirschfeld, *Geschlechtskunde: Auf Grund Dreissigjähriger Forschung Und Erfahrung Bearbeit*, vol. 4 (Stuttgart: J. Pittmann, 1930), 620. Karl Giese, Hirschfeld's assistant and partner after 1920, provided the caption; see Herrn, 124. My translation of the German is in brackets. See Rainer Herrn, *Schnittmuster des Geschlechts: Transvestitismus und Transsexualität in der frühen Sexualwissenschaft* (Giessen: Psychosozial Verlag, 2005). Hirschfeld believed that transvestism was a sexual variation on the spectrum, an expression of a gender feeling. See Hirschfeld, *Die Transvestiten* (Leipzig: Max Spohr, 1910).
17 Judith Butler, *Undoing Gender* (New York: Routledge), 8.
18 Natasha Seymour, "Representing Transgender Embodiment in Film and Culture: Looking beyond the Transition Narrative in Amazon's *Transparent*," *Somatechnics* 9, no. 1 (2019): 88. Seymour is drawing specifically on Jay Prosser's work in this quotation.
19 Seymour, 94.
20 Arguably, the entire season is about thwarted homecomings: Maura returns from Israel to find a German airbnb-er "occupying" her house; Sara and Len's effort to return to their heterosexual union is thwarted by design by Lila who triangulates their relationship; and Ali is still waiting for answers, having found temporary shelter at the camp, as instructed by the hallucinatory Black dentist.
21 For a discussion of the use of "ish," see Villarejo, "Jewish, Queer-ish, Trans."
22 I heard Gershom Scholem comment on this exchange at a James Joyce Symposium in Zurich in 1979, which he attended. I recorded this in several articles, including in an essay for Fritz Senn Festschrift; see Marilyn Reizbaum, "Sennschrift: james jews," in *A Collideorscope of Joyce*, eds. Ruth Frehner and Ursula Zeller (Dublin: Lilliput Press, 1998).
23 Seymour discusses how film narrativizes transgender experience by investing in two projects: first, transliteracy; the second, "is best described by Prosser as establishing the constitutive significance of somatic feeling,'" 90. In Jay Prosser, *Second Skins: The Body Narratives of Transsexuality* (New York: Columbia University Press, 1998).
24 Liz Raftery, "Transparent: Here's the Real Story Behind Caitlyn Jenner's Season 3 Cameo," *TV Guide*, September 25, 2016, https://www.tvguide.com/news/transparent-caitlyn-jenner-season-3-cameo/.
25 Jonathan Freedman, "'Transparent': A Guide for The Perplexed," *LA Review of Books*, April 10, 2016, https://lareviewofbooks.org/article/transparent-a-guide-for-the-perplexed/.

Part 5
Concluding and Transitioning

15

Run from Your Parent's House

Transfeminism and Abraham's Blessing

SLAVA GREENBERG

Award-winning *Transparent* became well known for its premise as the tale of Maura's gender transition at an older age while parenting three adult children. The first three seasons explore themes of gender, sexuality, and family ties in light of their Jewishness. In the fourth season, and the series' musical finale, the focus shifts from Maura to her youngest child, Ari, not only discovering their own gender identity but also their spiritual role in the family and the overall community. The Pfeffermans go on a trip to Israel, which sets Ari on their Abrahamic journey; they separate from their mother and independently question gender, religious, and territorial divides.

I focus on Maura's youngest child's journey by offering a transfeminist Jewish interpretation of the biblical Abrahamic narrative. Ari's narrative, which gradually becomes the center of the series, shifts to focus on a journey for the discovery of their (Ari's) own gender identity; in addition, they replace their parent as a spiritual guide. Like the Abrahamic figure, Ari begins by leaving their parent's house, going forth into Israel. Unlike Abraham, they discover queer and trans Palestinians living under Israeli occupation, immerse (*tvila* Jewish ritual bathing) in the Dead Sea, witness the divine revelation of a goddess, change their own name, and finally return to their parents' house to become a blessing for others while they are still alive.

Jewish studies scholar Judith Plaskow has issued a call that the time has come to upend the gender binary and interrogate how it functions within Judaism: "It is time to undertake a thorough, critical investigation of the persistence of gender roles, leading to a new phase in the transformation of Judaism in which the liberal community takes a hard look at the ways its structures continue to assume and support the gender binary. Transgender awareness and activism are crucial elements in moving to this next stage."[1] If Plaskow is correct, then *Transparent* suggests some ways trans and gender nonconforming Jews may not only be included in religious services but also push against the gender and other binaries. *Transparent*'s challenge of the gender divide is made by citing, referencing, and reimagining the mythological call to the biblical figure of Abraham: "Go forth from your land, your birthplace, your father's house, to the land that I will show you" (Genesis 12:1).

I use Joy Ladin's transfeminist theology in my analysis of *Transparent*'s televised version of a nonbinary Abraham. Ladin posed questions such as, "Do religious traditions speak to trans experiences as they do to other human experiences? Can trans experiences illuminate religious texts and transition, or does including trans perspectives in religious life require 'transing' traditions, changing them in ways that represent fundamental breaks with tradition?"[2] *Transparent*'s interpretation of the biblical verse "Go forth" and "from your father's house" adds questions about the meanings entailed in leaving a home—through trans perspectives of displacement, migration, and housing precarity. Diving into the manifestations of going, leaving, or running away from (gender) roles assigned at birth allows for reconnection and reconciliation of the two parts of the verse. Ari runs away from their parents' house; however, to fully complete their quest (as assigned by the series), they must finally return there.

In what follows, I explore trans and gender-nonconforming ways of being in contemporary Judaism, through a televised version of Abraham, as portrayed in *Transparent*. The interconnection between the text's temporal and spatial gaps allows for a polysemic reading. It not only gives way to a renewed exploration of the two parts of the verse (the divine call to "go forth" and "from your father's house") but also adds another possible reading of the conclusion to Abraham's biblical story. In the first two sections in what follows, I explore both parts of the verse; in the third, I describe *Transparent*'s alteration of the origin as it adds yet another call, which I argue is transfeminist: "Return to your parents' house, to care for your community," advocating for action and spiritual leadership with the urgency of movements such as "If Not Now."

Go Forth to Yourself, for Yourself

The ritual of being included in the Abrahamic covenant with God, and the precepts Jewish babies assigned male are obliged to undertake, involves a circumcision eight days after birth. This is followed by the ritual of accepting the obligation of the commandments imposed by the gender divide: the bat mitzvah for girls at the age of twelve and the bar mitzvah for boys at thirteen. The rituals do not only distinguish girls from boys but also (at least in more Orthodox communities) through access to publicly reading the Torah. Furthermore, the rituals also reinforce the gender divide by separating the options on the basis of gender: a feminine bat or a masculine bar. The same issue arises with the attempt to find a gender-neutral alternative to the masculine-assumed "Go forth" call—in Hebrew, *Lekh Lekha*. The absence of gender-neutral language becomes a barrier for nonbinary Jews and requires the creation of new names, terms, and practices. However, *Transparent*'s fourth season and musical finale intentionally cite, quote, and paraphrase the call to go forth. This requires viewers to rewatch both, allowing them to fully enjoy the intertextual meanings that lie within these conversations. Although Ari's quest in the fourth season alludes to incidents, places, and events from Abraham's biblical narrative, these can only be fully understood after watching the musical finale. The finale directly paraphrases the Go Forth call in the song "Run from Your Father's House" and later quotes it in the sermon that Ari gives during shiva, the mourning rituals after Maura's death.

In *Transparent*, Ari's character becomes a contemporary nonbinary Abraham figure. In the fourth season Ali (as Abram), leaves their parent's house on a journey to become Ari (as Abraham) and create a blessing for families, communities, and nations. The biblical text and its creative interpretation navigate the series' musical finale, in which Ari sings the Go Forth portion for their belated "bart mitzvah" (a multigendered amalgamation of the feminine bat and the masculine bar mitzvah). In *Transparent*'s version of the story, the call to set off on this self-reflective journey results in Ari—the contemporary version of Abraham—realizing that they are nonbinary, changing their name, and taking on a spiritual leadership role in their family and the trans community.

This allegory of the Go Forth verse adds to the vast explorations of this divine call, particularly those reading it as an urge to set off on one's own journey.[3] The Hebrew Lekh Lekha might mean go to yourself, in your own way, or go on the path that would isolate you from your country and homeland, your father's house, and from all connections that you previously had. Within this mitzvah (precept), the going is a goal of its own. This inner calling aids in times of crisis, in crossroads, and so Lekh Lekha can be seen as a blessing of one's chosen path.[4]

In *Transparent*, Ari explains the story to their siblings while cuddling in their recently deceased mother's bed: "If you leave your parent's house and go out into the world and do something different than what they taught you, then you will be blessed . . . that your life will be blessed. And . . . everyone who's nice to you gets blessed, and everybody who's mean to you gets cursed."[5] In this moment, after their parent recently died, Ari connects with their siblings through their own nonbinary interpretation of the Go Forth verse. They explain it as an urge to leave a parent's house and go on an independent path that bears the promise that this journey will eventually be fruitful. This act of sharing with their siblings allows Ari to reject not only assigned gender expectations but also to transform their lastborn patterns of dependency into dependable spiritual guidance.

The ambiguity of these two words—"go" and "forth"—leaves space for multiple trans and gender nonconforming interpretations. Aviv and Erlichman suggest that although *Lekh lekha* means "Go to yourself," it also utilizes changing one's name as part of a public covenant, marked by the transformation in the story. This "takes place when the Divine changes people's names: Abram to Abraham and Sarai to Sara.... Changing names to mark spiritual and physical transformation is thus a deeply Jewish value and is also common among queers, especially transpeople."[6]

Joy Ladin's transfeminist approach to Lekh Lekha focuses on its opening verse by comparing her lived experiences as a trans woman to those of Abraham. Noting how the actions of trans people are at times viewed and narrated externally from cisgender points of view, Ladin reads around, before, and after Abraham's actions. Ladin reminds us that prior to this divine call, Abraham had faithfully fulfilled his firstborn role by following his father from his native city, Ur of the Chaldeans, to the city of Haran. Consequently, the Lekh Lekha call becomes a commandment to create oneself, in and through various ways. For both Ladin and Abraham, becoming oneself involves physical transformation.[7] In Abraham's case, circumcision transformed him from the head of a single nomadic household into "the father of a multitude of nations." God has marked this transformation by changing his name from Abram to Abraham (Genesis 17:5). Abraham's abandonment of his firstborn role was a private family matter. His name change, however, publicly signified his transformation into a different kind of man, a kind of man who had never before existed, one for which even the Torah does not provide a name: a Jewish man, whose circumcised body attests to his covenant with God.[8]

Ladin's transfeminist perspective evokes at least two possible interpretations of the contemporary Lekh Lekha portrayal in *Transparent*, one focusing on Maura and the other on Ari. Like Abraham, Maura begins her journey later in life by leaving the house in which she raised her children with her ex-wife. Also, like Abraham (Abram) she changes her name to mark the transition. One year into her transition, she is invited as a keynote speaker at a Judaism and gender conference in Jerusalem. Her spiritual journey to the "promised land" is unrelated to her transition and focuses on reconciliation with her father, who abandoned her as a child. Maura's journey ends with her realizing that gender nonconformity runs in her family: her aunt was trans, and now her child is coming out as nonbinary. Finally, as with the biblical figure of Abraham, the narrative continues, telling the offspring's stories while connecting them to their Jewish and queer-trans lineage.

That lineage demonstrates the blessing of Go Forth with each generation crossing the gender divide on its own terms. Although Maura and her aunt Gittel have crossed the divide, Ari's journey rejects it altogether. One scene, in which the family reaches the Wailing Wall and is forced to split according to binary genders, makes the gender divide visible. The ancient wall in Jerusalem is significant to Jews, Muslims, and Christians. The Wailing Wall is sacred to Jews because it is the closest and most accessible remains of the Jewish Temple. Ever since its occupation by the State of Israel in 1967, it has been under Israeli control and Jewish Orthodox rule, regulating gender segregation (by both legal and illegal means). They have prevented women from praying freely, wearing prayer shawls, and reading from the Torah, collectively and aloud.[9]

The anthology *Balancing on the Mechitza: Transgender in Jewish Community* is the first volume to have taken up this topic. It uses the gender divide (*mechitza*) as a springboard to address trans and nonbinary perspectives of Judaism and gender.[10] In *Transparent*, Ari does not only have to decide which side of the gender divide to choose on their trip to the Wall but also what this choice may entail. Although this goes (unrealistically) smoothly for the transgender mother, Maura, her gender-nonconforming child is faced with a different experience.[11]

The Pfeffermans arrive at the Wailing Wall and the camera pans left to right—from the men's side to the women's—pausing on the divide itself. This gender segregation is naturally accepted by everyone, including their trans mother, Maura, but not by Ari. Ari's discomfort with the divide is rationally explained in terms of gender equality when Ari notices that "the men have about three times as much of the wall space." However, that is not enough to convince the rest to revolt. "Yeah, but it's tradition," their older sister responds and moves on. She joins her mothers and aunt on the women's side while her spouse, brother, and grandfather go to the men's side. Ari feels discomfort in this gender-segregated space (known as gender dysphoria), looks around, and finally wears a kippah and crosses over to the men's area.[12] Despite physically crossing the divide, Ari does not mean to stay on either side. The physical and metaphorical divides in Ari's narrative emphasize the divide's use in the oppression and policing of women's and girls' bodies, and in many of the scenes, its rejection is explained through feminism.

Transparent offers a contemporary version of Lekh Lekha (the Hebrew masculine form of Go Forth), in singular-plural, or in nonbinary form, *Lekhu Lakhenm* (the Hebrew merging of masculine and feminine forms in plural). The intellectual, spiritual, and emotional rejection of the gender divide comprises Ari's go forth journey. In this version, the covenant with God/dess does not require any physical transformation but rather a spiritual one. Ari has to abandon the traditional role of a lastborn or youngest child in need and grow into a spiritual leader for their family and community. Ari has to leave their "father's house," represented through their trans mother. Maura's "house" is her lineage of belated gender transition and crossing of the gender divide, within which Ari must reject their roles assigned at birth. Ari must go so far as to reject the gender divide in order to be blessed and to bring blessings on those around them. According to *Transparent*, the contemporary Abraham must leave their parent's house to find a way to give back to their community by eliminating the divide.

Run from Your Parent's House

Trans and feminist perspectives expand on the "forth" part of the verse by interpreting it as "for yourself," but the same perspectives might also be applied to the rest of the verse: "from your birthplace and from your father's house" (Genesis 12:1). Investigating the statement of "leaving your parent's house" through transfeminist perspectives and experiences of trans and queer people lead directly to issues of displacement, abandonment, homelessness, immigration, and medical tourism.[13]

For many trans and gender-nonconforming people, leaving their parents' house is not a choice—indeed, for many it is the only way to survive. Queer and trans studies scholar Aren Aizura interrogates mobility through terms such as travel, migration, displacement, and tourism as subjected to divisions of ethnicity, class, geography, language, gender, and sexuality. Quoting American studies scholar Caren Kaplan, Aizura commented on the circulation of travel tropes: "immigrants, refugees, exiles, nomads, and the homeless also move in and out of these discourses as metaphors, tropes and symbols but rarely as historically recognized producers of critical discourses themselves." I follow these observations in my exploration of *Transparent*'s adaptation of Go Forth, and particularly the return.[14]

Aizura studied the trope of leaving and returning through transsexual travel narratives. These have been pervasive within Euro-American cultural productions and also "often [involve] the protagonist returning ready to take their proper place in the social field." In Ari's case, this is a renewed place in the family and Jewish community. Aizura suggested that "in classical journey narratives also, the geographical metaphor's meaning relies on a clear distinction between 'here' and 'elsewhere' [...] familiar/strange; home/away; centre/periphery; West/East; civilization/barbarism; rootedness/traversal; domestic/foreign; same/other."[15] In Ari's journey, many of these binaries collapse when they are introduced to the Palestinian queer collective and nightlife in Ramallah.

Although the biblical text minimizes the weight of the act of leaving by omitting the actual word (leave) and implying it instead (go forth ... from ...), *Transparent* amplifies it by replacing "go" with a much more urgent "Run!" as it appears in the song in the musical finale.[16] Both the "house" and the "running" in the series are simultaneously literal and figurative. The series' narrative is framed by Maura's house, the childhood home where the siblings grew up, as both a physical and metaphysical link to Jewish heritage, inheritance, and generational trauma. The series' pilot centers on Maura's announcement to her three adult children that she does not want her house anymore. The siblings get into an argument about who should get their "father's house" (this is before she comes out to them). Maura resolves the argument by deciding to give it to her firstborn, Sarah. In the finale, however, viewers realize that Maura had in fact left her house to her chosen family rather than her birth family. In her will, she says the house should go to her friend Davina, a trans woman of color, who gave her a home and cared for her throughout her transition, and its profits should go to support the trans community, an innovative form of tithing.[17] Davina's interpretation of this tithe is in offering a home (and not just housing) to trans and gender-nonconforming youth. Thus, the final moments of the series illuminate the circumstances in which many queer and trans youth leave their parents' homes.

In a study on the abandonment of LGBT youth, Caitlin Judge suggests that "while the exact number of runaways and homeless youth in the United States each year is unknown, various sources estimate that at any given time, between 500,000 and 2.8 million youth are homeless. Of those youth, between 20% and 40% identify as LGBT."[18] According to a status report on hunger and homelessness in America's cities, over 8 percent of transgender adults who came out to immediate family while growing up were kicked out as a result. Ten percent chose to run away from home (32 percent of whom did so before the age of 15). Among transgender adult respondents whose family had kicked them out of the house, nearly three-quarters (74 percent) experienced homelessness at some point in their lives—almost three times as much as respondents who had not been kicked out after disclosing their trans identity to their families (28 percent of whom experienced homelessness).[19]

The "house" in *Transparent* serves as a recurring allegory of un/desired inheritance from our ancestors. Maura—and Ari as well, to a lesser extent—is preoccupied with the symbolic aspects of the home in their heritage, inheritance, and lineage of depression and trans experiences in the family. Maura learns more about her family history and decides to share it with the rest of the family.

Questions about genes and inheritance come up when Maura and Ari meet Moshe—their father and grandfather, respectively—for the first time. Moshe is forced to explain why he left Maura, her sister Bryna, and her mother Rose with their abusive grandfather. He explains that he left Rose because of her depression. Ari asks, "Why was Grandma Rose depressed?" Moshe immediately yells: "Why? Because of the fucking Holocaust. Have you ever heard of it? I'm trying to explain to you, some families got out. But no family got out clean." For Rose, immigration did not fully constitute an escape from the Holocaust because its memory kept haunting her in Los Angeles. After this outburst, Moshe explains that his abandonment also may have been motivated by the death of Rose's trans sister, Gittel. Moshe is making the point that escaping an unwanted house is not entirely possible for everyone. It is not until the end of the visit that Moshe explains to Maura that Gittel was trans, "like you." For the first time, Maura learns that she descends from a line of Jewish trans women who eventually created more accomodating homes than those of their birth.

For Ari, though, it is the return part of the journey that allows a reconnection, despite not being quite "transformed." Although Abraham never looked back, Ari's journey cannot be concluded in a faraway land. Ari's journey is different from Abraham's, not only in the lack of a physical transformation but also in its nonlinear migration; this contemporary nomadic tale ends with settling back down where they originated.

Return to Your Parent's House? From Healing Oneself to Healing the World

In *Transparent*'s contemporary references to the Abrahamic journey, Ari runs from their parent's house, discovers their gender identity in a Palestinian queer and trans collective (i.e., "elsewhere"), changes their name, and becomes a nonbinary priestess. However, the series' musical finale ends with Ari's path to becoming a rabbi through amending, healing, and repairing the world (and particularly its gender divisions). At its conclusion, the finale provides a glimpse into the future after Ari has become a nonbinary rabbi. They return to their parent's house for Shabbat (Friday night) dinner—hosted by its current matriarch and owner, Davina with the trans youth from the local LGBT center. This final return is a way of amending binary and patriarchal interpretations of Judaism, mostly attributed to the Orthodox stream, and illustrating another path.[20]

Before I demonstrate how the finale avoids the "returning transformed" narrative of self-healing and moves toward a healing of the world, I must first address the two years that transpired between the fourth season and the series finale. This is crucial to understanding the unique aspects that make returning home particularly unsafe for some women of trans experience and gender nonconforming people.

In November 2017, two months after the fourth season aired, Jeffrey Tambor, the actor who played Maura, was fired following complaints of sexual harassment made publicly by actresses Van Barnes and Trace Lysette, two trans women who worked with Tambor on set. Barnes had worked as Tambor's assistant on the show and accused him of subjecting her to unwanted physical contact and lewd remarks. This took place following the pilot episode after the series had already been criticized by the trans community for casting Tambor, a cisgender man, rather than a transgender actress.

Thinking that *Transparent* was over, creator and writer Joey Soloway published their own version of what went on behind the scenes in the 2018 book *She Wants It: Desire, Power and Toppling the Patriarchy*. Similar to some parts of the series' finale, the book sought to repent, repair, and finally attempt to heal the world. The finale's repair (in Hebrew, *tikkun*) was thus realized in creatively finding a way for Maura, or rather her spirit, to be played by a transgender actress.

In their book, Soloway described what happened to trans women on the set of *Transparent* from their (Soloway's) point of view. Their account starts from the moment they learned about the abuse and ends before they thought about adapting their sister Faith Soloway's theater musical into a televised episode. Joey Soloway shared that for a time, after the show was canceled, they blamed it on the women who came forward; however, they write, "I had to remind myself that it wasn't Van's or Trace's fault for being willing to speak. This happened because of Jeffery and how his male privilege, his place in the patriarchy, blinded him to how his actions affected others."[21] After receiving emails from *Deadline*, *The Hollywood Reporter*, and *Variety* requesting comment on Van Barnes's Facebook post (in which she came forward about Tambor's harassment), Soloway and the other writers started working on a version of the fifth season without Maura.[22]

From the transfeminist perspective, the feminist movements of #MeToo and #TimesUp had left the women who spoke up in particular and trans women in broad, behind. Even though Tambor was eventually fired from *Transparent*, *Variety* reported that "Tambor's career is still alive; he has a starring role on Netflix's *Arrested Development* reboot. Lysette wasn't surprised Tambor seemed to take a softer hit compared to other industry heavyweights singled out in the #MeToo movement, since she, Barnes, and most of his accusers are transgender women."[23]

In fact, it is not Ari's character who returns "transformed" in the show's finale but *Transparent* as a series. For the finale, Faith Soloway played a bigger role in the production and creative process. Whether the passage of time allowed for a different perspective or whether due to changes in the creative process, this transformed production emerged and spoke in a different language. In this iteration, *Transparent* utilizes a different space, genre references, beat, and soundtrack, and Tambor was replaced with transgender actress Shakina Nayfack.

In their book, Joey Soloway writes that Faith had been showcasing "all the songs she'd been writing over the years for an imaginary *Transparent* musical."[24] Before she came to work on *Transparent*, she had been "mounting rock operas in Boston, folk songs, light operas, and sweet arias.... Now, five years later she had a stack of songs about our family and the Pfeffermans. She was also writing songs about gender long before our parent came out, with names like 'NeverGenderland,' an absurd *Fantasia*-inspired amusement park you could visit where you could be anyone you need to be."[25] The book ends with Soloway crediting their sister with the casting of Nayfack to play Maura. Soloway saw her in the theatrical musical and wrote: "Shakina is trans and Jewish and her name means 'goddess' in Hebrew, or 'the great feminine,' or 'she who holds space with love and patience,' and I got chills as she started singing. Like she was giving a kind of resuscitation to Maura."[26] Later on, Nayfack plays Ava, a version of Maura's spirit in the televised finale.

The self-healing, created by replacing Maura with a stand-in (Ava) following her passing, allows Ari to begin a new spiritual journey. This new journey is no longer geographical or gender-transition related; however, it does require the rejection of roles assigned at birth. Ari seeks to change the binary prepositions in Judaism by creating their own path.

I read Soloway's attempts at amending the situation in the book and series' musical finale, as well as Ari's journey, through Jewish interpretations of repair. Scholar and rabbi James Jacobson-Maisels suggests that the kabbalistic (Jewish mystical tradition) meaning of *tikkun olam*—"repairing the brokenness of both God and the world"—has evolved into a contemporary affirmation of "social and political activism."[27] The intersection of *tikkun atzmi* (self-healing/mending) and *tikkun olam* (world-healing/mending) lies in the understanding that "self-transformation, to be genuine, must always be directed outward as well as inward."[28] Jacobson-Maisels concludes with, "We do not wait to achieve complete self-reflection before pursuing a perfected world but, as the Zohar book [Kabbalah text] teaches us, we start with it each day, committing ourselves to the inner healing necessary for the true outer healing to take place."[29]

Ari's return to their parent's house begins as self-healing and quickly becomes part of their tikkun olam. Maura's house, which in the first episode of *Transparent* was the bone of contention between the siblings, becomes the form through which Ari can be blessed. In the finale, the siblings learn that Maura had left her house to Davina. As with the biblical Go Forth, here, too, we see the journey from an external point of view: not only had Maura disinherited her firstborn (and all her children) from this wealth, she gave it to unhoused queer and trans folks. We are only given a glimpse into a possible mindset of caring for chosen family members in need of a home. Maura had left the house to Davina and its profits to the local LGBT center. Ari's place at this new table enables them to both bless their new trans family and be blessed by their presence. In so doing, the show creates a double *tikkun*, both for Ari and for the show's creator, Joey Soloway.

This trans and gender-nonconforming perspective, added to *Transparent*'s take on the Lekh Lekha portion, draws from feminist analyses of Abraham's story. Perry Dane suggests that Abraham's story is protofeminist, with a protofeminist message, being a story of a succession of women. This is because in the conclusion of the Go Forth chapter, not only does Yitzhak succeed his father Abraham, but Sarah also becomes the mother of all Jews.[30] *Transparent*'s transfeminist and gender-nonconforming perspective emphasizes the aspects of care, accountability, and responsibility in leaving one's parent's house, as well as the need to return to it.

Searching for the traces of Abraham's responsibility toward his father, and by extension his brother, nieces, and nephews whom he had left behind, I reread another possible note with which to end the story. Although Abraham never returned in person, and his father passed away shortly after Abraham left, his path had blessed those he left behind. In this, the Bible does not allow for the neglect of one's loved ones. Abraham's blessing was passed on to his remaining family in Haran. In Genesis 25, Abraham is told that his niece and sister-in-law (Haran's daughter and her uncle Nahor's wife) had eight children (Genesis 25: 20–23). This echoes the perspective woven within *Transparent*'s finale: you can choose a family, and turn away from birth family and roles assigned at birth, but it is a journey.

Transing the Gender Divide in Judaism

Transparent's musical finale presents some of the more disputed issues within Judaism that surround trans people's participation in religious life: Maura's death (including her funeral service, shiva, and inheritance) and Ari's *aliya la'torah* (the ritual of reading the Torah on stage in the synagogue) on their bart mitzvah. Despite Reform Judaism's critiques of the Orthodox stream's narrow view of Judaism as the written Jewish Law (in Hebrew, *Halakha*) only,[31] it was not until 2009 that the Reform movement officially stated that "gender is not so important" to Jewish religious practices.[32] *Transparent* itself avoids these issues altogether in Maura's narrative; it is only through Ari's character that the series targets gender hierarchies and not only divisions.

In his book *Generation of Perversions*, published the same year *Transparent* premiered, Idan Ben-Ephraim, an Orthodox rabbi, specifies and expands the question of participation of trans Jews to many everyday aspects of Orthodox precepts. He discusses and rules on most of the issues raised by the show and on issues such as gender-affirming surgeries (prohibiting them), dress and head covering, and more. In general, Ben-Ephraim recognizes binary trans men and women as valid men and women and treats them as such in his rulings. By so doing, his approach may be considered more liberal than *Transparent*'s, which cast a cisgender man to play a trans woman. If we were to judge Maura's actions through Ben-Ephraim's rulings, it seems the show excludes and denies her access to most of the precepts discussed in *Generation of Perversions*. Maura's choice to be cremated spares the series from having to address questions of burial and purification.

A similar reading of Ari's character, which problematizes gender hierarchies, illuminates the misogynist aspects of the rulings in Ben-Ephraim's book. Two scenes from the finale focus on Ari praying—once privately with their siblings and once publicly. In the former, Ari is seen saying Kaddish (a Jewish prayer commonly recited on behalf of the dead) over their mother while she is cremated, and in the latter, they are making aliya la'torah for their bart mitzvah during the shiva (mourning ritual of sitting for seven days). According to Ben-Ephraim's ruling on the Mourner/Orphans' Kaddish prayer, although Ari is nonbinary, their Kaddish is still "kosher."[33]

According to Ben-Ephraim, a person assigned female at birth can publicly say the Mourner/Orphans' Kaddish in a synagogue as long as they appear masculine. However, he also offered a stricter version in small print, stating, "And even while saying *Orphan's Kaddish*, one of the public should say it with him."[34] Under this perspective, appearances count the most—that is, as long as Ari passes as masculine, they are permitted to say Kaddish over their parent. *Transparent*'s writers made this even easier as the Kaddish is said privately, within the family, together with a cisgender man partially saying it with them.

During Ari's bart mitzvah, they sing the verses of Lekh Lekha and "Run from Your Father's House" song, the song that inspired this essay. This ritual is also acceptable in Ben-Ephraim's ruling on the issue of aliya la'torah. Ben-Ephraim argues that in the case of "a woman who turned herself into a man, if this man is drawn closer to Judaism and comes to pray in the synagogue, it is permitted to let him read from the Torah publicly, and all according to the [instructions of the] Moreh [in Hebrew, teacher, rabbi, community's spiritual leader]."[35] Therefore, as a masculine-presenting person who was assigned female at birth, Ari is allowed to read from the Torah with the approval of their rabbi, who is present in the scene.

From a binary trans perspective, *Generation of Perversions* is just as (if not more) "liberal" or "trans-friendly" as *Transparent*. However, from a transfeminist perspective, we cannot overlook the utilization of trans issues to reinforce not just the gender binary, but also gender hierarchies through the devaluation of women. Ben-Ephraim, unapologetically and in concurrence with Orthodox premises, writes that in the case of Mourner/Orphan's Kaddish, "a man turned himself into a woman, it is clear that this woman should not be allowed to say the prayer, despite the fact that she had been a man from her inception."[36] With regard to reading the Torah, he rules that in the case of "a man who turned himself into a woman, this woman should not be permitted to say *Kaddish* neither from the women's side of the synagogue's divide nor at home."[37]

Reading *Transparent* through Ben-Ephraim's (binary) transinclusive book illuminates the transmisogynist casting of a man to play a woman. This casting, unintentionally, unconsciously, and indirectly has contributed to the pool of "cis-face" representations of trans women and caused direct harm to at least two trans women on set. Simultaneously, reading Ben-Ephraim's book through *Transparent* brings forth not only the book's affirmation of the gender divide but mainly its misogyny. Both texts draw from and add to the biblical narrative. Exploring them through a transfeminist theology, however, allows unveiling the different appropriations of Abraham's story. Although some *halachic* responsas (body of written decisions and rulings) base their devaluation of women, trans, and gender nonconforming people on interpreting

Abraham's covenant with God—and particularly the ritual of circumcision—as linked to the masculine body, *Transparent* uses the divine call as a springboard to address trans and gender-nonconforming journeys from healing oneself to healing the world.

Notes

1. Judith Plaskow, "Dismantling the Gender Binary within Judaism: The Challenge of Transgender to Compulsory Heterosexuality," in *Balancing on the Mechitza: Transgender in Jewish Community*, ed. Noach Dzmura (Berkeley, CA: North Atlantic Books, 2010), 203.
2. Joy Ladin, "In the Image of God, God Created Them: Toward Trans Theology," *Journal of Feminist Studies in Religion* 34, no. 1 (2018): 54.
3. Rashi's interpretation of this story, through the Gemara and the Midrash, explains Lekh Lekha as the drive to leave one's father's house for one's own good and happiness.
4. Yair Barkai, "Lekh Lekha—Lekh Le'hanaatkha," Parashat Lekh Lekha, *Daf Shvui: Jewish Studies Faculty* 1242 (Ramat Gan: Bar-Ilan University 2018), 1–2.
5. *Transparent*, Season 5, "Musical Finale," Amazon Prime Video, September 27, 2019.
6. Caryn Aviv and Karen Erlichman, "Going to and Becoming Ourselves: Transformation and Covenants in *Parashat Lech Lecha* (Genesis 12:1–17:27)," in *Torah Queeries: Weekly Commentaries on the Hebrew Bible*, eds. Gregg Drinkwater and Joshua Lesser (New York: New York University Press, 2009), 24–25.
7. Ladin, "Trans Experiences and the Torah," 44.
8. Ladin, "Trans Experiences and the Torah," 48.
9. Women of the Wall is a nonprofit organization advocating for women's right to pray at the Western Wall since 1988. See: https://www.womenofthewall.org.il/.
10. Noach Dzumra, "Introduction: The Literal and Metaphorical *Mechitza*," in: *Balancing on the Mechitza: Transgender in Jewish Community*, ed. Noach Dzmura (Berkeley, CA: North Atlantic Books, 2010), xiii.
11. Gender segregated spaces, and often "women-only" ones are bases for exclusion and discrimination of transpeople and trans women in particular. The most obvious example is the anti-trans laws denying access to public bathrooms, which have been at the heart of political struggle in U.S. history. See Max Strassfeld, "Transing Religious Studies," *Journal of Feminist Studies in Religion* 34, no. 1 (2018): 37–53.
12. This scene was filmed on the Paramount lot and Jimmy Frohna, the director of the episode, invited Rabbi Susan Goldberg, one of the show's rabbi consultants, to bless the set. See J. Joey Soloway, *She Wants It: Desire, Power and Toppling the Patriarchy* (New York, NY: Broadway Books, 2018), 196.
13. Trystan T. Cotton, "Introduction: Migration and Morphing," in *Transgender Migrations: The Bodies, Borders, and Politics of Transition*, Trystan T. Cotton (New York: Routledge, 2012), 1.
14. Aren Z. Aizura, *Mobile Subjects: Transnational Imaginaries of Gender Reassignment* (Durham, NC: Duke University Press, 2018), 17–18.
15. Aren Z. Aizura, "The Persistence of Transgender Travel Narrative," in *The Bodies, Borders, and Politics of Transition* (New York: Routledge 2012), 149.

16 Lior Zaltzman, "There's a Horrible Holocaust Song in the 'Transparent' Finale," *Kveller*, October 3, 2019, https://www.kveller.com/theres-a-horrible-holocaust-song-in-the-transparent-finale/.
17 Tithing is also linked to feminist activism by Ann Ferguson: "To constitute ourselves to prioritize world distributive justice, we must involve ourselves in personal and political practices that place us I imaginative community with those oppressed by economic want ... Also middle-class and wealthy feminists could agree to tithe a considerable percentage of their income for redistributive projects ... Such tithing symbolizes a moral attack on consumerist preoccupations and is part of the process of reconstituting oneself away from the status-que." See Ferguson, "Feminist Communities and Moral Revolutions," in *Feminism and Community*, eds. Penny A. Weiss and Marilyn Friedman (Philadelphia: Temple University Press, 1995), 389.
18 Caitlin "Casey" Judge, "Thrown Away for Being Gay: The Abandonment of LGBT Youth and Their Lack of Legal Recourse," *Indiana Journal of Law and Social Equality* 3, no. 2, art. 5 (2015): 260–280.
19 Adam P. Romero, Shoshana K. Goldberg, and Luis A. Vasquez, *LGBT People and Housing Affordability, Discrimination, and Homelessness*, Williams Institute, School of Law (Los Angeles: University of California Los Angeles, April 2020), 17.
20 The gender divide is a leading bone of contention between Orthodox and liberal Jews; Orthodoxy claims that "sex" is intended to help rule whether one is obligated to, or exempt from, a certain precept. Liberal Jews, on the other hand, argue that "gender" expression should not exclude anyone from practicing religion, nor should a physical transformation determine one's belonging to the community. Reliance on the gender binary is linked to the origin of Judaism: Abraham's covenant with God as marked on the bodies of Jews assigned male at birth, through circumcision. This physical transformation, if not surgical intervention, however, is also the origin of the weight placed on visible sexual organs in Jewish law.
21 Soloway, *She Wants It*, 223.
22 Soloway, *She Wants It*, 219.
23 Christi Carras, "'Transparent's' Trace Lysette on Accusing Jeffrey Tambor of Sexual Harassment: 'It Was Hell,'" *Variety*, August 7, 2018, https://variety.com/2018/tv/news/transparent-trace-lysette-jeffrey-tambor-sexual-harassment-1202898144/.
24 Soloway, *She Wants It*, 231
25 Soloway, *She Wants It*, 231.
26 Soloway, *She Wants It*, 238.
27 James Jacobson-Maisels, "Tikkun Olam, Tikkun Atzmi: Healing the Self, Healing the World," in *Tikkun Olam: Judaism, Humanism, and Transcendence*, eds. David Birnbaum, Martin S. Cohen, and Saul Berman (New York: New Paradigm Matrix Publishing, 2015), 353.
28 Jacobson-Maisels, "Tikkun Olam, Tikkun Atzmi," 354.
29 Jacobson-Maisels, "Tikkun Olam, Tikkun Atzmi," 380.
30 Perry Dane, "Hanging by A Thread": A D'var Torah on Parshat Lech Lecha," Social Science Research Network, last modified May 5, 2020, https://ssrn.com/abstract=3480737, p. 12.
31 Ronit Irshai, "The Construction of Gender in Halakhic Responsa by the Reform Movement: Transgender People as a Case Study," *Journal of Modern Jewish Studies* 18, no. 2 (2019): 163.
32 Irshai "The Construction of Gender," 170.

33 According to Idan Ben-Ephraim: "[In the case of] a woman who turned herself into a man, if this man comes into a synagogue to say *kaddish* over his deceased relatives, he is permitted to reply 'amen' however, this is true for *kaddish* said in prayers before '*alienu leshabeah*,' also known as the *Orphan's Kaddish* and said to elevate the soul of the deceased." See Idan Ben-Ephraim, *Generation of Perversions: Issues in Actual Surgeries in Halakha* [Halachos of Transsexual surgery and more] Dor Tahapukhot: Besugiyat Nituchim Actualiim BaHalakha (Hebrew) (Jerusalem, 2004), 164. (my translation hereafter).
34 Ben-Ephraim, *Generation of Perversions*, 164.
35 Ben-Ephraim, *Generation of Perversions*, 163.
36 Ben-Ephraim, *Generation of Perversions*, 164.
37 Ben-Ephraim, *Generation of Perversions*, 163.

Chapter 16

La-La-Lech-Lecha: *Transparent*'s Musical Finale

WARREN HOFFMAN

When Joey Soloway, the creator of the hit TV show *Transparent*, announced in mid-October 2018 that the show's final season would consist of a single extended-length musical episode, the news, for many fans, was a bit head-scratching. The Pfeffermans, the show's neurotic, self-obsessed Jewish family, would sing? Music had played a role throughout the series, but actual live musical numbers? It might have seemed far-fetched, but it would not be a unique phenomenon. A number of TV shows including *Buffy the Vampire Slayer*, *Scrubs*, and *Riverdale* also had one-off musical episodes as part of their runs.

Yet in watching the *Transparent* finale, having the characters sing not only felt right, it seemed sort of inevitable.[1] The Pfeffermans had long been trying to figure out who they were as individuals. Over the course of four seasons, they had expressed themselves through sexual deeds, gender exploration, and other performative acts, sometimes successfully, sometimes not. Now, through the genre of the musical, an art form defined by characters bursting into song, the Pfeffermans would be able to find their voices, literally, that they had been searching for. The entire show, after all, was predicated on the characters, predominantly Maura, the show's central figure, trying to come to terms with who they are and how to fully reveal themselves. If the show is about "coming out" in the broadest sense of the expression, not just as trans but as queer, as Jewish, as sexually obsessed, then the characters being able to sing their emotions becomes the fullest manifestation of their complicated and conflicted journeys.

The finale of *Transparent* picks up more or less where season 4 ended. The Pfeffermans had gone to Israel where youngest child, Ari, felt a new connection to their Jewish roots, son Josh worked through his issues around sexual addiction, and daughter Sarah rekindled things with her ex, Len. The family's transmatriarch Maura was looking to have gender-confirmation surgery, but the finale opens not with this plot development but with Maura's sudden death, leaving the entire Pfefferman clan to grieve and plan a funeral, which in this case involves the cremation of Maura's body, an unorthodox practice in Judaism.[2]

Over the course of the almost two-hour musical episode, the Pfefferman children process their grief, deal with the loss of their family home, and come to terms with their overbearing mother, Shelly Pfefferman, who has recently taken up acting and improv. This being a finale, there are of course many loose strings to tie up from previous seasons, and indeed, virtually every significant secondary character makes an appearance at the shiva for Maura where past issues and relationships can, like Maura herself, be put to rest.

But what about the singing? How does it fit into the larger arc of *Transparent*? Musical theater scholar Scott McMillin argues that "often a number seems to express a character's deep feeling, as though song and dance can reach into the area of subtext and transform the private motivations found there into performability.... If the subtext is to be explored by the realistic actor in the legitimate theater, it is to be changed into accessible song and dance formats in the musical. There is no subtext the musical cannot get to, and once gotten to, the hidden motive will be obvious to everyone, transformed into a different beat, into a melody that can be shared, into a lyric others can join."[3] The logic of most texts, whether they be novels, movies, or straight plays, is that although the words on the page or those said out loud may tell us a great deal about what the characters are feeling or thinking, such modes of performances often have limits as to what they reveal. This is because many texts, as McMillin notes, not only have subtexts percolating beneath their surfaces but because most human beings, for a variety of reasons, do not communicate everything they are feeling out loud.[4] Although this may be due to an individual not having the words to express themselves or simply because to nakedly communicate certain feelings would be difficult, scary, or traumatizing, people tend to speak via detour, hesitation, and incompletion. That is, except if the character is in a musical.

Musicals and related arts like opera function on a completely different level from most other art forms. Modern musicals are grounded in the notion that the book and songs are tightly interwoven, but the truth is that song operates on another level, one that is able to elevate and free the characters to express openly whatever they are feeling. This is why musicals are typically such exciting and beloved art forms as the songs transport both the audience and the characters to a state of pure emotion, whether that be unadulterated joy, heartbreaking loss, or something in between. From *Dreamgirls*'s "And I Am Telling You" to *Carousel*'s "Soliloquy," songs such as these free the character from what cannot be spoken and instead allow, or rather demand, that they sing to express their truth.

Singing enables *Transparent*'s characters to experience a new level of self-expression, one that permits them to further their journeys of self-exploration. In fact, the organizing theme of the show's finale is journeys, going so far as to invoke one of the greatest spiritual journeys of the Bible, that of Jewish patriarch Abraham. A major theme, musically and otherwise, that runs through the episode is the chanting of the verses of the Torah portion Lech Lecha. Ari Pfefferman, who now identifies as nonbinary, laments that they never got to have a bar/bat mitzvah, which would have featured Lech Lecha as their Torah portion. This section of the Torah, Genesis 12:1–3, focuses on God telling Abram, who has not yet become Abraham—another transition of sorts—to "Go for yourself from your land, from your relatives, and from your father's house to the land that I will show you. And I will make of you a great nation; I will bless you, and make your name great, and you shall be a blessing. I will bless those who bless you, and him who curses you I will curse; and all the families of the earth shall bless themselves by you." From this, Abram, Sarai, and Lot set off for the land of Canaan. Ari not only chants the Hebrew of Lech Lecha, but Faith Soloway, the composer of the musical finale (and Joey Soloway's sister), wrote a song for Ari called "Father's House," which sets the biblical text to music (see figure 16.1).

It is little wonder that the Soloways have chosen these lines for Ari, if not for all the Pffefermans, so pregnant are they with the meaning of self-discovery and

FIGURE 16.1 Ari Pfefferman (Gaby Hoffmann) sings "Father's House," which uses the Torah portion Lech Lecha as a metaphor for the journey of gender exploration. *Transparent.* "Transparent Musicale Finale," Season 5:1. Written by Louisa Hill, Eleanor Jean, and Chloe Keenan, directed by Joey Soloway, September 27, 2019.

exploration. Going from their "father's house" has layered meanings in *Transparent*. For Maura, it was the house of patriarchy. Her *zayde* (grandfather), who we meet in flashbacks in season 3, episode 8, with the musical title, "If I Were a Bell" from *Guys and Dolls*, tries to keep Maura trapped in the framework of masculinity, threatening to kick Maura out of the house if she does not conform to a more traditional gender identity. For Maura, leaving her father's house is the story of coming out as trans, and in doing so, finding the blessings of peace and wholeness that she has been seeking from an early age. For the Pfefferman children, going from their father's house (or in this case, Moppa's house) means finally growing up and seeing themselves as adults with the agency to take control of their own lives. Sarah, Josh, and Ari are literally leaving their home in this episode as they learn that Maura bequeathed the house to her good friend Davina and not to them; the family cannot go again home, even if they want to.

But the Hebrew construction of Lech Lecha can have another meaning: *Lech* means "go," which would have been sufficient enough of a command if God simply wanted Abram to leave his homeland and make a new nation, but what does *lecha* signify? Although translated as "go for yourself," it can also be translated as "go into yourself" or "go to yourself," turning this phrase not just into a physical command of movement but a commandment of introspection to see who you are and who you will become. For Abraham, his journey was not just one of movement but one of ontological change as he became the first Jew.[5] This indeed is what Maura and all of the Pfeffermans have been trying to do throughout *Transparent*'s seasons: look deeply within themselves and figure out who they are.

The Lech Lecha journey does not end there. God tells Abraham that by "going forth" from your land and your father's house, "I will make of you a great nation." The nation in *Transparent*, though, is not only the Jewish people; rather, it is the formation of a new queer, transpositive space in which the manifestation of multiple genders and sexualities is not only accepted, it is the new norm. *Transparent*, the show, as it narrated Maura's journey through multiple seasons, had itself been moving to this moment in which a new trans "nation" is formed. The episode opens with Maura's death, but it concludes with a firm eye toward the future, a future that is multiracial and trans.[6]

We witness this new future in two moments in the episode. During Maura's funeral, a bumbling rabbi keeps making errors as he eulogizes Maura's life. Davina steps in to save the day and interrupts him with a song that she and the trans youth of the community have prepared: "Let Her Be Okay." Although not suggesting that Judaism is without purpose in this moment, the shift to Davina and multi-racial trans youth offers up the possibility of a rich future for another community that will become "great" and "blessed," precisely because of how individuals like Maura and Davina left their own houses to forge paths forward for the trans community. This promise of a new fruitful nation is visually sealed at the end of this episode in a quick cutaway. The Pfefferman house, now owned by Davina, has been transformed once again. It is no longer the father's house, the house of patriarchy, but a house where Judaism, queerness, and trans identity not only coexist but flourish, as Ari leads the household through the ritual of blessing the Shabbat candles. Like the Jews, a new people has been formed.

Ari's connection to Lech Lecha, to a journey of self-exploration, and to their own bar/bat mitzvah completes a narrative that began not even with the first episode but in the show's iconic opening credits. Created by Zackary Drucker and Rhys Ernst, the grainy videotape footage that opens each episode intercuts two worlds: scenes from old VHS footage of bar mitzvahs and clips from the 1968 documentary *The Queen* about the 1967 New York Miss All-America Camp Beauty Pageant. This interwoven footage, all of which features dancing, sparkle, and performance, is about what it means to be a man, both in the Jewish sense of one's bar mitzvah ("Today I am a man"), but also in the gendered queer sense, calling into question not just what it means to perform as a man but what it means to perform any gender identity, for that matter.[7] What makes one a "man"? Is it biology, social conditioning, clothing, or religious ceremony? The fact that it can be rooted in all of these things and in none of them reveals just how fluid and arbitrary definitions of gender can be. The bar mitzvah ceremony is a performative rite of passage that "magically" turns a Jewish boy into a Jewish man. Taking advantage of the fact that the entire Pfefferman clan and family just happen to all be in the same place at the same time, Josh, with the help of Rabbi Raquel, enables Ari to finally have a "bart mitzvah," incongruously perhaps, at Maura's shiva. Forget that the timing is off and that it is a Sunday when the Torah is not read; the Pfeffermans have never really played by the books when practicing their Judaism.[8] In both chanting the Hebrew, but also by singing "Father's House," Ari performs their own sense of gender *and* Judaism. And it is by singing and performing that Ari (like the bar mitzvah boys and drag queens of the opening credits) can claim an identity for themselves.

Much of the finale's music by Faith Soloway leans toward the maudlin and toward introspection, but the episode is not without moments of levity. Howard, the Pfefferman's lawyer, and Davina sing a sprightly number called "Goddamn House," while Rabbi Raquel, backed up by campers at her Jewish girls retreat, sings the sexy and comical "Sit in It" about how the Pfeffermans have to come to terms with their grief. What these numbers remind us of is that the musical, in its seemingly nonsensical burst-into-song moments, is often viewed as a gay form of expression. Gay men are stereotypically associated with musical theater, and there is often something camp (and campy) and queer about musicals themselves in their flamboyancy—they are not subtle—and their excess of emotion that syncs with the lives of the Pfeffermans, characters who, too, are anything but diminutive or shy.[9] The musical, in its larger-than-life sensibility, offers audiences a different way of seeing the world. If the world is conceived of as a place with boundaries of how people should act and behave as well as perform gender and sexuality, then the musical throws all that out the window with modes of performance that are nonrealistic, often utopic, and imaginative. Where the real world traps individuals, the musical frees them.[10]

This desire for freedom is perhaps most craved by Shelly Pfefferman, the family's self-absorbed, but also mistreated and misunderstood, mother who harbors the secret of her own sexual abuse as a child. Forced by society into the role of the dutiful Jewish woman who should marry and have children, Shelly's world is thrown for a loop when her ex-husband, now Maura, comes out as trans.[11] While trying to be sympathetic to Maura's needs and new life, Maura's coming out causes Shelly to question her own life. Was her entire relationship with Maura a sham? Shelly's desire to take hold of her own life begins not in season 5, but via another live musical performance in the season 3 finale when she sings Alanis Morissette's "Hand in My Pocket" while on a cruise with her family. Continuing to draw on live performance as a way to express her inner unresolved trauma, in the musical finale, Shelly has written a play about her family that she is rehearsing with a bunch of doppelganger actors at her local synagogue. When her children show up to the rehearsal space to confront Shelly about her desire to move Maura's funeral service to accommodate her rehearsal schedule, the situation blows up. Shelly proclaims, "I have so much inside of me" and then launches into her big number called, "Your Boundary is My Trigger." Shelly's words evoke the lyrics of perhaps the most famous musical mother of all time, Mama Rose from *Gypsy*, who in her iconic eleven o'clock number "Rose's Turn," says "What I got in me—what I been holding down inside of me—if I ever let it out, there wouldn't be signs big enough!"[12] Shelly, of all the Pfeffermans, has sadly been the most repressed, and so when her issues all come bursting out of her, the result is a number that is perhaps the most Broadway and elaborate in nature of the entire episode, complete with set, costumes, lights, and choreography. (See figure 16.2)

Transparent most broadly utilizes the musical genre as an antidote to real life in its treatment of death, and more specifically, in its evocation of the Holocaust. The show, up until this point, has interwoven the lives of the Pfefferman family with key moments from Jewish history and culture. Season 2 features a number of flashbacks in which we see how Maura's aunt Gittel (born Gershon) was involved in the queer Weimar Germany salons of Magnus Hirschfeld, while season 4, episode 6 has the Pfeffermans heading to Israel where they grapple with both Jewish American ties to Israel as well as the Israeli-Palestinian conflict, which features the family singing "What's the Buzz?" from the musical *Jesus Christ Superstar*. Even though the show explains how Maura's mother and grandmother came to America and escaped the Holocaust, it has never really been a Holocaust-centric series. In the final episode, though, discussion of the Holocaust enters the picture when Sarah's children become confused and think that Maura's body being cremated has something to do with gas chambers and crematoriums. It is a darkly humorous moment to be sure, and one that makes its reappearance at the episode's conclusion when Shelly says that

FIGURE 16.2 Shelly Pfefferman (Judith Light) finally claims the spotlight in her *Gypsy*-esque "Rose's Turn"-inspired moment in "Your Boundary is My Trigger." *Transparent*. "Transparent Musicale Finale," Season 5:1. Written by Louisa Hill, Eleanor Jean, and Chloe Keenan, directed by Joey Soloway, September 27, 2019.

Jews need some sort of antidote to the Holocaust. In what may be one of the most questionable musical numbers ever written, the entire cast sings a number called "Joyocaust," in which Shelly and Ava, an actor from Shelly's play, sing, "We need a Joyocaust/ for all the lives we've lost/ This pain in all of us/ Remains at quite a cost./ Six million/ ain't no joke./ We win for losing folk./ Need a celebration of the soul/ For this extermination Super Bowl." As Jenny Singer describes it, the number is "intentionally grotesque" and both "pretty brilliant, but embarrassing."[13] The musical as the supreme over-the-top form of expression, becomes by the show's logic, the best format to combat death, even a scenario as large as the Holocaust itself. It is a gutsy move by the Soloways to be sure, but one on which many a musical has stood.[14]

Maura's life may have ended in *Transparent*, but in some ways her death was irrelevant; like Abraham in Lech Lecha, her friends and family were already on their own journeys of discovery and exploration that would continue irrespective of Maura. The Pfeffermans will surely have more growing and soul-searching in front of them, but the world of the musical has given them a new language through which to chart their own journeys, both physical and spiritual. This may be where we leave the Pfeffermans, but Soloway lets the characters go out with a big finish that is worthy of their crazy and messy lives.[15]

Notes

1 Although I think a case can more than be made for a musical episode of *Transparent*, it should be noted that many critics and fans found this final episode to be disappointing and even outright bad. For some "pans" of the finale, see Ben Travers, "'Transparent' Review: Amazon's Musical Finale Strikes the Wrong Chord, Too

Many Times," *IndieWire*, September 28, 2019, https://www.indiewire.com/2019/09/transparent-finale-review-musical-ending-amazon-1202177103/; Judy Berman, "*Transparent*'s Excruciating Musical Finale Hits One False Note after the Next," *Time*, September 25, 2019, https://time.com/5682200/transparent-musicale-finale-review/; Naomi Gordon-Loebl, "Not Kidding: Transparent's Bizarre Musical Finale," *The Nation*, September 27, 2019, https://www.thenation.com/article/transparent-musicale-finale-review/; Rich Juzwiak, "The *Transparent Musicale Finale* is a Transgenre Letdown," *Jezebel*, September 20, 2019, https://themuse.jezebel.com/the-transparent-musicale-finale-is-a-transgenre-letdown-1838257856.

2 The sudden death of Maura and the absence of Jeffrey Tambor who played Maura from the finale, was, as many fans of the show know, connected to allegations of sexual misconduct by Tambor toward several cast members. Soloway felt it would be inappropriate for Tambor to return to the show under these circumstances leading to this plot development.

3 Scott McMillin, *The Musical as Drama* (Princeton, NJ: Princeton University Press, 2006), 76.

4 Of course, soliloquies, although not used much in TV, also involve direct address to the audience.

5 In what is not too far of a stretch, I believe, Abraham also goes through a bodily transformation of sorts, also related to gender and tied to his becoming a Jew. In Genesis 17:23, he circumcises himself, his son Ishmael, and other men, thereby entering into a physical covenant with God.

6 One might argue that this moment mirrors an important moment in the bible: the death of Moses (Deuteronomy 34:1–8). After having led the Israelites through the desert, Moses never actually gets to enter the promised land and actually see the fruit of all his labors.

7 For more on this, see Stephen Vider, "Why is an Obscure 1968 Documentary in the Opening Credits of *Transparent*?", *Slate*, October 24, 2014, https://slate.com/human-interest/2014/10/transparents-opening-credits-are-a-lesson-in-the-history-of-gender.html.

8 *Transparent* has been full of Jewish ritual and holiday moments, all performed with a variety of less-than-traditional accuracy. Other episodes show the Pfeffermans celebrating Yom Kippur (season 2, episode 7) and Shabbat (season 3, episode 5).

9 The question of whether musicals are "camp" or "campy," which are different concepts, can be difficult to parse at times. Of all of Susan Sontag's "notes on camp," the point that most defines "camp" for me is note number 23, "In naïve, or pure, Camp, the essential element is seriousness, a seriousness that fails." In other words, a piece of art that does not mean to be funny but ends up so anyway can often be considered "camp." On the other hand, art that knowingly winks at the audience and embraces its silly, over-the-top aesthetics would be deemed "campy." The *Transparent* musical finale falls into both categories. Numbers like Rabbi Raquel's "Sit in It" seem to be campy, but Shelly's "Your Boundary is My Trigger" registers more like camp. For more, see Warren Hoffman, "The 2019 Met Gala is Wacky, Gorgeous, and Fun ... But It Isn't Camp," May 7, 2019, *Medium*, https://medium.com/@whoffman18/the-2019-met-gala-is-wacky-gorgeous-and-fun-but-it-isnt-camp-205ea1233afa.

10 Other movie musicals that use the musical form itself on a metalevel to represent a break with reality include *Chicago* (2002) and the Chilean film *A Fantastic Woman* (2017), which also features a transwoman at the center of the story.

11 This is not entirely new territory for queer Jewish stories. William Finn and James Lapine's 1992 musical *Falsettos* opens with Marvin telling his wife Trina that he is

leaving her and their son Jason to move in with his gay lover Whizzer. In act two, Trina sings the ballad "Holding to the Ground" where she sings, "I was sure growing up I would live the life/ My mother assumed I'd live. / Very Jewish/ Very middle class/ And very straight/ Where healthy men/ Stayed healthy men/ And marriages were long and great." William Finn and James Lapine, *Falsettos* (New York: Samuel French, 1995), 130–131.

12 Arthur Laurents, *Gypsy* (New York: Theatre Communications Group, 1959), 104.

13 Jenny Singer, "The 'Transparent' Musical Finale: Terminally Jewish and Endearingly Hard to Watch," *Forward*, October 3, 2019, https://forward.com/schmooze/432636/the-transparent-musical-finale-is-obscenely-jewish-and-endearingly-hard-to/.

14 Consider, for example, the ending of the watershed musical *Oklahoma!* (1943), which changed musical theater forever. The show's villain, Jud Fry, dies at the end of the musical, but that does not stop the cast from singing the joyous title number at the conclusion to send the audience out on a high note.

15 As this book was being edited, a live stage musical based on the TV series, simply titled *A Transparent Musical* and written by the show's creators, premiered at the Mark Taper Forum in Los Angeles from May 20 to June 25, 2023.

Conclusion

BRETT KRUTZSCH

In May 2023, *Transparent* transitioned again. What first started as a streaming television series that turned into a movie for its finale transformed once more and became a musical stage production. Premiering in Los Angeles, the epicenter of the fictional Pfefferman clan, *A Transparent Musical* allowed *Transparent* to return to popular culture in a new form and with an opportunity to correct the issues that had haunted the show since its genesis.[1]

Transparent was always a show of paradoxes to those paying attention to its reception. Beloved by television critics, industry executives, awards committees, and, as this volume attests, Jewish studies scholars, the series was also a source of disappointment to many transgender Americans. That frustration began with the casting of cisgender actor Jeffrey Tambor as the show's lead transgender character. Tambor as a trans woman was, in Christian parlance that *Transparent*'s character Colton might use, the show's original sin. For many transgender Americans, that casting choice alone, not to mention storylines about primarily privileged, upper-middle-class white people, rendered the show out of touch with contemporary transgender politics. *Transparent* may have been the first streaming series ever to win a Golden Globe for Best Television Series, but transgender viewers concurrently shunned the show.

A Transparent Musical endeavored to redeem *Transparent*'s original sin and featured a transgender actress as Maura Pfefferman. Several other original cast members in the musical also identified as trans or nonbinary. And all three of the musical's creators, including the original series creator, Joey Soloway, identified as nonbinary or trans.[2] If actual transgender people were sidelined at the series' start, trans people were central to the show's reinvention as a musical stage production.

Reinvention, as several contributors to this book note, is a central theme in *Transparent*. Nothing, the show demonstrates time and again, is inherently permanent—not gender, not sexuality, not religious traditions. Everything can change, and everything can become queerer. In *Transparent*'s world, queerer is better. And so, a television show can become a movie musical, and that movie musical can become a theatrical production. With characters bursting into song and choreographed dance numbers, *Transparent* became even queerer, and for transgender audiences, possibly better.

In the transformation from screen to stage, what did not change was *Transparent*'s focus on Jews. The musical retains the series' emphasis on Jewish identity. As this volume has demonstrated, *Transparent* was a landmark show not only for its depiction of a trans woman in a main role but for its constant attention to Jewish culture, rituals, and history. In a media industry that Jews have dominated for decades, *Transparent* managed to become the "Jewiest show ever" and introduced viewers to an Ashkenazi family that does not want to assimilate, that sneers at the dominant Christian culture, and that queers Jewish traditions.[3]

In the years since *Transparent*'s 2014 debut, several new shows have made trans, Jewish, and queer identities central to their storytelling. Transgender characters, and trans and nonbinary actors, are prominently featured on such shows as *Euphoria*, *Pose*, *The Politician*, and *Heartstopper*. And since *Transparent*'s award-winning first season, queer Jewish characters have appeared on *Schitt's Creek*, *Difficult People*, *Andi Mack*, *Better Things*, and other programs. *Transparent* opened a door for more trans, queer, and Jewish visibility, and several shows have followed in its path.

Although *Transparent* ushered in a new era of transgender, queer, and Jewish storylines on television, what are we to make of the fact that since *Transparent*'s premiere, the situation for transgender, queer, and Jewish Americans has become more precarious, possibly even much worse? In the years since the show's debut, we have witnessed a horrific rise in anti-trans violence—especially against transgender women of color, a dramatic upsurge in antisemitism, a U.S. president who defended white supremacists who chanted, "Jews will not replace us," mass shootings in synagogues in Pennsylvania and Texas, and a barrage of anti-trans legislation across the country. Although no television show prior to 2014 featured a transgender character in a lead role, transgender adolescents in Arkansas, Oklahoma, and Utah could still access gender-affirming care if they had supportive parents, which by the debut of *A Transgender Musical* in 2023, they could no longer do.

Since *Transparent*'s premiere, Christian nationalist politicians have specifically targeted transgender, queer, and Jewish Americans and, in many instances, they have tried to erase their presence. School districts across the country have banned books with Jewish and queer themes, like *Maus*, the graphic novel about the Holocaust, and *The Purim Superhero*, a children's book about a Jewish kid with two gay dads.[4] In several places, schools have been forbidden from supporting trans and nonbinary students, drag queens have been prohibited from reading to children, and educators have been barred from teaching about gender and sexual diversity and often from teaching about America's history of racial violence. Such suppression and the targeting of queers and Jews in particular—as season 2 of *Transparent* reminds us—resembles the rise of 1930s European fascism and the decline of democracy.

Greater media visibility of transgender, Jewish, and queer people through *Transparent* and the many shows that followed it did not, we can now say with nearly a decade of reflection, lead to ever-expanding equality and more safety throughout the country. Although some political gains did happen, most notably the Supreme Court's decision in 2015 to allow same-gender couples to marry, anti-LGBTQ legislation has increased dramatically, with the bulk of it directed at transgender and nonbinary Americans. As a queer, Jewish philosopher of gender, Judith Butler says about the rise of anti-trans violence and legislation following *Transparent*'s much-lauded first two seasons, "It is always possible to be an object of public fascination or a visual icon of trans life that cisgendered people want to consume visually at the same time that the legal and economic situation for trans people remains bad, or worsens."[5] As transgender people have become a more common feature in American media, so has a hostile backlash within American politics that paints transgender people as dangerous to the country's children, as mentally ill, or both.

But here, too, *Transparent* holds a lesson. As this volume has made clear, one of *Transparent*'s strengths is its ability to portray the past and present *together*. Scenes of trans people in 1930s Berlin alongside twenty-first-century Los Angeles remind us that progress does not inherently come with the march of time and that trans people, queers, and Jews have long posed threats to those who want a conservative Christian order. The show insists on weaving together histories of what the Nazis destroyed with the present day. And now, to watch *Transparent* as the teaching of history itself is under attack is to be reminded why trans, queer, and Jewish visibility matters greatly, even if it generates a backlash.

In response to the horrifying abundance of anti-trans legislation, anti-queer violence, and antisemitism, *Transparent* seems as important as ever. As Rabbi Raquel, the ethical center of the show, offers in the third season premiere while reflecting on the Passover story alongside the present day by saying to herself and to us, the audience: "You're waiting for a miracle. You're waiting for the sea to part. Well, that's an old miracle. So what about this? What if the miracle was you? What if you had to be your own Messiah? Then what?"[6]

Transparent offers an answer. The show suggests that the path to repairing the world is through queering it. Rigid boxes, unchangeable identities, and strict traditions are the ways of the fascists. Liberation comes not through assimilation but through upending our gender, sexual, and religious norms. Everything can change. A television series can become a movie. A boy can become a woman. A woman can become a rabbi who prays to Mother Goddess. *Transparent* shines a queer Jewish gaze on the Christian-dominated world and finds it wanting then rejects it and imagines a queer alternative where, at the end of the movie finale, we see trans and queer adolescents of multiple races, religions, and ethnicities lighting Shabbat candles, and in so doing—we can imagine, we can hope—they are welcoming in a time of queer peace.

Notes

1. *A Transparent Musical* began its first run on May 20, 2023, at the Center Theatre Group in Los Angeles and officially opened on May 31, 2023. For more on the production, see Logan Culwell-Block, "Daya Curley, Peppermint, Sarah Stiles, More to Star in *A Transparent Musical* at Center Theatre Group," *Playbill*, April 12, 2023, https://playbill.com/article/daya-curley-peppermint-sarah-stiles-more-to-star-in-a-transparent-musical-at-center-theatre-group.
2. MJ Kaufman and series creator Joey Soloway wrote the book for *A Transparent Musical* and Soloway's sibling, Faith Soloway, who wrote the music for the movie finale, wrote the production's musical lyrics.
3. Debra Nussbaum Cohen, "How Jill Soloway Created 'Transparent'—The Jewiest Show Ever," *Forward*, October 21, 2014, https://forward.com/culture/207407/how-jill-soloway-created-transparent-the-jewiest/.
4. See Philissa Cramer, "Florida School District Removes 'Purim Superhero,' a Book about a Jewish Kid with 2 Dads," *Jewish Telegraphic Agency*, April 21, 2022.
5. Judith Butler in Diane Tourjee, "Why Do Men Kill Trans Women? Gender Theorist Judith Butler Explains," *Vice*, December 16, 2015, https://www.vice.com/en/article/z4jd7y/why-do-men-kill-trans-women-gender-theorist-judith-butler-explains.
6. *Transparent*, Season 3, episode 1, "Elizah," Amazon Prime Video, September 23, 2016.

Acknowledgments

This book is an indirect outgrowth of the "*Transparent*: A Multi-Disciplinary Symposium" held at the University of Rochester in December 2016. Dreamed up by three Jewish academics in a Chinese restaurant, hosted by the Susan B. Anthony Institute for Gender, Sexuality, and Women's Studies, and sponsored by the Department of Religion and Classics, the Center for Jewish Studies, and the Humanities Project, the symposium brought together an international group of scholars to delve into what was then a relatively new series. A good number of those in attendance are represented in this volume, along with fellow travelers who later joined us along the way. A great deal of thanks goes out to all involved with the symposium, especially Jane Bryant, Joshua Dubler, Rachel Haidu, Jason Peck, and Caleb Rood. Joan Saab was particularly instrumental in the program's organization and the early work on this volume. A special acknowledgment goes out to *Transparent*'s creator, Joey Soloway, for their help in connecting us to members of the *Transparent* team, resulting in consultants Zachary Drucker and Rabbi Susan Goldberg and actor Alexandra Grey joining us in Rochester—a true gift.

This volume moved well beyond the symposium, however, and we want to thank our matchmaker, Rebecca Alpert, for introducing the two of us and suggesting we work on this book together. This volume took several years to come to fruition, and we wish to thank all the contributors for their insights, commitment to the project, and patience. Beyond those providing content, Rio Hartwell provided a keen editorial eye, Elisabeth Maselli and Christopher Rios-Sueverkruebbe championed the project at Rutgers University Press from the beginning, and Carah Naseem ushered it through the final process—for this work, we are grateful. Also worthy of thanking are the anonymous reviewers whose careful readings made the volume even stronger. *Blessings beyond the Binary* received subvention funding from the University of Rochester's

Susan B. Anthony Institute for Gender, Sexuality, and Women's Studies, the Office of the Dean, and the Center for Jewish Studies.

And finally, we would like to thank our families. Our husbands, Rob Nipe and Kevin Williams, patiently listened to countless conversations about *Transparent* (whether they were interested or not) and Zoe and Ashe Nipe—members of this first generation to live proudly beyond the binary—cheered the book along. We are so lucky to have these queer and Jewish families.

Selected Bibliography

Abrams, Nathan. *The New Jew in Film: Exploring Jewishness and Judaism in Contemporary Cinema.* New Brunswick, NJ: Rutgers University Press, 2012.
Antler, Joyce. *You Never Call! You Never Write! A History of the Jewish Mother.* New York: Oxford University Press, 2007.
Antler, Joyce, ed. *Talking Back: Images of Jewish Women in American Popular Culture.* Hanover, NH: Brandeis University Press, 1998.
Beachy, Robert. *Gay Berlin: Birthplace of a Modern Identity.* New York: Vintage, 2015.
Bial, Henry. *Acting Jewish: Negotiating Ethnicity on the American Stage and Screen.* Ann Arbor: University of Michigan Press, 2005.
Boyarin, Daniel, Daniel Itzkovitz, and Ann Pellegrini. *Queer Theory and the Jewish Question.* New York: Columbia University Press, 2003.
Brook, Vincent. *Something Ain't Kosher Here: The Rise of the "Jewish" Sitcom.* New Brunswick, NJ: Rutgers University Press, 2003.
Buhle, Paul. *From the Lower East Side to Hollywood: Jews in American Popular Culture.* New York: Verso, 2004.
Crasnow, S. J. "On Transition: Normative Judaism and Trans Innovation." *Journal of Contemporary Religion* 32, no. 3 (September 2017): 403–415.
Crenshaw, Kimberlé Williams. "Mapping the Margins: Intersectionality, Identity Politics, and Violence Against Women of Color." In *The Public Nature of Private Violence*, edited by Martha Albertson Fineman and Rixanne Mykitiuk, 93–118. New York: Routledge, 1994.
Dose, Ralf. *Magnus Hirschfeld: The Origins of the Gay Liberation Movement.* Translated by Edward H. Willis. New York: Monthly Review Press, 2014.
Dzmura, Noach, ed. *Balancing on the Mechitza: Transgender in Jewish Community.* Berkeley, CA.: North Atlantic Books, 2010.
Erdman, Harley. *Staging the Jew: The Performance of an American Ethnicity, 1860–1920.* New Brunswick, NJ: Rutgers University Press, 1997.
Freedman, Jonathan. "'Transparent': A Guide for The Perplexed." *LA Review of Books*, April 10, 2016. https://lareviewofbooks.org/article/transparent-a-guide-for-the-perplexed/.
Freeman, Elizabeth. *Time Binds: Queer Temporalities, Queer Histories.* Durham, NC: Duke University Press, 2010.

Gilman, Sander. *Jewish Self-Hatred: Anti-Semitism and the Hidden Language of the Jews*. Baltimore: Johns Hopkins University Press, 1986.

———. *The Jew's Body*. New York: Routledge, 1991.

Hess, Linda M. "My Whole Life I've Been Dressing up like a Man: Negotiations of Queer Aging and Queer Temporality in the TV Series Transparent." *European Journal of American Studies* 11, no. 3 (2017).

Hoberman, J., and Jeffrey Shandler, eds. *Entertaining America: Jews, Movies and Broadcasting*. Princeton, NJ: Princeton University Press, 2003.

Ladin, Joy. "In the Image of God, God Created Them: Toward Trans Theology." *Journal of Feminist Studies in Religion* 34, no. 1 (2018): 53–58.

———. *Through the Door of Life: A Jewish Journey Between Genders*. Madison: University of Wisconsin Press, 2013.

Moss, Joshua Louis. "The Woman Thing and the Jew Thing: Transsexuality, Transcomedy, and the Legacy of Subversive Jewishness in Transparent." *From Shtetl to Stardom: Jews and Hollywood*. Lafayette, IN: Purdue University Press, 2017.

Nadell, Pamela S. *Women Who Would be Rabbis: A History of Women's Ordination, 1889–1985*. Boston: Beacon Press, 1998.

Parsemain, Ava. *The Pedagogy of Queer TV*. Cham, Switzerland: Palgrave Macmillan, 2019.

Pearl, Jonathan, and Judith Pearl, *The Chosen Image: Television's Portrayal of Jewish Themes and Characters*. Jefferson, NC: McFarland, 1999.

Shandler, Jeffrey. *Jews, God, and Videotape: Religion and Media in America*. New York: New York University Press, 2009.

Showalter, Elaine. *Sexual Anarchy: Gender and Culture at the Fin de Siecle*. New York: Bloomsbury, 1991.

Soloway, Joey. *She Wants It: Desire, Power, and Toppling the Patriarchy*. New York: Random House, 2019.

Stanley, Eric A., Johanna Burton, and Tourmaline Gossett, eds., *Trap Door: Trans Cultural Production and the Politics of Visibility*. Cambridge, MA: MIT Press, 2017.

Strassfeld, Max. "Transing Religious Studies." *Journal of Feminist Studies in Religion* 34, no. 1 (2018): 37–53.

Sumerau, J. E., Lain A. B. Mathers, and Ryan T. Cragun, "Incorporating Transgender Experience Toward a More Inclusive Gender Lens in the Sociology of Religion." *Sociology of Religion* 79, no. 4 (2018): 425–448.

Villarejo, Amy. *Ethereal Queer: Television, Historicity, and Desire*. Durham, NC: Duke University Press, 2014.

———. "Jewish, Queer-ish, Trans, and Completely Revolutionary: Jill Soloway's Transparent and the New Television." *Film Quarterly* 69, no. 4 (2016): 10–22.

Weber, Donald. *Haunted in the New World: Jewish American Culture from Cahan to the Goldbergs*. Bloomington: Indiana University Press, 2005.

Westbrook, Laurel, and Kristen Schilt, "Doing Gender, Determining Gender: Transgender People, Gender Panics, and the Maintenance of the Sex/Gender/Sexuality System." *Gender & Society* 28, no. 1 (2014): 32–57.

Zimman, Lal, Jenny L. Davis, and Joshua Raclaw. *Queer Excursions: Retheorizing Binaries in Language, Gender, and Sexuality*. Studies in Language and Gender. New York: Oxford University Press, 2014.

Notes on Contributors

SARAH BUNIN BENOR is a professor of contemporary Jewish studies at Hebrew Union College—Jewish Institute of Religion (Los Angeles), adjunct professor in the University of Southern California linguistics department, and director of the HUC-JIR Jewish Language Project. Her books include *Becoming Frum: How Newcomers Learn the Language and Culture of Orthodox Judaism* and *Hebrew Infusion: Language and Community at American Jewish Summer Camps*.

JODI EICHLER-LEVINE is a professor of religion studies and serves as the Berman professor of Jewish civilization at Lehigh University. She is the author of *Painted Pomegranates and Needlepoint Rabbis: How Jews Craft Resilience and Create Community* and *Suffer the Little Children: Uses of the Past in Jewish and African American Children's Literature*.

JOSHUA FALEK is a PhD candidate at York University in gender, feminist, and women's studies. Their work has been published in *Rhizomes, New Centennial Review, Canadian Journal of Disability Studies,* and *Cultural Studies*.

JENNIFER GLASER is an associate professor of English at the University of Cincinnati. She is the author of *Borrowed Voices: Writing and Racial Ventriloquism in the Jewish American Imagination*.

SLAVA GREENBERG is an assistant professor of film in the Department of Media Studies and Amsterdam School for Cultural Analysis at the University of Amsterdam. He is the author of *Animated Film and Disability: Cripping Spectatorship*.

WARREN HOFFMAN is the executive director of the Association for Jewish Studies. He is the author of the books *The Passing Game: Queering Jewish American Culture* and *The Great White Way: Race and the Broadway Musical*.

BRETT KRUTZSCH is the assistant director of the New York University Center for Religion and Media and editor of its award-winning magazine, *The Revealer*. He is the author of the book *Dying to Be Normal: Gay Martyrs and the Transformation of American Sexual Politics*.

JOSH LAMBERT is the Sophia Moses Robison associate professor of Jewish studies and English at Wellesley College. He is the author of *The Literary Mafia: Jews, Publishing, and Postwar American Literature* and *Unclean Lips: Obscenity, Jews, and American Culture*, which won a Jordan Schnitzer Book Award from the Association for Jewish Studies.

KATHRYN LOFTON is the Lex Hixon professor of religious studies, American studies, history, and divinity at Yale University. She is the author of *Oprah: The Gospel of an Icon* and *Consuming Religion*.

SHAUL MAGID is a distinguished fellow in Jewish studies at Dartmouth College and a senior fellow at the Center for World Religions at Harvard. He is the author of nine books, including *American Post-Judaism: Identity and Renewal in a Post-ethnic Society*, *Hasidism Incarnate: Hasidism, Christianity, and the Construction of Modern Judaism*, and *Meir Kahane: The Public Life and Political Thought of an American Jewish Radical*.

RANEN OMER-SHERMAN is the JHFE endowed chair in Judaic studies at the University of Louisville. He is the author or editor of five books, including *Imagining Kibbutz: Visions of Utopia in Literature and Film* and *Amos Oz: The Legacy of a Writer in Israel and Beyond*.

SHARI RABIN is an associate professor of Jewish studies and religion at Oberlin College. Her first book, *Jews on the Frontier: Religion and Mobility in Nineteenth-Century America* was the winner of a National Jewish Book Award.

MARILYN REIZBAUM is the Harrison King McCann professor of English at Bowdoin College. She is the author of *Unfit: Jewish Degeneration and Modernism*, *James Joyce's Judaic Other*, and coeditor with Kimberly J. Devlin of *Ulysses, En-gendered Perspectives: Eighteen New Essays on the Episodes*.

NORA RUBEL is the Jane and Alan Batkin professor in Jewish studies and chair of the Department of Religion and Classics at the University of Rochester. She is the author of *Doubting the Devout: The Ultra-Orthodox in the Jewish American Imagination* and coeditor of *Religion, Food and Eating in North America*.

MARTIN SHUSTER is the Isaac Swift distinguished professor of Jewish studies and professor of philosophy at the University of North Carolina at Charlotte. He is the author of *How to Measure a World? A Philosophy of Judaism*, *New Television: The Aesthetics and Politics of a Genre*, and *Autonomy after Auschwitz: Adorno, German Idealism, and Modernity*.

KERSTIN STEITZ is an associate professor of German and the German program director in the Department of World Languages and Cultures and affiliated faculty in the Jewish Studies Program at Old Dominion University. She is the author of *Dichterische Holocaust-Wahrheit und -Gerechtigkeit: Fritz Bauer und die literarische und filmische Bearbeitung des Frankfurter Auschwitz-Prozesses (1963–1965)*.

JARROD TANNY is an associate professor of history and the Charles and Hannah Block distinguished scholar in Jewish history at the University of North Carolina at Wilmington. He is the author of *City of Rogues and Schnorrers* and *The Seinfeld Talmud*.

Index

Abraham (biblical figure): Ari's interpretation of, 86; as biblical patriarch, 165, 247–253, 264–265, 268, 269n5; divine imperative, 60, 110, 167; as exile, 27, 57; nomadism of, 53–54
Abrahamic covenant, 248, 250–251, 259
Abrahamic narrative, 247–253
Abrams, Nathan, 37
Academy Awards, 5
Ahmed, Sara, 234
Aizura, Aren, 252
Al Chet, 44, 99, 203, 206
Allen, Woody, 114–115, 131
All in the Family (TV series), 138–139
"And I Am Telling You" (song), 264
Andi Mack (TV series), 272
And Just Like That . . . (TV series), 12
androgynes, 161
anti-LGBTQ legislation, 273
anti-queer violence, 273
antisemitic discourse, 118, 216, 218–219
antisemitism: Levinas on, 73–74; 99, 149, 218–219; upsurge in, 272–273
anti-trans legislation, 273
anti-trans violence, 3, 5, 156, 272–273
Antler, Joyce, 115–116
Arrested Development (TV series), 255
Ashkenazi, 2, 6, 50n9, 94, 110, 155, 203; non-Ashkenazi characters, 133
Ashkenormativity, 185
Assassination Nation (TV series), 5

assimilation, 273–274
Association for Jewish Studies, 8, 31n12
Athirat, Canaanite goddess, 160–161
atonement, 37, 40–41, 43–44
Auerbach, Erich, 53

Baddiel, David, 7
Barnes, Van, 7, 254–255
Bayer, Vanessa, 28
BDS (Boycott, Divest, and Sanction Israel), 132, 186
belle juive (beautiful Jewess) trope, 178–181, 184
Ben-Ephraim, Idan, 257–258
Ben Gurion, David, 240
Benjamin, Walter, 69–75, 79n45, 79n47, 80n50
Better Things (TV series), 272
Bhanji, Nael, 239
Bial, Henry, 39, 47
Bible: Abraham's journey, 264; Abram and God's demand, 53; elastic view of gender in Hebrew, 57; Lech Lecha Torah portion, 264; Levinas on Abraham's desert nomadism, 53; Maura's death and Jewish practices, 257; Moses' death mirroring Maura's, 269n6; queer theory and diversity of God's creation, 167–168; responding to God's call in pivotal moments, 109–110. *See also* Torah
Billings, Alexandra, 5

283

Black Jews, 6–7, 185
Bloom, Rachel, 187
Bonhoeffer, Karl, 225
book burning, 107, 220–221, 223–224
"Book of Life, The" (*Transparent* episode), 23, 36–38, 42–43, 47
Boym, Svetlana, 143–145, 147
Bridget Loves Bernie (TV series), 2, 131
Broad City (TV series), 130
Broadway, 93–94
Brown, Simone, 91
Bunker, Archie (All in the Family character), 138–139
Butler, Isaac, 57, 62n5
Butler, Judith, 3, 23, 54, 79n44, 236, 273
Buzz (*Transparent* character): bonds with older Pfeffermans over Yiddish, 48–49; corrects Ari's non-traditional holiday greetings, 100, 107; deceitful boyfriend of Shelly, 132; present at family events, 44, 134, 241; supports Maura's transition with Yiddish phrase, 241

cable television, 19–20
Cahan, Abraham, 148
Cahan, Benjamin, 9
California, 148, 152–153; Jews in, 176–177, 185
camp, 266
Camp Kohenet, 189
Canaan, land of, 264
Carbado, Devon W., 215
Carousel (musical), 264
Cashman, Tammy (*Transparent* character): marriage to Sarah, 132, 133–135, 137, 148–149, 202; renovation of Pfefferman home, 42, 146
Cavell, Stanley, 69–70
Central Conference of American Rabbis (CCAR), 12, 160, 171
Chabon, Michael, 60, 150
Chesnutt, Charles, 148
chosenness, 229–233, 238, 240–242
Christianity, 122–123, 132–133, 135; Josh's conversion, 164–165
Christian nationalism, 272
chrononormativity, 201–204
circumcision, 60, 118, 249–250, 259, 260n20
cisnormativity: critiqued in *Transparent*, 153, 159; definitions, 10, 59, 106; family structures and, 176, 180–182, 189–190; Jewish masculinity and, 126; queer temporality versus, 205, 207; transgender experience and, 168
Colton (*Transparent* character): conversion to Christianity, 121–123; as goy from Jewish perspective, 100, 133–134; Josh's relationship with, 58, 121–122, 184–185; rejection of Pfeffermans, 136, 185
confession, 31, 37, 39, 42–44, 135, 164
Cornwall, Susannah, 156
Cox, Laverne, 3
Crasnow, S. J., 28, 33, 58, 88
Crazy Ex-Girlfriend (TV series), 187–188
Crenshaw, Kimberlé Williams, 215
Croce, Jim, 1, 13n2, 147, 243n2
crossdressing, 27, 149, 152, 217–218, 225
Curb Your Enthusiasm (TV series), 37, 40–42, 131

Dallas Buyers Club (film), 5, 71
Dane, Perry, 256
Danish Girl, The (film), 5
Davina (*Transparent* character), 45–46, 100–101, 104, 189, 240–241, 253, 265–266
dayenu, 88
deadnaming, 13n1, 155n37, 170n8, 217
demonic, the, 132, 134, 138–139
de Szegheo Lang, Tamara, 145
Diamond, Neil, 130, 139
diaspora, 57, 60, 124, 136, 151–153, 239
diasporic Jewish male, 10, 114–115, 122–126
Difficult People (TV series), 27, 187–190, 272
Doniger, Wendy, 161
Dose, Ralf, 218, 227n16
drag queen, 105, 146, 266, 273
Drake, 7, 28
Dreamgirls (musical), 264
Drucker, Zackary, 146, 208, 266
Dzmura, Noach, 4, 84

East Side Jews, 26, 109, 181
Egypt, 58, 110, 166–167
Eilberg, Amy, 175
Elizah (*Transparent* character), 56, 101, 105
Emmy Awards, 4
Englander, Nathan, 24, 52
Entourage (TV series), 37, 40–42
epigenetics, 73–74, 79n49, 152, 210, 239
Ernst, Rhys, 146, 266

Etzioni, Amitai, 38, 44
Exodus, 66n33

"Father's House" (song), 264, 266
feminist spirituality movements, 90
Fiddler on the Roof, 116, 179
Fleischman, Joel, 39
Foer, Jonathan Safran, 24, 150
Frank, Rachel "Ray," 175–177, 180
Freedman, Jonathan: on intergenerational trauma, 44; Klezmer America, 130; Maura's persecution versus Gittel's, 221; *Transparent*'s creative liberties with Weimar history, 227n13; on *Transparent*'s depiction of trauma, 221; use of flashbacks to depict family trauma, 243; works on Jewish American identity, 42, 53, 58
Freeman, Elizabeth, 147, 200–202, 205, 210, 217
Frieden, Ken, 61
Freud, Sigmund, 219
Friedan, Betty, 183
Friedländer, Benedict, 235
Friedman, Bruce Jay, 115
Friedman, Joshua, 24, 33

Gaza, 151
gematria, 242
gender-affirming care, 272
gender-affirming surgery, 104, 247
gender confirmation surgery, 87, 89, 100, 217–218, 225, 263
Genesis, 57, 110, 167–168, 248–250, 252
gentiles, 10, 39, 134–137
Gershon (*Transparent* character). *See* Gittel
Gilded Age, 177
Gilman, Sander, 113n16, 118, 219
Gittel (*Transparent* character): aunt of Maura Pfefferman, 121, 210; as Gershon (birth name), 214; murder of, 94; as transgender woman in Holocaust, 214–215, 217, 224–225
"Goddamn House" (song), 266
Go Forth, 246, 248–252
Goldberg, Rabbi Susan, 109, 181, 259n12
Goldbergs, The (TV series), 2, 8, 37–39, 41, 48, 131
Golden Globe Awards, 4, 19, 179, 271
goy/goyish, 121–122
Grau, Günter, 221

Greenburg, Dan, 115
Gypsy (musical), 267–268

Halberstam, Jack, 146–147, 153, 183, 201, 204
Hammerman, Shaina, 6
"Hand in My Pocket" (song), 151, 267
Handmaid's Tale, The (TV series), 188–189
Haran, 250, 257
Havdalah: concluding the Sabbath, 42; Maura interrupts with Kaddish, 132; as queer feminism, 185–186; transitional ritual, 164, 166; in *Transparent*, 26, 28, 99
Herrn, Rainer, 217–218, 224–225
Heschel, Susannah, 92
heteronormativity. *See* cisnormativity
heteropathic memory, 222
Hirsch, Marianne, 154n32, 201, 222
Hirschfeld, Magnus: anti-Semitic reception of work, 218–219, 235; feminist and trans politics, 230; Institute for Sexual Science, 214, 216–218, 220–224; lack of scholarship on Jewish background, 234–235; pioneering work on homosexuality and gender dysphoria, 148; reclaimed as first Jewish trans activist, 214, 217; Scientific Humanitarian Committee co-founder, 148; sexual spectrum, 236; theories of homosexuality and femininity, 235; in *Transparent*, 149, 152; "transvestite" and sexual intermediacy, 149, 217; and Walter Benjamin, 79n45
Hogan's Heroes (TV series), 131
Holocaust: and collective Jewish trauma, 29, 119, 124; and commemoration of LGBTQ victims, 226; destruction of Hirschfeld's Institute for Sexual Science, 214–215; and epigenetic inheritance of trauma, 79n48; and Gittel's deportation as transgender woman, 208, 214–215, 224–225; and Jewish continuity, 121; and Jewish genocide, 226; "Joycaust" as questionable antidote to, 267–268; and Maura's family history, 214; Nazi persecution of homosexuals and transgender individuals, 214, 225; Pfefferman family's gallows humor about, 99; and post-Holocaust European Jewish life, 150; and postmemory media, 210; and queer temporality in *Transparent*, 209, 211, 217; and recovery of pre-Holocaust Jewish archives/life, 150, 155n33;

Holocaust (cont)
and revisiting from LGBTQ perspectives, 214, 217; and similarities/differences in Jewish and transgender experiences, 214–215, 224–226; as touchstone of contemporary Jewish experience, 29; and *Transparent*'s evocation through musical genre, 267–268
How to be a Jewish Mother (book), 115
Hunter, Lourdes Ashley, 5

Idyllwild Wimmin's Festival: context of feminist music festivals, 205; Maura attending with Ari and Sarah, 73, 189, 240; Michigan Womyn's Music Festival (MichFest), 89–90, 212n39, 216; transphobia at, 58, 61, 221. *See also* Michigan Womyn's Music Festival
impotence, 115, 118, 120, 126
Institute for Sexual Science: destruction by Nazis in 1933, 62, 72, 149; employed trans people, 154n30; first of its kind, 148; founding in 1919, 148
intersectionality: Black feminism, origins in, 113n22, 214–215; emphasis in *Transparent*, 214, 216, 219–220, 224–226; as heuristic and analytical tool, 215; in queer Holocaust memorialization, 225–226; rejection of singular identity categories, 222–223
Israel: American Jewish identity and, 134–135, 150–151; as catalyst for Josh and Shelly's personal growth, 126; deconstruction of binaries in, 136–137; gender divisions in, 165–166; Holocaust memory and, 65n31; Jewish Diaspora and, 239; Jewish state, as envisioned, 124; Maura's experience in, 136, 151–152; normative Israeli identity, juxtaposed with American Jewishness, 114–115; Occupation, the, 65n31, 137, 151; Pfeffermans' trip to, 114–115, 124–126, 132–138, 149–153, 165–166; season 4 depiction of, 136–138, 149–153; as transformative for Ari, 137–138, 166; transgender community in, 66n33; untenable binaries, 136–139; Wailing Wall gender segregation, 165–166, 251; Zionism and, 124, 239
Ivry, Sara, 9, 115

Jacobson-Maisels, James, 256
Jazz Singer (film), The, 41, 50n9, 50n19, 130–131, 139, 178
Jenner, Caitlyn, 6, 242
Jesus Christ Superstar, 91–92, 94, 136, 138, 240, 267
Jewface, 7, 100
Jewish American princess stereotype, 178–179, 184, 187
Jewish mother stereotype, 114–116, 178–179, 187
Jewishness: communal versus individual, 99; criticism of *Transparent*'s portrayal, 6–7; ethnic versus religious markers, 101–102; gendered aspects of, 165; and the gentile Other, 132–135, 137; as indelible identity, 120; in language use, 98–99; and Maura's transition, 114–115; post-assimilated, 135, 138; repetition and unsettlement, 243; vestigial presence in language, 162–163
Jewish studies, 3–4, 8, 22, 24, 186, 211
Jonas, Regina, 175
Joyocaust, 94, 103, 153, 190, 268
Judge, Caitlin, 253

Kaddish, 28, 99, 108, 164, 257–258, 261
Kaplan, Caren, 252
Kemp, Jonathan, 169
Keshet, 12
Kierkegaard, Søren, 60
Kirshenblatt-Gimblett, Barbara, 93
Klausner, Julie, 187, 190
Kohan, Jenji, 29
Kornhaber, Spencer, 23
Kotel (Western Wall), 137. *See also* Western Wall
Kushner, Tony, 60

Ladin, Joy, 88, 248, 250
Law & Order (TV series), 2
Lech Lecha: Ari's canceled bat mitzvah and nonbinary identity, 27, 108; characters' journeys and self-exploration, 57, 60, 264–265; introspection and ontological change, 265; Jewish tradition of renaming and transformation, 64n24; Soloway's ethos, 57; as theme in *Transparent*, 57, 108, 264–265
Lekh Lekha, 248–252, 258. *See also* Lech Lecha

Len (*Transparent* character), 42–43, 132–133, 138
Leslie (*Transparent* character): contrasted with Rabbi Raquel, 186–187; dismissive of Jewishness, 229; and Israel/Palestine politics, 132–136; and Sarah Pfefferman, 186–187, 238
"Let Her Be Okay" (song), 265
Levinas, Emmanuel, 53–57, 73–74
Libii, Kobi, 185
Light, Judith, 60, 151
Lila (*Transparent* character), 133, 138, 244n20
Lot (biblical figure), 264
Love, Heather, 145–146, 200, 203, 208
Lyfe (*Transparent* character), 137
Lyons, Margaret, 23
Lysette, Trace, 7, 254–255

male menstruation, 219
Mama Rose (character in Gypsy), 267
Männerbund, 235
Marvelous Mrs. Maisel, The (TV series), 2, 31–32n14, 36, 41
Maus (graphic novel), 150, 154, 273
McMillin, Scott, 263
Michigan Womyn's Music Festival, 63n11, 89–90, 205, 212n39, 216. *See also* Idyllwild Wimmin's Festival
mikvah, 9, 28, 84, 88, 187, 189
Moshe (*Transparent* character), 136, 149, 151–152, 253
musicals, 263, 266–268, 269n9–10

National Center for Transgender Equality, 6, 14n22
National Day of Unplugging, 25–26
National Jewish Population Survey, 24, 32n23
National Socialism: deportation and murder during Holocaust, 131, 214–215, 224–226; fascism and targeting of LGBTQ communities, 273; and Jewish "science," 214; Nazi destruction of Magnus Hirschfeld's Institute for Sexual Science, 214–215; parallels to contemporary targeting of Jews and LGBTQ groups, 273; and persecution of Jews, 11, 29, 121, 124, 150, 155n33, 208, 267–268; *Transparent*'s depiction of, 214–215, 217

Nayfack, Shakina, 255
Nazism. *See* National Socialism
Nef, Hari, 5, 12, 149
Netflix, 3, 19–21
New York Miss All-America Camp Beauty Pageant, 266
New York Times, 12, 43, 177
Ngai, Sian, 145
Nielsen Company, 21–22
Nitzan (*Transparent* character)), 125–126
Nomadism, 53, 57, 62n2
Northern Exposure (TV series), 39, 41, 49
Nussbaum, Emily, 22–23, 31n13–14

Ochs, Vanessa, 85
Oedipus Wrecks (film), 115, 118
Orange Is the New Black (TV series), 3, 7, 29
Ovadia, Duvid (*Transparent* character), 106, 108–109, 133–134, 184–185

Paley, Grace, 57
parallel montage, 215, 223–224
Parsemain, Ava Laure, 3, 6
Paskin, Willa, 23, 32n16
Pfefferman, Ali. *See* Pfefferman, Ari
Pfefferman, Ari: Bat mitzvah, 27, 83–87, 94, 103, 258, 266; chanting Lech Lecha, 86, 91–94, 108, 264; contrasted with Rabbi Raquel, 186–187; critiquing binary Judaism, 187; flashbacks, 221–224, 238; parallels to Abraham, 249–254, 264–266, 268; relationship with Leslie, 132–133, 206; in the series finale, 87, 190; similarity to "The Jazz Singer's" Jack Robin, 47–48; Spanx ritual, 87–88; subverting security theater at airport, 91–92; theory of intersectionality, 230, 242; as "true" protagonist, 46, 137–138; vision at Idyllwild, 90
Pfefferman, Josh: asserting Jewish identity, 100; attempts at atonement on Yom Kippur, 43–44; childhood sexual abuse by Rita, 118; Christian son Colton, relationship with, 121–122, 133, 184; coping with loss of baby, 48; effeminacy and transphobia, embracing religious practices, 99; failed attempts at fatherhood, 61; failures of, 204; gentile characters, rejection by, 134; healing relationship with

Pfefferman, Josh (cont)
Shelly in Israel, 126; impotence and anxiety over sexuality, 114, 117–118; Israeli hypermasculinity, confrontation with, 124–126; Jewish identity of, 100, 119–120; learning about spiritual practices, 99; need for clear boundaries, 57; Rabbi Raquel, relationship with, 99, 117, 120, 164, 183–184, 203; seeking freedom from, 125; self-loathing and oppression as diasporic Jew, 115, 119; self-negating path, 57; sex addiction support group, joining, 126; Shelly, relationship with, 61, 94, 99–100, 115–117, 121–124, 126; as stereotypical Jewish mother's son, 115–117; temporarily converts to Christianity, 184; use of Yiddishisms, 100

Pfefferman, Maura: asserts womanhood, 120; birthday party, 100, 241; candle-lighting ritual, 85, 101, 240; casting controversy, 5–6; coming out as trans, 58, 61, 158, 265; cremation, 257; death of, 263, 265; feelings about Israel, 138, 165; gender transition, 56, 61, 63n11, 85, 88, 104–105; gives family home to Davina, 256, 265; identifies with Jesus, 92–93; interrupts Havdalah with Kaddish, 164; meets Israeli father, 151–152

Pfefferman, Sarah: failed marriage to Tammy, 89–90, 132, 146, 148, 202–203; Israel trip, impact of, 138; Jewish identity, practice, and rituals, 42–44, 99–100, 108–109, 132, 164, 184–186, 233, 240; pleasure, queerness, and sexual needs, 157, 184, 203–204, 206; seeking awe and spirituality, 99–100, 108–109; transformation in season 3, 134

Pfefferman, Shelly: blames self for Raquel's miscarriage, 121; "Joyocaust," 94, 103; moves beyond caricature as her history of trauma is explored, 151; relationship to religiosity, 99–100; relationship with Josh begins healing in Israel, 126; at Sarah's wedding, 103, 105; synagogue as social hub, 44; tension with Maura's trans identity and community, 241; as underdeveloped character, 61

Pfefferman family: dysfunctional dynamics and relationships, 1, 36–37, 60–61, 115, 133–134, 148; ethnic and religious identity, 2, 72, 99–100, 103–104, 132–135, 148–150, 157–165, 186–187; family and Israel, 115, 124–126, 135–138, 152; growth and self-discovery, 115, 124–126, 137–138; Holocaust trauma and legacy, 60, 72, 103, 214, 222; Jewishness as both ethnic and religious, 2, 99–100, 103–104; Maura's death, 262–263; musical numbers, 103, 267–268; neurosis and self-absorption, 1–2, 23, 60–61, 115, 133–134; perceived as "Jewish gentiles" by Israeli relatives, 135–136; reconciliation and forgiveness, 36–37; rituals and practices, 148–150, 157–158, 163–165, 186–187; Yom Kippur observance, 36–37, 40–43

philanthropy, 24, 30, 35n52
pinkwashing, 151
Piper, Adrian, 67, 75n1
Plaskow, Judith, 248
Portnoy, Alexander (*Portnoy's Complaint* character), 117–125, 128
Portnoy's Complaint (novel), 114–115, 117–118, 124, 136
Portnoy template, 115, 120, 126
Preminger, Otto, 138
Priesand, Sally, 175

Qadesh, gender variant priests, 160–161
Queen, The (documentary), 146, 266
queer studies, 145, 147, 153, 159, 167, 169
queer subjectivity, 145
queer temporality, 146–147
queer theory, 95n3, 144, 146, 159, 167, 204, 211

rabbinical assembly, 4, 170–171n15
Rabbi Raquel (*Transparent* character): absence from season 4 and Israel/Palestine storyline, 186–187; admonishment of Josh on Yom Kippur, 43, 174, 203; on being "your own Messiah," 273; breakup with Josh, 164; cleanses self of Pfeffermans in mikvah, 187; embrace of expansive Judaism, 190; helps Ari become Jewish adult in "bart mitzvah," 189; influence on Pfefferman children's religiosity, 99; modeled Rabbi Goldberg, 181; screaming at Sarah for shallow spirituality, 186; sermon, 55–56; visiting

mikveh, 164; as voice of normality and common sense, 58; yarmulke and empty womb as sites of gendered anxiety, 120–121, 182–183
Reboot (organization), 33n30; cultural impact and initiatives, 24–27; founding and funding sources, 24–25; influence on Joey Soloway, 26; National Day of Unplugging, 25; rebooting rituals, 26–28; relationship with *Transparent*, 25–27, 34n35; Sukkah City project, 25
Redmayne, Eddie, 5
Reform Judaism, 2, 4, 12, 101, 160, 171n23, 175–177, 257
Reklis, Kathryn, 12, 181–182
Robertson, Ritchie, 118
Rose (*Transparent* character), 89, 165, 220, 224, 253; Ari and Rose witnessing Gittel's fate, 207–208; gender transition as process, 89; and intergenerational trauma, 210
Rosenberg, Jordy, 148
Rosenberg, Roberta, 28, 43
Rosenblatt, Kate, 128n30
"Rose's Turn" (song from Gypsy), 267–268
Rushkoff, Douglas, 33n33

Salah, Trish, 147
Sameth, Mark, 57–58, 63n15
Sasso, Sandy Eisenberg, 175
Satlow, Michael, 160
Saturday Night Live (TV series), 23, 28
Schafer, Hunter, 5
Schindler's List (film), 25, 220
Scholem, Gershom, 240, 244n22
Schulman, Michael, 1
Scientific Humanitarian Committee, 148
Second Wave Feminism, 179, 205
security theatre, 91–93
Seinfeld (TV series), 2, 131
sexology, 62, 148, 214, 219–220, 238
sexual abuse, 150–151, 267
sexual dysfunction, 114–115, 118–120
Seymour, Natasha, 239
Shabbat, 26, 38, 42, 94, 99, 101, 163–164, 166, 240, 254, 266
Shachar-Hill, Essie, 12
shamans, 161
sheitel, 163
She Wants It (memoir), 5, 23, 63n8, 63n12, 65n26, 65n31, 254, 259n12

Shimkovitz, Mel, 28
Shoulson, Jeffrey, 60, 61
shtetl, 119, 158
Silverman, Sarah, 7
Singer, Jenny, 2, 268
"Sit in It" (song), 266
Six Feet Under (TV series), 180–181
smith, s. e., 6
Sollors, Werner, 147–148
Solomon, Alisa, 233–234
Soloveitchik, Joseph, 37, 41, 49
Soloway, Faith, 255–256, 264, 266
Soloway, Joey: based on Soloway's family, 3; came out as queer and non-binary, 153n6, 190; casting Tambor as trans woman, criticism for, 5, 232; on characters constantly transforming, 52–53, 55, 57, 59; collaborative *Transparent* set, 58; early influences and creative process, 109, 181; hired more trans crew, 5; Holocaust, queering the, 226; Jewish and trans histories, on linking, 214–215; musical finale, 255; Reboot, and, 26, 28; reinterpretations of antisemitic stereotypes, 219; Tambor fired for misconduct, 255
Spanx, 87–88, 93
Spiegelman, Art, 150, 154
Spielberg, Steven, 25, 131, 220
Spinoza, Baruch, 166
Stanley, Eric A., 3
Steiner, George, 60
Strassfeld, Max, 4, 83, 88–89, 139n4, 167
streaming media, 4, 19–21, 24, 27, 29, 271
Streisand, Barbra, 179–180
Stuever, Hank, 3
Summit, Jeffery, 87
Sunden, Jenny, 147
Super Bowl, 268
Sutton, Katie, 226n1

Talmud, 4, 79, 139, 161, 165, 243
Tambor, Jeffrey, 5, 144, 151–153, 232, 254–255, 271
tashlich, 44–46, 88, 93
Tel Aviv (Israel), 136, 152, 226
Tevye (Fiddler on the Roof character), 116, 138
Thai Buddhism, 167
Thurm, Eric, 36, 38–39, 44
tikkun atzmi, 256

Torah: chanting Torah portion Lech Lecha, 86–87, 93, 264; father's obligations in teaching Torah, 160; musical finale and spiritual journeys theme, 264; queering Torah chanting practice, 87; recontextualization of traditional ritual, 27–28; trans issues and aliyah la'torah, 257–258. *See also* Bible

trans actors, 3, 5, 23, 149, 152–153, 271–272

transfeminism, 247–253

trans history, 146, 150

transitioning, 230, 236, 238–239, 241

transphobia, 95, 120, 125, 152, 209

trans studies, 147, 149, 152

transvestite, 149, 217–218, 224–225, 226n1, 235

Trap Door (book), 3

Turim, Maureen, 216, 221

Twersky, Luzer, 220

Ulrich, Karl Heinrich, 235

Ulysses (book), 240

University of Rochester, 8

Unorthodox (TV series), 8, 13n8

U.S. Transgender Survey (2015), 161–162

VanDerWerff, Todd, 22

Vicki (*Transparent* character), 105, 133, 241

Viddui, 164

Vider, Stephen, 146

Villarejo, Amy, 232–233

Von Braun, Christina, 218–219

Warshow, Robert, 69–70

WASPs, 19, 118, 124, 148, 233

Watts Belser, Julia, 91

weddings, 42, 103, 121, 148–149, 174, 186, 189–190

Weimar Germany, 214, 216–221, 224, 235

Wertheimer, Jack, 35n51

Western Wall, 12, 91–92, 108, 136–137, 259

West Wing, The (TV series), 40

Wheel of Fortune (TV series), 242–243

whiteness, 105; criticism of *Transparent*, 226n2, 232–233; ethnicity as marker of, 148; Jenner's experience and, 6; Pfeffermans' assimilation and, 59

white privilege, 6, 138, 168

white supremacy, 6, 79n45, 272

Wilcox, Melissa M., 87, 95n4

wilderness, 56, 90–91, 93, 166

Yentl (film), 179–182

Yerushalmi, Yosef, 70, 75, 75–76n4, 77n29

Yeshivat Maharat, 175

Yetta (*Transparent* character), 216–217

yichus, 115, 118

Yiddish, 98–104, 115–116, 120, 217, 241

Yom Kippur, 36–41, 48–49, 135, 163–164

Young, Nikki, 169

"Your Boundary is My Trigger" (song), 267–268, 269n9

Zionism, 65, 124, 136, 239